RULES OF THE GAME

THE AMERICAN RETROSPECTIVE SERIES

RULES OF THE GAME

THE BEST SPORTS WRITING FROM
HARPER'S MAGAZINE

◆

Preface by Roy Blount Jr.
Introduction by Matthew Stevenson
Edited by Matthew Stevenson and Michael Martin

FRANKLIN
SQUARE
PRESS

NEW YORK

Published by Franklin Square Press, a division of Harper's Magazine
666 Broadway, New York, NY 10012

First Edition

First Printing 2010

ISBN: 978-1-879957-58-9
Library of Congress CIP data:
    Rules of the game : the best sports writing from Harper's magazine /
    preface by Roy Blount; edited by Matthew Stevenson and Michael Martin.
        p. cm. — (The American retrospective series)
     ISBN-13: 978-1-879957-58-9
     ISBN-10: 1-879957-58-2
    1. Sports—United States. 2. Sports stories, American. 3. Sports
    literature—United States. I. Stevenson, Matthew Mills, 1954- II.
    Martin, Michael. III. Harper's magazine.
     GV704.R85 2010
     796'.0973--dc22
                         2009048196

Book design by Deborah Thomas
Cover design by Renée Khatami

Manufactured in the United States of America.

10 9 8 7 6 5 4 3 2 1

Contents

PREFACE

Roy Blount Jr.

"THE DEMANDS MADE on consciousness by mere existence in the world to-day," wrote Bernard DeVoto in *Harper's Magazine* in 1937, "are so great that there must be constantly available ways of lowering consciousness and escaping to simpler levels, to muscular and instinctive levels where the exigent demand for thinking is not felt." Unlike DeVoto's views on corsets, in the same essay (as we shall see), that reflection holds up pretty well today, if we lose the hyphen.

The word *sport* comes from *disport*, literally "to carry away." In the nursery rhyme, when the cow jumped over the moon, and so on, "The little dog laughed to see such sport." Sports are amusing. And childish. And otherworldly. In 1602, Richard Carew on the sport of hurling: "The ball in this play may be compared to an infernal spirit, for whosoever catcheth it, fareth straightways like a mad man, struggling and fighting with those that go about to hold him. You shall see them retiring home as from a pitched battle, with bloody pates, bones broken and out of joint, and such bruises as serve to shorten their days. Yet all is good play, and never attorney nor coroner troubled."

Then, too, some people find sport in watching dogs fight to the death. And Congressional hearings have recently called attention to evidence that playing pro football causes brain damage, such as leads to early-onset senility. "We are now getting a sense of what we were watching" in that sport in recent years, wrote the longtime *New York Times* sports columnist George Vecsey. "We were watching people be maimed. For our enjoyment."

Oof.

"Sacrifice your body," coaches urge: put all of your force into the other fellow lest he or she put his or hers into you. Central to the fascination with sports is the experience, personal or vicarious, of artfully getting all of your oomph into a leap, a swing, a dash, a punch, a tackle. In the real world—unless you are fighting for your life or trying to lift a car off a loved one—such a consummation is not only extremely unlikely but ill-advised. The rules, gear, and venues of sport are meant to let people fly through the air and collide securely, like tots tossed up and caught by parents or cartoon characters temporarily squashed by falling anvils. Players aren't tots or cartoon characters, but they derive fellowship, highs, and admiration from pretending to be; and the big-time pros among them are paid outlandishly, until adulthood catches up with them. Even people who do sport just for recreation and fitness, if they do it as intensely as the sport seems to call for, are likely to mess up their backs or wear out their knees.

Hence the poignance arising from stories—fine examples in this book— by or about people who must give up their games at last. What Gary Cartwright is washed up from is sportswriting, old-school. These days sportswriters industriously file online updates, analyze clauses in multimillion-dollar contracts, and work up new mathematical models for quantifying heretofore unstatistical values such as percentage of heart shown per point per minute of play, corrected for shape of stadium. In Cartwright's day, sportswriters were out trying to jump over the moon. Cartwright touches on the capacities of his colleague, the late Bud Shrake, "the accidental winner of a Chili Rice Eating Contest one time while serving as contest referee." Cartwright himself can look back and "know this: in a time my memory cannot identify, in a place I cannot remember being welcome, there is someone's voice, full of respect and anticipation, saying, 'For Chrissake, here he comes again!'

I don't claim to have approached the mythic status of Cartwright or Shrake, or that of Pete Axthelm, whose still-definitive book about self-destructive inner-city basketball legends (*The City Game*, excerpted in *Harper's* and here), and who died young, himself, of a wasted liver. But I was out there among them many a night, going all out, in emulation of the players we were covering. When you are feeling a little too sozzled to carry on, I was advised by a Pittsburgh Steeler friend of mine who would die before he was sixty, you should "drink through it," just as, when you're hurt, you should "play through" the injury.

Very period, that. As is Peter Schrag's 1970 story about Lester McClain, the first African-American football player in the Southeastern Conference. "In the background hangs the specter of change and revolt, not merely among black athletes, but among all young men and women. References to riots and demonstrations creep incessantly into the discussions of collegiate sports." And McClain's coach: "It's sad that Negroes as a race lack stable leadership."

And Bernard DeVoto, holding forth peculiarly regarding the effect of sport on women's wear: "Fifteen years ago the sex put away its corsets in order to be athletic; now it has had to put them on again in order to smooth out the muscles produced by athletics. . . . [T]he corset is one of the most stable and constant elements in our civilization."

And John R. Tunis in 1938, more or less sportively disgruntled by the vulgar new phenomenon of radio-broadcast tennis: "And what will the Davis Cup be in 1960? Will . . . the Stock Exchange close as the matches between the United States and Japan are played and televised to hundreds of millions of fans . . . and will the star of the Japanese team commit hara-kiri on the center court rather than return defeated to be killed in Japan by an angry populace?"

That is a great thing about an anthology of any sort of writing from a magazine as venerably edgy as *Harper's*: you get lots of periods, and the stuff from the early ones is in some ways fresher than it was then, or at any rate just as fresh: I give you George Plimpton in 1977 on luncheon with Muhammad Ali and Marianne Moore, John Chamberlain on the eccentricities of Branch Rickey, and Mark Twain in 1906 on pursuing a "deceitful" wild turkey mother over "much of the United States" one day in his youth.

And one more shout out to my old friend Axthelm, in 1970, celebrating the legendary player known in Harlem as "The Helicopter": "As Knowings goes up, the crowd shouts 'Fly, Copter, fly,' and seems to share his heady trip." ✦

INTRODUCTION

Matthew Stevenson

NOT EVERY READER will immediately associate *Harper's Magazine* with articles about sports. Essays, short stories, reporting, even poetry, come more readily to mind. But since it was founded in 1850, *Harper's* has been publishing articles about what in the nineteenth century might have been called "the sporting life."

This collection of sports writing spans more than a hundred years in the magazine's history. The earliest article, "Yachting in Kiel," by James B. Connolly, about German ships large and small, was published in 1903. The most recent, "Mudville," by Lewis H. Lapham, ran in 2008, just after former Senator George Mitchell released his report on the widespread use of illicit drugs within major league baseball. In between, the magazine has published many articles about tennis, bowling, college football, gymnastics, wrestling, car racing, sailing, soccer, dog tracks, and baseball, which is the most popular sport in the pages of *Harper's*. In many ways, *Harper's* and baseball (both can be thought of as national pastimes) come of age in the late nineteenth century and flourish during the twentieth.

The book begins with Gary Cartwright's lament about the decline in the quality of sports writing and ends with Rich Cohen's "The Boys of Winter," an essay about the long careers of certain athletes, like ice hockey's Gordie Howe and baseball's Cal Ripken. In between are several delightful illustrations by Tom Wolfe, who for many years touched on the folly of professional sports in his drawings for the magazine, under the rubric "In Our Time." And nearly all the pieces confirm the observation of Joseph Epstein (for many years the editor of *American Scholar* and here the author of "Obsessed with Sports") that sports are a common language across the barriers of race, economics, and age.

A number of the articles collected here were published in the last thirty-five years, when Lewis H. Lapham was editor of *Harper's Magazine.* He held that job, except for two years, between 1976 and 2006—a stretch of longevity that, had he been managing a baseball team, would have won him first-ballot admission to the Hall of Fame. During these years, Lewis wrote the monthly editorial column, first called the Easy Chair and later Notebook. Two Notebook columns are reprinted here. One is "Mudville"; the other is about his long friendship with George Plimpton.

George Plimpton has probably written the most articles about sports in the magazine's long history. In 1963, he went with the poet Marianne Moore to the World Series and wrote about it for *Harper's*, and he was still contributing to the magazine when he died in 2003. An excerpt from *Paper Lion*, Plimpton's account of his training with the Detroit Lions, ran first in *Harper's* in January 1966. He also published pieces about the America's Cup in Newport (he watched it with President John F. Kennedy), the culture of the baseball bullpen, and Muhammad Ali's attempts at poetry ("These Sporting Poets," included here).

Another close friend of Lewis Lapham's was A. Bartlett Giamatti, later president of Yale University, whose sports articles in *Harper's* may have been one of the reasons the owners of professional baseball made him their commissioner. Now it seems commonplace, but in the 1970s and 1980s it was revolutionary for a distinguished Yale professor to be writing in a serious monthly magazine about Tom Seaver or boxing.

When *Harper's* writers turn their attention to sports, however, they are in search of more than just a game. Former New York Yankee and *Ball Four* author Jim Bouton said that Pat Jordan's *A False Spring* was the best account that he had ever read about trying to make it to the major leagues. In these pages, Jordan scouts a prospect who has been compared favorably to the legends of the game, only to find someone missing life's cutoff men. For anyone who grew up in New York in the 1960s, the Rucker basketball tournament played in Harlem, described here by Pete Axthelm, has aspects of an urban legend. Lord Nicholas Bethell writes about the 1972 chess matches between Boris Spassky and Bobby Fischer, but "A Poisoned Russian King" reads just as well as an account of the Cold War. Shirley Jackson, author of "The Lottery," finds parallels, lightly sketched here, between chance and the evil spirits of Little League baseball.

Mark Twain published many of his celebrated essays in *Harper's*. The Twain essay included in this collection ("Hunting the Deceitful Turkey") describes his shortcomings as a hunter, but it can be read as a parable on how hard it is for a writer to understand the subject about which he is writing (or maybe hunting). Bernard DeVoto's essay about the madness of the exercise craze, in which he suggests that no one ever went broke selling sporting goods to Americans, might have been written within the past ten years—not in 1937.

DeVoto wrote the Editor's Easy Chair column from 1935 to 1955, a period that might well be considered one of the golden ages of monthly magazines, and certainly of *Harper's*. It was an era when Frederick Lewis Allen was editor and E. B. White was writing his column One Man's Meat. DeVoto wrote frequently about the American West. In the history of *Harper's,* he is an important link between Twain's nineteenth-century excursions to California and the need, later articulated in DeVoto's Easy Chair columns, to preserve the West.

If there is a thread that links the articles in this collection, it is that the writers use sports or the occasion of a game to write about the larger issues of race relations, poetry, international politics, language, childhood, history, death, urban affairs, and—in the case of the former baseball player Bernie Carbo—hair styling. In the early years, *Harper's* published articles about the games themselves—for example, an exciting U.S. Open or a memorable World Series—but by 1903, James B. Connolly, writing about yachting at Kiel, was suggesting that Germany's affection for competitive sailing, not to mention Baltic fleets, might one day have a darker goal than simply winning a cup at a regatta's closing dinner.

In a similar political vein, John R. Tunis uses tennis and the Davis Cup to make the point that nationalism is as fatal to sports as it is to peace. Better than any urban sociologist, the Canadian writer Guy Lawson takes readers into the underworld that is hockey in rural Canada, something he knew well from his own playing days. And the collection is richer for having essays from Wilfrid Sheed, Peter Schrag, Robert H. Zieger, David James Duncan, and John Chamberlain, for whom sports are a point of departure, not just a score.

Anthologies of all kinds of writing sometimes end up on vacation-home side tables. If that, at some future date, is the fate of this collection, I will not be disappointed. Some of the most pleasurable reads that I can remember have been from browsing books in strange houses and coming across writers who were, at least for me, new. That's how I felt in the *Harper's* archive when I came across Leo Katcher's 1959 story (reprinted here) on gambling and horse racing. One of my favorite books is a used one that I bought in 1976, when I was studying at Columbia University and just before I started work-ing at *Harper's*. It had the title *Great American Essays*, and my copy was paper-back and fairly worn. I read and reread the essays in that book for years, and found that many of the pieces had first been published in *Harper's*—perhaps another reason that I admire the essays and writers represented here, and am confident they will survive for generations. ✦

PART I: THE BLEACHERS

✦

Confessions of a Washed-Up Sportswriter

Confessions of a
Washed-Up Sportswriter

(April 1968)

Gary Cartwright

"Listen, Tojo and Hirohito and you Nomuru and you Kurusu, and all the
rest of you heathen sons of heaven, you won't understand this, it'll be far
over your pagan heads, but, even so, you ought to hear about it."
        —C. E. McBride, Kansas City *Star,* March 27, 1944.
        Reprinted in *Best Sports Stories 1944* (Dutton).

CREW SLAMMER NEVER made *Best Sports Stories.* He never got farther than the
bulletin board at the Fort Worth *Press.* He was a victim of the industry, for he
collided time and again with the mentality ceiling that bears down on every
newspaper I know anything about. Nevertheless, I believe that Crew Slammer
in his way was a better sportswriter than C. E. McBride, Stanley Woodward,
or even Red Smith. He was inquisitive, sardonic, satirical, cynical, opinion-
ated, hedonistic, and what intelligence he had was easily offended. He hated
sport. "To watch it," he thought, "is a deadly bore." Baseball was something
that the twentieth century had a right to do without. Spectator golf ranked in
importance with bridge tournaments and Junior League rummage sales.
Football, tennis, hockey, and boxing interested him for aesthetic reasons.
Crew Slammer fancied that he wrote like Hemingway. A typical lead describing a junior swimming meet would begin, "In the late summer of that year
we lived in a house in a village that . . ."

Crew Slammer was like all my friends in those days. He wanted more. He
had a competitive drive to be the best. Why did he become a sportswriter?
That is the question we were all trying to answer. Inevitably we turned to the
Best Sports Stories anthology, there to prosper or rot. I am sad to say that Crew
Slammer did not prosper, but pretend you don't know that for a while. For
Crew Slammer was a myth, a symbol of our tragic graveyard, a commentary

19

on conditions. He lived only in our imaginations, which of course means that he lived nonetheless.

When I started writing sports in 1958 at the *Press,* I already knew something about basic reporting. I covered the night police beat for two years at the Fort Worth *Star-Telegram,* much to the despair of a night city editor named Ed Capers who used to tell me, "Your trouble is, your fingers are too fast for your mind." I thought he had it backwards, so I quit and joined the sports staff of the *Press.* Instinctively I realized that the only way to move forward was to change newspapers every two years—a pattern I followed to the Dallas *Times Herald,* the Dallas *Morning News,* and finally the Philadelphia *Inquirer,* where, like Crew Slammer, I became a victim of the mentality ceiling. But almost every important thing I learned, I learned at the *Press.*

The Fort Worth *Press* is one of those dilapidated brick-box institutions that Scripps-Howard used to stake between the railroad yard and the farmers' market. Its city room with the eras of dirt and the rancid smell of machine oil reminds you of a train depot in a college-size town. For years it has been vanishing in a cloud of soot, and momentarily it will reappear as a parking lot. It is maintained as you would maintain a shoe box of old letters by a few faithful servants who are nearing retirement age. Good writers have come and gone, and the others have joined the scenery. I cannot visualize the *Press* city room without calling up Delbert Willis, the one-legged city editor who periodically takes a leave of absence to hunt for the Jap who got him; Caroline Hamilton, a husky, old-maidish feature writer in cowboy boots; or Marvin Garrett, a meek silver-haired farm and county editor. Marvin is sitting at his desk, barely visible behind an enormous mound of publicity releases (which we would sometimes take, turn over, and use for copy paper in times of austerity), and all day he is shuffling papers and clucking.

The *Press* is P.M., meaning that it publishes in the afternoon, and that we had to report at 6:00 A.M. The morning dark does things to the creative man. My friend and fellow sportswriter Dan Jenkins used to complain that it made his hair hurt. His wife would set her alarm for 3:00 A.M., watch his hair from her side of the bed, and make notes, but they never isolated the problem. I never made it at 6:00 A.M., but I came close that first day. Twelve minutes late, in a panic, peeling off coat and sweater as I climbed the single flight of dark stairs, I smashed glue-eyed through the swinging gate that separated Sports from the other departments. Suddenly I realized that the only other person in the room was Puss Erwin, a retired postman who had signed on as our bowling writer. Puss was hunched over his typewriter, drinking vodka from a paper cup and puzzling over the previous night's bowling averages. It was the dead of winter, so the heater—the coal chute, we called it—was running full blast. Puss had removed his coat, tie, and shirt, and draped them over the back of his chair. He didn't know me yet, but I guess he had heard I was coming to work at the *Press*. He wouldn't look up. Between sentences he muttered: "You'll never make it, son." I knew he was right. Half an hour before deadline, our slot man, Sick Charley Modesette, arrived. Charley had been out all night, looking for his car. There was a professional detachment about Charley, a combat residual bred in men who have learned to expect nothing. "All the bastards slept in again, huh?" Charley observed, and started plugging the first edition with old pictures and dated syndicated columns by Joe Williams and Harry Grayson. We made deadline with seconds to spare. It was always this way.

Many times I put out the paper alone. All the sportswriters did. We staggered in, tore the night's run of copy from the United Press machine, selected the stories according to the page dummies supplied by the advertising department, assigned headlines and wrote them, clipped box scores and other trivia from the morning *Star-Telegram*, selected pictures and sent them to the engravers, made up the cutlines, then hurried to the composing room where a printer named Max would be waiting to change everything. Like Charley, Max was a professional. All he ever said was, "Who the hell do you think you are?"

We survived on the assumption that no one read our paper anyhow. It is the same feeling you get on a college newspaper or on mind-expanding drugs. There are no shackles on the imagination; there is no retreat, only attack. One of my jobs was to make up little "brights" or boxes:

> John Doughe made a hole-in-one yesterday at Glen Lakes Country
> Club when a snake swallowed his tee shot, a dog swallowed the snake,
> and an eagle carried off the dog, dropping him in the cup after collid-
> ing head on with a private plane flown by Doughe's maternal twin.

We went heavy on the irony. Under these circumstances you might think we got a lot of letters to the editor, but I don't remember any.

II

The starting salary for a college graduate was about $45.67 a week. It went up in pennies. For that reason we ate our meals at the Lavender Cafeteria.

Three biscuits soaked in cream gravy cost 26 cents. Cowboy Hardley, a photographer, favored gravy over cantaloupe, which cost slightly more but got results from those of us who had to watch him eat it. Cowboy was a chow hustler. We called him Everman Fats for his hometown of Everman. He would bet his breakfast against yours that you wouldn't finish.

I did not know it at the time, but the *Press* sports staff was ten years ahead of the game. In 1955 the *Press* was perfecting what most, but not yet all, sports staffs believe they have just created: a competitive art form. Significant television competition was years away, but already the *Press* was rebelling against the stiff, bleak who/what/when/where architecture of its predecessors, exposing myths, demanding to know why, and treating why as the only question. It was funny about 1961 when *Newsweek* devoted its press section to the wry progressive sports editor of *Newsday,* Jack Mann. *Newsday* hired good, creative writers. They worked as a unit, pruning clichés from wire copy, pepping up hard news by tracing angles all over the country, barreling over dogma where they confronted it. Was Yogi Berra a lovable gnome, like it said in *Sporting News*? Did he sit around reading comic books and eating bananas? Or was he a noncommunicative boor whose funniest line was, "How the hell would I know?" *Newsday,* the magazine pointed out, demanded an answer.

There was no way for *Newsweek* to know it, but sports editor Blackie Sherrod had been preaching a better anarchy at the *Press* in 1950. Sherrod surrounded himself with such men as Dan Jenkins and Bud Shrake, now well-known and excellent writers at *Sports Illustrated,* not to mention the irresponsible Crew Slammer. He let them write from the gut.

What obsessed us all was the species. We could watch for hours out the window of the *Press* composing room which overlooked the New Gem Hotel, where God knows what the Negroes were up to, speculating out loud what the species might otherwise become. Without sport, what would Mickey Mantle do? He would drive a fork lift, Crew Slammer was certain. Joe Kuharich would be night watchman for a company that manufactures caskets. Joe Namath raised carrier pigeons and sold hubcaps. Roger Maris operated a liquor store on the Illinois–Missouri border. Bud Wilkinson was Norman Rockwell's chauffeur, and Vince Lombardi operated an academy for the sons of South American dictators. Rice football coach Jess Neely, a slight, shallow-faced man with a Southern drawl who has since retired, was a kindly Southern scientist who devoted his life to crossbreeding the boll weevil with the bull elephant. He always seemed to be at cross purposes.

It was a great joke, of course, but after a while Jess Neely did suggest something unusual. I remember being assigned to do what we called a jock-strap story after an SMU–Rice game in Houston about 1960. It appeared from the press box that Rice lost the game because Neely refused to gamble on fourth down late in the fourth quarter when the alternative was certain defeat. In the twenty minutes before deadline I had to race to the Rice dressing room to gather some quotes from Neely and write six hundred words. All I could think to ask was, "Coach Neely, what were you thinking out there on fourth down?" Neely gave me a sorry scowl and said, "Why, young man, to score more points than my opponents, naturally." At the time I questioned his sincerity. Now that I am older and wiser I believe that Neely was answering as well as he knew how. Frank Howard, the former coach at Clemson, was one of the best men I ever interviewed. In a situation much like the one Neely found himself in, Frank Howard first talked about the other team ("Those big old fine-looking athletes"), then concluded, "We were gonna get our tails whipped, it was a question of by how much."

In most cases the argot of the sports industry can be traced to the sports pages. An American Football League player discussing the ability of a rival kickoff-return man observed recently, "He good! He good! He have developed the knack to alter directions on a dime." He read that somewhere. On the other hand, originality and imagination can be trouble, as Darrell Royal frequently discovers. Royal, the University of Texas football coach, thought himself amusing a few years ago when he likened the rival team from Texas Christian to "a bunch of cockroaches." And he was. The trouble started because a few sportswriters stopped short of explaining that while TCU had not won many games, it had occasionally risen to the moment and spoiled a good thing for someone else. This slip is still a psychological spook anytime TCU plays Texas.

Press conferences such as this one are hazardous. Sportswriters are too absorbed by their own questions to understand the answers. Harold Ratliff, sports editor for the Associated Press in Texas, is the dean of the press conference because he has made himself a focal point for years. Harold likes to bait his subject. He is always asking coaches to predict how much they will win by, or better yet say something rotten about the opponent. While he is never successful, he believes that he is. A recent AP story out of Dallas begins, "Coach Tom Landry of the Dallas Cowboys professed concern over his team's future Wednesday although the Cowboys hold a three-game lead . . ." On the face of it, this is a strong story. Good Lord, the entire future of the Cowboys? Well, not quite, as the story goes on to explain. What happened, I am certain, is that Ratliff asked Landry something like, "Coach, your team about has it [the championship] wrapped up, wouldn't you say?" Landry would not. Landry pointed to the difficult schedule in the final weeks of the season, and he said, "We could still lose it . . . "

III

I remember a discussion that several of us had with Landry one afternoon. The subject was "field position," a term you hear more frequently from college coaches than professional coaches. The concept of the game of football is attack and retreat, the same as war. The ultimate object is to capture the opponent's goal, but a secondary consideration is keeping the ball as far as possible from your own goal line. Professional teams with their superior striking power are less cautious about field position, but no less concerned, as Landry was explaining. After taking some time to ferment his question, Ratliff cornered Landry and asked, "Tell us, Tom, what do you consider the best field position?" I looked at Landry. He didn't need anyone to remind him to answer with care. He said, "Harold, I am personally attracted to my opponent's one-inch line."

I respect Landry. One reason is that he defended me before a mob of super-fans who wanted to know why Landry had neglected to have me fired for writing terrible things about his team. (It somehow amazes the super-fan to learn that writers are not hired or fired by the teams they are assigned to cover.) Landry told them, "You have to remember one thing, when the game is over and we're all feeling bad about losing, he is the one with the typewriter." I have thought about what Landry said. Especially in the escaping minutes after a night game, plunging into the irretrievable deadline, I have written my story upside down and backwards and then hoped to hell I could find a first paragraph to justify it. Don Meredith, the Cowboys' quarterback, is a good friend of mine, but one afternoon when he failed to rise to the occasion, I started my game story:

"Outlined against a gray November sky, the Four Horsemen rode again: Pestilence, Death, Famine, and Meredith."

Meredith read it and thought it was funny. His fans did not. Fans of Kansas City Chiefs linebacker Sherrill Headrick thought it was funny when I wrote that he had "the face of an Oklahoma chicken thief." Headrick's wife did not. Buddy Dial's wife canceled her subscription to the Dallas *Morning News* when I wrote that he had been benched because Landry felt he wasn't playing well. I didn't even write that. I was drunk. Three friends wrote it for me. I have done as much for them. Sportswriters will pull you out of a ditch.

All of our hearts went out to the old sportswriter from the Rio Grande Valley—I forget his name—who stumbled into the Cotton Bowl Press box one New Year's Day. Someone on the field fired a cannon and he fell out of his chair. I asked him, "Didn't you get to bed last night?" He said, "Damn near. Only missed it about that far," holding his hands to indicate a foot or so.

IV

Professional football players are easily the best educated, most congenial, and most sensitive group of athletes I know. They have a different kind of courage, almost masochistic.

I fell into the habit of dropping by the Cowboys' training room before a game. It was the warmest place in any stadium, but I also needed a B-12 shot or something more stimulating. No one talks about it, but training rooms are portable pharmacies. It is the trainer's job to have his forty men ready by Sunday afternoon. If a player is injured, they shoot him full of cortisone. If his pain threshold is low, they give him morphine or another opium deriva-tive. If his metabolism is skimpy, they give him amphetamine. When Commissioner Pete Rozelle outlawed the free use of amphetamines a few years ago, several players and maybe a few sportswriters were ruined. I suspect the National Football League was on the verge of a scandal. Certainly Big Daddy Lipscomb didn't help the image by taking an overdose of horse. Rozelle got pep pills out of the aisles and under the tables. One trainer got around the rule by putting out two pots of coffee, one straight and the other laced with dope. It was explained to me recently by an NFL player, "Every man lets the trainer know his requirements. When you get to the stadium there is a paper cup of whatever you need waiting in your locker."

Almost any football player would be astonished to have explained to him the deliberate change that football has made to his body chemistry. Ernie Stautner, a wide, strong, innocent, hard-living former defensive end who now coaches for the Cowboys, nearly died from being given the wrong drug before a game in Cleveland. Stautner should have been in the hospital that day, but he was determined to play for the Pittsburgh Steelers. After the team doctor inadvertently stoked him up with 1,200 milligrams of Demerol instead of

Novocain, he *was* in the hospital, dying he suspected. "Nurses and doctors were running around like a British comedy," he told me later. "I kept thinking: I'm just a statistic now. I thought about this testimonial dinner they were having for me in two weeks back in Pittsburgh. Boy, that's gonna be a dead affair! Pittsburgh! Boy! That's the irony—the only team in the league I never wanted to play for, and here I was dying on their time."

Someone called a priest and Stautner made his final peace with The Maker. "Father," he said weakly, "I don't have much time, so if it's okay with you I'll just hit the highlights."

V

Just as an athlete, if he's any good, will rise to the occasion, so will a sportswriter. That is the essence of his profession, and one of the reasons there are so few good sportswriters. The other reason is editors. Unfortunately, there is not a hint of a parallel between the average coach and the average newspaper editor. There was an abundance of writing talent in Texas at the time when Crew Slammer and the rest of us still considered the impossible dream to be a dateline from College Station. Few sports editors were talented enough to recognize it. The Dallas *Morning News'* Bill Rives had Tex Maule working the slot. His reasoning was that it took more judgment to arrange stories than it did to write them. Maule hated the job. Now he is senior editor at *Sports Illustrated* and one of the top sportswriters in the country. Roy Terrell, *SI's* assistant managing editor, was stuck away somewhere in Corpus Christi.

The sportswriters everyone heard of in the 1950s were Jesse Abramson, New York *Herald Tribune*; John Carmichael, Chicago *Daily News*; Red Smith, New York *Herald Tribune*; Maxwell Stiles, Los Angeles *Mirror*; Ed Danforth, Atlanta *Journal*; Earl Ruby, Louisville *Courier-Journal*; Milton Gross, New York *Post*; Joe Williams, New York *World-Telegram & Sun*; Jimmy Cannon, New York *Post*; Prescott Sullivan, San Francisco *Examiner*; Tim Cohane, *Look*; Bob Hunter, Los Angeles *Examiner*; Si Burdick, Dayton *News*; Shirley Pavich, Washington *Post*.

As E. P. Dutton & Co., Inc. spread the word in its anthologies of *Best Sports Stories,* names like Furman Bisher, Atlanta *Journal*; Jack Murphy, San Diego *Union*; Murray Olderman, NEA; and Bill Rives, Dallas *Morning News,* joined the pack. Still later, Blackie Sherrod clamored over the wall of the Fort Worth *Press,* found an outlet at the Dallas *Times Herald,* and became—along with two Los Angeles columnists, the *Times'* Jim Murray and the *Herald*

Examiner's Mel Durslag—one of the best day-in day-out sportswriters in the business. These men worked for the big papers and covered the big stories, and E. P. Dutton & Co., Inc., sorted them out each year for recognition. Others, such as Dan Jenkins and Bud Shrake, would occasionally break through on pure ability. The men in *Best Sports Stories* wrote with a diversity of styles and emphasis which only helped to confuse a novice. I can't think of his name but there was an old-timer from Philadelphia who started every game story like this: "Army's powerful Cadets defeated Navy's game but out-manned Midshipmen for the second straight year here Saturday, 14–6, before a crowd of 81,342." The second sentence was always, "Army won the toss and elected to receive." Having created that, he tacked on the play-by-play and got drunk. We could see that this style went nowhere. We were in danger of being replaced by the ape.

As far as I know, this exercise is still tacked to the bulletin board of the Fort Worth *Press:*

By CREW SLAMMER
The World's Greatest Sportswriter

Baltimore, Nov. 27—Late in the fourth quarter when Army's Black Knights of the Hudson had traveled on their bellies long enough to be mistook for Arlington National Cemetery, and had risen in an agonizing mass and smashed the United States Navy's football team to bobbing bits and pieces, Army coach Red Blaik craned his neck toward the score board clock, whispered to an assistant, and squirmed off in the direction of the men's room. Army had won, 23 to 7, and Blaik was ready to wash his hands of the whole affair.

Conditions conspired to prevent this from being a flawless opening paragraph. After all, it was written for the bulletin board, not the five-star final. Crew Slammer was 1,500 miles away, emptying the wastebasket, when Army defeated Navy. There was something else, though, which Bill Rives (by then assistant managing editor of the Dallas *Morning News*) explained to me a few years later: "You can't use *men's room* in a family newspaper!" I also learned from Rives that you can't use "Jap-a-Nazi Rat" in a family newspaper, even when you are quoting Jules Feiffer's *Great Comic Book Heroes.*

VI

Rives looked like an aging Rudolph Valentino. He was a fanatic for words. The walls of his department were posted with signs ordering KEEP IT SHORT! or WRITE LIKE YOU TALK! The trouble was, neither Rives nor any of the other name writers followed those orders. Maxwell Stiles would open a story on the United States Women's golf championship: "Last Saturday at the Waverly Country Club in Portland I saw the face of America peer at me through a pair of dark eyes alight with the radiant glory of one who has brought honor and dignity to her native land." Then we would study Sherrod, painting his first impressions of a Kansas sophomore named Wilt Chamberlain: "If they're going to let him play basketball . . . they ought to let the Grand Canyon play ditch." Rives would start: "Julius Nicholas Boros, swarthy-skinned son of Hungarian immigrants, captured the National Open championship Saturday with a score of 281, one over par." And *Best Sports Stories* would leap on it.

Dan Jenkins could mock them all with his sweep and simplicity: "Tommy Bolt, with astonishing ease, won the 1958 U.S. Open golf championship today on a vicious course that broke Sam Snead in two days and wrenched Ben Hogan's wrists." And who was Jenkins? He was our first big-timer from the Fort Worth *Press*. He wrote for *Golf Digest*. He could be counted on to have a pocketful of press-box tickets or parking passes. Any time he passed Ben Hogan on the veranda of Colonial Country Club, Hogan was as likely as not to say, "Hi, fella," the only two words Hogan used well. An ex-TCU football player named Red ("How's ya mom and them?") Marable had even confided to friends in high places that he did not want to hit Jenkins, merely "grab him and shake him around."

Bud Shrake followed hard behind Jenkins. He is a giant of a man with a poet's soul and a lumberjack's appetite. He was the accidental winner of a Chili Rice Eating Contest one time while serving as contest referee. Shrake is an enormously talented sportswriter and a keen observer of the species. For a while Shrake and I shared an apartment in Dallas. From time to time a well-known college football coach from a big-time school whose name I will not mention would show up with a bag of groceries, often on the night before a major game. We would eat and drink until about 3:00 A.M., then drive through town looking for girls. We never talked football.

Shrake had a suspicious habit of being with me each time I disgraced myself, my newspaper, and my country. I have always reacted in curious ways to the pressures and exigencies of my profession. It was not Shrake who suggested that I dress up like a waiter, crash the Fort Worth Colonial Country Club's first (and last) annual poolside luau and fashion show, and leap off the three-meter diving board, spraying dinner rolls among the floating orchids.

Yet Shrake had an invitation and I had none. He helped me find a linen closet in the basement, and he was there when Club manager Virgil Bourland intercepted me on the way to the poolside. "What's this?" Bourland asked, lifting a roll from the wicker basket. "Them's rolls!" "What for?" Bourland challenged. "For hungry people." Bourland asked, "Is this some kind of joke?" and I assured him that hunger is never a joke, stomping away indignantly and crouching in the hedges while a search party was organized. It was not Shrake who threw up all over Michigan State football coach Duffy Daugherty when Daugherty told a nauseous joke (punch line: "I don't know what it *is*! I found it in my nose) in the hotel suite of "Coach of the Year" Murray Warmath. It was me. Yet Shrake was a ready accomplice, I confess, just before that, when we ripped off Warmath's bedding, contrived an effigy, and hung it from his transom, much as his students at the University of Minnesota had been doing earlier in the year. Shrake was clear across the room when I took off my clothes and sang "Danny Boy" at Blackie Sherrod's Christmas party. He was there when I swung at and missed Norm Van Brocklin at a night spot in Birmingham. And he had grave reservations the time we found a dead carp on the banks of a gravel pit, and had it cooked and served to Bill Rives, a Catholic. The answers to why we do such things are buried with the minute and uncelebrated details of the events themselves, and maybe too fragile for the Freudian window sash. I know this: in a time my memory cannot identify, in a place I cannot remember being welcome, there is someone's voice, full of respect and anticipation, saying, "For Chrissake, here he comes *again*!"

VII

Influenced in part by men like Blackie Sherrod, Dan Jenkins, and Bud Shrake, almost all sportswriters were experimenting with words in the name of literature by 1960. It is impossible to overestimate the damage this has done to subsequent sportswriters, as this lead, selected at random from the October 22, 1967, Dallas *Morning News* suggests:

Houston—There was mutiny of SMU's Good Ship Destiny here

Saturday night and the Rice Owls found themselves marooned all alone on the Southwest Conference's unbeaten Isle of Desire.

In the fifth paragraph the writer lets you in on the secret: Rice defeated SMU, 14 to 10.

Dan Jenkins is probably the best sportswriter I have ever read, but until he went to *Sports Illustrated* it was difficult to plead his case. Take the creative mind and lash it to a pillar in the city room some Saturday night. Bombard it with the rattle of Western Union printers. Give it headlines to write and other people's stories to read and paste up, and you will understand why from time to time rats have been trained to play the piano. Boredom may be the mother of genius; certainly it comes equipped with its own safety valve.

Boredom is the reason why at the Dallas *Times Herald* in 1960 we came to invent the mythical football power from Metcalf R. The name honors the late newspaper poet James J. Metcalf (the R. stands for nothing in particular, it just sounded better than Metcalf U. or Metcalf Poly). On any Sunday among the agate lines of type telling who won, a *Times Herald* reader was privileged to find the results of the Metcalf R. game. Metcalf R. scheduled such worthies as Indiana McGruder and Southeastern Oklahoma Central, and always won by three points.

Do not suppose this went unchallenged. On one occasion when the Metcalf R. score was accidentally lost on the composing-room floor, a neighbor of the city editor complained. This complaint was the inspiration for our next move: the invention of the Corbet Comets, a small high-school football power of unspecified classification.

The Comets streaked along on the energies of their twin halfbacks, Dickie Don and Rickie Ron Yewbet—named for TCU football coach Abe Martin's speech pattern ("We gonna play some foobuhl, yewbet we are!"). Every Friday night we inserted under a 14-point headline a paragraph celebrating Corbet's newest triumph. Corbet did not lose for two seasons, in which time Rickie Ron got mumps and died. Someone had blue and black Corbet window decals printed, and someone else suggested a story to the editor of the women's page when E. O. (Shug) Kempleman, Corbet Ford dealer, donated the world's largest tuba to the Fighting Corbet Band. Later, when I worked for the Dallas *Morning News,* someone slipped in to print the results of the city of Corbet municipal elections. F. D. Orr defeated E. O. (Shug) Kempleman, 43 votes to 38. Rives, by then an assistant managing editor, blamed me. He called me "flip" and suggested that I read *The Texas Almanac* sometime and grow up.

What is much harder to forgive is what Rives did to my "Study in Black and White" story, the year that the Mississippi State basketball team conquered everyone except its state legislature. There was a law in Mississippi prohibiting integrated sports events. On the day before the MSU basketball team was supposed to leave for the NCAA tournament in Louisville, this law was stretched to include sports events anywhere in the world so long as they involved state teams from Mississippi.

This was a banner story anywhere in the country. No one had to tell me to place a long-distance call to the captain of the MSU team. I don't remember the captain's name, but I remember that he was surprisingly candid. To his way of thinking there was justice in the fact that the Mississippi State basketball team could not claim a national championship until it had played and beaten teams of Negroes. In a touching aside, he told what happened the night of his senior dance in his hometown of Poplarville, Miss. That night, some of the town rednecks kicked down the jail door, hauled out a Negro named Parker, tied him with rope, and threw him in the river. The MSU captain could not remember what the victim had done to rile the population, but the lynching dampened his heart where it would never dry. "The night of our senior dance!" he repeated. "Imagine." I wrote the story straight and Rives killed it. He gave this reason: "This puts the Dallas *News* in a position of taking sides." Well, my God, what if it does? Rives could have just dropped it there. Instead, in an amazing burst of rationale, he added, "If it were a wire-service story, maybe it would be different. But this story . . . this story is written by our own man. Our own man!"

Rives wasn't there a few years later when the *Morning News* destroyed another story, this one considerably closer to home. I learned from a friend that Dallas Country Club was discreetly planning to drop its annual invitational tennis tournament rather than open it to Arthur Ashe, a Negro. The friend put me in touch with an influential club member who confirmed the story and added, "We can't very well have an invitational tennis tournament without inviting the best player in the country. And the mossbacks who run this place can't very well bring themselves to let Arthur Ashe in the front door."

For several years running I had been assigned to cover the tournament. I didn't like it, but there it was in my assignment folder. Dallas Country Club is where The Establishment that Dallas claims does not exist runs the city, including both of its newspapers. Hence the annual DCC Invitational Tennis Tournament was displayed by both Dallas newspapers as you would display WORLD WAR THREE . . . right up till the moment when my story that the whole thing had been dropped was dumped in the editor's wastebasket. After a day and a half of soul-searching, I learned, the rival Dallas *Times Herald* also reached the conclusion that there was no story here.

Then an unfortunate thing happened. *Sports Illustrated* got wind of the story and printed it completely, including the part which made mention of the fact that *Times Herald* executive editor Felix McKnight was a board member at the Country Club. McKnight is a onetime sportswriter and wire-service reporter with a reputation as a no-holds-barred newsman. It was shortly after McKnight took over that *Times Herald* staff members adopted a motto for their paper: "We wait until the bandwagon gets rolling, then throw ourselves under it."

VIII

By this time I knew I would never be a good sportswriter. Yet to turn away from the only profession you have ever known would not be an easy thing. Especially a profession with all those beautiful conflicts of interest. Sportswriters get in free, to sports events or most anything else. They are fed and liquored and given unusual considerations. There are cocktail parties, and wealthy sportsmen with yachts and planes and private islands in the Bahamas, and moonlight jobs in communications. The pay is poor but no one bothers to live on his salary.

There is no spectacle in sport more delightful than witnessing members of the Baseball Writers Association, who invented the box score, trampling each other at the buffet table. The first time I actually saw Dick Young, the New York *Daily News'* very good baseball writer, he was smearing deviled egg on the sleeve of Arthur Daley's sport coat and discussing Casey Stengel's grammar. Ben Hogan was rude and gruff but he impressed me when I learned that the caviar at his annual press party cost $45 a jar. Tony Lema had a genius for public relations at least as great as his genius for golf. Champagne Tony! I covered his funeral. It was an assignment that I did not want, but I was there, thinking that it may be years before I taste champagne again. They served some on the flight home. Bear Bryant used to insist that the way to handle a sportswriter was with a fifth of Scotch. Sportswriters deplored this attitude, but no one ever thought to sue Bear Bryant.

Editors across the land dove for their memo pads a few years ago when the trade magazine, *Editor & Publisher,* exposed the practice of permitting sports teams to pay traveling expenses for writers assigned to cover them. The practice still exists. Some editors see no special evil in the fact that their writers accept cash per diem from the team, usually $25 a day for room and meals. I know a sportswriter who accepts per diem *and* signs for all expenses. The team pays double, but this is how he keeps a daughter in college.

W. O. McGeehan is credited with drafting the industry's code. "If it's a bribe," McGeehan allegedly told a public-relations man, "it's not enough. If it's a gift, it's too much." Still, ethics is a nebulous question to a profession that has never really defined its purpose. To report? To expose? To speculate? To entertain? To criticize? To subsist and endure? A good sportswriter does it all. I do not know a sportswriter who would accept, say, one hundred dollars to print something he did not believe.

On the other hand, I can believe damn near anything. In 1960 after I had written that their training camp was "A Mickey Mouse Operation," an official of the Dallas Texans (now the Kansas City Chiefs) put an envelope into my shirt pocket. It contained, I learned after I had thanked him and walked off, three one-hundred-dollar bills, the only three I had ever seen. It was an offer in the nature of a living allowance, for we were guests at the training camp. The club was training in the spartan quarters of the New Mexico Military Institute in Roswell. In keeping with tradition, sportswriters lived there too. Windowpanes and indoor plumbing had not yet weakened NMMI, which I suppose was part of the reason the Texans selected it as a training site, aside from the fact it was cheap. I had been sitting on my cot, sweating and drinking gin from a chipped coffee cup, when destiny happened by the open window—Paul Miller, a defensive end who once trained with the uptown Los Angeles Rams. Miller was a constant but authoritative bitcher. He became the source for my Mickey Mouse story. The morning after it appeared in print, this club official pushed the three bills in my pocket. All he said was, "I guess things haven't been too easy on you guys these last few weeks."

Well, it was true: they had not. What is more, I had seen the Texans' owner Lamar Hunt squander that much money warming up the engines of his airplane. The Hunts were perhaps the richest family in the world. Lamar and all of his brothers and all of his children and all of his brothers' children each inherited $20 million at birth. Bunker, his older brother, is fat and right-wing to a fault, but I liked him and had traveled places with him in his airplane. I think of Bunker now, half-asleep on the team bus waiting outside the Polo Grounds in New York . . . bitter cold, blowing snow, Christmas music, and the blind blue faces of the people outside in the crowding darkness. An old woman in a stocking cap stomped her feet to keep from freezing. A boy—he couldn't have been ten—pressed close to a burning trash basket. Something stirred Bunker; he started and saw them too. He looked at them a while, then he told me, "Boy hi-dy, that's what I call 'The Great Unwashed.'"

I carried the three hundred dollars with me all morning. I really was broke, having ripped through my expense money from the *Times Herald* in defense of sanity. But I gave back those three bills. I finally realized they were payment for all the Mickey Mouse stories I would ever write.

That is the only time anyone ever offered me money. There is a more subtle practice, however—hiring sportswriters to do program stories or other inconsequential writing jobs for the team they are assigned to cover. It pays well, up to $50 for a couple of pages. I could nominally consider myself a professional writer, so I accepted this sort of arrangement. It is about the same as baseball writers accepting $25 a game to serve as "official scorer."

The answer to conflict of interest, Texas E. Schramm used to explain, is to write positive. Schramm is president and general manager of the Dallas Cowboys, but he learned the business as publicity man and later general manager of the Los Angeles Rams. Los Angeles was and still is a sportswriters' holy place. Athletes step softly. Management is generous. Nevertheless, a big game is a big game, and tickets can be hard to come by.

When the Rams' management prohibited passing out free tickets to the 1951 championship games in the Coliseum (in accordance with league rules), local newspapermen talked it over and decided that the event was not worth covering. They stuck by the position until the Rams reassessed their own and purchased at full price from the league office several hundred "complimentary" tickets.

As a publicity man, Schramm sometimes wrote a column under the by-line of a well-known Los Angeles sportswriter. While Schramm slanted the columns in favor of his employers, he wrote nothing that the columnist might not have written for himself, had he been up to it. All Schramm did was accent redeeming qualities. Ex-Tulane publicity man Larry Karl provided a similar service for a New Orleans sports columnist in the 1950s. Karl would write the column, deliver it, fix it with a standard headline, and tuck it in the columnist's typewriter. On one occasion Karl appendaged the column with a personal note—"Ed" (or whatever), "the plane leaves at noon." He discovered how far things had gone when the message appeared in print as the final sentence to the column.

Let me make one thing plain: most sportswriters have no business in journalism. They are misfits looking for a soft life. The worst sportswriters are frustrated athletes, or compulsive sports fans, or both. The best are frustrated writers trapped by circumstances. Westbrook Pegler called sportswriters "historians of trivia," but Pegler learned his craft by writing sport. Scotty Reston, Heywood Broun, Damon Runyon, Ring Lardner, and Paul Gallico wrote about sport. Winston Churchill covered cricket during the Boer War. The *New York Times'* John Kieran was a sportswriter, but he was much more. When students at Yale protested that a *sportswriter* had been invited to address them, Kieran delivered his speech in Latin.

Sportswriting should be a young man's profession. No one improves after eight or ten years, but the assignments get juicier and the way out less attractive. After eight or ten years there is nothing else to say. Every word in every style has been set in print, every variation from discovery to death explored. The ritual goes on, and the mind bends under it. Ask a baseball writer what's new and he'll quote you the record book. Baseball writers are old men, regardless of age. Crew Slammer contended it was the sport that made it so, but all sport has a tedium that eventually gets too heavy for the human soul. Men who have traveled the deadly dull cycle too often are forever deafened to what they started to say. One writer with the Philadelphia *Bulletin* has been with the Philadelphia Eagles Football Club so long that he refers to them as "we." Difficulty with pronouns is a terminal sign for the journalist.

A writer whose ear is gone can become an editor, which is to say he can become a censor and accountant. Newspaper editors pretend to be appointed guardians of the old mentality ceiling ("write to the sixth-grade reader": never mind why he is sixth-grade), yet in reality they *are* the mentality ceiling. Crew Slammer and the rest of us formulated the theory that the higher a man climbs in the newspaper business, the less he becomes. It must be like a pencil sharpener up there.

I never did learn the name of the man in The Tower who had me fired from my last job as sports columnist of the Philadelphia *Inquirer.* I saw him once. He was pale and, as I recall, walked with a limp. I believe the last time he came down from The Tower was in '07, to overturn a *Bulletin* truck or something. His reason for letting me go was he couldn't understand what I was writing. I appreciated his position. ✦

THE FINAL SEASON

(JANUARY 1977)

George Plimpton

I SUPPOSE THE average athlete begins to wonder when his career is going to end almost as soon as he starts it—knowing that it either can be shortened with devastating swiftness by an injury or eventually reach the point at which the great skills begin to erode. As time goes on, and the broadcasters begin to refer to the athlete as a "veteran" and the club begins to use high draft choices to acquire young collegians to groom for his position, the player has to decide whether to cut it clean and retire at the top—as Rocky Marciano, the heavyweight champion, did—or wait for some sad moment—Willie Mays stumbling around in the outfield reaches of Candlestick Park—when the evidence is clear not only to oneself but to one's peers that the time is up.

Bubba Smith, the great Baltimore defensive end, thought of the process as being symbolized by a small, monkeylike figure he called "Rigor," "Mr. Rigor Mortis," who sometimes reached up out of the grass and slowed him down getting to the ball carrier. Smith told me once, "And then one year he jumps on your back. Sometimes you can brush him off, but every year he gets heavier and grips harder. I've seen him riding the backs of others. He's right around somewhere. Look yonder—he might be just behind the door. Maybe he's behind that curtain over there."

Two summers ago I was driving up to Green Bay, Wisconsin, with a football player who had much of this on his mind. His name was Bill Curry, a veteran center (that unhappy designation) who was on his way to the Packers' training camp where he was going to give football one more try. He had started there ten years before under Vince Lombardi, and now his career, which had been most illustrious with the Baltimore Colts, had come full circle to the club where it had begun.

On the way, we spent one night in the Hotel Pfister in Milwaukee, where we happened to run into Don Drysdale, the cranelike ex-Dodger pitcher, who was working on the California Angels broadcasting team and had been in the booth at the ball park that afternoon for an Angel–Milwaukee game. Curry recognized him, and the three of us sat down in a corner of the hotel's tap room.

They exchanged news. Curry talked about going back to Green Bay and he admitted that he worried about making it. He had a long curved scar, white and new, crossing his kneecap from a fearsome injury suffered while he was with the Houston Oilers, and he had no idea how the leg was going to hold up. Maybe the decision would soon be made for him.

Drysdale grinned, and, with the avuncular attitude of someone who has already gone through it, said that in his case it had been a very easy decision to make—and a very quick one.

Curry winced slightly and said he wanted to hear about it.

Well, the fellow who made it easy for him, Drysdale began, was Roberto Clemente, the great Puerto Rican player for the Pittsburgh Pirates. Clemente always gave him fits at the plate. The distinguishing characteristic of Clemente's base hits was their ropelike trajectory, the ball hit at buzzing speeds, and every time he came up to bat against him, Clemente seemed to hit the ball straight up the middle. Drysdale said he never could face him without thinking of the terrible thing that had happened to Herb Score, the Indians' pitcher, when Gil McDougald hit the ball back into his face and almost blinded him. He'd stand on the mound and look down at Clemente and the Score thing would pop into his mind and he'd give an involuntary shudder. It got so bad, Drysdale told us, that when he delivered the ball, he flinched at his follow-through and tucked his head down a bit.

One day Clemente came up against him in a Dodger–Pirate game in Pittsburgh and drilled one. It was a line drive base hit into center field. Drysdale could hear the ball hum by his ear. Then he had the sensation of a bug crawling on his neck. He flicked at it. Leaning down for the rosin bag, he noticed a runny substance on his finger, and, still feeling the irritation, he reached up and discovered his ear was bleeding: the ball had actually taken the skin off the top of his ear on its way out to center field.

"That was enough for me," Drysdale said. "I remember the first game I pitched in the major leagues, and the last one, and I'm telling you I remember the last one better."

Curry and I left the hotel early the next morning, planning to arrive in Green Bay before noon. Bill seemed preoccupied and kept referring back to

Drysdale's story of the evening before. I asked him if moments like that were likely to come along in football—excluding a sudden wicked injury—a moment, like Drysdale's nicked ear, when a player knew he was finished.

"I'm not sure you can tell so easily," Bill said. "But you can tell. The difference is perhaps a half a step in speed. Just several weeks of not quite getting there would tell you. I won't know until I get in a couple of exhibition games."

We drove along in silence for a while—the countryside, green and beginning to shimmer in the July heat, slipping by.

"Curious," Curry said. "I can never think of the Pfister Hotel back there in Milwaukee without remembering Ray Nitschke—who was just the best middle linebacker there ever was—at the end of his career."

"He was a friend of yours?" I asked innocently.

"Friend?" Curry's hand came off the wheel and made a fist. I thought he was going to slam it down on the horn.

"What was wrong with him?" I asked.

"He was just about the embodiment of my despair at Green Bay," Curry said. "The guy was driven by an intensity which was simply demonic. I don't know another way of describing it. I remember Dan Pastorini, when I was with the Oilers, telling me about Nitschke's intensity even during the *coin toss* at the beginning of an Oiler–Packer game. The captains were all standing out there at the fifty-yard line. Nitschke was out there jawing at the referee who was going to flip the coin: 'All right, goddammit! Come on, ref, toss the goddam coin! Let's get it over with! I want the hell out of here! Let's get this game going!' He really frightened Pastorini.

"When I first signed with Green Bay, in 1964, I was in awe of Nitschke. Off the field he looked professorial: glasses, a high, balding dome. In uniform he looked massive and powerful and mean. The awe soon became tempered by a sort of hatred. At practices he'd appear on the field padded to the hilt—forearms, hands, everything—and you came to know it was going to be a long, tough day. Sometimes things got so bad that Jerry Kramer, Bob Skoronski, Fuzzy Thurston, and Forrest Gregg would gang up and beat the daylights out of him just to slow him up, because he'd run around clotheslining people and crashing into them, even the quarterbacks. He'd be always yelling in that rough, nagging voice of his, 'Come on, let's have some ent'usiasm. Let's get ment'ly . . . ' He came from the back side of Chicago somewhere. Just a constant stream of chatter until finally Lombardi—although he liked a lot of spirit—would call out:

"'Hey, Nitschke.'

"'Yes, sir?'

"'Shaddup.'

"But what he was—well, he was Lombardi's instrument to instill fear. Lombardi would say something like 'I'm going to use fear on you guys, it motivates you. I'm going to make you afraid. I know you're not afraid of the physical aspects of football, or you wouldn't be here. But you *are* afraid of embarrassment in front of your peers. That's what I'm going to do to you, embarrass you, humiliate you until you do the job.'

"I didn't really know what Lombardi meant until one day he said, 'Well, now we're going to have a blitz drill.' In a blitz drill, the middle linebacker comes charging toward the line, The center is supposed to drop straight back about three yards, set his feet, and then hit the middle linebacker before he gets to the passer. Nitschke was at middle linebacker, and I wasn't at all afraid of him. But the first time he hit me was the hardest I'd ever been hit in my life. He knocked me down. A bit stunned, I got up and I thought, Well, I'll hit him that way next time. But I couldn't seem to do it! It's a skill that takes time to cultivate, to drop back that quickly and get your feet set. Of course, Nitschke had some advantages. He was a veteran player and a great linebacker; also he knew the snap count and he knew the plays. Not only that, but he would jump the snap count. He'd come up close to the line of scrimmage and be almost by me before I could hit him. And I was not allowed to cut him low in the legs because he had bad knees. I never did get to where I could block him on those plays. Once he broke my headgear with his forearm. On another occasion he snapped my chin strap with just the sheer force of his blow. Every time I missed him, Lombardi would go into a tantrum: 'Godammit, Curry, can't you move! Can't you do anything!' And then a strange thing happened: I began to dread those practice sessions with blitz drills—with a fear that I had never experienced before in my whole life. I suddenly understood about the fear that Lombardi said he was going to instill in us."

I asked Bill what would have happened if he'd gone to Lombardi and said, "Goddammit, Nitschke's beating the snap count on me. Why the hell doesn't he play it square?!"

"Oh boy!" Curry said. "If I'd've done that, he would've said, 'Goddammit, son, I didn't ask you to come and tell me how to conduct drills. If you can't block him, then get your ass off the field! I don't ever want to see you again!'

"One day this strange thing happened with Nitschke," Curry went on.

"Do you know what a cut block is? You drive out at the man as if you were going to hit him about chest high, and when he lunges to meet you with his forearm you suddenly dip down and hit him around the knees and knock him down. It's a technique that I've made a living off of for almost my whole career. Well, you don't do it in practice. It's just an unwritten rule—no, it's almost a *written* rule. You just *don't cut* your teammates; it's too dangerous to their knees. This day we were practicing running plays. Lombardi was always fussing around the huddle and sticking his head in. 'All right now, I want you to run a thirty-six.' Bart Starr, the quarterback, didn't like that sort of thing. He'd say: 'Wait just a minute. I'm running this huddle.' And Lombardi would step back. But this time Lombardi stuck his head in and he stayed there. He said: 'Curry, I want you to cut Nitschke.'

" 'What!'

"He said, 'I want you to cut Nitschke down on his ass!'

"Not only did Nitschke have a couple of bad knees, as I was telling you, but he did not even have any knee pads, or thigh pads! But what was I going to say to Lombardi? Nothing. I snapped the ball and I fired out and I cut Nitschke, really knocked him down. I thought he'd probably get up and just kill me; he'd kick me in the face or something. He didn't say a word. Everybody called: 'Hey, good block! That's-a-way to git 'im,' 'cause everybody got mad at Ray during practice for always knocking people's heads off. So I was kind of proud of myself and very relieved. I came back to the huddle beaming. Lombardi stood there. He wasn't smiling or anything. He said: 'Hit him again.' I just went pale, 'Oh no. Oh, Jeez, what . . .' So I went out, and I cut him down again. Nitschke did not say a word. When I got back Lombardi said: 'Now, see there? You got him.'

"So Lombardi would do things like that to try to build your confidence and to help you, I suppose, and also because maybe he felt that Nitschke needed a taste of that notion Lombardi had about fear."

"I like it that he never complained," I said.

Curry looked across at me. "You can have him," he said. "The rest of my time with Nitschke was a steady, humiliating, demeaning punishment. All my life my reaction has been, if you push me, or cross me, I'll fight. I fistfight a lot. On the field I play at a high level of combativeness. It's just not civil out there. One afternoon Ray hit me a lot; he snapped my chin strap. Then he hit me again. So I hit him and I started pushing at him—exactly the sort of preliminaries that invariably lead to a fistfight. But he wouldn't do me the favor of hitting back; he wouldn't deign to fight a rookie. He said, 'Kid, what the hell's wrong with you?' Like flicking off a mosquito. It humiliated me. With everybody looking on, I couldn't even get the satisfaction of getting my ass whipped by this guy.

Four years later, after I had become a Colt, we went back to Green Bay to play the Packers. I kept thinking of Nitschke. I told the Baltimore coaching staff, 'I'll bet they're going to blitz a lot because they think Nitschke can beat me.' They were skeptical, because, according to their scouting reports, the Packer defense blitzed only 5 percent of the time, and rarely with the middle linebacker. Of course I was hoping they'd try, because by this time I had become much more proficient in the art of picking up blitzes.

"That day Nitschke blitzed 75 percent of the plays. It started with the first play of the game, and it went on all the way through. He never touched the quarterback, never got within five yards of him. It was one of the most satisfying games of my whole career. I *hit* him and struck him down. All of this sounds so vindictive—and it was. I took tremendous pleasure in using every *ounce* to smash him with, because of all the humiliation he had caused me.

"Then, the last time I saw him was in 1972. I was with the Oilers, and we were in Milwaukee to play the Packers in our third exhibition game. I walked into the lobby of the Pfister Hotel, looked around, and there was Nitschke. It was as if I'd walked through a time warp. There he sat, with his gleaming dome, surveying what had been his for many years. He was trying to struggle back for his fifteenth year as an NFL linebacker, but, from what I was hearing through the grapevine, he was not making it. I felt very awkward trying to speak to this man who had broken me into the NFL in such a rigorous fashion. The conversation went something like 'Gee, Ray, how are you? How's Jackie? How're the kids?' 'Oh, Bill, they're fine. We just got a little girl'— they've adopted, I think, three children now. Then there was an awkward pause, and he suddenly blurted out: 'Bill, I can play. I can go. I can do it.' And I said, 'Well, I heard you were going to play tonight.' He said, 'I don't know about that, but I can go.' He looked at me and he said, 'If I do get to play, you better buckle it up.' I said, 'Well, I've always had to buckle it up against you.' He said, 'Yeah, but I'm fighting for my life this time.' Man, it was sad!

"That night it was worse. The game was bad, as usual. We got behind by 17 to nothing in just a matter of half a quarter; we came back and made it 17 to 14 but then went on to lose the game by something like 34 to 14. With about five minutes left, 50,000 people in County Stadium began to chant: *'We want Nitschke! We want Nitschke!'* I stood on the sidelines watching Ray. He didn't move. It was as if he were a statue. It reminded me of Dan Sullivan's great line about John Unitas: 'Unitas is the only guy whose number they tried to retire while he was still in the jersey.' That was what was happening to Ray, and it was very sad. They never did put him in the game.

"After the game I ran over to him and took the hand of this man who had stomped me physically and emotionally during my first two years with the Packers, and I said, 'Ray, I've never thanked you for what you did for me.' I meant it sincerely, because he helped to make me a lot tougher than I'd ever been. He had not gone about it very pleasantly, but he had meant to help me improve, and I think we both knew that. And I said, 'Ray, I've never thanked you.' He said, 'Yes you have. There're a lot of ways of saying thanks besides verbally.'

"I watched him run off the County Stadium field for the last time. That big number sixty-six and that unique gait of his, leaning forward, huge shoulders and arms pumping slightly, skinny calves. I realized that I had just touched a legend and was seeing him brought down by the very sport he had helped build. I've seen the same happen to Unitas and Tom Matte and others.

"Players think their careers are going to go on forever. Most of them don't prepare for the day it ends. They don't take off-season jobs. Their excuse is 'Well, there's always July,' meaning that another training season is rolling around, one more July, and everything will be as it always was."

Bill Curry did not make it with the Packers that season. His knee held up better than he thought it would, but he developed a hamstring muscle-pull that kept bothering him. During most of the scrimmages he stood on the sidelines watching two younger centers taking turns at his position.

Quitting was not as hard as he imagined it was for a man like Nitschke. But it had been a closing out, a frightening sense of cessation, and when he told me about it over the phone I remembered Dylan Thomas's line "After the first death there is no other."

Yes, Bill said. He thought that was an appropriate enough sentiment. ✦

DOWN AND OUT AT WRIGLEY FIELD

(AUGUST 2001)

Rich Cohen

WHEN THE CHICAGO Cubs last won a World Series, the automobile was still a new and untrusted invention and the electric light was not yet twenty years old. In the years since the fifth game of that series, most of the European monarchies have collapsed, two world wars have been fought, Communism has risen and fallen, and disco has come and gone and come again. Losing year after year, sometimes in the last weeks of the season, more often in the middle of August, the Cubs have become a symbol of futility, the blind, never-ending hope of a hopeless people. Before his death, Jack Brickhouse, the great Cubs play-by-play man, excused the team by saying, "Everyone is entitled to a bad century."

For the Cubs, the current season has thus far played out like a dream. The team collected twelve straight victories in May and early June, a feat it had not accomplished since 1936—a year in which, incidentally, the Cubs did not reach the World Series. Despite the fact that such stretches come along once every five or six years in the manner of a remission that, for a time, masks the true direction of the disease, even the most cynical of fans clings, in a secret place hidden beneath the heckles and beer, to the belief in eventual victory. But if 2001 is indeed the breakthrough year, if the new century indeed ushers in a rebirth of the franchise, these rooters will lose a treasure more valuable than any World Series ring: they will lose an enduring, dependable, nearly mystical relationship with loss.

Last August, hoping to discover the secret of this relationship, I checked into a hotel just off Michigan Avenue on the North Side of Chicago and prepared to "cover" the Cubs. The team had just come off a winning streak that had left them a few games below .500 and a half dozen games behind the division-leading St. Louis Cardinals, whom, in a few days, they would face at Wrigley Field. In other words, I had arrived at that most heartbreaking moment of any Cubs year: the false spring.

I went for walks along Rush Street, in and out of the bars. At Harry Caray's on Kinzie and Dearborn, watching the Cubs on television, I heard a big guy in a SHUT UP AND DRINK YOUR BEER T-shirt refer to a towering Sammy Sosa home run as a "God Ball." He then picked a fight with an old man in a Brewers hat, saying, "Look at your boys! In last place! We are in a solid third! All we got to do is sweep this series, sweep the next series, and go from there."

On State Street, I ran into a friend who had just returned from New York, where he had made his first visit to Yankee Stadium. The Yankees were great, of course, but he thought the stadium a disgrace. No one familiar with Cub fans would find this judgment at all unusual: the prevailing aesthetic is, of necessity, beauty above victory. Anyone else might argue that Yankee Stadium, no matter how monstrous, is a treasure. Why? Because winning has made it beautiful. On the other hand, Wrigley Field, no matter how picturesque, might be considered an eyesore, because losing has made it ugly. The true Cub fan believes the opposite. My friend said, "I'll tell you what, kid, that stadium, it sure made me appreciate what we got right here at Wrigley Field."

Wrigley Field is a trim configuration of red brick and steel. Built in 1914, it was first home to the Chicago Whales of the old Federal League. By the time the Cubs moved here in 1916, they had already won their last World Series. Over the years, with the destruction of most other early twentieth-century ballparks, Wrigley has emerged as a lone witness to the glorious dead-ball era. After generations of artificial turf and multipurpose stadiums, a new generation of architects has come to emulate Wrigley, building snug down-town parks in Baltimore, Cleveland, and Houston. For the most part, though, these stadiums are mere approximations, with none of the mood, or feeling, or grime, of the real thing, none of that terrible history. Wrigley Field is, after all, where, in the 1932 World Series, Babe Ruth supposedly called his shot, pointing two fingers at center field, then hitting a home run into those very seats.

When I went to the games as a kid, I sat in the bleachers, home of the sport's most rabid fans. For a bleacher bum, it was a signal achievement to so incense an enemy outfielder that he climbed the wall in an attempt to get at you. I was at a game in which Omar Moreno of the Pirates started that climb only to be pummeled and covered in beer. Of course, such a climb was made possible by that most famous feature of Wrigley: the ivy, the lush green ivy, which softens all that red brick.

Now, here is the disturbing part: that ivy, that beloved, ticket-selling ivy, is a direct outgrowth of management's realization that the Cubs might never again win a World Series. In 1931, when chewing-gum magnate William Wrigley died, he left the team to his son, P. K. Wrigley, who refused to waste company resources on baseball; he decided that fans must instead be given a reason other than player competence to go to the park. "The fun . . . the sunshine, the relaxation. Our idea is to get the public to go see a ball game, win or lose," said P.K., who then told a young Bill Veeck, who would later become one of the greatest impresarios in the history of baseball, to plant the ivy. It was his way of selling the fans the sunshine.

I grew up in the Chicago suburbs, about fifteen miles up Lake Michigan from Wrigley Field. In the summers, if I was not at the beach, or shopping for records at one of the stores uptown, or scanning the radio for my all-time favorite song, "Rhinestone Cowboy," I was riding the public bus to Evanston, where I caught the elevated train, which threaded its way through a private world of red brick and fire escapes down to the ballpark. On the way I often read the sports section of the *Chicago Tribune*, or else a book about Cubs history. In school we studied the heroes and gods of antiquity, but for me the Cubs supplied a far handier mythology: the great teams of the eighties (the 1880s). The Cubs, a charter member of professional baseball, known first as the White Stockings, and then, in succession, as the Orphans, the Colts, and the Cubs, played in the Congress Street Grounds, the "nicest park in America," with 2,000 grandstand seats and velvet-curtained luxury boxes. Championships were won in 1880, 1881, 1882, 1885, and 1886. These were the teams of the legendary Cap Anson, who first devised the strategy wherein players run out of position to back up other players and, in another first, called for the banning of black athletes from the game. In his autobiography, Anson wrote of an early minority hire:

> Clarence was a little darkey that I had met sometime before while in Philadelphia. . . . I had togged him out in a suit of navy blue with brass buttons, at my own expense, and had engaged him as a mascot. He was an ungrateful little rascal . . .

There was Mike Kelly, a hard-drinking Irishman from the West Side, the first catcher to communicate with the pitcher in a secret code of often comical hand signals. There was Billy "The Evangelist" Sunday, who, before scaring sinners with his fiery prophecies of hell, was a speedy, base-stealing outfielder. In 1906, behind the awesome double-play combination of Tinkers to Evers to Chance, the team posted the best record in major-league history, winning 116 games. After each victory, the players went drinking at Biggio Brothers Saloon on Polk and Lincoln Streets. In later years came Grover Cleveland Alexander, a once great pitcher who came back from the First World War shell-shocked. When Alexander fell into seizures on the mound, the infielders would shield him from view. In the biopic, Alexander was played by Ronald Reagan, who himself, as a young man, had called play-by-play for the Cubs.

William Wrigley took control of the Cubs in 1921 and fielded pennant-winning teams in '32, '35, and '38. These teams boasted such superstars as Kiki Cuyler, Hack Wilson, Billy Jurges, Babe Herman, and Rogers Hornsby. In 1932, Jurges was shot in a hotel room by a jilted lover in a black veil, an episode borrowed by Bernard Malamud for his novel *The Natural.* In 1929, Hornsby batted for a .380 average with 149 RBIs. Hack Wilson, a squat alcoholic of a power hitter, still holds the record for most runs batted in (190) during a single season. After retirement, Hack became a drifter. In 1948, when he died, his body went unclaimed for three days. Nineteen years earlier, in 1929, when the Cubs had lost the World Series, Wilson told a train of badgering reporters, "Let me alone now, fellows. I haven't anything to say except that I am heartbroken and that we did get some awful breaks."

In 1953 the club signed its first black superstar, Ernie Banks, a Hall of Famer who encouraged hope in the fans, beginning each season with a little poem, such as, "The Cubs will come alive in sixty-five," or, "The Cubs will be heavenly in sixty-sevenly." In my own childhood there were the Reuschel brothers, fat, mustachioed, glasses-wearing screwballers who, to me, looked like the newspaper's photos of John Wayne Gacy. On my baseball card, the Reuschels, Rick and Paul, are pictured over the words BIG LEAGUE BROTHERS. In this era, due to years of futility—the team had not even been in the post-season since 1945—a certain ugliness grew up between fans and management, peaking in 1983, when, during a postgame press conference, skipper Lee Elia attacked the bleacher bums, saying,

Eighty-five percent of the people in this country work. The other fifteen percent come here and boo my players. They oughta go out and get a fucking job and find out what it's like to go out and earn a fucking living. Eighty-five percent of the fucking world is working. The other fifteen percent come out here. A fucking playground for the cocksuckers.

CUBS 7, CARDINALS 3

Each day the Cubs lineup was posted, with slight variation, in the clubhouse. It was a collection of found parts, as is often the case: Damon Buford, a center fielder, who came in a trade from Boston; Joe Girardi, a born-again Christian from Peoria, Illinois, who started with the Cubs a decade ago and had returned to finish his career in Chicago; Mark Grace, the blond-haired, goateed first baseman, who before and after each game smoked a cigarette at his locker; Willie Greene, a third baseman from Milledgeville, Georgia, by way of the Toronto Blue Jays; Ricky Gutierrez, an edgy, error-prone shortstop, a free agent from the Houston Astros; Chad Meyers, a twenty-five-year-old infielder who looked like a sitcom sidekick on the WB (a Cubs fan from Nebraska, Meyers was, as a kid, certain the Cubs were always "just about to win it"); Brant Brown, an outfielder who, in 1998, had dropped a routine fly ball that almost kept the team out of that year's postseason play.

At three o'clock, only the pitchers were in uniform, among them Kerry Wood, a lank, sullen-faced Texan who was once thought to be the savior of the team. In 1998, at twenty, in only his fifth start, Wood struck out twenty batters, tying a major-league record. A few months later he blew out his pitching arm; he was still recovering from the surgery. In his locker he had mounted a Big Mouth Billy Bass, the talking mechanical fish, which, on occasion, he let answer the press queries: "I run on batteries, don't need no gas, I'm the Big Mouth Billy Bass."

Sammy Sosa, the great star of the Cubs, showed up shouting, a man of entrances. Although the players in the clubhouse were listening to Pearl Jam, Sosa plugged in his radio and began playing salsa music, the sound of his native Dominican Republic. Someone turned up the Pearl Jam. Sosa turned up the salsa. For a moment, the sunny Caribbean faced off against the once grungy Pacific Northwest. Sosa closed his eyes and started to dance. Today, and each day, it ended with the Pearl Jam turned down and turned off. It was not hard to tell how Sosa's teammates felt about this.

Standing in front of his locker, Sosa took several practice swings, which, like his body, were short and compact. In 1998 he had kept pace with Mark

McGwire in a contest to break the single-season home-run record. Sosa had finished four homers behind McGwire. There are those who called Sosa a hot dog, error-prone, strikeout-prone, a one-way player who padded his statistics with meaningless late-game long balls. Earlier in the season, when the front office threatened to trade Sosa, there had been a tremendous uproar from the fans, who, in exchange for all that losing, expect at least one superstar. After a loss in which Sosa homered with the bases empty and struck out with the bases full, I asked him if he changed his approach depending on the situation—shortened his swing, stepped up in the box. He said, "I just hit the ball as hard as I can."

By five o'clock the reporters had gathered in the clubhouse. They stood in a tight little knot like boys at a high school dance, waiting for some sign from a pretty girl across the floor. Now and then, one of these reporters would plunge in with his tape recorder; depending on whether he was welcomed or rebuffed, the reporter would return saying, "Wow, what a regular guy!" or, "Can you believe how much money those dumb fucks make?"

To reach the field we followed the clatter of cleats through a dank tunnel into the dugout. At eye level the grass, which in the middle of the season was already parched, stretched away to the power alleys. The bench was crowded with that gaggle of former players, broadcasters, and hangers-on that make up the courtier class of the national game. A few hundred fans had gathered for batting practice. They shouted, "Sammy! Sammy! Sammy!" I found myself in a conversation with Joe Girardi. In the clubhouse, I had seen Girardi, and everyone else, naked, and I was struck by his body, which seemed to me old-fashioned, a body from the Great Depression: thick torso and heavy arms, social realism, a WPA poster. He had spent the previous four seasons in New York, where he won three World Series. How could he now play for a team that never wins, has never won, and, it seems to many of us, never will win?

"When I was in third grade, I wrote an essay about how I would play for the Cubs," Girardi said. "Ten times a summer, I drove with my father from Peoria just to see the games." Back then, his favorite players were Ron Santo, a third baseman who, as a broadcaster, still travels with the team, and Jose Cardenal, remembered mostly for his vertiginous Afro, on top of which, the cherry on the ice-cream sundae, perched his cap. Cardenal is credited with the worst excuse ever given for missing a game: he once told his manager he could not play because his eyelid was stuck open. "When I left the Cubs that first time, I was crushed," said Girardi. "I had always wanted to be a Cubbie."

I asked why the team never wins.

"The Yankees have a hundred-million-dollar payroll. Our club is sixty million. And there is also all the money spent on the minor leagues and free agents, signing kids from the Dominican, from Puerto Rico. But it's more than that. In New York, you go into spring training expecting to get to the World Series. You feel it when you walk in the clubhouse—the pictures of all those Yankee greats, the monuments. There is something special about putting on the pinstripes. In Chicago, they hope for a good season, maybe the play-offs."

"But they have pictures here at Wrigley Field," I said. "The Cub greats, Hack Wilson, Kiki Cuyler."

"Yeah, but just think about those pictures," he said. "Still shots, each player by himself. In Yankee Stadium, it's group shots, the team celebrating on the mound, in the clubhouse, the champagne, winning it all. Here you won't see that."

When Girardi went to take batting practice, I wandered out onto the field. The players chirped and fluttered around the cage like birds; players from the Cubs and players from the Cardinals met one another with backslaps and hugs. "In our day, there was no fraternizing," Ron Santo told me. "You never saw one team up watching the other team hit. Never saw a guy hugging the other guy. You walked across the white lines, money was not the criteria. Winning was." Sosa greeted every Latin player on the Cardinals, then wandered over to the seats, the crowd bubbling before him like surf. He spotted two friends from the Dominican and led them out onto the field. They were potbellied, sleepy-eyed, with slow, sad smiles; one wore a silk shirt decorated with naked girls, fast cars, tropical sunsets.

I walked over to a circle of beat reporters, three of them: a young banana-shaped one; a middle-aged, balding, red-haired one; and an old stately one with no hair at all. I said hello. Without a word, each turned his back on me. It took me some time to realize that these reporters, who after each game filed stories for the *Tribune,* the *Sun-Times,* and a third paper I had never heard of, were actually participants in the Cubs' perpetual loss and naturally took a pride in the project that made it necessary to resent someone like myself, who had come aboard the *Titanic* to snap a few shots before shoving off. Of course, that ship was at least heading toward a conclusion, a climax. The Cubs, on the other hand, were and are forever adrift.

The only friend I made among the press was a kid entirely untouched by the stinking heartbreak of history. His name was Nick, and he was on summer break from Drake University in Iowa. He had landed a part-time job writing about the Cubs for his hometown newspaper in Oak Park. A few times a week Nick went to the clubhouse and, without the least hesitation, pulled aside his favorite players. Before this game, he had talked to some of the Cardinals, even to Will Clark, rumored to be the crankiest man in the league.

Nick said, "Can I ask you some questions, Mr. Clark?"

Mr. Clark said, "Get the fuck away from me, kid."

Nick told me that Mr. Clark had stunk of beer.

Nick led me up to the press box, high above home plate. As we talked, I could see the lake, blue and crowded with sailboats, beyond the apartment buildings. The game was a sellout, standing room only, men and women at the back of the bleachers in sketchy outline. To some, this remained the best explanation for the Cubs' woes: if a team with a losing record sold 40,000 tickets on a Monday night and drew, win or lose, 2 million fans a year, while the White Sox, in first place on the South Side of the city, could not even sell out on a Saturday afternoon, what was the incentive? Why should the Tribune Company, which owns the Cubs, spend millions to build a winning team if, all these years later, the fans were still willing to pay for sunshine? "We hear a lot of that," Kevin Tapani, a Cubs pitcher, told me. "But I don't know of any player that says, 'We've got a sold-out crowd, let's lose.'"

Of course, Tapani, at thirty-six, was precisely the sort of player a team might go after if it was not determined to win; that is to say, yes, Tapani tried to win, but perhaps, at this point in his career, he was no longer good enough to win consistently. And yet—the Cubs *did* spend money. Not so much as the Dodgers or the Orioles but more than some successful teams (the Kansas City Royals, the Oakland A's), and they traded for players and hired managers who had won elsewhere. A Cubs fan therefore learns to distrust the easy answers and to accept each moment, each game, for what it is, not for where it is leading, which is nowhere. A victory, any victory, is a victory. Like tonight, for example, with a warm breeze off the lake, and the sun going down (ah, that beautiful Cubs sunshine), and the team at last stirring to life. Jeff Huson, a journeyman third baseman, with teeth as small and perfect as white Chiclets, drove a ball down the left-field line, scoring the winning runs. And then we were following the ramps down to the clubhouse, where the players, having already changed into Nike shower sandals and gym shorts, ate fried chicken off Styrofoam plates and watched SportsCenter on ESPN. There was music, there was clowning. Cubs win! Cubs win!

CARDINALS 4, CUBS 2

Three hours before the first pitch, Carol Slezak, a columnist for the *Sun-Times,* was in the dugout, looking for a story. Baseball is a world of men, and so it was strange and pleasing to see a woman on the field. Some of the older Latin coaches commented on Slezak's eyes, her legs. "You are making me uncomfortable," she said. "Stop it." A year ago, Slezak had written a column about Sosa's music, how it had become an irritating and never-ending soundtrack. Sosa and Glenallen Hill (since traded) had pulled her aside and yelled at her. "Do you know how angry Sammy's teammates are at you?" Hill said. "They love Sammy."

"Do you want to hear what Sammy's teammates say about his music?" asked Slezak.

Sammy told her, "Fuck my teammates."

Today, Carol was in a pregame panic. Her deadline was a few hours away and she had yet to find a subject. Players suggested she write about the heat. "I have a policy," she said. "No stories about weather." Mark Grace greeted her in a large way and sat at the end of the bench, determined to help. Each generation, there is one Cub who seems, for fans, to stand for the team. For the last several years that had been Grace. Previously, it had been Ryne Sandberg, Bill Buckner, Rick Monday, Ernie Banks. One of the great things about baseball is that, by setting these players, whose careers overlap, in a time line, you can link yourself clear back to Mike Kelly and Johnny Evers. After suggesting several stories, which Carol dismissed, Grace said, "What about the heat?"

Grace took off his hat, rubbed his scalp. A few weeks earlier, several Cubs had shaved their heads in a gesture of solidarity. Grace was lucky; he looked good. Some of the other guys had emerged knotty-skulled, or bug-eyed, or jug-eared. Grace talked about being thirty-six. In the minor leagues, the Cubs were developing Hee Seop Choi, a Korean power-hitting first baseman, to take his position. To a player like Grace, this was what the end must look like—a husky nobody from the minors with no feel for the game.

Mark Grace was the classic Cub playing in a pointless doubleheader on an August afternoon with the wind blowing in and nothing on the line but a flutter at the bottom of the standings. Only a player like Grace, who got the joke of being a Cub[1] and still reveled in it, could possibly explain to me how and why it was that each Cub season began and ended in futility.

I asked him if there was any thrill to being the spoiler, stopping some other team from making the play-offs—often the only role left for the Cubs. "No, I don't take a whole lot of pleasure in it," he said. "But the last thing you want is somebody clinching on your turf, mobbing, pouring bubbly on your field."

Sosa emerged from the tunnel and shouted, "I just took a big shit. It feels good when you take your big shit."

The temperature at game time was 91 degrees. In the fifth inning, the umpire left the game due to heat exhaustion. I asked Carol Slezak if the players were upset after such a loss, and she said, "They pretend to be." The next day, in the *Sun-Times,* I read her story about how exceptionally hot it was at the game.

CARDINALS 5, CUBS 1

Even after a player retires from the Cubs, he remains a hero in Chicago, a god in the pantheon of loss. For players traded to the team this is a consolation. The smart ones, who understand a thing or two about history, must know that they will never be part of a dynasty here. Kevin Tapani remembers when he learned of his trade to the team: "Everyone around here tells you the history and says, 'Now you are a part of it. You're one of the lovable losers.' And so you think, 'Well, I was not a loser to start with, I did not come here to lose, I will not carry on like a loser.'" Some deluded Cubs even speak of being part of the team that at last breaks the streak. But fans—some of us, anyway, who know the truth—pity the talented young prospect who, having won in Little League, high school, and everywhere else, finds himself on the

---

[1] *At the end of the season, Grace would leave Chicago; unwanted, he would sign a two-year contract with the Arizona Diamondbacks. At the press conference he would say, "I know we play [the Cubs] nine times this year, and I want to kick their butt nine times. . . . I gave my heart and soul for thirteen years to the Chicago Cubs." Cub greats have often met a dubious end. In my era, Bill Buckner was traded to Boston at the end of his career, where, in game six of the 1986 World Series, he let a routine grounder hop between his legs, costing the Red Sox their first championship since 1918. This inevitably leads to Mike Royko's Cubs theorem: If you want to determine the outcome of any particular baseball game, simply calculate which team has more ex-Cubs. That's your loser. There are exceptions to this rule—players who go on to win Cy Young Awards and pennants elsewhere—but these usually result from awful deals. The worst trade in team history sent twenty-four-year-old Lou Brock to St. Louis, where he would rewrite the record books, in exchange for thirty-seven-year-old Ernie Broglio, a warhorse of a pitcher who would retire a year later.*

Cubs. *Hope you enjoyed the ride, friend. Because, barring a trade, your winning days are over.* In return such a player, if he is good enough to make an impression, is given the city. Chicago loves its Cubs as it loves no other athletes. The Cubs personify Chicago's striving, the pride that locals take in even the smallest construction, the sense that the rest of the country, especially New York City, is giving us the high hat.

This love was in evidence a few minutes before yet another afternoon game against the Cardinals, as Ryne Sandberg, who for twelve seasons was the star of the Cubs, wandered across the infield to shouts and cheers. In 1994, Sandberg, the highest-paid player in the game, had returned millions of dollars and gone into early retirement, saying he wasn't happy with his performance. He came back in '96, found that he had lost his swing, and retired again. It was like watching someone grow old in public. He was now an instructor with the team. On the field, he wore prefaded jeans and a button-down shirt and moved with the stiffness one expects in a retired athlete, his glossy, handsome face turning red in the sun.

For every Cub fan, there is a season, an inning, an at bat, when all hope is lost, when, at long last, he becomes disillusioned and realizes with dread certainty that no matter how good its prospects the team will never win. "The better they look," my father[2] had warned, "the bigger the heartbreak." For some, hope was lost in 1969, when, after decades of loss, the management fielded an uncharacteristic collection of future Hall of Famers and all-stars. By September 1 the team was in first place by eight games. After each victory, Ron Santo, the third baseman, would jump up and click his heels. A song that year had the fans singing, "Hey hey, holy mackerel, no doubt about it, the Cubs are on their way!" By mid-September they had been overtaken by the expansion New York Mets, who went on to sweep the World Series. "The Mets were not a team you worried about," Santo told me. "It was divine intervention. God just lived in New York that year."

For some, hope was lost in 1989, when the Cubs, with Mark Grace at first base, were swept in the play-offs by the San Francisco Giants. For some it was in 1998, with Sosa hitting all those homers and the team still looking pathetic in the play-offs. For me it was 1984 and the collapse of the great team

---

[2] *A New Yorker, my father had urged me to follow the Dodgers or the Yankees, the teams he had watched as a kid. He worried that in cheering for the Cubs I would come to accept losing as the natural condition of things and so ruin my life.*

anchored by Ryne Sandberg, who that year won the National League MVP. In 1981 the Wrigley family had sold the franchise to the Tribune Company, filling the loyalists with hope. Whereas the Wrigleys had refused to spend top dollar on talent, often trading away their best prospects and, what's worse, evincing a kind of country-club racism, for years signing no black players and then signing only a few, the Tribune Company was a cash-rich empire. For the first time in years real money was spent on the Cubs. A new general manager was brought in, and soon he had built the first team I ever really cared about. That team had Lee Smith, the fire-throwing relief pitcher, and Rick Sutcliffe, the red-headed ace, and Harry Caray, the great broadcaster, the true visage of the Cubs, who told you not what players were averaging but what they *should* be averaging were the world a decent place. "He's really up around .400," Harry would say. "He's hit the ball well, but at people." Harry said that the Cubs infield was not only the most competent in the game but by far the best looking: "Sandberg: classical good looks. Bowa: scrappy, sinewy, and sexy. Cey: just look at that guy! Durham: what woman would not love Bull Durham?"

The team won the National League East by six and a half games. In August several Cubs, including Sutcliffe and Durham, released a country song that my brother called "a crime—an idiotic, stupid, jinx-inducing crime." The song went like this: "As sure as there's ivy on the center-field wall, the men in blue are gonna win it all." And: "We're on top and looking down and picking up more steam." And: "There's been lots of talk about no lights in Wrigley Park, we don't care, if we make it there, we'll play in the dark."

The Cubs at that time were the only professional team without lights—a fact that, from time to time, was suggested as a reason for their woes. When the team played night games on the road, so went the reasoning, they were out of sorts, up past their bedtime. In 1984 the commissioner of baseball was more concerned with the fact that no night games at Wrigley meant the league would be robbed of prime-time TV revenue. As a result, the Cubs, in a great miscarriage of justice, were stripped of their home-field advantage, which, in the best-of-five play-off, proved crucial. I skipped school to attend the first game, which the Cubs won in a blowout. I followed game two at school, checking the score between classes on TV: another victory. The Cubs then went to San Diego, where they had to win only one of the next three games to clinch a trip to the World Series. In each game the Cubs went into the seventh inning with the lead. In each game they choked. The final blow came with a home run by Steve Garvey, the square-jawed Padres first baseman at the end of his career. The footage of the ensuing trot, Garvey pumping his fist, suggested everything that is wrong with the world.

Arizona 11, Cubs 2
Arizona 11, Cubs 3
Arizona 5, Cubs 4

Sooner or later every Cubs fan, if he is at all reflective, comes to realize that if the Cubs were somehow to cast off the past and win, they would no longer be the Cubs. There is a thrill in victory, yes, but there is a certainty in defeat, and is losing not, in the end, more righteous than winning? Sure, the team might enjoy the arrogance of victory for a season or two, or three, or however long it lasted, but it would thereby destroy the more interesting part of its identity. It would become just another club that won not long ago and is now not so good and not so bad. *The first shall be the last and the last shall be the first.* But what of those in the middle?

Since 1908, ninety-two teams have had hard luck, like the Red Sox, who have not won the World Series in eighty-three years, but the Red Sox have often gone deep into the Series. Perhaps there is more of a sting to the near miss, but the deep pain, the good stuff, is only to be had by never even coming close. If one must lose, it may as well be spectacularly, as was the case with the series I saw in Arizona. Everything went wrong. Every play was botched. Every player stank. If this were a movie I would title it, simply, *Three Days in August.*

The Diamondbacks play in a kind of terrarium, a vast biosphere in the center of Phoenix with a retractable roof and seats running clear up to the great glass panels. It was well over 100 degrees out there in the desert, but inside it is always a brisk 72; there is even a kind of autumn crispness in the air. Each player's equipment had been hung in lockers on the far side of the clubhouse. Unfortunately, Sosa's locker was at some distance from an electrical outlet, and thus he could not plug in his radio. A work crew was brought in to run an extension cord across the floor, which a pitcher proceeded to trip on.

Across the room sat a table with a pile of magazines, on top of which was a *Sports Illustrated* Where Are They Now? issue that showed William "Refrigerator" Perry, a lineman for the Bears, once a famous athlete in Chicago, in a hard hat and work clothes, over the words, "Bricklayer, Aiken, South Carolina." The Cubs walked by this magazine as if it had nothing to do with them. They watched, on DVD, the scene in *Fast Times at Ridgemont High* in which Judge Reinhold, caught masturbating in the bathroom, says, "Doesn't anyone around here knock?" Sosa made the jerk-off motion—a locker-room gesture so basic and true it was like a revelation.

In the dugout, Mark Grace was talking with Joe Garagiola, himself a former catcher and now the vice president and general manager of the Diamondbacks. Grace told Garagiola that he considered himself a throwback, an old-fashioned player, demonstrated by the fact that, among other things, he did not wear batting gloves, saying he prefers "the feel of the wood." Since he was a rookie, he said, the big change in the game had been pitchers, who no longer intimidated in the same way. If, as a young Cub, he had come to the plate following a home run, he could have expected the next pitch to be a fastball at his back, "between the one and the seven." Now, Grace said, pitchers were so nervous about getting tossed from a game that "the best ball to hit is the one right after the home run." The following night, after Sammy Sosa's long home run off Randy Johnson, the next pitch is a fastball, to Grace, "between the one and the seven."

HOUSTON 5, CUBS 4
HOUSTON 10, CUBS 7

With each loss, the clubhouse grew noticeably darker. There was no music during the losing streak, no chatter. Only the sound of Sosa talking with reporters about his most recent home run—a moon shot that kissed the outer glass of Enron Field before falling back into the seats. With each home run, you could see the chasm widening between Sammy and his teammates. "I never really watch the ball," Sosa said. "I put my head down and run the bases. But I know I got that one good." In the locker room, Tim Worrell, a pitcher who gave up a homer that meant a lot more than Sammy's, sat with his head in his hands. A coach, stationed before a VCR, with two empty beer cans at his side, watched the home run, freezing the frame just prior to the disaster: Worrell in his follow-through, the ball hanging like a pigeon over the plate. The coach took notes, rewound, lived through the terrible moment again, then hit fast-forward: the batter, with lickety-split cartoon speed, dashed around the bases to score.

I think I wanted to travel with the Cubs and see them suffer in return for all of the suffering they have caused me. But being on the road with the team in a true slump—well, I guess I had no idea how awful it would be: the stillness of the clubhouses, the eyes on the floor, the jumpiness. Mark Grace saying, "I'm 0 for this road trip, and that really sucks," and after every game the manager, Don Baylor—why does a manager wear cleats?—making his statement to the press, the general of an army in perpetual retreat: "Defensively, we've gone from the bottom to second in the league." Or, "That was a home run people can talk about for years. . . . Unfortunately, it comes as part of another loss." It was hard to imagine how the Cubs would ever win another game.

Eventually I put the problem to the man charged, hopelessly, with fixing it. "What this club has always done is lose," Baylor told me. "So even if you have to change the players, you need to find a way to switch the mind-set. You have to find winning players who will talk about winning and not about how the organization has never won."

General Manager's Office

One afternoon in Chicago I met with Andy MacPhail, the president and general manager of the Cubs, in his office at Wrigley Field. MacPhail, who won two World Series with the Minnesota Twins, descends from baseball royalty. His grandfather Larry MacPhail, the owner of the Brooklyn Dodgers, helped pioneer night baseball in the major leagues. His father, Lee MacPhail, was the general manager of the Yankees and the Orioles and the president of the American League. For Andy, a neatly dressed middle-aged man with blond hair and wire-rimmed glasses, turning the Cubs around is perhaps the only way he can outdo his father and grandfather, both members of baseball's Hall of Fame. "The Cubs have not been good enough at bringing players through the system," he told me. "Other clubs have done it better. You don't have to look further than the Yankees, who've been going to the World Series ad nauseam in the nineties. People think it's the payroll, but look at Bernie Williams, Derek Jeter, Andy Pettitte, Mariano Rivera—all of them come from the Yankees system. That's what we need to do, and I'm confident that we're doing it. We're going to have our share of players coming up. I can see them in the pipeline."

I asked if there wasn't something greater at play with the Cubs. A corporation-wide funk, a mental or emotional block, a culture of loss.

"To be honest, I have been trying to figure that one out myself," he said, "and here is what I realized: through different ownerships, managers, general managers, players, equipment managers, the one constant has been the ballpark, the vagaries of playing in Wrigley Field. In Minnesota, in the dome, we had AstroTurf, 70 degrees, and no wind, every day. You could customize your team to the environment where you played. You can't do that here. One day the wind is howling straight in from the lake; the next day it's howling straight out. You really have to be good all the way around."

"What about the Cubs teams that were good but still lost?" I asked. "How do you explain '69 and '84?"

"I don't think that there is a curse, if that's what you mean."

In 1945, when the Cubs last went to the World Series, the owner of the Billy Goat Tavern, not allowed to bring his goat into the park, is said to have hexed the team—a curse some fans say explains '69 and '84, and all the rest of it.

I told MacPhail what Ron Santo had told me on the road. "Once you win it, and establish that you are a winning club, it becomes easier," said Santo, who in his playing career never won anything. "When you have won and somebody comes to this organization, they cannot look back and say, 'Well, we haven't won since 1908, or even been there since 1945.'"

"I hate to disagree with a Cub legend," said MacPhail, "but I can't get into the occult. My problem is wins and losses, supply and demand. Do you really think Bill Buckner or Leon Durham was thinking about 1969? I don't think it's in the players' minds. I do think that it is popular with the fans to have teams that represent futility. They like to have lovable losers. Even in the years where we were pretty good, they are slow to recognize it, or believe it, or want to believe it. Now, I find that personally repugnant, and I am going to die trying to change it."

Cubs 15, Houston 5

When it happens, it happens fast. One moment the Cubs cannot string together two hits, or turn a double play, or steal a base. The next minute they are driving the ball all over the field, sliding into clouds of dirt, racing around the bases. The beat reporters typed furiously into their laptops, adjectives flying everywhere. A press-box announcer said that the fifteen runs scored by the Cubs ties their season record set in May in a game against Montreal, which the Cubs lost 16–15. In the clubhouse after the game, it was V-E Day all over again, music cranked up, players goofing in the showers. There were whoops, shouts, backslaps. In the aftershock of a high ten, I was racked by a memory that filled me with shame: In the sixth grade I was on a hockey team, the Winnetka Warriors, that had started the season 0 and 13. In our fourteenth game we beat a team from up north. Afterward, as the two teams stood side by side, we started to sing, "We are the Champions!" The other team, who knew they had lost to the biggest losers in the league, waited until we reached the line, "No time for losers." That's when the brawl broke out. I fought for my team, of course, but I was ashamed doing it. And that's pretty much how I felt watching the locker-room party after the Cubs beat the Astros. There was something self-deceiving in the whole crummy display.

At night when I can't sleep, I sometimes think back on my travels with the Cubs, and it is always the same image that first comes to mind: I was in the clubhouse in Arizona after another defeat. The room was somber, the players dressing quickly in front of their lockers. Several reporters had gathered around Mark Grace, who had caught that Randy Johnson fastball between the shoulder blades—retaliation for Sosa's long home run; Grace had staggered and collapsed.

As Grace buttoned his shirt, one of the reporters said, "Looked like Johnson didn't have his best stuff out there."

"Oh, I don't know," said Grace. "The one that hit me felt pretty good."

You could already see the bruise. It was red and blue, and within it was a darker bruise left by the stitches on the ball. Over the next several days, this wound would develop like a photograph of yet another painful season for the Chicago Cubs.   ✦

OBSESSED WITH SPORT

(JULY 1976)

Joseph Epstein

I CANNOT REMEMBER when I was not surrounded by sports, when talk of sports was not in the air, when I did not care passionately about sports. As a boy in Chicago in the late forties, I lived in the same building as the sister and brother-in-law of Barney Ross, the welterweight champion. Half a block away, down near the lake, the Sullivan High School football team worked out in the spring and autumn. Summers the same field was given over to baseball and men's softball on Sundays. A few blocks to the north was the Touhy Avenue Fieldhouse, where basketball was played, and lifeguards trained, and behind which, in a softball field frozen over in winter, crack-the-whip, hockey, and speed skating took over. To the west, a block or so up Morse Avenue, was the Morse Avenue "L" Recreations, a combined pool hall and bowling alley. Life, in short, was games.

My father had no interest in sports. He had grown up, one of the ten children of Russian Jewish immigrant parents, on tough Notre Dame Street in Montreal, where the major sports were craps, poker, and petty larceny. He left Montreal at seventeen to come to Chicago, where he worked hard and successfully so that his sons might play. Two of his boyhood friends from Notre Dame Street, who had the comic-book names of Sammy and Danny Spunt, had also come to Chicago, where they bought the Ringside Gym on Dearborn Street in the Loop. All the big names worked out at Ringside for their Chicago fights: Willie Pep, Tony Zale, Joe Louis. At eight or nine I would take the El downtown to the Ringside, be introduced around by Danny Spunt ("Tony Zale, I'd like you to meet the son of an old friend of mine. Kid, I'd like you to meet the middleweight champion of the world"), and return home with an envelope filled with autographed 8-by-10 glossies of Gus Lesnevich, Tammy Mauriello, Kid Gavilan, and the wondrous Sugar Ray.

I lived on, off, and in sports. *Sport* magazine had recently begun publication, and I gobbled up its issues cover to cover, soon becoming knowledgeable not only about the major sports—baseball, football, and basketball—but about golf, hockey, tennis, and horse racing, so that I scored reputably on the Sport Quiz, a regular department at the front of the magazine. Another regular department was the Sport Classic, which featured longish profiles of the legendary figures in the history of sports: Ty Cobb, Jim Thorpe, Bobby Jones, Big Bill Tilden, Red Grange, Man o' War. I next moved on to the sports novels of John R. Tunis—*All-American, The Iron Duke, The Kid from Tomkinsville, The Kid Comes Back, World Series,* the lot—which I read with as much excitement as any books I have read since.

The time was, as is now apparent, a splendid era in sports. Ted Williams, Joe DiMaggio, and Stan Musial were afield; first Jack Kramer, then Pancho Gonzales, dominated tennis; George Mikan led the Minneapolis Lakers, and the Harlem Globetrotters could still be taken seriously; Doc Blanchard and Glen Davis, Mr. Inside and Mr. Outside, were playing for Army, Johnny Lujack was at Notre Dame; in the pros Sammy Baugh, Bob Waterfield, and Sid Luckman were the major T-formation quarterbacks; Joe Louis and Sugar Ray Robinson fought frequently; the two Willies, Mosconi and Hoppe, put in regular appearances at Bensinger's in the Loop; Eddie Arcaro seemed to ride three, four winners a day. Giants, it truly seemed, walked the earth.

All learning of craft—which sport, like writing, most assuredly is—involves imitation, especially in the early stages; and I was an excellent mimic. By the time I was ten years old I had mastery over all the big-time moves: the spit in the mitt, the fluid infield chatter, the knocking of dirt from the spikes; the rhythmic barking out of signals, hands high under the center's crotch to take the ball; the three bounces and deep breath before shooting the free throw (on this last, I regretted not being a Catholic, so that I might be able to make the sign of the cross before shooting, as was then the fashion among Catholic high-school and college players). I went in for athletic haberdashery in a big way, often going beyond mimicry to the point of flat-out phoniness—wearing, for example, a knee pad while playing basketball, though my knees were always, exasperatingly, intact.

I always looked good, which was important, because form is intrinsic to sports; but in my case it was doubly important, because the truth is that I wasn't really very good. Or at any rate not good enough. Two factors accounted for this. The first was that, without being shy about body contact,

I lacked a certain indispensable aggressiveness; the second, connected closely to the first, was that, when it came right down to it, I did not care enough about winning. I would rather lose a point attempting a slashing cross-court backhand than play for an easier winner down the side; the long jump shot always had more allure for me than the safer drive to the basket. Given a choice between the two vanities of winning and looking good, I almost always preferred looking good.

I shall never forget the afternoon, sometime along about my thirteenth year, when, shooting baskets alone, I came upon the technique for shooting the hook. Although today it has nowhere near the consequence of the jump shot—an innovation that has been to basketball what the jet has been to air travel—the hook is still the single most beautiful shot in the game. The rhythm and grace of it, the sway of the body off the pivot, the release of the ball behind the head and off the fingertips, the touch and instinct involved in its execution, make the hook altogether a balletic thing, and to achieve it is to feel one of the most delectable sensations in sports. That afternoon, on a deserted side street, shooting on a rickety wooden backboard and a black rim without a net, I felt it and grew nearly drunk on the feeling. Rain came down, dirt washed in the gutters, flecks of it spattering my clothes and arms and face, but, soaked and cold though I was, I do not think I would have left that basket on that afternoon for anything. I threw up hook after hook, from every angle, from father and farther out, off the board, without the board, and hook after hook went in. Only pitch darkness drove me home.

I do not say that not to have shot the hook is never to have lived, but only that, once having done so, the pleasure it gives is not so easily forgotten. Every sport offers similar pleasures, the pleasures taken differing by temperament: the canter into the end zone to meet a floating touchdown pass, or the clean, crisp feel of a perfect block or tackle; the long straight drive or the precisely played approach shot to the green; the solid overhead; the pickup on the tricky short hop or the long ball down one of the power alleys. Different sports, different pleasures. But so keen are these pleasures—pleasures of execution, of craft completed—that, along with being unforgettable, they are also worth recapturing in any available way, and the most available way, when reflexes have slowed, when muscle no longer responds so readily to brain, is from the grandstand or, perhaps more often nowadays, from the chair before the television.

Pleasures of the Spectator

I have put in days on the bench, but years in my chair before the television set. Recently it has occurred to me that over the years I have heard more hours of talk from the announcer Curt Gowdy than from my own father, who is not a reticent man. I have been thoroughly Schenkeled, Mussbergered, Summeralled, Cosselled, DeRogotissed, and Garagiolaed. How many hundreds—thousands?—of hours have I spent watching sports of all sorts, either at parks or stadiums or over television? I am glad I shall never have a precise answer. Yet neither apparently can I get enough. What is the fascination? Why is it that, with the prospect of a game to watch in the evening or on the weekend, the day seems lighter and brighter? What do I get out of it?

What I get out of it, according to one fairly prominent view, is an outlet for my violent emotions. Knee-wrenching, rib-cracking, head-busting, this view has it, is what sports are really about, with sports fans being essentially sadists, and cowardly sadists at that, for they take their violence not at firsthand but at second remove. Enthusiasm for sports among Americans is little more than a reflection of the national penchant for violence. Military men talk about game plans; the long touchdown pass is called the bomb. The average pro-football fan, seeing a quarterback writhing on the ground at midfield as a result of the ministrations of Joe Greene, Carl Eller, or Lyle Alzado, twitters with glee, finds his ultimate reward, and declares a little holiday in the blackest corner of his heart.

But this is a criticism that comes at sports by way of politics. To believe it one has to believe that the history of the United States is chiefly one of rape, expropriation, and aggressive imperialism. To dismiss it, however, one need only know something about sports. Violence is indubitably a part of some sports; in some—hockey is an example—it sometimes comes close to being featured. But in no sport—not even boxing, that most rudimentary of sports—is it the main item, and in many other sports it plays no part at all. A distinction worth insisting on is that between violence and roughness. Roughness, a willingness to mix it up, to take if need be an elbow in the jaw, is part of rebounding in basketball, yet violence is not. Even in pro football, most maligned of modern American sports, more of roughness than of violence is involved. Roughness raises the stakes, provides the pressure, behind execution. A splendid because true phrase has come about in pro football to cover the situation in which a pass receiver, certain that he will be tackled upon the instant he makes his reception, drops a ball he should otherwise have caught easily—the phrase, best delivered in a Southern accent such as Don Meredith's, is "He heard footsteps on that one, Howard." Although a part of the attraction, it is not so much those footsteps that fill the stands and the den chairs on Sunday afternoons as it is those men who elude them: the Lynn Swanns, the Fran Tarkentons, the O. J. Simpsons. The American love of violence theory really will not wash. Dick Butkus did not get us into Vietnam.

Many who would not argue that sports reflect American violence nevertheless claim that they imbue one with the competitive spirit. In some who are already amply endowed with it, sports doubtless do tend to refine (or possibly brutalize) the desire to win. Yet sports also teach a serious respect for craft. Competition, though it flourishes as always, is in bad odor nowadays; but craft, officially respected, does not flourish greatly outside the boutique.

If the love of violence or the competitive urge does not put me in my chair for the countless games I watch, is it, then, nostalgia, a yearning to regain the more glowing moments of adolescence? Many argue that this is precisely so, that American men exist in a state of perpetual immaturity, suspended between boy- and manhood. "The difference between men and boys," says Liberace, "is the price of their toys." (I have paid more than $300 for two half-season tickets to the Chicago Bulls games, parking fees not included.) Such unending enthusiasm for games may have something to do with adolescence, but little, I suspect, with regaining anything whatever. Instead, it has more to do with watching men do regularly and surpassingly what, as an adolescent, one did often bumblingly though with an occasional flash of genius. To have played these games oneself as a boy or a young man helps immeasurably the appreciation that in watching a sport played at professional caliber one is witnessing the extraordinary made to look ordinary. That a game may have no consequence outside itself—no effect on history, on one's own life, on anything really—does not make it trivial but only makes the enjoyment of it all the purer.

The notion that men watch sports to regain their adolescence pictures them sitting in the stands or at home watching a game and, within their psyches, muttering, "There, but for the lack of grace of God, go I." And it is true that a number of contemporary authors who are taken seriously have indeed written about sports with a strong overlay of yearning. In the men's softball games described in the fiction of Philip Roth, center field is a place akin to Arcady. Arcadian, too, is the outfield in Willie Morris's memoir of growing up in the South, *North Toward Home*. In the first half of *Rabbit Run* John Updike takes up the life of a man whose days are downhill all the way after hitting his peak as a high-school basketball star—and in the writing Updike himself evinces a nice soft touch of undisguised longing. In *A Fan's Notes,* a book combining yearning and self-disgust in roughly equal measure, Frederick Exley makes plain that he would much prefer to have been born into the skin of Frank Gifford rather than into his own.

But most men who are enraptured by sports do not think any such thing. I should like to have Kareem Abdul-Jabbar's sky hook, but not, especially for civilian life, the excessive height that is necessary to its execution. I should like to have Jimmy Connors's ground strokes, but no part of his mind. These are men born with certain gifts, gifts honed by practice and determination, that I, and millions along with me, enjoy seeing on display. But the reality principle is too deeply ingrained, at least in a man of my years, for me to even imagine exchanging places with them. One might as well imagine oneself in the winner's circle at Churchill Downs as the horse.

Fantasy is an element in sports when they are played in adolescence—an alley basket becomes the glass backboard at Madison Square Garden, a concrete park district tennis court with grass creeping out of the service line becomes center court at Wimbledon—but fantasy of this kind is hard to come by. Part of this has to do with age; but as large a part has to do with the age in which we live. Sport has always been a business but never more so than currently, and nothing lends itself less to fantasy than business. Reading the sports section has become rather like reading the business section—mergers, trades, salary negotiations, contract disputes, options, and strikes fill the columns. Along with the details of business, those of the psychological and social problems of athletes have come to the fore. The old *Sport* magazine concentrated on play on the field, with only an occasional digressive reference to personal life. ("Yogi likes plenty of pizza in the off-season and spends a lot of his time at his teammate Phil Rizzuto's bowling alley," is a rough facsimile of a sentence from its pages that I recall.) But the magazine in its current version, as well as the now more popular *Sports Illustrated,* expends much space on the private lives of athletes—their divorces, hang-ups, race relations, need for approval, concern for security, potted philosophies—with the result that the grand is made to seem small.

On the other side of the ledger, there is a view that finds a shimmering significance in everything having to do with sports. Literary men in general are notoriously to be distrusted on the subject. They dig around everywhere, and can be depended upon to find much treasure where none is buried. Norman Mailer mining metaphysical ore in every jab of Muhammad Ali's, an existential nugget in each of his various and profuse utterances, is a particularly horrendous example. Even the sensible William Carlos Williams was not above this sort of temptation. In a poem entitled "At the Ball Game," we find the lines "It is the Inquisition, the/Revolution." Dr. Williams could not have been much fun at the ball park.

THE REAL THING

If enthusiasm for sports has little to do with providing an outlet for violent emotions, regaining adolescence, discovering metaphysical truths, the Inquisition or the Revolution, then what, I ask myself, am I doing past midnight, when I have to be up at 5:30 the next morning, watching on television what will turn out to be a seventeen-inning game between the New York Mets and the St. Louis Cardinals? The conversation coming out of my television set is of a very low grade, even for sports announcing. But even the dreary talk cannot put me off—the rehash of statistics, the advice to youngsters to keep their gloves low when in the field, the thin jokes. Neither the Mets nor the Cards figure to be contenders this year. The only possible effect that this game can have on my life is to make me dog-tired the next day. Yet I cannot pull myself away. I want to know how it is going to end. True, the score will be available in the morning paper. But that is not the same thing. What is going on here?

One thing that is going on is the practice of craft of a very high order, which is intrinsically interesting. But something as important is involved, something rarer in contemporary life, the spectacle of which gives enormous satisfaction. To define this satisfaction negatively, it is the absence of fraudulence and fakery. No small item, this, when one stops to think that in nearly every realm of contemporary life fraud and fakery have an established—some would say a preponderant—place. Advertising, politics, business, and journalism are only the most obvious examples. Fraud seems similarly pervasive in modern art: in painters whose reputations rest on press agentry; in writers who write one way and live quite another; in composers who are taken seriously but whose work cannot be seriously listened to. At a time when *image* is one of the most frequently used words in American speech and writing, one does not too often come upon the real thing.

Sport may be the toy department of life, but one of its abiding compensations is that, at least on the field, it is the real thing. Much has been done in recent years in the attempt to ruin sport—the ruthlessness of owners, the greed of players, the general exploitation of fans. But even all this cannot destroy it. On the court, down on the field, sport is fraud-free and fakeproof. With a full count, two men on, his team down by one run in the last of the eighth, a batter (as well as a pitcher) is beyond the aid of public relations. At match point at Forest Hills a player's press clippings are of no help. Last year's earnings will not sink a twelve-foot putt on the eighteenth at Augusta. Alan Page, galloping up along a quarterback's blind side, figures to be neglectful of that quarterback's image as a swinger. In all these situations, and hundreds of others, a man either comes through or he doesn't. He is alone out there, naked but for his ability, which counts for everything. Something there is that is elemental about this, and something greatly satisfying.

Another part of the satisfaction to be got from sports—from playing them, but also from watching them being played—derives from their special clarity. Sports offer clarity of a kind sufficient to engage the most serious minds. That the Cambridge mathematician G. H. Hardy closely followed cricket and avidly read cricket scores is not altogether surprising. Numbers in sports are ubiquitous. Scores, standings, averages, times, records—comfort is found in such numbers. ERA, RBIs, FGP, pass completions, turnovers, category upon category of statistics are kept for nearly every aspect of athletic activity. (Why, I recently heard someone ask, are records not kept for catchers throwing out runners attempting to steal? Because, the answer is, often runners steal on pitchers, and so it would be unfair to charge these stolen bases against catchers.) As perhaps in no other sphere, numbers in sports tell one where things stand. No loopholes here, where figures, for once, do not lie. Nowhere else is such specificity of result available.

Clarity about character is also available in sports. "You Americans hold to the proposition that it is self-evident that all men are created equal," I not long ago heard an Englishman say, adding, "it had better be self-evident, for no other evidence for it exists." Sport coldly demonstrates physical inequalities—there are the larger, the faster, the stronger, the more graceful athletes—but it also throws up human types who have devised ways to redress these inequalities. One such type is the hustler. In every realm but that of sports the word *hustle* is pejorative, whereas in sports it is approbative. Two of the hustler breed, Pete Rose of the Cincinnati Reds and Jerry Sloan of the Chicago Bulls, are men who supplement reasonably high levels of ability with unreasonably high levels of courage and desire. Other athletes—Joe Morgan and Oscar Robertson come to mind—bring superior athletic intelligence to bear upon their play. And Bill Russell, late of the Boston Celtics, who if the truth be known was not an inherently superior athlete, blended hustle and intelligence with what abilities he did have and through force of character established supremacy.

Whence do hustle, intelligence, and character in sports derive, especially since they apparently do not necessarily carry over into life? Joe DiMaggio and Sugar Ray Robinson, two of the most instinctively intelligent and physically elegant athletes, brought little of either of these qualities over into their business or personal activities. Some athletes can do all but one important thing well: Wilt Chamberlain at the free-throw line, for those who recall his misery there, leaves a permanent picture of a mental block in action. Other athletes—Connie Hawkins, Ilie Nastase, Dick Allen—have all the physical gifts in superabundance, yet, because of some insufficiency of character, some searing flaw, never come near to fulfilling their promise. Coaches supply yet another gallery of human types, from the fanatical Vince Lombardi to the comical Casey Stengel to the measured and aptly named John Wooden. The cast of characters in sport, the variety of situations, the complexity of behavior it puts on display, the overall human exhibit it offers—together these supply an enjoyment akin to that once provided by reading interminably long but inexhaustibly rich nineteenth-century novels.

In a wider sense, sport is culture. For many American men it represents a common background, a shared interest. It has a binding power that transcends social class and education. Some years ago I found myself working in the South among men with whom I shared nothing in the way of region, religion, education, politics, or general views; we shared nothing, in fact, but sports, which was enough for us to get along and grow to become friends, in the process showing how superficial all the things that might have kept us apart in fact were. More recently, in Chicago, at a time when race relations were in a particularly jagged state, I recall emerging from an NBA game, in which the Chicago Bulls in overtime beat the Milwaukee Bucks, into a snowy night and an aura of common good feeling that, for a time, submerged the enmity between races; laughing, throwing snowballs, exuberant generally, the crowd leaving the Chicago Stadium that night was not divided by being black and white but unified by being Bull fans. Last year's Boston–Cincinnati World Series, one of the most gratifying in memory, coming hard upon a year of extreme political divisiveness, performed, however briefly, something of the same function. How much better it felt to agree about the mastery of Luis Tiant than to argue about the wretchedness of Richard Nixon.

In sports as in life, character does not much change. I have recently begun to play a game called racquet ball, and I find I would still rather look good than win, which is what I usually do: look good and lose. I beat the rum-dums but go down before quality players. I get compliments in defeat. Men who beat me admire the whip of my strokes, my wrist action, my anticipation, the power I get behind the ball. When this occurs I feel like a woman who is complimented for the shape of her bottom when it is her mind she craves admiration for, though of course she will take what praise she can get.

R. H. Tawney, the great historian of religion and capitalism, once remarked that the only progress he could note during the course of his lifetime was in the deportment of dogs. For myself, I would say that the chief progress in the course of my lifetime has been in the quality and variety of athletic gear. Racquets made of metal, aluminum, wood, and fiberglass, balls of different colors, sneakers of all materials and designs, posh warm-up suits, tube socks, sweatbands for the head and wrist in various colors and pipings; only the athletic supporter, the old jockstrap, remains unornamented, but perhaps even now Vera or Peter Max is at the drawing board. In any event, with all this elegant plumage available, it is a nice time to be playing ball again.

Sports can be impervious to age. My father-in-law, a man of style, seriousness, and great good humor who died a year ago in his late sixties, was born in South Bend, Indiana, and in his early manhood left the Catholic Church—two facts that conjoined to give him an intense interest in the fortunes of the teams from Notre Dame. He loved to see them lose. The torch has been passed on. I now love to see Notre Dame lose, and when it does I think of him and remember his smile.

When I was a boy I had a neighbor, a man who, after retirement, had a number of strokes. An old man and a young boy, we had in common a love of sports, which, when we met on the street, was our only topic of conversation. He once inspected a new glove of mine, and instructed me to rub it down with neat's-foot oil, place a ball firmly in the pocket, wrap string tightly around the glove, and leave it like that for the winter. I did, and it worked. After his last stroke but one, he seldom left his house. Afternoons he spent in a chair in his bedroom, a blanket over his lap, listening to Cub games over the radio. It was while listening to a ball game that he quietly died. I cannot imagine a better way.   ✦

THE CITY GAME

(October 1970)

Pete Axthelm

BASKETBALL IS THE city game. Its battlegrounds are strips of asphalt between tattered wire fences or crumbling buildings; its rhythms grow from the uneven thump of a ball against hard surfaces. It demands no open spaces or lush backyards or elaborate equipment. It doesn't even require specified numbers of players; a one-on-one confrontation in a playground can be as memorable as a full-scale organized game. Basketball is one game for young athletes without cars or allowances—the game in which the drama and action are intensified by its confined spaces and chaotic surroundings.

Every American sport directs itself in a general way toward certain segments of American life. Baseball is basically a slow, pastoral experience, offering a tableau of athletes against a green background, providing moments of action amid longer periods allowed for contemplation of the spectacle. In its relaxed, unhurried way, it is exactly what it claims to be—the national "pastime" rather than an intense, sustained game crammed with action. Born in a rural age, its appeal still lies largely in its offer of an untroubled island where, for a few hours, a pitcher tugging at his pants leg can seem to be the most important thing in a fan's life.

Football's attraction is more contemporary. Its violence is in tune with the times, and its well-mapped strategic war games invite fans to become generals, plotting and second-guessing along with their warriors on the fields. With its action compressed in a fairly small area and its formations and patterns relatively easy to interpret, football is the ideal television spectacle. Other sports have similar, if smaller, primary audiences. Golf and tennis belong first to country-club members, horse racing to an enduring breed of gamblers, auto racing to Middle Americans who thrive on its violent roaring machines and death-defying risks. But basketball belongs to the cities—and New York, from its asphalt playgrounds to the huge modern arena that houses the profession-

73

al basketball champions of the world, is the most active, dedicated basketball city of all.

The game is simple, an act of one man challenging another, twisting, feinting, then perhaps breaking free to leap upward, directing a ball toward a target, a metal hoop ten feet above the ground. But its simple motions swirl into intricate patterns, its variations become almost endless, its brief soaring moments merge into a fascinating dance. To the uninitiated, the patterns may seem fleeting, elusive, even confusing; but on a city playground, a classic play is frozen in the minds of those who see it—a moment of order and achievement in a turbulent, frustrating existence. Basketball is more than a sport or diversion in the cities. It is a part, often a major part, of the fabric of life. Kids in small towns—particularly in the Midwest—often become superb basketball players. But they do so by developing accurate shots and precise skills; in the cities, kids simply develop "moves." Other athletes may learn basketball, but city kids live it.

The New York Knickerbockers, champions of the National Basketball Association, are not direct products of the city's playgrounds. Like all professional teams, they have been assembled by drafting and trading to amass the best available athletes from across the country. Geographically and socially, they could hardly have more diverse backgrounds. The coach, Red Holzman, was a pure New York ballplayer; the captain, Willis Reed, is from the black rural South. The other stars include black products of city streets and the white son of a bank president. Yet as they rose to the summit of basketball, the Knicks became inextricably identified with the city they represented.

The media, based largely in New York, have fallen in love with the Knicks and with basketball, giving the sport its first taste of heavy television coverage, national-magazine cover stories, and all forms of advertising and promotion. New York's rich citizens also joined the love affair, and the traditionally scruffy pro basketball audiences were replaced by a chic new breed in Madison Square Garden. And in the playgrounds, the kids, too, responded to the Knicks, acknowledging that a New York team was at last bringing a rare playground art to new levels of perfection. The Knicks seemed ideal symbols of the traditions of New York basketball, and if the media portrayed the Knick stars as larger than life, the playground kids understood that too.

The first week of May, when the Knicks won the championship, had been a brutalizing, feverish ordeal for most New Yorkers. United States armies were marching into Cambodia and a shocked young girl was screaming silently from the front pages of newspapers and magazines, in terrible, haunting testimony to the four murders at Kent State University. Demonstrators were assembling near the United Nations and in the Wall Street area, pleading almost hopelessly to a government they knew wasn't listening. Then the city's darkest fears took shape, as mobs of Wall Street construction workers unleashed the small hatreds and resentments that had been building within them for years, and descended on the young people who their President had reassured them were merely bums. On the afternoon before the final Knicks game against the Los Angeles Lakers, the workers came down to bully the kids at close range. Aided by Wall Street clerks, they went on a spree, ganging up on the kids, kicking them when they were on the pavement, and leaving scores of bloody victims while policemen stood placidly by.

The politics of hate and polarization had thrust deep into New York's consciousness, and few people on either side could relish the sight of open war between Nixon's newly unleashed Silent Majority and opponents of the war. Some of the spectators who came to watch the Knicks that night may have wondered just how much they could still care about a game. Then the Knicks showed them. They didn't solve the world's problems, any more than playground games cure the ills of the ghetto. But the Knicks and Lakers did offer a moment of high drama, a brief and necessary escape from reality—a transcendent experience that, in the end, is all anyone can ask of a great sporting event.

Basketball has always had this special quality for the boys of New York's streets. Two decades ago, it fed the dreams of the Irish athletes on famous playgrounds like the one on 108th Street in Rockaway, Queens. Those playgrounds produced Bob Cousy and Dick McGuire and other superb playmakers and brilliant passers; they also spawned countless athletes who were almost as accomplished but never made it to college and did not achieve public recognition. On Kingsbridge Road in the Bronx, tough, aggressive Jewish youths grew into defense-minded, set-shooting stars; some led the colleges of the city to national prominence in the late 1940s, but still others faded before the public ever learned their names. With money available for cars and stereos and surfboards, the hunger vanished from many white playgrounds, and so did top-caliber basketball. But the blacks of Harlem and Bedford-Stuyvesant more than filled the void. Some made it to colleges and into the pros, helping to reshape the game with their flamboyant moves. Still others failed to find a niche in college or the pros, but endured as playground heroes, facing the challenges of the best of each new generation of players, occasionally proving themselves against pro players who return to the parks for summer games.

Each ethnic group and each generation of street ballplayers produced its special styles and legends, and each left its colorful brand on the sport. But more than that, each built a distinctive kind of pride—partly ethnic or racial, partly athletic, but much more than the sum of those parts. Veterans of playground ball describe it in terms of individuality, status, manhood; they also talk of the way it brings kids together. If the Knicks brought a special pride to all New York, they were only multiplying the feeling that the playground kids have always understood.

Occasionally the two distinct worlds of New York basketball converge. A playground idol such as Connie Hawkins joins the Phoenix Suns and comes into the Garden to challenge the Knicks; Knick stars like Bill Bradley and Willis Reed appear at 155th Street and Eighth Avenue to enter Harlem's most prestigious summer competition, the Rucker Pro Tournament. These confrontations are always electric. Hawkins may pack the Garden, while a Reed or Bradley will add hundreds to the overflowing crowds at a Rucker game. And if a playground star like Herman ("Helicopter") Knowings or Harold ("Funny") Kitt goes up to block a pro's shot or stuff a basket over a pro defender, he creates myths that endure long after the score of the game is forgotten.

A morning rain had left wide shallow puddles in the asphalt, and some of Saturday night's litter had washed down from the corners of the small park, giving the basketball court a grimy and abandoned look. The green- and red-tinted glass of discarded wine and whiskey bottles glinted in the sunlight that was just breaking through; the surrounding wire fence was scarred every few yards by unrepaired holes. Within hours the court would be fairly dry, the debris would be kicked aside, and the games—raucous, exuberant pickup affairs or perhaps even full-scale epic battles featuring local titans—would fill the Sunday afternoon with excitement. But for the moment the playground, set back from Seventh Avenue near 130th Street, seemed silently evocative of its illustrious past. Walking across it, Pat Smith was lost in thought.

Smith, who played for several seasons at Marquette University in Milwaukee, is twenty-four now, and years of studying in a less basketball-oriented city have rendered him out of shape for the highest caliber of playground competition back in Harlem. Yet he remains a cultural hero on the streets. He was a classic Harlem product, a six-foot three-inch center who spent his college career outleaping and outfighting six-foot ten-inch rivals. He never had any illusions about his basketball future: very weak eyesight made him a terrible outside shooter and limited him to center, and six-foot three-inch centers—regardless of their jumping ability—are not sought after by the pros. But at Benjamin Franklin High School in Harlem and then at Marquette, Smith had used moves and muscle and a fierce instinct for domination to delight his Harlem followers.

The second reason for Smith's prestige was equally important: he had "made it." Like most ghetto youths, he had faced tremendous adjustment problems when he arrived on a predominantly white campus. In his first months at Marquette, he had fought everyone who seemed unable to understand his ghetto jargon, his racial pride, or his competitive fury. He was so combative that teammates and friends nicknamed him "The Evil Doctor Blackheart." The name stayed with him, but the attitudes that produced it began to change. He became extremely popular on campus, did well scholastically, and developed a deep bond with his coach, Al McGuire. In Smith's senior year, that bond faced its ultimate test. For reasons that neither man has ever confided, McGuire suspended Smith for most of that season—and, incredibly, the two men grew closer than ever. Most black athletes who encounter such crises and find their basketball eligibility running out drift back home, feeling lost and exploited, and lacking a college degree. Smith stayed at Marquette through the suspension, then remained two more years before earning his degree in 1970. The reasons for his remarkable determination are as shadowy as the man himself sometimes seems, but it made the Evil Doctor a figure to be respected back home. And though he is intent on building a future outside Harlem, Smith returns home often, to be troubled once again by friends who have succumbed to drugs, to be enraged by conditions, and to remember some of the good things about growing up:

"The old Rucker tournament was held in this park," Smith said, gesturing to one of the trees alongside the court. "When I was a kid I'd climb up into that tree. I'd stake out one of the branches early in the morning and just sit up there all day. A guy with a cart would come by and I'd yell for him to hand me up some lemon ices, and I'd eat one after another. There was no way anyone could get me to come down while the games were going on. I was in a world of my own, sitting up above the crowd and watching the great ones come in and do their thing...."

The Rucker tournament is actually not a tournament but a summer league in which teams play one another through the weekends of July and August. Established in 1946 by a remarkable young teacher named Holcombe Rucker, it was originally intended mainly to keep kids off the streets and in school by encouraging them in both studies and basketball. Rucker's idea was to give dignity and meaning to pickup games by adding referees, local publicity, and larger audiences; it worked, and gradually the Rucker tournament expanded to include divisions for young athletes from junior high school through the pro level. A project that had begun with four teams and one referee began to offer basketball from morning until dark in various Harlem parks, before crowds estimated as high as five thousand. It remains the pinnacle of playground ball in New York, attracting stars from both pro leagues, members of touring teams like the Harlem Globetrotters, as well as the best players of the regular pickup games of the city.

The pro section of the Rucker tournament had long since been moved to another storied playground on 155th Street and Eighth Avenue, but the lure of a decade-old game remained in that Seventh Avenue park for Pat Smith. Near the knots of women engaged in Sunday conversation on church steps, grown men in boys' uniforms joined small children in formation for one of the minor parades that still serve some Harlemites as straggly symbols of unity and pride. Young, educated, and militant, Pat Smith had very different ideas about black dignity; moments earlier he had been depressed by what he felt to be the Sunday delusions of some of his people. But now, under the tree that had once been his reserved seat, he recalled a game of street basketball at its best:

"It was the kind of game that established citywide reputations. Clinton Robinson was playing. Jackie Jackson was there. So was Wilt Chamberlain, who was in his first or second year of pro ball at the time. . . . " He savored each name as he spoke it; this was a very special honor roll. Some of the names, like Robinson's and Jackson's, would be familiar only to the ghetto kids who once worshiped them; others, like Chamberlain's, would be recognized by every basketball fan. But to Smith and many others they were all gods, and their best games were Olympian clashes.

"Chamberlain and Robinson were on the same team along with some other greats, and they were ahead by about fifteen points. They looked like easy winners. Then, up in the tree, I heard a strange noise. There were maybe four, five thousand people watching the game, and all of a sudden a hush came over them. All you could hear was a whisper: 'The Hawk, the Hawk, the Hawk is here.' Then the crowd parted. And the Hawk walked onto the court."

"The Hawk" was Connie Hawkins. When you ask ghetto basketball fans to cite the very best players ever to come out of New York, you find much disagreement; but a few names are invariably included, and one of them is the Hawk. Yet for years he seemed fated to become one of those virtually forgotten playground stars. Connie made his reputation at Brooklyn's Boys High in the late 1950s, but when he was a freshman at Iowa in 1961, he was linked to a gambling scandal. His chief crime had been naïveté in talking to glad-handing gamblers, and he had never been indicted or even accused of trying to shave points or fix games. But his college career was shattered and for almost a decade he was an outcast, barred from the NBA, laboring in the short-lived American Basketball League and then in the American Basketball Association as it struggled for survival.

In 1969, after a prolonged legal battle, Hawkins won a million-dollar lawsuit and readmission to the NBA as a member of the Phoenix Suns. He quickly justified everything the playground kids had been saying about him for years. At the time of the game Smith described, Hawkins was a year or two out of Boys High, a man without a team. Yet he was the most magnetic star in Harlem.

"The crowd was still hushed as they called time out," Smith remembered. "They surrounded the man. They undressed the man. And finally he finished lacing up his sneakers and walked out into the backcourt. He got the ball, picked up speed, and started his first move. Chamberlain came right out to stop him. The Hawk went up—he was still way out beyond the foul line—and started floating toward the basket. Wilt, taller and stronger, stayed right with him—but then the Hawk hook-dunked the ball right over Chamberlain. He *hook*-dunked! Nobody had ever done anything like that to Wilt. The crowd went so crazy that they had to stop the game for five minutes. I almost fell out of the tree.

"But you didn't get away with just one spectacular move in those games. So the other guys came right back at the Hawk. Clinton Robinson charged in, drove around him, and laid one up so high that it hit the top of the backboard. The Hawk went way up, but he couldn't quite reach it, and it went down into the basket. Clinton Robinson was about six feet tall and the Hawk was six feet eight, so the crowd went wild again. In fact, Clinton had thrown some of the greatest moves I'd ever seen, shaking guys left and right before he even reached the Hawk.

"Then it was Chamberlain's turn to get back. Wilt usually took it pretty easy in summer games, walking up and down the court and doing just enough to intimidate his opponents with his seven-foot body. But now his pride was hurt, his manhood was wounded. And you can't let that happen in a tough street game. So he came down, drove directly at the hoop, and went up over the Hawk. Will stuffed the ball with two hands, and he did it so hard that he almost ripped the backboard off the pole.

"By then everybody on the court was fired up—and it was time for the Hawk to take charge again. Clinton Robinson came toward him with the ball, throwing those crazy moves on anyone who tried to stop him, and then he tried to loft a lay-up way up onto the board, the way he had done before. Only this time the Hawk was up there waiting for it. He was up so high that he blocked the shot with his *chest*. Still in midair, he kind of swept his hands down across his chest as if he were wiping his shirt—and slammed the ball down at Robinson's feet. The play seemed to turn the whole game around, and the Hawk's team came from behind to win. That was the Hawk. Just beautiful. I don't think anybody who was in that crowd could ever forget that game."

In March of 1964, Boys High of Brooklyn faced Benjamin Franklin High of Harlem in the old Madison Square Garden, on Eighth Avenue and 50th Street, for the public-high-school championship of New York. Boys won the title; but the result was quickly overshadowed by a seat-slashing, bottle-throwing melee that resulted in the end of high-school ball in the Garden and established a negative landmark in city basketball. The riot occurred against the backdrop of the city's first black school boycott; and it happened on St. Patrick's Day, when many patrolmen who might have handled the crowd were out parading. But administrators were not much interested in the details or causes of the disturbance. It was much easier to run from the problem than to solve it. So the Public School Athletic League moved its tournaments into small neutral gyms, and the black stars who dominate high-school ball in the city were swept quietly out of sight.

Since that time, the Garden has promoted a series of fights featuring Latin-American boxers with their bottle-throwing followers. It has had rallies for such public figures as George Wallace. But the young black ballplayers have not reappeared. While the Knicks turn on the city, its most talented young stars play in virtual secrecy in musty gyms and youth centers and playgrounds, before only their peers and a handful of college scouts. While the media fall in love with the Knicks, a top high-school star searches in vain for a paragraph or two in the *Times* on his team's victories. A year ago, the Boys High team went to New Haven, Connecticut, to face Hillhouse High for the informal championship of the East. Boys won by a point. It was the team's forty-sixth consecutive victory. And it drew more attention in New Haven in one day than Boys had gathered in New York with the forty-five wins that preceded it. The irony was not lost on the athletes. The struggle to establish an identity is basic to city basketball, but many black kids in New York have learned that their identity is a well-kept secret to the general public.

The bitterness was not readily apparent at the playground on 135th Street near Lenox Avenue. The June afternoon was warm and the basketball was very good. The games were just pickup affairs, with five-man teams being assembled on the spot to challenge the winners of whatever game was in progress. But a few pro players dropped by, as well as several Globetrotters and the established stars of the neighborhood, and somebody said that it was the best ball you would find in Harlem short of the Rucker tournament itself. The cars were double-parked all the way down the block, and the crowd was three deep alongside the high fences.

Then one athlete, who didn't want to give his name, began talking about it all, and there was an edge on his voice: "Sure there are good players here, and good ones who have made it in college and the pros. But don't try to write this up as a beautiful breeding ground for future stars, because for every star you hear about, there are many more who never escaped. I mean, I can look back on the group that I grew up with down on 111th Street, and I can tell you all about the one or two who are playing college ball, and it will make a great story. But there were twenty of us. And now maybe fifteen are on drugs and three are dead or just gone, who knows where? So how much do the two lucky ones count?" The kid sounded very old. He said he was twenty-one.

The less fortunate grow old even faster, leaving the bright moments behind them on the courts as the real world drags them down to earth. There is a sustaining power to basketball in the playgrounds: a young athlete walks into a bar or luncheonette and hears people say, "That's the dude that dunked on Lew up at Rucker." The admirers want to talk to him, to ask advice, to be near the star, and maybe that sense of importance and identity will keep a kid going for weeks. But if he is a dropout and he is broke, and the hustlers and pushers are around him with their cars and fancy clothes, the magic of his game can begin to wear off. Sooner or later, stuffing a basketball through a hoop is not quite enough to transcend the reality of his life.

"At one point in most guys' lives," said Keith Edwards, a Harlem ballplayer and youth worker, "basketball is the top priority, because it is the one escape valve from the ghetto. But once the paths toward college or pro ball are closed to an athlete, merely playing the game is not as much of an escape. Then the kids get offered a much easier escape, an escape to within themselves, in drugs. A few years ago, I would have said that the athletes I knew looked ninety percent to ball, ten percent to drugs. Now, the ratio is reversed. The kids are looking to drugs ninety percent of the time. And they are destroying themselves."

Everyone in Harlem has watched the process of destruction, but no one feels it more acutely than the ballplayers. "You see somebody who can do everything on the court," said Pat Smith. "You know that his playing can open up a whole new world to him. It gives you a feeling of excitement. It makes you build high hopes. And when you watch him start to deteriorate, it tears you apart." Smith paused, shying momentarily from the subject. Two of Smith's nine brothers have died on the Harlem streets; another was a dope pusher at the age of fourteen. Six years away at school in Milwaukee have not erased the streets from Smith's life. "There's such great waste of humanity," he said slowly. "Such tragic waste." And then the memories came pouring out, a remarkable testament to the darkest side of basketball in the city:

"I remember when I was just developing as a ballplayer, early in high school. I played a lot with a guy named Artie. I never knew his last name, just Artie. He played often at Millbank Center, and his team was known for winning a lot of local tournaments. Artie was capable of scoring every way: jump shots, hooks, lay-ups, set shots. His scoring totals were forty to fifty points every game. When I knew him, Artie was about twenty-eight, and he was trying to make a comeback. From alcohol. He was a wine drinker. That shows you how far back it was—people still ruined themselves the slow way with wine, instead of drugs.

"Anyway, Artie had been in a hospital, trying to dry out and recuperate. When he started playing again, he was probably a step slower than he once was, but he still had those fantastic shots. He took an interest in me for some reason, and he picked me to play with him in pickup games whenever he could. When we played together, he would teach me, and he would also get so many good passes to me that I was sure of getting twenty-five or thirty points—while he still got his fifty.

"But after a few months he began showing up less at the playgrounds. Then he didn't come at all. And one day I was on the street and somebody asked if I'd heard about Artie. Then the guy told me. They'd found Artie dead in a hallway. He drank himself to death.

"There was another guy we knew only by his first name, Frank," Smith said. "He came from uptown, around 155th Street, but he would come down to our neighborhood around 128th Street to play. He was a strong guy, very good-looking, with a great build. I didn't know him well, I didn't know what high school he was from, but I always assumed that he had the potential to go on and start for some college team.

"Then we heard the news. Frank had tried to rob a drugstore. The storekeeper had a gun, and Frank got shot in the back. He was paralyzed from the waist down. He was maybe nineteen years old, and it was all over for him.

"People still see him, in his wheelchair. When anyone goes up in that neighborhood they look for him. He's about twenty-four now, and he tries to take the thing very well. Talking to him, you can hardly realize that he knows he'll never walk again. But the way he hides his pain only makes it hurt more to look at him and think of what he could have been.

"Dexter Westbrook was one of the few big men that ever came from the uptown playgrounds," said Smith. "For some reason, most of the taller guys happened to play downtown around 135th Street or 128th Street, while the players up at 155th were known more for quickness and ball-handling. But Dexter was about six feet eight, and he was a super big man. Playing with so many fast little guys, he developed the quickness and moves of a guard. He had a beautiful left-handed jump shot, and could do everything with the ball.

"Dexter went to Providence College for a while. Then he failed out and came home and worked in a few jobs in the poverty program. But with his size and talent, everybody insisted that he could still make the pros, and two or three years ago he tried out. I forget which team it was, but word got back to Harlem that Dexter was doing great. He was the high scorer and the best rebounder in rookie camp; nobody could touch him. Then it came time for the routine physical examination, and he couldn't pass it. There were needle tracks on his arms.

"Now this was a man who could have made it big. But he just couldn't seem to adjust his mind to bigger things than what's here in Harlem. The last time I heard of Dexter was in the summer of 1969. There was a robbery on

Riverside Drive, and he was arrested for taking somebody's wallet. His drug habit had gotten beyond his means. Like it always does."

If it hurt Smith to talk of his contemporaries, it seemed to wrench him more to turn to younger kids. "I saw guys I played with get ruined, and it was bad, but it wasn't always unexpected," he said. "You go to school or play a lot of ball with a guy and you get an idea whether he can make it. But watching kids come up, you lose that perspective. You somehow hope they'll all make it. And you forget that the drug thing is much worse now than it was when you were in school yourself. You forget that escaping the streets is harder than ever. And then you see what happens to a kid like Kenny Bellinger.

"Kenny earned a city-wide basketball reputation when he was still in junior high school. I was a senior in high school when I played against him, and he was still in ninth grade. But he couldn't go on playing against kids his own age, because he was too good. He was always looking for older guys to challenge, and he always held his own. A lot of high-school players waited to see where he would decide to go, and we were glad when he chose Franklin. He was a cinch to make all-city, and he had a great future ahead of him.

"Then one day, I was walking on 111th Street between Seventh and Eighth avenues, and I saw four or five squad cars. I asked somebody what was going on, and people said that a lady's purse had been snatched, and someone had run into one of the buildings with it. The next thing we knew, there was a helicopter over the buildings. The purse-snatcher was on the roofs, and they were trying to spot him. Nobody had ever seen the police use a helicopter before, but somebody said that the purse belonged to a white lady with some influence. Anyway, it looked like they were fighting the whole Vietcong instead of looking for a purse.

"Suddenly all the cops rushed into an alley, and in a few minutes the word spread: the thief had tried to hurdle a six-foot gap between the buildings, and he hadn't made it. I went home, and I didn't find out until the next day that the kid who had plunged into the alley had been Kenny.

"I couldn't believe it. I thought there must have been a mistake. Kenny couldn't have risked so much . . . and anyway, he could have leaped a six-foot gap with no problem at all. So I went up onto the building and checked out the gap, and it was more like fifteen feet. Then it began to sink in. All that potential was gone. Whether it was drugs or despair or what, Kenny hadn't been able to stay straight. One more victim. Kenny was sixteen years old when he died.

"Boobie Tucker was also in junior high when he first came around to play with us older guys," Smith said. "He was about six feet nine, but he wasn't as advanced as Kenny Bellinger. He was still clumsy and uncoordinated. He didn't know how to take advantage of his size. But while I was at Franklin and he was in junior high, he would come to our gym and try to learn, and we watched him develop into a really good ballplayer. He learned to get position under the boards for rebounds, and he practiced a short jump shot until he could make it regularly. Here was a kid only about sixteen, and he was six feet nine, and still growing: he might have had the world in front of him. The year I went away to college, he started playing for Franklin.

"Every so often I'd ask somebody about Boobie. First I heard that he was coming along fine, scoring nicely. But gradually the other rumors reached me: 'Yeah, Tucker's on stuff. . . . Yeah, he's snorting pretty heavy. . . . Yeah, Tucker's strung out.' Boobie stopped playing altogether and went out onto the streets. And finally I learned that he had died of an overdose. It was a shock, because he hadn't been strung out for that long. He probably hadn't even developed an expensive habit yet. But of course when times get hard, pushers will put anything into that white bag and sell it. Some guys have shot up rat poison and died instantly.

"It was a terrible, frustrating thing to imagine Boobie dead. I felt very close to his career, because I'd watched him develop from a clumsy kid into a ballplayer. Day to day, I'd seen the improvements. I'd watched him work at the game, and I couldn't help thinking he would be repaid for all that work.

"But the one thing I wasn't thinking about, the one thing you never think about, I guess, until it's too late, was that the pusher was watching him develop, too."

In the litany of quiet misfortunes, it may seem almost impossible to select one man and give him special importance. Yet in the stories and traditions that are recounted in the Harlem parks, one figure does emerge above the rest. Asked about the finest athletes they have seen, scores of ballplayers in a dozen parks mention Connie Hawkins and Lew Alcindor and similar celebrities. But almost without exception, they speak first of one star who didn't go on: Earl Manigault.

No official scorers tabulate the results of pickup games; there are no composite box scores to prove that Manigault ranked highest among playground athletes. But in its own way, a reputation in the parks is as definable as a scoring average in the NBA. Street ballplayers develop their own elaborate word-of-mouth system. One spectacular performance or one backwards, twisting stuff shot may be the seed of an athlete's reputation. If he can repeat it a few times in a park where the competition is tough, the word goes out that he may be something special. Then there will be challenges from more established players, and a man who can withstand them may earn a "neighborhood rep." The process continues in an expanding series of confrontations, until the best athletes have emerged. Perhaps a dozen men at a given time may enjoy "city-wide reps," guaranteeing them attention and respect in any playground they may visit. And of those, one or two will stand alone.

A few years ago, Earl Manigault stood among the loftiest. But his reign was brief, and in order to capture some feeling of what his stature meant in the playground world, one must turn to two athletes who enjoy similar positions today. Herman ("Helicopter") Knowings, now in his late twenties, is among the most remarkable playground players; he was a demigod before Manigault, and he remains one after Earl's departure. Uneducated and unable to break into pro ball, the Helicopter has managed to retain the spring in his legs and the willpower to remain at the summit after many of his contemporaries have faded from the basketball scene. Joe Hammond, not yet twenty, is generally recognized as the best of the young crop. He has not finished school or vaulted into the public spotlight, but, like Knowings, he picks up money playing in a minor league, the Eastern League—and returns home between games to continue domination of the parks.

The Helicopter got his name for obvious reasons. When he goes up to block a shot, he seems to hover endlessly in midair above his prey, daring him to shoot—and then blocking whatever shot his hapless foe attempts. Like most memorable playground moves, it is not only effective but magnetic. As Knowings goes up, the crowd shouts, "Fly, Copter, fly," and seems to share his heady trip. When he shoves a ball down the throat of a visiting NBA star, as he often does in the Rucker tournament, the Helicopter inflates the pride of a whole neighborhood.

Like Connie Hawkins, Knowings can send waves of electricity through a park with his mere presence. Standing by a court, watching a game in progress, the Helicopter doesn't have to ask to play. People quickly spot his dark, chiseled, ageless face and six-foot four-inch frame, and they make room for him. Joe Hammond is less imposing. A shade over six feet, he is a skinny, sleepy-eyed kid who looks slow and tired, the way backcourt star Clinton

Robinson appeared during his reign. But, like Robinson, Hammond has proved himself, and now he stands as the descendant of Pablo Robertson and James Barlow and the other backcourt heroes of the streets.

The kings of playground ball are not expected to defend their titles every weekend, proving themselves again and again the way less exalted players must. But when a new athlete begins winning a large following, when the rumors spread that he is truly someone special, the call goes out: if he is a forward, get the Helicopter; if he's a guard, let's try him against Joe Hammond. A crowd will gather before the star arrives. It is time for a supreme test.

Jay Vaughn has been in such confrontations several times. He saw the Helicopter defend his reign, and he watched Joe Hammond win his own way to the top. He described the ritual:

"When I first met the Helicopter, I was only about seventeen, and I was playing with a lot of kids my age at Wagner Center. I was better than the guys I was playing with and I knew it, so I didn't feel I had anything to prove. I was playing lazy, lackadaisical. And one of the youth workers saw how cocky I was and decided to show me just how good I really was. He sent for the Helicopter.

"One day I was just shooting baskets, trying all kinds of wild shots, not thinking about fundamentals, and I saw this older dude come in. He had sneakers and shorts on and he was ready to play. I said, 'Who's this guy? He's too old for our games. Is he supposed to be good?' 'The coach sent for him,' somebody told me. 'He's gonna play you.'

"I said to myself, well fine, I'll try him, and I went out there one-on-one with Herman Knowings. Well, it was a disastrous thing. I tried lay-ups, jump shots, hooks. And everything I threw up, he blocked. The word had gone out that Herman was there, and a crowd was gathering, and I said to myself, 'You got to do something. You're getting humiliated.' But the harder I tried, the more he shoved the ball down into my face. I went home and thought about that game for a long time. Like a lot of young athletes, I had been put in my place.

"I worked out like crazy after that. I was determined to get back. After about a month, I challenged him again. I found myself jumping higher, feeling stronger, and playing better than ever before. I wasn't humiliated again. But I was beaten. Since that time, I've played against Herman many times. He took an interest in me and gave me a lot of good advice. And now, when I see he's going to block a shot, I may be able to fake and go around him and score, and people will yell, 'The pupil showed the master.'

"Then, of course, he'll usually come back and stuff one on me. . . .

"Joe Hammond was playing in the junior division games in the youth centers when I was in the senior games," Vaughn said. "He was three years younger than me, and sometimes after I'd played, I'd stay and watch his game. He wasn't that exceptional. Just another young boy who was gonna play ball. In fact, at that time, I didn't even know his last name.

"Then I carne home from school in the summer of 1969, and one name was on everyone's lips: Joe Hammond. I thought it must have been somebody new from out of town, but people said, no, he'd been around Harlem all the time. They described him and it sounded like the young kid I'd watched around the centers, but I couldn't believe it was the same guy. Then I saw him, and it was the same Joe, and he was killing a bunch of guys his own age. He was much improved, but I still said to myself, 'He's young. He won't do much against the older brothers. They've been in business too long.'

"But then I heard, 'Joe's up at 135th Street beating the pros. . . . Joe's doing everything to those guys.' I still didn't take it too seriously. In fact, when Joe came out to Mount Morris Park for a game against a good team I was on, I said, 'Now we'll see how you do. You won't do anything today.'

"Now I believe in him. Joe Hammond left that game with seven minutes to go. He had forty points. Like everybody had said, Joe was the one."

Earl Manigault played at Benjamin Franklin High School in 1962 and 1963, then spent a season at Laurinburg Institute, the North Carolina prep school that has steered so many ghetto stars toward colleges. Earl never reached college, but when he returned to Harlem he was the king of his own generation of ballplayers, the idol for the generation that followed. He was a six-foot two-inch forward who could outleap men eight inches taller.

But he was also a very human ghetto youth, with weaknesses and doubts that left him vulnerable. Lacking education and motivation, looking toward an empty future, he found that basketball could take him only so far. Then he became the image of the hellish side of ghetto existence. Earl is now in his mid-twenties, a dope addict, in prison. On the playgrounds Earl was a powerful magnetic figure who carried the dreams and ideals of every kid around him as he spun and twisted and sailed over all obstacles. When he fell, he carried those aspirations down with him.

"You think of him on the court and you think of so many incredible things that it's hard to sort them out," Bob Spivey, who played briefly with Earl at Franklin, said. "But I particularly recall one all-star game in the gym at PS 113, in about 1964. Most of the best high-school players in the city were there: Charlie Scott, who went on to North Carolina; Vaughn Harper, who went to Syracuse, and a lot more. But the people who were there will hardly remember the others. Earl was the whole show.

"For a few minutes, Earl seemed to move slowly, feeling his way, getting himself ready. Then he got the ball on a fast break. Harper, who was six feet six, and Val Reed, who was six feet eight, got back quickly to defend. You wouldn't have given Earl a chance to score. Then he accelerated, changing his step suddenly. And at the foul line he went into the air. Harper and Reed went up, too, and, between them, the two big men completely surrounded the rim. But Earl just kept going higher, and finally he two-hand dunked the ball over both of them. For a split second there was complete silence, and then the crowd exploded. They were cheering so loud that they stopped the game for five minutes. Five minutes. That was Earl Manigault."

Faces light up when Harlem veterans reminisce about Manigault. Many street players won reputations with elaborate innovations and tricks: Jackie Jackson was among the first to warm up for games by picking quarters off the top of the backboard. Willie Hall, the former St. John's leader, apparently originated the custom of jumping to the top of the board and, instead of merely blocking a shot, slamming a hand with tremendous force against the board; the fixture would vibrate for several seconds after the blow, causing an easy lay-up to bounce crazily off the rim. Other noted leapers were famous for "pinning"—blocking a lay-up, then simply holding it momentarily against the backboard in a gesture of triumph. Some players seemed to hold it for seconds, suspended in air, multiplying the humiliation of the man who had tried the futile shot. Then they could slam the ball back down at the shooter or, for special emphasis, flip it into the crowd.

Earl Manigault did all of those things and more, borrowing, innovating, and forming one of the most exciting styles Harlem crowds ever watched. Occasionally, he would drive past a few defenders, dunk the ball with one hand, catch it with the other—and raise it and stuff it through the hoop a second time before returning to earth.

"I was in the eighth grade when Earl was in the eleventh," Charley Yelverton, now a star at Fordham, recalled. "I was just another young kid at the time. Like everybody else on the streets, I played some ball. But I just did it for something to do. I wasn't that excited about it. Then there happened to be a game around my block, down at 112th Street, and a lot of the top players were in it—and Earl came down to play. Well, I had never believed things like that could go on. I had never known what basketball could be like. Everybody in the game was doing something, stuffing or blocking shots or making great passes. There's only one game I've ever seen in my life to compare to it—the Knicks' last game against the Lakers.

"But among all the stars, there was no doubt who was the greatest. Passing, shooting, going up in the air, Earl just left everybody behind. No one could turn it on like he could."

Keith Edwards, who lived with Earl during the great days of the Young Life team, agreed: "I guess he had about the most natural ability that I've ever seen. Talent for talent, inch for inch, you'd have to put him on a par with Alcindor and the other superstars. To watch him was like poetry. To play with him or against him—just to be on the same court with him—was a deep experience.

"You can't really project him against an Alcindor, though, because you could never picture Earl going to UCLA or any place like that. He was never the type to really face his responsibilities and his future. He didn't want to think ahead. There was very little discipline about the man...."

And so the decline began. "I lived with the man for about two or three years," Edwards said, "from his pre-drug period into the beginning of his drug period. There were six of us there, and maybe some of us would have liked to help him out. But we were all just young guys finding themselves, and when Earl and another cat named Onion started to get into the drug thing, nobody really had a right, or was in a position, to say much about it."

It didn't happen suddenly. On the weekends, people would still find Earl Manigault at the parks, and flashes of the magnetic ability were there. Young athletes would ask his advice, and he would still be helpful; even among the ones who knew he was sinking deeper into his drug habit, he remained respected and popular. But by early 1968 he seldom came to the parks, and his old friends would find him on street corners along Eighth Avenue, nodding.

In the summer of 1968, Bob Hunter was working on a drug-rehabilitation program. He looked up Earl. They became close, building a friendship that went deeper than their mutual respect on a basketball court. "Earl was an unusual type of addict," Hunter said. "He understood that he was a hard addict, and he faced it very honestly. He wanted to help me in the drug program, and he gave me a lot of hints on how to handle younger addicts. He knew different tricks that would appeal to them and win their trust. And he also knew all the tricks they would use, to deceive me into thinking they were getting cured. Earl had used the tricks himself, and he helped me see through them, and maybe we managed to save a few young kids who might have gotten hooked much worse.

"But it's the most frustrating thing in the world, working with addicts. It's hard to accept the fact that a man who has been burned will go back and touch fire. But they do it. I have countless friends on drugs, and I had many more who have died from drugs. And somehow it's hard to just give up on them and forget that they ever existed. Maybe you would think that only the less talented types would let themselves get hooked—but then you'd see a guy like Earl and you couldn't understand. . . . "

Some people hoped that Earl would be cured that summer. He did so much to help Hunter work with others that people felt he could help himself. Hunter was not as optimistic. "The truth is that nobody is ever going to cure Earl," he said. "The only way he'll be cured is by himself. A lot of people come off drugs only after they've been faced with an extreme crisis. For example, if they come very close to dying and somehow escape, then they might be able to stay away from the fire. But it takes something like that, most of the time."

Earl was not cured, and as the months went on the habit grew more expensive. He broke into a store, and he is now in prison. "Maybe that will be the crisis he needs," Hunter said. "Maybe, just possibly. . . . But when you're talking about addicts, it's very hard to get your hopes too high."

Harold ("Funny") Kitt went to Franklin three years behind Earl Manigault. When Funny finished in 1967, he was rated the best high-school player in the city, largely because he had modeled himself so closely after Earl. "We all idolized Earl in those days," Kitt said. "And when you idolize somebody, you think of the good things, not the bad. As we watched Earl play ball, we had visions of him going on to different places, visiting the whole world, becoming a great star, and then maybe coming back here to see us and talk to us about it all.

"But he didn't do any of those things. He just went into his own strange world, a world I hope I'll never see. I guess there were reasons. I guess there were frustrations that only Earl knew about, and I feel sorry for what happened. But when Earl went into that world, it had an effect on all of us, all the young ballplayers. I idolized the man. And he hurt me."

Beyond the hurt, though, Earl left something more. If his career was a small dramatization of the world of Harlem basketball, then he was a fitting protagonist, in his magnitude and his frailty, a hero for his time. "Earl was quiet, he was honest," Jay Vaughn said, "and he handled the pressures of being the star very well. When you're on top, everybody is out to challenge you, to make their own reps by doing something against you. One guy after another wants to take a shot, and some stars react to all that by bragging, or by being aloof from the crowd.

"Earl was different. The game I'll never forget was in the G-Dub (George Washington High) tournament one summer, when the team that Earl's group was scheduled to play didn't show. The game was forfeited, and some guys were just looking for some kind of pickup game, when one fellow on the team that forfeited came in and said, 'Where's Manigault? I want to play Manigault.'

"Well, this guy was an unknown and he really had no right to talk like that. If he really wanted to challenge a guy like Earl, he should have been out in the parks, building up a rep of his own. But he kept yelling and bragging, and Earl quietly agreed to play him one-on-one. The word went out within minutes, and immediately there was a big crowd gathered for the drama.

"Then they started playing. Earl went over the guy and dunked. Then he blocked the guy's first shot. It was obvious that the man had nothing to offer against Earl. But he was really determined to win himself a rep. So he started pushing and shoving and fouling. Earl didn't say a word. He just kept making his moves and beating the guy, and the guy kept grabbing and jostling him to try to stop him. It got to the point where it wasn't really basketball. And suddenly Earl put down the ball and said, 'I don't need this. You're the best.' Then he just walked away.

"Well, if Earl had gone on and whipped the guy thirty to nothing, he couldn't have proved any more than he did. The other cat just stood there, not knowing what to say. The crowd surrounded Earl, and some of us said things about the fouling and the shoving. But he didn't say anything about it. He didn't feel any need to argue or complain. He had everyone's respect and he knew it. The role he played that day never left anyone who saw it. This was a beautiful man." ✦

MENS SANA IN CORPORE SANO

(APRIL 1979)

Tom Wolfe

"We'll give you a full scholarship, and you won't have to take but one class a week during basketball season, and you'll have your own apartment, rent free, and eleven hundred dollars a month for books and supplies and incidentals, and a Corvette for yourself and a Caprice Classic for your folks, and when you graduate you'll be able to read the newspaper and the stereo ads and add and subtract on a portable calculator and direct-dial anywhere in the world."   ✦

Tennessee Lonesome End

(MARCH 1970)

Peter Schrag

THE SCENE IS like a tribal memory, a fantasy of the race. In the last triumphant moments of the afternoon, the rays of the low autumn sun filter through the banners of the Confederacy, softening the colors. *Mississippi 21, Tennessee Nothing; Mississippi 24, Tennessee Nothing; Mississippi 31, Tennessee Nothing; Mississippi 38, Tennessee Nothing.* "Rebs Put Big Squeeze on Big Orange 38–0." The intensity, hysterical, catatonic, is of the moment, but the currents that give it life are beyond football, flowing from some underground source which rises here. At the end of the game the shades of Horace Benbow and Temple Drake—Faulknerian ghosts in camel's hair coats and bouffant wigs—will wander across the field, greeting other ghosts, replaying the game through the exits, through the parking lots, through the lobbies of Howard Johnson's Motor Lodges and Holiday Inns, through bars and country clubs, far into the evening and through the night, shouting To Hell With Tennessee, To Hell With Vanderbilt, To Hell With Georgia Tech.

It is an eternal celebration of time defied. The clock on the field measures no dimension except the ritual itself, no continuity beyond the formal hour of quarters, halves, and minutes to go. The clock is a liar. Individuals live in other continuities, but here, in this Southern stadium in Jackson, Mississippi, the crowd does not. On the Tennessee side, a young woman in an orange suit, with orange jewelry, orange boots, and an orange ten-gallon hat, watches the hopeless progress of defeat, and screams obscenities at the team, her face contorted with rage. Her husband, similarly dressed, humiliated now not only by his costume but by his partner, understands. "Don't be so hard on those boys," he says to her, loud enough so that all around can hear. "They're fighting all our battles for us." It is not a joke. Battles, he knows, can be lost, but Bruce and Bobby, Charlie and Archie, their achievements committed to memory, will return, eventually with new names, to fight the clock another day. The New

South is there, somewhere, in glass and steel and electronics, but this is where youth eternally verifies the past. To defy time is the greatest of heroic acts.

The Negro is time's intruder. From the beginning, the battles were fought by white men while the great Southern black athletes went to Negro colleges which were even more undistinguished academically than the white universities which refused to take them—to the A and I's, to Grambling and Morgan State—and later to the Big Ten, the Big Eight, and the Pacific Coast. Black athletes have begun to predominate in professional football and, increasingly, in college football as well, and the Southeastern Conference—Alabama, Auburn, Florida, Georgia, Kentucky, LSU, Ole Miss, Mississippi State, Tennessee, Vanderbilt—has begun to suffer, even if the worshippers at Ole Miss and Alabama don't quite know it yet. A year ago, Bobby Dodd, then the Georgia Tech athletic director, declared, patronizingly, "It's just amazing how good the Negro athlete is if given a chance," a remark that must have sounded peculiar, even in the South, at a time when black players had won the National Football League rushing championship six years in succession and the National League baseball batting title seven years of the previous eight, and when virtually every professional basketball star was a Negro.

But Southern football has remained white. The confrontations took place at the schoolhouse door where they were symbolic, not in the stadium or the locker room where they might have gone straight to the heart. The SEC is more than a collection of universities which compete in football and other sports—and winning games, despite assertions to the contrary, may be only one of its considerations. It is the facade, the structure of a ritual, where the fantasy of superiority can be maintained not only by regional isolation, but by an athletic schedule that rarely exposes the region's teams to the real behemoths of national football.

In 1966, a few politically astute liberals—people not so much interested in football as in social change—tried unsuccessfully to persuade the federal government to bring legal pressure on deep-South universities to recruit and play Negroes: in Alabama, they knew, the most influential man was not George C. Wallace but Paul "Bear" Bryant, the university's football coach. "They didn't understand in Washington that it was important they were thinking about lofty things like education," one of those liberals said later. "But can you imagine what would have happened if we could have separated Bryant from Wallace, if there had been pictures in the papers of the Bear and some black football star kneeling together in church?"

Then three years ago—almost, it seemed, by accident—it began to happen, not at Alabama or Ole Miss, but at Kentucky and Tennessee, where the passions of football and race, always running together, were channeled by a sense of the inevitable. Lester McClain, six foot three, 198 pounds, came from Nashville as Tennessee's first black recruit. There had been abortive efforts to integrate Southern football before; players were recruited but didn't come or didn't stay; some, according to the coaches in the Conferences, were academically unqualified, and one quit after playing a few games. McClain, who was signed as a companion to another black player who later withdrew, received the last of Tennessee's quota of football scholarships in 1967. (Football scholarships cover room, board, tuition, and a little free cash; they are controlled by the coaches, not the university, and it is rare, if not impossible, for a student not on scholarship to play varsity ball.) "The high schools had started to integrate," said Tennessee's head coach, Doug Dickey, "and we figured it was time for us to do something." Since then Dickey has recruited several more; in 1969 three black men were playing varsity ball for Tennessee, Jackie Walker as a linebacker, Andy Bennett as a second string halfback, and McClain as the starting split end. (There are now also a few Negro athletes in other sports—at Tennessee, Auburn, Florida, Kentucky, Georgia Tech, and Mississippi State.) Walker, Bennett, and McClain are all highly skilled athletes, but none is a Jimmy Brown or an O. J. Simpson. "I think it was easier that way," one of the Tennessee coaches said recently. "The pressure on a superstar would have been that much greater."

Ole Miss leads 21–0. McClain, wearing Number 85, lines up wide to the right, three or four yards beyond the tight end. He cannot hear the snap count of the quarterback, Bobby Scott, over the screaming spectators. When he sees the ball snapped he runs, almost lopes, ten yards downfield, cuts sharply to the inside, and takes the pass from Scott, then turns and gains perhaps another three yards before he is tackled. First down, one of the few Tennessee will get that afternoon. "Hey nigger," someone yells from the Ole Miss stands. McClain, who can hear nothing but the crowd, returns to the huddle. "Hey Leroy," the man screams again. Laughter in the twentieth row. "What you doing givin' that ball to a nigger." Last year, in Knoxville, when Tennessee beat Ole Miss 31–0, McClain scored two touchdowns. Some of the Mississippi fans, one of the Tennessee coaches said, were yelling nigger there, too, but McClain didn't hear them either.

McClain never said it was hard; you have to say that for him. It is a long way from the old preacher's place outside Nashville—the thirty acres, the hogs and cows, the seven children spread over two generations—to the University of Tennessee in Knoxville, to Bill Gibbs Hall where the jocks live, to Mississippi Memorial Stadium, where the sun sets behind the banners of the South and the band plays "Dixie." (How did it feel to be playing there, you ask later, and he answers, "I've never seen so many Confederate flags.") For five years the road began at 6:30 A.M. every day, forty miles across the city to the black high school where he started to play football; two hours on a bus every morning, two hours every afternoon; then, after integration (in his senior year) to Antioch High where he learned the style and etiquette of the black player on the white man's field: don't be the second man on a tackle (he thinks, playing defense for Antioch) some referee might call a penalty (though, in fact, none ever did); don't be obtrusive. "I played ball and people got to know and like me. Then I did the same thing when I got to Tennessee. Maybe the word will get around that black people click just like other people. Maybe the next guys won't have to do this."

At first, in the early conversations in the trophy room of the Athletic Building, you think that perhaps he hasn't thought much about what he has to do, or what others are now doing. (Or is he putting you on?) Has he heard about the revolt of the black athletes, the 1968 Olympic boycott, the suspension of black football players at Wyoming and Indiana and other places who protested racism in their own schools or among their opponents? "Why," he asked at one time, "do they always play 'Dixie'?" but he didn't pursue the question. McClain will have nothing to do with the Black Student Union at Tennessee (there are some 300 black students of a total of 23,000 on the Knoxville campus), and will remain alone rather than mix too much with anyone, black or white. He doesn't date students at Tennessee; there is a girl at home and, occasionally, he spends an evening with girls he meets through "the people who work here," meaning the maids and cooks. Between the lines he tells you that clusters of blacks make him uncomfortable, but he has also learned, somewhere, that the price of integration is not to ask too much of white men either. His roommate, a "fifth string" quarterback, is white (Bennett and Walker room together). "The BSU wanted me to participate in a protest but I didn't understand what they were complaining about. Maybe it's because I live over here with the other athletes, but I didn't have the complaints they had. If I'd wanted black separatism I could have gone to Tennessee A and I."

Knoxville (AP) —Tennessee's Lester McClain says being the first Negro to play varsity football in the Southeastern Conference has posed no problems at all.

"I haven't given it any thought," said McClain, who returns to his hometown of Nashville Saturday to play against Vanderbilt. "There have been no problems or incidents of any kind," McClain said. "To the fellows on the team, I feel like I have been just one of the guys from the beginning.

"So far as our opponents are concerned, there have been no problems. Sometimes one of the players will say 'nice block' or 'that was a nice catch.' When we beat Mississippi (in 1968) several of their players sought me out to congratulate me."

McClain was named SEC Lineman of the Week for catching two touchdown passes against Kentucky in Tennessee's 24–7 victory over the Wildcats Saturday. It was the third time this season McClain had caught two TD passes in a game. He grabbed two against Georgia Tech and two more against UCLA.

On the afternoon before the game, two large buses stop at the side of the empty stadium, and the Tennessee players—for the moment ranked as the sixth-best football team in America—file out, silent in their orange blazers and their too-tight trousers. The cold East wind and the deserted stadium make this a moment of unspeakable loneliness. You have seen lines of young men like this in other places, at induction centers and military schools, and you wonder whether any of them really want to be there. They walk quietly into the dressing room under the concrete stands and reappear on the field a few minutes later, this time in orange sweat suits and helmets, and begin to run their plays and practice their kicks. Sometimes, after a good catch or a long kick, they whoop and cheer, but their voices are inadequate to the stadium, and the sound, swept by the wind, is almost meek. Between plays McClain stands cross-armed, usually alone, warming his hands under his armpits. It is something one may have learned from poverty in cold places.

"What I want to do," McClain had said, "is to make money." He came to college hoping to be an engineer because he had been good in mathematics in high school, "but when I got here, I discovered it was another world, so I switched to accounting." We were sitting on the steps of Gibbs Hall, stopping occasionally to chat with another player. "I had a little trouble in accounting, too, but I'm doing all right now. They'd be talking about some company—the other students knew about it—but living in the country I hadn't even heard of it." He speaks about his childhood, about a family in which, a decade before, no one could have expected to go to college, let alone to the University of Tennessee, which didn't begin to integrate until 1962. Saturday, for the Georgia Tech game, he will have ten visitors: three brothers, their wives, one of their children, his parents, and his girl who works as a bookkeeper in Nashville. His parents hadn't wanted him to play football, were afraid that he might get hurt, but his brother, now forty-two, encouraged him. When they saw his first press clippings from high school his parents dropped their objections. It was, even then, a possible way out. *"Hey Lester," says a passing player, "I saw your picture in the paper again." "That wasn't me," McClain answers, "that was my brother."* What does he talk about with them, you ask, and now he answers a little indefinitely: "Business sometimes, or maybe the high-school teams that we follow; or maybe movies or movie stars or music. We talk about girls, but never our own girls, and we never talk about politics. In politics people have different views and it breaks up friendships if you talk about it."

And then, riding in the Olds 442 that his brother gave him, there are dreams and fantasies, but the dreams are tempered by some deep hard sense of reality that seems almost strange on that early fall evening. "I'll play pro football if they pay me for it; otherwise I'll stick to accounting. Everybody would play pro ball if he had the chance. But what I'd really like to do is be an actor like Jimmy Brown, maybe play in a movie. Not really act, but be in a movie." The world eventually is at the end of some road, in a big city, maybe Atlanta, but not in the rural South, not around here. And then he speaks about the world he is already in, a world between worlds: "I went back to a game at a black high school in Memphis and felt like a stranger. If I went to an all-white affair I'd feel like a stranger, too. I feel at home in a place that's integrated."

We stopped at Shoney's Restaurant for ice cream, the black athlete from Nashville, the Jewish writer from New York, talking now about how people grow up, how kids learn, about life in the streets and in the country, and about the subtle things one has to learn, each of you knowing that in a situation like this some things must be left unsaid. McClain tells of the Cotton Bowl game in Dallas the previous New Year's Day. There had been some hope that if Tennessee was up and Texas down it might be a close game, but it turned out to be the other way around, and Texas won easily. During the week in Dallas, McClain said, "some of the guys went clubbing. I didn't like Dallas—everybody walking around in ten-gallon hats and cowboy boots. I don't want to wear a ten-gallon hat and I didn't go clubbing. Some of the guys asked me to go along; I thought it was nice of them to ask me. There wasn't anything to do in Dallas; I didn't know where to go, didn't know any places, so I went home the day after the game." Then what's the point of it all, what's the use, you ask, and he says it does make a difference. "I know one guy—from Selma; his daddy won't have anything to do with black people. He told how he's discovered that black people click just like other people. He asked me to his wedding." The waitress brings our check—McClain has to get back to his dormitory for the 11:00 P.M. curfew. "It's good to talk like this, it's a load off you," he says. "It's been real nice serving you," says the waitress, like a recorded announcement.

Tennessee has just beaten Georgia Tech 26–8. In the team meeting room out-side the showers, the orange carpet is littered with pieces of discarded tape and empty cans of Gatorade. Three or four young boys—all of them white—stop McClain on his way out, ask for his autograph, and wait quietly while he signs on programs and scraps of paper. He walks on toward the door leading into the stadium, meeting Walker and Bennett near the exit, and the three emerge togeth-er. Outside there are more autographs for waiting boys, handshakes from the par-ents of some of the other players, and an embrace from Marcia, the girl from Nashville. Bennett and Walker go on together; McClain and Marcia, arm-in-arm, walk alone across the field, up the steps on the other side, and finally into the street. On the way they are stopped several more times—handshakes, congratula-tions, introductions—and when they arrive at the reception outside Gibbs Hall (held after each home game) they are absorbed into the chatter of the crowd, into the orange blazers and the tailored autumn dresses. It is like a fraternity party on a homecoming weekend, now familiar and jocular, now formal and awkward. At the edge of the crowd Andrew McClain, the older brother, tells Lester of the fam-ily plans to drive to Birmingham for the Alabama game and then, when Lester and Marcia stop to talk to the fiancée of one of the other players, Andrew speaks about his own youth during the Depression. "Lester," he said, "will have it a lit-tle better." Resting against the fender of a parked car, McClain's seventy-year-old father, his wrinkled hands folded across his middle, looks absently at the orange pompon that Marcia brought back from the game.

If football is the major ritual of the South—its religion, its dream, its secret life—it is also a world unique to itself, a million-dollar enterprise directed by professionals, played by "amateurs" (for pride, for money, for an education), and surrounded by hordes of managers, publicists, soothsayers, and assorted hangers-on, paid and unpaid, who live in the reflected glory of Saturday afternoon. One does not have to remain among them long to understand how bruised hips, pulled groin muscles, and twisted knees can become major events, how and why athletes—black and white—become chattels, or why, for that very reason, the one-dimensional assessment of players takes on that fundamental honesty which is interested, above all, in winners. All these things make it easier to integrate Negro athletes than Negro students. If every man is property, if self-effacement, good conduct, and discipline (not to mention strength and speed) are the highest virtues, then one can treat Negroes and athletes in precisely the same way: they're all boys. But for that reason, also, the Negro athlete may turn out to be the Trojan horse in the locker room. If he decides to rebel in the name of black freedom, how long will it take the white players to decide that they're niggers, too, and that curfews, dress codes, and special dormitories are for children, for boys, not for men?

"I don't understand what's the matter with mankind," a sportswriter from Nashville says. "They're all crazy, letting those good colored players go North. The best thing that's happened to this place is getting Lester McClain. You know what Bear Bryant told me? He told me Southeastern Conference football would never be great again until they removed the restrictions."

What restrictions?

"I don't know that they got any rules; it's just that there might be trouble, but people would accept it, just like they accepted it here. They keep saying that the colored players can't make it academically, but that's just an excuse. They're all taking players who aren't geniuses."

"Why don't they take them in under the Poverty Program," asks a visiting football scout from the Dallas Cowboys. "If they can't qualify under SEC rules (the Conference imposes minimum standards for athletes) they'd have a year for remedial work. Then, if they don't flunk out, you could give 'em football scholarships."

"Lester's just perfect," says another sportswriter. "He must have been raised well. His father's a preacher down in Nashville."

What about the revolt of the black athletes elsewhere? "Oh, you can tell," says the scout. "You can spot the troublemakers."

The hypotheses abound and the rumors flow, and the variables become almost too numerous to manage: coaches are professionals who want to win, and will play anyone who can help them do it; the people of Mississippi and Alabama, perhaps even the people of Tennessee, would never support teams dominated by black players; it is better not to get stars who are black since they would be too threatening to the faithful; it is imperative to get stars, if you are going to recruit black players at all, so there is no doubt that their scholarships and their presence on the team are justified. And as the recognition of the potential value of black athletes increases, so do the defenses. "Sure, those black boys can run," said someone from Ole Miss, "because they're built differently, their legs are different. It's their bones. Houston had a fellow—I can't remember his name—he could run but he was yellow."

The Conference rules, you are told by the reasonable people, have made it difficult for black athletes to qualify academically, yet there is no evidence that SEC regulations are more stringent than those in any other Conference. Somehow Dickey has managed to get Negro players while Bryant at Alabama and Johnny Vaught at Ole Miss have not. (This fall, Mississippi State played two outstanding black athletes in its freshman football game against Ole Miss; Mississippi State won 51–0 and that may create more pressure than all the civil-rights cases in the world.) "We're seeking athletes regardless of color," said Vaught, who has the highest lifetime winning percentage of all college football coaches in the country. "We signed a couple," meaning they had signed letters of intent—mini-contracts, "but one didn't qualify academically and the other decided to go elsewhere. We would have liked the boy from Vicksburg [now the starting quarterback at Michigan State]. He's an exceptionally fine boy." Vaught claims that he has sought athletes at all-black high schools in the state. "They're all supposed to be integrated now," he said, but there is considerable doubt about the diligence of his pursuit. In 1966 Vaught had said that when Ole Miss integrated he didn't expect to be around anymore. Ole Miss fans, he says now, would support the team even if there were black players—after all, he added, there are many Negro students on campus—but others in Oxford aren't so sure. "They'd accept it," said someone on the Ole Miss staff, "but they sure as hell wouldn't like it." Whatever the hypotheses (could any black man, indeed, play for a team calling itself the Rebels; could any crowd waving Confederate flags cheer his touchdown?) the fact is simply that there are none. In Jackson, a gentleman representing the White Citizens' Council was asked if the Council had a policy about black and white athletes playing on the same team. "No," he said, "we don't have a policy on that. But I'll make one up. We're against it."

On Thursday they begin to assemble: the advance men, the early travelers, the big-bellied men with their bulbous class rings, the bourbon-pickled loud-voiced women, debouching from Cadillacs and chartered planes, how-ya-doin' through the lobbies of motels, starting the party, greeting the arrivals—To Hell With Ole Miss, To Hell With Tennessee. "City Greets Vols for Nippy Reb Tiff." Each week they march through the South, armies of the faithful, forsaking their vacations for six or ten three-day football weekends, carrying their cushions, their bottles, possessed by what they can no longer possess, filling the void with noise. "Wasn't that a helluva game . . . we kicked to 'em but it hardly went past the line of scrimmage . . . Missed you in Memphis . . . The lot's right at the bottom of the hill, you turn right . . . You know Mrs. Davis, and this is her sister . . . To Hell With Tennessee." Sometimes they charter trains: $100 per person, Knoxville to Birmingham, for sleepers, club car, two breakfasts and Saturday dinner, sometimes they fly or drive. "In Birmingham or Jackson you can feel the electricity, the excitement," someone had said. "They're really proud of those teams; maybe it's because they haven't had much else to be proud of." If this is what it's like to be an adult, who would ever want to grow up? To Hell With Ole Miss. Mississippi goddamn. By the time they arrive at the game, they have given voice to the secret meaning, have, as it were, invented words for what words can't express. (It happens to be, through ironic coincidence, Youth Appreciation Week.) The big grudge, the longings and passions denied, cannot be played out, for when youth ends, so does life, and so little grudges, which can be adjudicated here and now, must replace them. Before the season began, a sportswriter had observed that Ole Miss seemed to have the horses for another good year, and Steve Kiner, Tennessee's All-American linebacker, countered that some people can't tell horses from mules. It was the sort of remark that nice boys aren't supposed to make, an insult, if you will, to the race, and it helped give this game its higher cause. Archie Manning, Mississippi's sanctified quarterback, moreover, had been reduced, on buttons worn by Tennessee rooters, to "Archie Who?"

Going into the game, Tennessee is undefeated, with a record of 7–0; Ole Miss has lost three, one of them to the University of Houston, whose team is integrated. When the announcer reads the starting lineups at Mississippi Memorial Stadium, he lists only ten starters for the Tennessee offense. McClain's name is omitted. At the same moment, according to the papers, Richard M. Nixon is preparing to watch Ohio State–Purdue on television, and the 500,000 people who came to Washington to protest the Vietnam war are gathering for their final rally. In Mississippi Memorial Stadium, a local minister reads the invocation: "God be with our fighting men in Vietnam who are fighting to keep our country free. In Jesus' Name, Amen." The Ole Miss band plays "The Star-Spangled Banner," and 47,000 people begin to scream, waiting for the battle.

In the background hangs the specter of change and revolt, not merely among black athletes, but among all young men and women. References to riots and demonstrations creep incessantly into the discussions of collegiate sports, and you are reminded, without ever having asked, that the orderly, disciplined life of the athlete is far more conducive to "getting an education" than the turmoil of a disrupted campus. "How can you study," someone asked, "if the university is closed down or the students are sitting in? The rooms in Gibbs Hall are kept clean; there are no drugs. These boys here have a chance to learn." On the Tennessee campus itself, several hundred students chartered buses to attend the second Vietnam Moratorium; the use of marijuana is extensive, and the number of freaks—people given to long hair, beads, and joss sticks—grows every year. On the evening after the Georgia Tech game they held an outdoor "Freak Concert"—bands, folk singers, guitars—attended by five or six hundred people who were not above shouting, "Kill the Pig," when the campus police car came around. And while Doug Dickey quietly integrated his football team, the undergraduates themselves elected Jimmie Baxter, a black Air Force veteran, as president of the Student Government. (At the University of Alabama, Diane Kirksy, a Negro, was one of the three finalists for 1969 homecoming queen—the winner was a Japanese American named Sue Shimoda—and at LSU the Student Government Association asked the university athletic director to begin active recruitment of black athletes.)

What you learn from people like Baxter, and from the freaks, is that slowly the base of student support, even at Tennessee, is beginning to erode beneath the old forms and institutions, and the new rituals—the ceremonial passing of the joint, for example—have started to replace them. In the months before Baxter's election there had been several protests—on women's hours, an open speaker policy, and black studies—which helped focus student sentiment. "I ran against the usual fraternity candidates," said Baxter, wearing an Afro, beard, shades, and a blue denim jacket. "I was the only one who

raised the issue of student power, and I got elected. This place is changing."
As you talk with people like him you reestablish contact with the newer student world, people who speak about the Vietnam war, and about reform. "The students aren't half as turned-on about football as they were a few years ago. Football is still supported—by the alumni, the administration, the trustees, by the whole state. The students know it's there, and most of them go to the games, but they're not as wild about it as they used to be. These older people come into the Student Center on Saturday before the games in their orange suits and coats, with their Tennessee neckties, and they stare at the freaks with their long hair. But they haven't any idea how silly *they* look. They'll support a team with a few black players"—everyone's for Lester, said someone else, because he's *our* nigger—"but if we got too many they'd begin to wonder if it was really their team. And we're never likely to have a black quarterback. That's not the role they imagine for Negroes."

And every day, the national black revolt comes closer. What Harry Edwards, then a teacher at San Jose State College, began in organizing the 1968 Olympic protest (first against participation by South Africa, then against American racism) has spread to major institutions in nearly every part of the country: black athletes demanding more black coaches and teachers, refusing to participate in competition against what they regard as racist opponents, insisting on better academic conditions—among them black studies programs—and better treatment on the campus.

> "Gradually," [wrote Edwards in his book *The Revolt of the Black Athlete*]
> most black college athletes begin to realize that their white employers, their
> teammates, even their fellow students, in spite of the cheers and adulations
> they shower upon them, regard them as something akin to super animals,
> but animals nevertheless. A black athlete on a white campus cannot afford
> to make mistakes or perform occasionally at a mediocre level. If he does, he
> does not play.
>
> If he fails academically, he is ridiculed; but if he quits he is despised. For
> he has not taken advantage of "the chance that his parents didn't have." He
> has failed those who had faith in him. . . . A black athlete himself may feel
> guilty even about the thought of quitting. But what he doesn't realize is that
> he can never prove himself in the eyes of white racists—not, at any rate, as
> a man or even a human being. From their perspective he is, and always will
> be, a nigger. From their perspective the only difference between the black

man shining shoes in the ghetto and the champion black sprinter is that the shoeshine man is a nigger, while the sprinter is a fast nigger.

The black athlete on the white-dominated college campus . . . is typically exploited, abused, dehumanized, and cast aside in much the same manner as a worn basketball.

The voices in the athletic offices intone the words "no trouble" like an incantation against evil spirits. Counting track runners, Tennessee now has eleven black athletes on scholarship. Track integrated before football. "You have to take into consideration what kind of guys these Negroes are. They're not marching or protesting. You know some guys have an inferiority complex about being colored. These guys fit right in. The fans have kind of adopted them." The coaches cannot bring themselves either to believe that there will be trouble here, or to refrain from discussing it. They treat their players equitably, and they believe in the validity of the order they maintain. "The revolt of the black athletes will be a passing thing," Dickey said. "They're following undisciplined leadership. The only place on the campus where there's still discipline is in athletics and fraternities. ROTC is almost gone in most places. It's sad that Negroes as a race lack stable leadership. But there's been no problem here. Sure, there have been some confrontations, between black and white, and between white and white, but football players, you have to remember, are combative types, and some of them can't always keep it on the field."

By the time the Tennessee offense gets the ball the first time, Ole Miss has already scored and the crowd is yelling for more. High in the Ole Miss stands someone has hung a hand-lettered banner: "No Fruit Sucks Like a Big Orange." McClain lines up wide to the right; Scott gives the ball to Curt Watson, the fullback, who cracks into the line for perhaps two yards. McClain, blocking downfield, hits the defensive halfback, Wyck Neely, a junior from Magee, Mississippi, drives him backward, and knocks him down, but Watson has already been stopped. McClain helps Neely up, and trots back to the huddle. Two plays later, on third and long yardage, McClain runs a pass pattern, ten yards downfield and clear, but Scott, looking for one of his other receivers, doesn't see him, and fails to make the completion. On the way back upfield, one of the Ole Miss defensive backs gives McClain a friendly pat on the rump. On fourth down, a bad punt gives Ole Miss the ball on the Tennessee 38, and a few plays later the Rebels score again.

The clock moves. During the Tennessee–Georgia Tech game, a sports-writer from Memphis was quick to point out to the visiting Yankee journal-ist that the band playing "Dixie" was not Tennessee's but Georgia Tech's. Does he know why there are no Negro cheerleaders, has he heard the story about the white Tennessee cheerleader who told a Negro applicant not to come back unless she brought her own black man so that no white boy would have to toss a black girl in the air? Sitting in a small campus office, Ralph Boston, a 1968 Olympic medal winner in the long jump, now an assistant dean of stu-dents, one of the few black men on the Tennessee staff, speaks about change: "It's coming here, too. You have to make some adjustments. If you're going to take black athletes or black students you can't just go on in the old way, expecting black kids to stand up when they play 'Dixie' or to accept the Confederate flag. It's silly to say that a kid can't play with a beard or a mous-tache, whether he's black or white. Joe Namath wins games with a moustache. I think some of these kids are angry, but they can't say much because they have to make it themselves first. There's a story about O. J. Simpson; he was supposed to have told the kids in Watts, 'Give me three or four years to make it, to make a real name as a football player, and I'll be back to help you.' But of course three or four years is a long time."

McClain says very little. They are all cordial, the athletes, the coaches, the flacks, but life around an athletic dormitory doesn't permit much privacy. One must learn, in this helpful, hospitable despotism, to keep one's mouth shut. "I don't think the papers are really telling very much about what's going on," he said one day at lunch. "One of the white guys on the team was saying that there must be something to the protest at Wyoming; they just wouldn't be doing all this without a cause." For people like McClain, football is the road to a better life; a means to an end. Some of the other black athletes, he said, have been doing some thinking, "but it wouldn't help 'em to say any-thing." For the coming summer, McClain himself already has several job offers from accounting firms "because they can't find enough black account-ants." He is, as he hoped, on the way to "another class of life."

A minute before the half, with the score 24–0, Scott attempts a long pass to McClain, who is a step or two behind the man who is covering him, but the ball is underthrown and the pass intercepted. "Hey nigger," shouts a young man from an end zone seat, "you be goin' to Jackson State with the other niggers." By now it is clear that the defeat is turning into a rout, and the crowd is beginning to cele-

brate. Everything is coming together again, the flag, the race, the time. The band marches, the eunuch steps and foppish costumes prance in unmanly counterpoint to the gladiators in the main event. "You're always hoping for the big play, hoping you can do something," McClain said later, but in the second half nothing changes. Kiner, still suffering from an injury, plays poorly, Walker is arm tackling, letting ball carriers run past him, and Archie Manning, never better, moves the Ole Miss team for two more touchdowns. The crowd, responding to the Archie buttons, begins to chant "Kiner Who? Kiner Who? Kiner Who?" (later some of them will send him vicious little postcards), while, in the Ole Miss cheering section, the students yell, rhythmically, "No School on Monday, no School on Monday." In Washington, at this moment, other kids are singing the songs of peace and listening to the last Moratorium speakers plead for withdrawal, and you remember how, a few weeks before, McClain, appearing at a pre-game pep rally, had made a V with his fingers, explaining that "usually this means peace, but on a Friday night, it stands for victory." In the last moments of the game Ole Miss intercepts a desperate pass by a second-string Tennessee quarterback, and, as the Mississippi substitutes go in to kill the clock, the defensive players, flushed, bouncing with triumph, come off the field and flash the V to their cheering fans. As the crowd disperses, Ross Barnett, former Governor of Mississippi, ghostlike, wanders around the end zone, greeting the scattered people who recognize him, and proclaims "Archie for Governor."

"What are you angry about?" you ask McClain for perhaps the third time, but there is still no answer. And then, for a moment, he speaks about Lew Alcindor, the great black basketball star who, after graduation, wrote about the racism he encountered while playing for UCLA. "You know," said McClain finally, "someday I'd like to tell my story the way Alcindor did."   ✦

Find Me a Writer

(FEBRUARY 1984)

Wilfrid Sheed

IT LOOKED LIKE fun when Spencer Tracy did it. Perched eternally in the best seat in the house, batting out his hard-boiled (but sensitive) copy in nothing flat, between wisecracks; then a few minutes with the superstar (who seemed overjoyed to see him) and off to Toots Shor's to collect his anecdotes. Sportswriting seemed like a neat way to make a living.

Its heyday was the Teens, Twenties, Thirties—any time before television. Sportswriters were lords, if not of the earth, at least of the afternoon editions. Some snob once started a rumor that the best prose was to be found in the sports pages, and in certain circles newspapers were rated by who they employed there. Well, why not? Ring Lardner, Damon Runyon, and Heywood Broun were pretty good contenders.

Nowadays, to watch the heirs of those titans traipsing across the tarmac hauling their dry cleaning from a fight in Cleveland to a basketball game in Detroit is to witness a fall of empire. Crowds form around Howard Cosell while a TV truck stands arrogantly by, its day's work done. Meanwhile the men with the dry cleaning board commercial flight 000 as anonymously as mailmen. No matter how they scurry, they will never catch up with the news, which went blinking out of town some time ago.

So what do they do, exactly? Heralds without news, eyewitnesses in a world of eyewitnesses—what remains to be said?

"The real object of sportswriting," says a friend of mine who does it, "is to keep readers away from the horrors in the rest of the paper." Thus sports continues its rounds as the Magnificent Evasion, since it also keeps us away from the bad news at home and in one's own psyche. Many men, and a spattering of women, talk about sports from morning to night for fear something else might get in. And strangers reach for it gratefully as a *lingua franca,* something to keep the chatter going while revealing nothing. As a form of cover

111

one invents a sort of "play" self as, say, a Red Sox fan, which one pushes ener-getically around the board in place of the real thing. It is no accident, I think, that this particular sport within a sport was invented in England, the home of fine acting and the very best spies.

Hence, the sportswriter's task would seem to be simply stoking up the nation's biggest conversation every day and throwing new items onto it from time to time. But there is nothing simple about it. Only to the ear of a wife does all sports conversation sound alike. In fact, the subject comes in millions of pieces, from local school football to Olympic boycotts, and every fan has his own hierarchy of interests, so that it's hard to arrange a coherent agenda even in a single saloon. A sportswriter is like a man trying to address a hun-dred saloons at once, not to mention dining rooms and bedrooms. And now, to add to his woes, he must wonder if "they" have seen this or that event on TV and know as much about it as he does.

TV has certainly scrambled what was already a confused picture. In the arts, critics are those who write for the people who already know the work in question, while reviewers are perennial introducers, booming out the names and credentials of new arrivals. Each task is agreeable enough in its thin-lipped way; but the sportswriter has to do both, because his clientele is mixed for him daily in unknown proportions.

For this reason, the locker room has become the favored arena of many a columnist, with the game serving as so much fodder for interviews. The recent hullabaloo about women in the locker room was based largely on this development. The public mind, being what it is, fell back on its *other* subject, and fantasized much hasty snatching of towels, attempts to interview in the shower, and all the other jolly things we like to think about. But if the story is in there, women writers obviously have to go in and get it, let the towels fall where they may.

What a flat story it generally is. Like many another club women have fought to get into, there isn't much *to* a locker room when you arrive. A score of articulate people can be found jabbering questions at a gaggle of tired and frustrated, or tired and elated, men who are not paid for eloquence. An artist like Red Smith can tease their mumbles into funny stories, and a safe-crack-er like Dick Young can extract better mumbles. But the rest are left scram-bling for the small coins, the "I hit the real good curve" and "we've been picking each other up all year"—thus contributing to another of the functions of sportswriting, as defined by a friend, namely "to keep those clichés circulating."

The phrase "in depth" usually has even less to do with these hairy confrontations than it does with a Washington press conference. The masters, the Smiths and the Youngs, have a certain small edge: the jocks remember them and occasionally treat them like friends and not answering services. But I suspect that even the best expect little from the postgame hog call. Only after the sweat has dried comes the quote; and by then frequently only the Smiths and Youngs, the trusted retainers, are around to hear it.

The quote they finally do pry loose seems these days to have less and less to do with the game that's just been played. Often the athletes appear to have seen the game slightly less well than the TV cameras, and have been known to mutter, "I'll have to see the films on that." What they do know about is their own grievances and those of their playmates and these the surliest of them seem willing to enlarge upon endlessly. "They treat us all like meat," says Dave Kingman, breaking a silence of several years. And if the great Steve Carlton ever breaks his monastic vows, one can bet it will be with some similar keening growl.

So the focus has shifted not just from the arena but from the whole world of liniment and leather and into the souls of men. These in turn divide into two departments: fiscal and medico-spiritual. A sportswriter so inclined can now write about money every day of the year without giving a thought to bats and balls. And if he can't, George Steinbrenner will help him. When the Yankee dictator, with his iron fist and his wooden tongue, observed that some of his batters were being thrown at, he hollered, in effect, "That may have been okay in the old days, but I pay these guys a lot of money." This startling evaluation of human life was all the more gripping for having gone, so far as I know, completely unquestioned. In the steamy bazaar of the sports pages, mowing down the peasants while sparing the millionaires seems almost as reasonable as boxing.

Just in case the fan in the street ever starts to choke on all the bankrolls he has to read about, along comes drugs to change the subject. Slightly. In fact, it is just a short stroll from one subject to the other. If athletes are going to be paid like movie stars, they are inevitably going to start acting like them, which includes, nowadays, snorting, mainlining, and—felicitous phrase—freebasing. After which, chances are they will find Jesus.

Back in the Fifties, the crusty Jimmy Cannon accused his young colleagues of being "chipmunks" because they asked so many personal questions. But the chipmunks must have sniffed something in the wind and foreseen a day when there would be no impersonal questions left. They were the first TV generation of Tracys, and they knew that the best seat in the house wasn't worth a single indiscreet remark from a famous ball player's ex-wife.

So the human-interest story went into place as a basic column—and mighty insipid stuff it could be, as Muscles McGurk conquered fear with the help of his priest and his seeing-eye dog. It needed a shot of something and it got a massive one: the great national shoot-up went coursing through these drab pieces, lighting them up like pinball machines. Even the news items began to read like *General Hospital*: shortstop agrees to rehabilitation, relief pitcher comes out of rehabilitation (but still looks kind of funny), basketball player disappears. All you needed to cover this circus was a degree in pharmacology and the soul of Rona Barrett.

Finding Jesus has, up to now, proved harder for our boys to handle than dope; in fact it could be called a downright handicap. The born-again game hero won't even tell you whether he hit the good curve or the bad slider before he launches into the Man Upstairs, and how *He* did it. Although I would dearly like to know how *He* did it and indeed would welcome a hot theological discussion in the clubhouse, followed by a pillow fight, these pious fellows seem to have given up thinking about anything at all, even the last thing they said. So a story about a born-again has to stress the lamentable drug years and the unfortunate bar brawls before homing in lightly on the homogenized happy ending. Sportswriters are versatile, but only a few of them—and those, specialists—can do much with uplift.

However, there is still work to be done in the other direction, the sin beat. When I covered Muhammad Ali back in 1975, I found myself, like everyone else, covering *for* him. Although he was clearly stepping out with a lady other than his wife, the writers agreed to a man simply not to see it. It goes against the grain of this (let's get it over with) remarkably decent profession to cover bedrooms—even when they begin to show in a subject's work. At the moment, with so many sinners turning themselves in voluntarily, one doesn't have to go looking for them. But even with privacy everywhere in tatters sportswriters sit on spicy stories with a frequency that would get them fired from other parts of the paper. Gallantly, I believe, many of them consider that stuff is simply unworthy of the sports pages.

Even if all the closets flew open at once, we would be left with the condition we came in with: namely, that sports, however described, are local and particular. Drive through Massachusetts or North Carolina on a fall Saturday and you will imagine that the state has been completely overrun by football teams: colleges with funny names like dummy corporations, high schools beyond measure—each demanding its mead of talk.

For this reason, there is hardly such a thing as a national sportswriter. Jim Murray of the *L.A. Times,* who is perhaps the closest, has no regular New York outlet. And when you do see a syndicated column in out-of-town papers it looks oddly abstract and out of place, like a paid ad, among the regional chatter. The syndicated writer must stick to national personalities like Pete Rose the Good or John McEnroe the Bad—but these are themselves commercial images, clumps of connected dots, brand names from another world. Or he can try to interest you in, say, some Dallas middle linebacker: but people have their own linebackers to worry about. Above all, he needs national subjects, which translates into endless coverage of championship fights, tennis players' manners, and the grotesque hype of the Super Bowl. All these matters fit quite comfortably into sports magazines, written by zealots for zealots, but seem like more fuss than they're worth in a daily paper. *Sports Illustrated* houses genuinely national sportswriters, but only for Sports-nation: if one wants a larger bowl to swim in one must still turn, like Lardner and Broun and Westbrook Pegler and so many others, reluctantly to other matters.

Meanwhile the best sportswriters remain what they always were, local guys talking to people they know about common, not manufactured, enthusiasms. Red Smith, to end this on a proper note of reverence, used to sweat out a column and then talk away several more of them at the nearest pub. Smith spanned several eras, so he is a useful gauge of possible change in the genus sportswriter. When he died two years ago at the age of seventy-six I doubt if there was a single apprentice in the game who didn't think of him as in some sense a model. And as long as the kids want to be like Smith, breasting the bar with a porkpie hat and a *Baseball Encyclopedia,* all the electronic flimflam in the world won't seriously modify this early American type. Upon rereading the old masters, I was startled to find that some of them barely seemed to know how each particular sport was played. What they knew were stories. And so do their successors. The stories may be different now, and fewer people may be listening, and conditions may be straitened, but Spencer Tracy lives—even if he is sometimes to be found in a broadcasting booth where the best announcers, like Vin Scully and Joe Garagiola, tell funny stories between pitches and frequently talk more like old sportswriters than young sportswriters do.

Even on film, it may still be the best way to do it. ✦

PART II: BOX SEATS

✦

THESE SPORTING POETS

PILGRIM'S PROGRESS

(DECEMBER 2003)

Lewis H. Lapham

If you come to my funeral,
Come dressed in red.
'Cause I got no business being dead.
　　　　—Langston Hughes

NEITHER HAS GEORGE Plimpton got any business being dead. Maybe later, when or if he could spare the time from one of the other projects on which he was embarked; certainly not now or yet. Such was the feeling among those of his friends (850 of them, all eligible for the adjective "best") who showed up for his party on October 14 at Cipriani on East Forty-second Street in Manhattan. The party had been on the calendar for six months, billed as "a revel" celebrating the fiftieth birthday of *The Paris Review* that George never had tired of editing since he sharpened his first blue pencil aboard a barge moored to a quay four miles downstream from the Louvre. He died in his sleep on the last Friday of September, at the age of seventy-six, in his apartment alongside the East River in New York, six miles upstream from the Brooklyn Bridge.

The altered circumstance changed the party into a requiem scored for dance band and indoor fireworks display. The guests came dressed in the equivalencies of red. Garrison Keillor introduced a literary program resembling an especially amiable issue of *The Paris Review*—selected poetry and prose declaimed by E. L. Doctorow, Billy Collins, Alec Baldwin, and Lee Grant. Kurt Vonnegut proposed the toast. "If anyone can come back from the dead and write about it," he said, "it will have to be George Plimpton."

None present doubted the proposition because the room was so crowded with affectionate remembrance of George that it was as if he had already come back, late as usual (delayed in traffic or detained by customs) but surely somewhere en route, bringing a sack of odd anecdote and eccentric observation—

death really quite different than one had been led to believe (a matter of changing trains or camera lenses rather than a final destination), the climate Mediterranean but invigorated by a heavy snowfall every second Tuesday, all the birds and animals capable of speech, the Atlantic seagulls better conversationalists than the London pigeons or the Chinese cranes.

If by midnight George was still nowhere to be seen in the flesh, he was everywhere present in the word, which spoke to the truth of the benediction pronounced by W. H. Auden (an occasional and valued contributor to *The Paris Review)* on the ancient alliance between reader and writer:

> *Time that is intolerant*
> *Of the brave and innocent,*
> *And indifferent in a week*
> *To a beautiful physique,*
> *Worships language and forgives*
> *Everyone by whom it lives.*

Film projections came and went on an immense screen behind the stage at the south end of the room larger than most Broadway theaters, the narrative montage matched to the chapters of George's long and happy pilgrimage from one thing to the next—George in Paris at the age of twenty-six, at the Café Tournon with Evan Connell, William Pène DuBois, and a mysterious lady known as "Gloria the beautiful cloak model"; George ten years later in New York, telling a joke to Jackie Kennedy, considering a manuscript with Marianne Moore; George in the uniform of a New York Yankee, frowning at the bat in the hand of Willie Mays; George on a football field and a flying trapeze; George in Hollywood being taught by John Wayne how to walk into a gunfight and a saloon; George alone at a desk with what he called "the melancholy task of writing."

The montage alluded to nearly every one of George's more than thirty published books about the graceful art of losing the ball or the match *(Out of My League, Shadow Box, Paper Lion)*, as well as to his wanderings off the page in company with the famous names that embodied the sense and sensibility of an age coincident with the second half of the century defined, even by French historians, as America's own. As the pictures passed across the screen (still photographs, scraps of television and movie footage, old postcards, stylish magazine portraits) they evoked among the assembled guests the echoes of long ago delight. Everybody remembered something else, another scene in another story testifying to George's generosity of spirit and kindness of heart. Some people mentioned their first meeting with George—on African safari in search of the white gorilla, poolside at one of Hugh Heffner's lingerie parties, playing a waltz of his own composition (his never-yet recorded "Opus One") on a piano at the Apollo Theater in Harlem, at the Ambassador Hotel in Los Angeles on the night that Robert Kennedy was shot. Other people referred to the last time they saw George—two days ago on a bicycle in Central Park, yesterday with an architect's blueprint of Ernest Hemingway's house in Havana, where George expected to find, if it hadn't been mauled by mice, the unpublished epilogue to *For Whom the Bell Tolls.* For five hours the recollections of time past but not lost filled the vast room like a drift of balloons held aloft in the updrafts of fond and corroborating memory.

I expect that George would have been well enough pleased with the proceedings to bestow upon the evening the honor that he was apt to express in the word "blowout." He understood the science of giving parties and knew that what was important was the spirit in which the wine was poured, not what the wine had cost, or where it came from, or whether it was temporarily housed in Venetian glass. For forty years his apartment on East Seventy-second Street had served as the headquarters tent for the New York literary crowd, the place where people went to redress the sorrows of Grub Street. For forty years no week went by in which George didn't give at least one party (sometimes preceded by invitations, often extemporaneously) in praise of a newly published book—a first novel, a volume of essays, an epic poem, a revised biography, a collection of short stories, a translation from the medieval Latin.

It didn't matter how many people were present—sometimes twenty-odd, sometimes upwards of 200—nor did it matter whether any celebrities were to be found, like Easter eggs, under the pool table or asleep in a chair. People didn't come with the thought of reading their names in the next day's papers. They came for the fun of it, drawn to the light of George's insatiable curiosity and irreducible enthusiasm. His manner was patrician, a consequence of his having been born in the arrondisement of old money and educated at schools (St. Bernards, Exeter, Harvard, Cambridge) that teach a diffident and self-deprecating tone of voice; his temperament was democratic. He valued people not because they were rich or famous but because they were his fellow pilgrims, outward bound, as he was outward bound, on the road to who knows where. One never knew who among them—the third baseman, the zoologist, the poet, the first violinist—might stumble upon something great.

I trace my first encounter with George to a winter evening in the Kennedy Administration, both of us standing with drinks in our hands in the long drawing room on East Seventy-second Street, looking out the window at a tugboat coming upriver against the current. I remember him correcting my impression of an author about whom I'd said something edged with sarcasm. You don't know enough about the man, George said; you forget that his great-great-grandfather commanded the Union artillery at Antietam, and you haven't read his monograph on the three-toed sloth. The remark was characteristic. During all the years in which I counted George a friend, I never once heard him speak unkindly of anyone with whom he was acquainted. He preferred the favorable interpretations of human nature, and he would listen to no malicious gossip—would walk away from any conversation in which it surfaced like a dead fish or a stale hockey sock.

During the two weeks between George's death and the revel at Cipriani, the New York news media bloomed with appreciative farewells from well-known literary figures (Norman Mailer, Robert Silvers, Peter Matthiessen, Elaine Kaufman, others too numerous to mention) who touched upon the same talents and traits of character (gracious after-dinner speaker, indefatigable optimism, intrepid bird-watcher, boundless energy, witty raconteur) on which, over the course of our friendship, I had come to rely as if upon the proverbial light at the end of the not always metaphorical tunnel. But of all the stories told about George's many qualities, the one I like the best I heard on Leonard Lopate's radio program from a caller who identified herself simply as Francie. She had graduated from Bennington College in 1975, and by way of doing a favor for a friend somehow associated with the school, George staged a fireworks show at the commencement ceremony. He instructed the Grucci family on Long Island, for many years his supplier of bespoke pyrotechnics, to make a rocket specific to each member of the departing class—different assortments of color, varied duration and shape of burst. As each student was handed his or her diploma, George fired off the custom-tailored thunder, meanwhile shouting, at the top of his voice, the name of the newly minted alumna or alumnus exploding downrange into the astonished future.

George conceived of the future as an empty canvas or a blank page, ripe with heroic possibility and never further away than the next best guess, the next play from scrimmage, the next sentence. What delighted him were the acts of courage and intelligence in whatever costume they made themselves manifest, and the city of New York he regarded as the Circus Maximus to which performers of every conceivable description came to enlarge—by a fraction of an inch or second, or maybe with a better choice of word or more graceful chord progression—the playing field of the human imagination.

As a writer George placed his trust in verbs and nouns, careful not to let the narrative go astray in the flowerbeds of showy adjectives. For the same reason he was equally wary as an editor, careful not to mess up somebody else's prose with decorative improvements. "Editing," he once said, "is much simpler than writing. The image that comes to mind is one of a sculptor (the editor) improving on the clay figure of a rabbit (a writer's manuscript), just a tuck here and there to make it better: the ear needs to be fixed up, and maybe the author forgot to put a tail on it."

Taking to heart that same instruction, I can think of no happier ending for this eulogy to an absent friend than George's own description of the place in which, with any luck, he now finds himself admiring the view and remarking on the weird variety of musical instruments. Twenty years ago I asked several New York editors to contribute to *Harper's Magazine* their notions, in a thousand words or less, of the perfect balance of form and content otherwise known as Paradise. George proposed a landscape more nearly akin to the classical Arcadia imagined by the ancient Greeks than to the baroque visions of Heaven and Hell dreamed of in the preachings of the Christian Church. The elegance and humor of the idea embodies George's civilizing spirit, and if I've subtracted a few sentences from the original text, I've done no more than find the rabbit in the hat:

An island. Something along the lines of the Seychelles—with a coastline of granite rocks, like Henry Moore sculptures, rising out of a warm tropical sea.

A few incidentals: a large and perfectly balanced boomerang, some bright-colored bathtub toys with small propellers and keys to wind them up, the ingredients and tools for making and setting off large aerial fireworks (along with an instruction booklet), athletic equipment, and a substantial amount of fishing gear, including a number of small red and white bobs.

The island compound would feature a dining pavilion among the palm trees, or a hall, rather, a somewhat baronial edifice with excellent acoustics, so that conversations, even very whispery ones, would not drift up into the rafters and get lost among the ceremonial flags. On hand would be an excellent butler, quite deaf, but faithful, and willing to help with the fireworks.

The compound would contain a number of guest houses. These small mushroomlike structures, set apart from each other, would all have views of the sea. They would be well appointed inside, each one having a white fan turning slowly on the ceiling and a large porcelain washbasin with a neatly folded, fluffed-up towel alongside. Every afternoon I would know my guests were being installed into these accommodations by the sounds of the houseboys chattering excitedly among themselves as they carried the baggage from the quay.

I would not see my guests before dinner, my own day being quite somnolent. Oh, a little boomerang tossing, perhaps, the construction of an aerial bomb or two, some bait-casting in the mangrove swamps, and surely a bit of a tub before dinner. (It's not that I would feel unfriendly toward my guests, simply that my personal pursuits, especially sitting in a tub winding up a small blue tugboat, would not be especially conducive to their companionship.)

The guest list would be composed of people I have never met. Not only that, they would be dead. Ludwig II, the mad king of Bavaria, dined alone with busts of various dignitaries—Louis XIV and Marie Antoinette among them—set on chairs down the length of the banquet hall at Linderhof, and carried on an animated if slightly one-sided conversation with them. My guests would be the real shades.

Many of them would be seagoing people—the captain of the deserted brigantine Mary Celeste; Joshua Slocum, who also disappeared at sea; Richard Haliburton, who may have fallen off the stern of a Chinese junk; and Captain Kidd, to discuss the whereabouts of his vanished treasure. Shubert, to inquire about the "Lost Symphony," and perhaps to persuade him to play a bit on the stand-up Yamaha in the corner.

Some of my dinner partner choices would be more quixotic. I've always wanted to know why Thomas Cromwell, Oliver's great-uncle, was so anxious to get Henry VIII to marry Anne, the daughter of the duke of Cleves. (The king took one look and hated her. The marriage took place but was never consummated, and Cromwell lost his head. Frightful error of judgment.) So he could have a brandy or two at dinner and perhaps give an odd little talk on matchmaking. And General James Longstreet. Why, I would ask, did he not roll up Cemetery Ridge when he had the chance?

I don't know how much of this it would be possible to take. So my Arcadia would also have a swift means of escape—preferably a drug-runner's cigarette boat with a deep rumble of a motor in it, which, after a time, would tie up at a New York pier where, waiting in a fine mist, there would be a yellow cab. ✦

THESE SPORTING POETS

(MAY 1977)

George Plimpton

I HAD VERY little idea what was going to come of it—the meeting arranged between Marianne Moore, the poet, and Muhammad Ali, who was the new champion then, just about to defend his crown against Ernie Terrell in Houston. It seemed quite an odd combination. She had expressed her hope of meeting him, as she and I were working on a project together—going to various events, mostly sports contests, and seeing how our artistic views of each compared—mine predictable and pedestrian, hers quirky and unexpected and illuminating: one saw something of the poetic process while sitting with her. We had been to a World Series game together, a football game, a zoo ("I am foolish about gorillas"), and a prizefight—the Floyd Patterson George Chuvalo fight at Madison Square Garden. It was after that fight that Miss Moore asked to meet Ali.

She loved athletes; she did not know how to account for people who could be indifferent to miracles of dexterity, though I often wondered how much she actually *knew* about sports—I mean, in the sense of the experts in the Third Avenue saloons who sounded like assistant coaches if you eavesdropped on them: they all seemed to know Tucker Frederickson, the ex-Giant; they could belabor a whole afternoon away with trivia contests, such as what major-league ballplayer had been an active player through *three* decades of baseball. Marianne Moore did not care about this sort of thing. I am not even sure that at the end of the games we attended she knew who had won. She was interested in the way pigeons dropped down out of the rafters, how a player wore his socks. She would have been entranced not by Minnie Minoso's longevity record (he was the one who played in three different decades) but by his first name, and she would have written it down in a tiny notebook she carried, just the name "Minnie" in a delicate spidery scrawl so that she could ponder it later. She loved ballplayers' names, and they would suddenly arrive in her conversation, quite unexpectedly, like a sneeze: Vinegar Bend Mizell was a particular favorite, the old Met pitcher, and she would say his name when she had a fancy to.

Another was Bill Monbouquette, the Yankee pitcher. One fine summer afternoon, when a small group of us were up at the stadium as guests of Mike Burke and the Yankee management, she peered out over the railing of the second-tier box and noticed that Monbouquette had a most disturbing habit at the end of his delivery, which was to cup his groin at the jockstrap and give it a little heft, as if to rearrange what was within. "That is interesting, what he does at the completion of his toss," she said, and our little group stared transfixed as, sure enough, he did it every time. It was an integral part of his pitching motion, surely quite unconscious since it was hardly a gesture one would think of oneself doing in front of 20,000 or so people, time after time. We discussed whether he should be told, whether an umpire should come out and say, "Hey, don't do that, please—our sensibilities!" or whether the television cameras ever lingered below his waist when he was pitching, and if he *were* told, what it would do to his pitching abilities—to realize suddenly that for the fifteen years or so of his career, he had been displaying across the country this faintly obscene peculiarity of his; it might just have kept Monbouquette from ever picking up a baseball again without blushing and having to drop it. Miss Moore was quite serene about what she had discovered. "There is an insouciance in that gesture which is appealing," she said. "He should not be told. We should keep mum." She wrote his name down in her little book. "Monbouquette," she said, just barely audible. "'My little bouquet.' Absolutely correct."

The rules, statistics, tactics, and the structure of the games we watched were of little interest. Indeed, she seemed lost in those vast sports arenas; people rushed to help her, the delicate tiny lady under one of the great hats she was famous for. I remember she caused a considerable flurry at Belmont Race Track by trying to bet 50 cents at the $10 window, a long line behind her, the great hat, and those immediately aft of it trying to get around to tell her she couldn't do such a thing.

SCARS OF BATTLE

Until she met Ali, Marianne Moore's favorite boxer was Floyd Patterson. She had met him at an autographing party to which she had been taken by a neighbor. The hostess was "Miss Negro Bookclub," a titular choice Miss

Moore found arresting; Sugar Ray Robinson was the chairman of the event. "His competence and unsensational modesty were very pleasing," she wrote me about the occasion. "I met Floyd Patterson and Buster Watson also, his assistant trainer. Floyd was very courteous, and I was very rude, interrupting Buster when he was talking to two other men. I resolved never to be so rude again. I bought books for some boys . . . and another for myself in which Floyd wrote my name and 'all the best.'"

She read the book with care—*Victory Over Myself.* She remembered phrases from it: "I never thought of boxing as a profession; it was a grind . . . but a way out for me and my family." Another was "Boxing is supposed to be a dirty business but it has made me clean and enabled me to do some good for others." I think that she was also moved by the description of Patterson's childhood: he was so intimidated and shy that he used to hide from the outside world in a cubbyhole he had discovered in the foundations of the New York Central tracks.

I arranged for a row of seats for his fight against Chuvalo. It was not at all clear that Marianne Moore was going to enjoy the evening. She had not been to a prizefight before, and people hitting each other was an activity she could not condone. A few days before the fight she wrote me: "Marred physiognomy and an occasional death don't seem an ideal life objective. I do not like demolishing anything—even a paper bag. Salvaging and saving all but dominate my life."

I asked her in the cab on the way to the fight if violence had ever intruded. It seemed an odd question to ask such a fragile person. "In Brooklyn I intercepted a small boy who laid down his schoolbooks to slug a classmate," she replied. "When I said, 'If you don't stop, I'll beat you up,' he said, 'He cursed my mother.' I said, 'Then it's justified, but lay off him.'" She closed her eyes, as if in thought, and then she said, "One time I was driving in a taxi going through the Bowery; I looked out and saw a man with a knife creeping up on another. The car was going quite fast, about as fast as we're going now, and I can't tell you what the end was." She made a small snorting sound. "Violence! I didn't know what it meant. If I was wild enough to come home late at night, I didn't know enough to be timid. Once I was amazed when my friend asked, 'Do you want me to go in with you to see if anyone's in the house?' I was astonished. Someone in the house? But now I have been trained to call out, 'Who is it?' and when I look out the little peephole I see my good friend, or a neighbor, and I feel craven."

Miss Moore was wearing her famous tricorne hat with its ship's prow effect; when she turned to speak it gave a sort of thrust to what she was saying, much like talking to a miner in the beam of the light from his helmet. Her tricorne fit nicely in the cab. She had others which would have required some jimmying around to fit—a great cartwheel of a stiffened felt hat that one had to get under if walking along beside her, skulking along Groucho Marx–like to hear what she was saying in her soft, erratic voice. She told me that she had picked the tricorne for the fight "because my other hats keep anyone behind me from seeing."

We picked up some friends to join us at the fight. Just as we were nearing the Garden, Miss Moore heard something from one of them about Chuvalo that shook her support of Patterson, namely, that Chuvalo was so incredibly poor at the start of his ring career that on one occasion he and his wife drove across Canada in a car so decrepit that the accelerator pedal had come off, and a part of the accelerator arm; Mrs. Chuvalo had to crouch under the dashboard and at a signal from her husband depress or raise what was left of the accelerator: "Bring her up a touch; we're coming into a town." Miss Moore was moved by this nearly to the point of shifting her allegiance. She asked to be told the story again.

It was obviously on her mind during the fight. We had good seats in the mezzanine, far enough away so that the physical side of the fight was not too pronounced. Still, at a solid blow, small gasps erupted from her. Once I heard her call out, "George!" Another time, "Floyd!" She had a small pad and pencil with her, though I never saw her write anything down. She seemed relieved when the fight was over. "Well, that's that," she said brightly, as if something especially wrenching had been completed, like a frightening circus act.

She wrote me subsequently when she had had time to consider things: "I did not enjoy the Patterson–Chuvalo fight at all until Floyd began to win and in the end suffered no major damage." But she could not rid herself of the Chuvalo accelerator story. "A moralist at heart, my notions of psychic adaptiveness and creativeness of muscular as well as mental endurance were enlarged by Mrs. Chuvalo's scars of battle with life when she held a finger in a fixed position to replace what should have been an automatic device in the car." She wrote that she had also been taken by the referee's performance: "The assiduous precision of the referee in seizing the angle most advantageous from which to see every trifle impressed me most—and his impeccable appearance—nothing sticking out or dangling. Swift and compact, the embodiment of vigilance."

She had also noticed Muhammad Ali at the fight—he had been sitting on the far side of the ring and had jumped up into it to talk with Patterson at the conclusion. When I next saw her, I asked if she would like to meet him. She nodded: "I do not see any reason why I should not meet someone who assures everyone 'I am the greatest' and who is a poet nonetheless."

Some weeks later I was able to arrange our tea through Hal Conrad, the fight publicist. For a reason that I have forgotten, we had it at Toots Shor's establishment in mid-Manhattan. The place was almost empty when Miss Moore and I arrived, about four in the afternoon. The late Toots Shor himself was there, but knowing that Ali was expected, he did not sit with us. He did not approve of Ali then, or perhaps ever, and he sat at the opposite end of the room studiously ignoring us. From our banquette, Miss Moore looked over and was impressed by him. She had heard that he had started in the restaurant business as a bouncer. I think she expected, or perhaps hoped, that he would "bounce" someone. "His haunt is quite peaceful," she said to me. "It makes the offices of bouncer seem hearsay; no killer instinct has made itself evident."

"No, no," I said. "I think he has other people to do that for him these days. Besides, there's no one in here for him to bounce except the waiters and you and me."

"Fancy," she said.

Presently Muhammad Ali arrived with Hal Conrad. He slid in behind the table and arranged himself next to Miss Moore. He gazed at her hat, which was the same tricorne she had worn to the fight. Almost immediately, as if she had yet to arrive, he turned to Hal and me and asked who she was and what he was expected to do. Had a photographer arrived?

Miss Moore listened attentively to what Conrad and I had to say about her—a great sports fan, one of the most distinguished poets in the country . . . "Mrs. Moore," said Ali, turning and looking at her, "a grandmother going to the fights?" She made a confused gesture and then had a sip of her tea.

He ordered a bowl of beef soup and a phone. He announced that if she were the greatest poetess in the country then the two of them should produce something together—"I am a poet, too," he said—a joint-effort sonnet, with each of them doing alternate lines. Miss Moore nodded vaguely. Ali was very much the more decisive of the pair, picking not only the form but also the topic: "Mrs. Moore and I are going to write a sonnet about my upcoming fight in Houston with Ernie Terrell. Mrs. Moore and I will show the world with this great poem who is who and what is what and who is going to win." A pen was produced. Ali was given a menu on which to write. He started off with half the first line—"After we defeat . . . " and left Miss Moore to write in "Ernie Terrell" in her spidery script—just to get her "warmed up." He wrote most of the second line "He will catch nothing . . . " expecting Miss Moore to fill in the obvious rhyme, and he was quite surprised when she did not. I could see her lips move as she fussed with possibilities. Finally, he leaned over and whispered to her, "'But hell,' Mrs. Moore."

"Oh, yes," she said. She wrote down "but hell." Then she wrestled with it some more, clucking gently, murmuring about the rhythm of the line, and then she crossed it out and substituted, "He will get nothing, nothing but hell."

Ali took over and produced his next line in jig time: "Terrell was big and ugly and tall." He pushed the menu over to her. His soup arrived. He leaned low over it, spooning it in, glancing over to see how she was coming along. While we waited, he told Conrad and me that he was going to try to get the poem out over the Associated Press wire that afternoon. Miss Moore's eyes widened—the irony of all those years struggling with *Broom* and the other literary magazines, and now to be with a fighter who promised instant publication over a ticker. It did not help the flow of inspiration. She was doubtless intimidated by Ali's presence, especially at his obvious concern that she—a distinguished poet—was having such a hard time holding up her side: in his mind speed of delivery was very much a qualification of a professional poet. He finished his soup and ordered another. The phone arrived and was plugged in behind the banquette. He began dialing a series of numbers, hotels most of them, but the people he requested never seemed to respond.

Finally, seeing that she had not got anywhere at all, he took the poem from her and completed it. It was not done in a patronizing way at all, but more out of consideration, presumably that every poet, however distinguished, is bound to have a bad day and should be helped through it. "Now let's see," he said as he began to write. He had moved close to her, so that she appeared to be looking down the long length of his arm to watch the poem emerge. "Yes," she said, "why not?" as he produced a last couplet. The whole composition, once he had taken over, took about a minute. With the spelling corrected, it read as follows:

After we defeat Ernie Terrell,
He will get nothing, nothing but hell.
Terrell was big and ugly and tall,
But when he fights me he is sure to fall.
If he criticize this poem by me and Miss Moore,
To prove he is not the champ she will stop him in four.
He is claiming to be the real heavyweight champ,
But when the fight starts he will look like a tramp.
He has been talking too much about me and making me sore.
After I am through with him he will not be able to challenge Mrs. Moore.

The stratagem of involving her in the poem, particularly as a pugilist herself, was clever: Miss Moore nodded in delight. She made a tiny fist. "Yes, he has been making me sore," she said.

A photographer arrived at the table—something of a surprise. He was from one of the wire services. I suspect that Muhammad Ali, knowing that he was meeting someone of distinction, if not quite sure *whom,* had arranged for the event to be recorded. Miss Moore did not seem to mind. She allowed Ali—who continued to dominate the afternoon—to dictate the poses. His idea was to have the photograph show the two of them at work on the poem. "We've got to show you *thinking,* Mrs. Moore," he said. "How you show you're thinking hard is to point your finger into the middle of your head." He illustrated, jabbing his forefinger at his forehead, closing his eyes to indicate concentration. She complied, pursing her lips in feigned concern as she pondered the menu poem. The photographer clicked away.

Miss Moore then expressed a wish to see the Ali shuffle—a foot maneuver which Ali occasionally did in mid-fight that made him look like a man trying to stay upright on a carpet being pulled out from under him. Ali said he would be delighted to show her the shuffle. He thought it would be best to do it out in the street, where he had room to do her a really *good* shuffle. When we walked outdoors, a crowd immediately formed—I think word had gone around the neighborhood that the fighter was in Toots Shor's place—so we went back through the revolving door, and he did the shuffle right there in the foyer. Miss Moore was delighted. She asked him to do it again, and when he went out and did the shuffle for the people in the street, she watched him through the revolving door.

"Well," she said when he had left. "He had every excuse for avoiding a performance. But he festooned out in as enticing a bit of shuffling as you would ever wish to see."

"He 'festooned'?" I asked.

"He certainly did. He was exactly what I had hoped to meet."

A WHIZ-BANG OF WORDS

Subsequently, I wrote Miss Moore to ask her what she had thought of her afternoon at Toots Shor's. What was her opinion of Ali as a poet?

She wrote: "Well, we were slightly under constraint. And the rhyme for Terrell (*hell*) being of one syllable is hardly novel. . . . Cassius has an ear, and a liking for balance . . . comic, poetic drama, it *is* poetry . . . saved by a hair from being the flattest, peanuttiest, unwariest of boastings."

She was especially pleased that the poem (which she thought might be titled "Much Ado About Cassius") showed a strong sense of structure, which indeed involved herself: "He begins by mentioning a special guest and concludes with mention of the same." She then went on to produce a whiz-bang of words about Ali.

> *The Greatest, though a mere youth, has snuffed out more dragons than Smokey the Bear hath. Mighty-muscled and fit, he is confident; he is sagacious, ever so, he trains. A king's daughter is bestowed on him as a fiancée. He is literary, in the tradition of Sir Philip Sidney, defensor of poesie. His verse is enhanced by alliteration. He is summoned by an official: "Come forth, Cassius." He is not even deterred by the small folks' dragons. He has a fondness for antithesis; he will not only give fighting lessons, but falling lessons. Admittedly the classiest and the brassiest. When asked, "How do you feel about being called by the British 'Gaseous Clay'?" his reply is one of the prettiest in literature. "I do not resent it." Note this: beat grime revolts him. He is neat. His brow is high. If beaten, he is still not "beat." He fights and he writes.*
>
> *Is there something I have missed?*
>
> *He is a smiling pugilist.* ◆

Hyperbole's Child

(DECEMBER 1977)

A. Bartlett Giamatti

It SUDDENLY BECAME clear to me, sitting in Madison Square Garden on September 29, watching the preliminary bouts to the Ali–Shavers fight, that the basis of sport is work. Running, jumping, lifting, pushing, bending, pulling, planting the legs and using the back—these exertions are essential to physical labor and to athletic competition. The closeness of a given game to the rituals and effort of work invests the game with dignity; without that proximity to labor, the game would be merely a release from work instead of a refinement of it. The radical difference between work and game, however, occurs when limits or rules are imposed on this labor, patterns which acknowledge that this new work, this sport, is not a matter of life and death. Whereas that work, the work of your back and arms, in field or mill, on ship or in forest, was crucial to your survival, and to the survival of those dependent on you, this work is different; it is delimited, separate, independent, a refinement of reality but distinct. This work is fully as serious and difficult as real work, but this unreal work is not coextensive with life. This work of sport, usually but not always at some predetermined point, will have an end. It will be over, not to begin again with the sun. This work, unlike that real work, does not sustain life in any immediate and practical way, such as providing food; but this unreal serious work does sustain life in the sense that it makes life bearable. It allows all of us to go back renewed to whatever real work we do, perhaps to go back for a moment redeemed. I have often thought that the world-wide appeal of soccer lies in part in its unabashed emphasis on penetrating the other's territory; partly in its wonderfully seamless and continuous quality, where no quarter is given, no pause taken, but like the tides men come and go; but mostly in its denial of the use of the hands. For the millions who work with their hands, there can be no greater relief than to escape the daily focus on those instruments of labor, and no greater confirmation of the centrality of hands to life than their denial in this sport.

These notions formed while I waited for the Ali–Shavers fight. I had been watching the undercard, and admiring the way Alfredo Evangelista of Uruguay would get his back into his punches, like a man digging a hole, and how the sheer expenditure of effort had forced Pedro Soto to fight Evangelista's fight until, in the eighth round, Soto was so badly punished by the patient, awkward digging of Evangelista that the referee stopped the bout. At this moment of victory, which is also a moment of reunion, as the men finish work and leave together, the crowd's attention was diverted from Soto and Evangelista by the presence of Ali, who suddenly appeared in the back of the Garden and roared through the aisles shaking his finger, surrounded by about ten of his entourage. The crowd responded with delight—"A-*li,* A-*li,* A-*li,*" they chanted; and when they turned from that spectacle, Evangelista and Soto were gone. If for most athletes and spectators sport is work conceived in some special way as play, for Muhammad Ali sport is work conceived as theater.

Ali has theatricalized his work in that, rather than continuing to serve his work as a worker, or slave, he has made what he does serve him as a setting. Ali has extended himself and boxing, the sport most like work, in the direction of theater by emphasizing the other being that lives beside the worker in every athlete, the actor. In the athlete worker and actor meet, the expenditure of energy and the power to give shape come together. Of course, workers "perform" tasks and actors work hard; the spectrum worker-athlete-actor is not a broad one and the three points are distinguished by emphasis more than anything else. As the athlete resembles the worker in the way he exerts his body, and in the way he catches the deep rhythms in work, so the athlete resembles the actor in the way he uses the body to express what I can only call an inner vision. Both athlete and actor release energy in order to restrain it and in restraining it, to give shape to a new idea. Both are judged effective or ineffective (that is what "good" or "bad" means in these two professions) by how well they execute what is set them; and for both athlete and actor execution depends not on inspiration or luck or the weather, inner or outer, but on coordination, economy of gesture, timing, good coaching.

It is Ali who has brought to the surface the actor in every athlete more successfully and obsessively than anyone else. Ali is in many ways profoundly bored, and he knows only one craft. In order to remain interested in what he must do, Ali has allowed the performer to erupt unchecked, burying the worker in him, the skilled artisan with extraordinary hands and legs and specific, worldly ambitions, under the sulfurous, scalding lava of his improvisations. Improvisation is the only way he has found to order the endless days: the monologizing, poeticizing, and prophesying, all that grimacing and exhorting and praying, is the style of a man who is not sure even he knows when his acts are simply acting, but who does know he does not care.

And when a fight is in view, and training is required, a regimen guaranteed to exacerbate boredom with brutal fatigue, Ali goes deeper into his protean reserves and whole dramas emerge. There is often the heroic beast fable—Ali will slay a dragon in the form of a Bear, a Rabbit, a Gorilla, or, lately, an Acorn. As time goes on, other subplots emerge. Howard Cosell once regularly took a part; occasionally whole countries, like Zaire, are cast. In recent years the press has been less and less willing to be the megaphone to this sideshow, but the press has no choice but to be megaphone when the source of news insists on defining himself as a barker. So we are treated to sermons, doggerel, parables, myths, even creations from whole cloth: "JIMMY ELLIS, SPARRING PARTNER, KNOCKS DOWN CHAMP TWICE TODAY." That particular story, out of Ali's Pennsylvania training camp some eight days before the bout, is a good example of the problems Ali poses and the problem he has.

Perhaps only a headline announcing the pope's intention to remarry would be as immediately unconvincing as the news that Ellis knocked Ali down twice in one round. The gloves used in sparring sessions weigh sixteen ounces apiece; Billy Carter would have trouble knocking over a schooner of Schlitz with one of those mitts. Then there is the fact that these two know each other well, having met more than twenty years ago in Louisville when they were both young teen-agers. Ali and Ellis cannot surprise each other and while Ellis would work for a man he could knock down, Ali would not hire a man who might even try it. Even once. But *twice!* Such an idea staggers the imagination.

Why put out the story then? In part because whereas the rest of us were born under a star, Ali was born under a rhetorical figure, hyperbole, defined by the great Quintilian as "an elegant straining of the truth." Surely Ali was also impelled by a realization that the advance sale for September 29 was slow; that the publicity, at the time of the Lance affair and a hot mayoral primary race in New York, had been soggy; and he was propelled by that instinct of his to hype the gate, to work his own crowd (as he would do as Soto and Evangelista finished work), to shill for himself, to be both the show and the man who hustled them into the tent. If there is one born every minute, Ali wants to be the midwife. But does that deep instinct justify putting out such a palpably transparent story as the one about being knocked down twice? No, that instinct does not justify straining the truth quite so inelegantly. An even deeper need justifies the story, the need to pump up once again the white man's hope to see the black champion beaten.

Here we engage Ali's deepest game, the only work he does with a will. While you are being encouraged to think he can be beaten, you are being allowed to understand that the form the encouragement takes is fraudulent. Your ability to see through the con undermines your belief in his vulnerability (he can't be beaten if he says he can) and reaffirms your faith in his theatrical mastery (knocked down twice, my foot! What a showman). You are now his. Ali has transformed all the potential spectators, the fight crowd, into something far different, an audience; he has enticed the naive, titillated the devoted, amused the jaded, outraged the mass; he has had it out with his opponent now in the press and on television for at least two weeks, his sense of pace impeccable, the whole spectacle building to the grand final number, the climax just before the last curtain, the weigh-in; and, most important, he has managed to legitimize race as an issue in the fight by making it part of the show, or, for those so inclined, the whole show. One so inclined is Ali, and the last scene is played.

At the weigh-in, the state lends whatever moral and legal credibility it has to the ritual of assessing the fighters' weight and physical fitness. They are always found to be fit. (Examinations and X rays conducted on September 28 could find no injuries, indeed no trace of trauma, resulting from the two knockdowns suffered by the champion during training.) And after the tape and scales, Ali takes over, and tears a passion to tatters, splitting the ears of the groundlings in the press, o'erdoing Termagant and out-heroding Herod, now the player, now the Prince, doing all the parts and, at the weigh-in on September 28, ranting at length about the theatrical nature of his ranting, exposing the structure of his illusion, the old actor getting himself worked up for the part, doing what Elvis Presley could no longer do, getting into the circle, recapturing the energy and interest to go out on stage by pretending to have it—all of this working precisely to the extent that all the hangers-on and reporters and onlookers and cuties and commission people and cameramen and friends and spies and flunkies and acolytes, who have seen it dozens of times, get pulled in, and begin to laugh and nudge and shake their heads and stamp their feet as if it were the first time; and yet, if you listen rather than acquiesce, at the center of this whirlwind of words and gestures and postures and poses the chosen epithet of the chosen opponent is chanted and honed and, finally, hurled like a knife at the man it signifies. The real fight is now almost over, as Ali turns on his opponent all the power of the opponent, turning the man's physical characteristics, his background, his class, his worth as a man against him. Ali deflects the opponent's strength from Ali, and now the opponent is left, in the weeks or hours remaining (for this process does not start at the weigh-in), to fight himself, to fight his ugliness or his awkwardness or his lack of education or, in the most savage blow of all, to fight his race. If the man is white, he is not allowed to be the White Hope. Ali bestows this duty as if it were a dukedom, and then watches while the opponent tries to figure out whether to hoist this load, and, if he will, how to gain a purchase on it, and, once it is up, where to take it. It is too easy.

With black fighters there is more sport, though the press here draws a line and the public does not, evidently, get the full force of Ali's treatment of black opponents. But the technique is clear. In calling Frazier a gorilla, or Shavers "shiftless," Ali simply unleashes the power of traditional racist epithets. He thus sets his black opponent to battling two chimeras, both now identified with himself. The opponent must confront his main sense of himself, his strength, his identity as a black man, as if it were a weakness; he must struggle with, rather than use, the source of his power, because this black champion has turned their race into a vicious insult. Lest the opponent miss the point to the burden that he alone now carries, Ali will during the fight clarify his status for him as he did for Shavers by calling him throughout the fight, according to reports, "nigger." It is a technique as simple, and decent, as rubbing your glove's laces on an opponent's swollen eye.

But while Ali has a black opponent fighting his blackness, he also has the other man fighting his whiteness. Everyone who fights Ali must be the white hope. The gate demands it, and hyperbole's child would have it no other way. Every opponent is the champion of that vast, hostile white mass that, since February 28, 1964, when Ali announced that he had a few months before joined the Nation of Islam, and especially since his refusal in Houston on April 28, 1967, to be inducted into the army, has wanted to see him knocked out. So, at least, Ali believes; and so believed the elegantly dressed, affable black man who sat behind me at the Ali–Shavers bout, and who laughingly insisted for fifteen rounds that I had come to see Ali beaten by my fighter, Shavers. But I believe that the act at Houston and the announcement about the Nation of Islam were themselves not the causes of an attitude, but the results of an even older attitude of Ali's. For those acts of 1967 and 1964 were acts of separation, of secession from black and white America's traditional assumptions about how to behave, and were themselves responses to the conviction, held by the boy who by his account in *My Own Story* felt a "deep kinship" with Emmett Till, that they wanted him out, and that he would dance inside and sting them before they could put him down and put him out.

Ali's boredom with training and fighting only masks a fear, a fear of being peripheral, a terror of being out, and that fear accounts for his need to be at the center of something, a stage, a ring, a Nation, a cosmic racial drama. His fear of being marginal accounts for the savagery of his desire to get in, to land the first blow, and for the outlandish intensity of his acting center stage, before the bell has ever rung or the lights have dimmed. Ali's sense of racial antagonism forces him to scorn his black opponents for being black, while at the same time smearing Frazier, Norton, Shavers with whiteface, grotesquely deforming the other's face in every way while trumpeting the beauty of his own, that clean-shaven, smooth, unblemished face so unlike the scarred, roughened laborers' faces his mocks. His is an extraordinary series of performances, culminating in the weigh-in, each scene contributing, as do rounds, to that overall accumulation of episode and pace and shaped energy we call a starring role. He has, particularly in the last year or so as preparation gets more and more difficult, set up the actual fight as an anticlimax to the weeks before it. And certainly the bout on the evening of September 29 was an anticlimax; for, regardless of what you saw on television, where closeups on intense faces covered a great deal of standing, leaning, peek-a-booing, clowning, missing, waiting, the Shavers–Ali fight was a good fight only once you had accepted how much less good a fighter Ali has become.

The real struggle goes on earlier, when Ali transforms the coming fight into a ghastly minstrel show, he never more black than when the other end man is daubed in white, the other never blacker than when Ali sneers at his color, the races locked together, at one and at odds, the whole a parody of race relations in every city street and union and school and firehouse and subway and unemployed black waking hour in America, the prizefight finally only a skirmish in the larger race war, this little battle masquerading as a show starring Muhammad Ali and a cast of everyone else.

Ali has known from the beginning what every good athlete learns: make him play your game, fight your fight, and you will beat him every time. But Ali has also learned a lesson kept from most athletes precisely by the pleasure of their work, a pleasure now beneath Ali, a pleasure in work insufficiently exhilarating to one who has the art born in him, the art of filling a scene: and that subtler lesson is that while you can only beat him if he fights your fight, you can destroy him if he acts in your play. If, like Othello, he will accept the role you set for him, you will master him as you master all scenes. And if you can make him play nigger and white racist all at once, surely you are the greatest and he is yours. This is, after all, an old drama and an old style, learned from the white slave-masters; they were the ones who based their play on others' brutal work and who forced the others to enact roles simply to survive. Ali, with his incredible gifts of body and mind, has brought the central drama of his people's history in America to a bright, gaudy life, for everyone to see. He has brought the patterns of work, play, and acting that commingle in slaves and athletes to the surface, and he has refined his techniques for communicating, through the media, what those old patterns mean.

Sitting in Madison Square Garden on September 29, I did not think Ali beat Shavers; even giving Ali all the even rounds, I scored the fight for Shavers, 8–7. I do not think Ali beat Shavers this September any more than many think he beat Ken Norton in September of 1976, or beat Jimmy Young in the spring of 1976. I also do not believe that Ali, at this point, really cares what anyone thinks, or cares what really happened. The fights in the ring, vastly remunerative, full of effort and clowning, are only incidental to the real battle. I believe he will participate in the ring fights longer than he should because he cannot stop until he has fought down the need, compounded of fear and fury, to act out completely what, in his view, it is to be black in America, to be always living at the margin, on the edge, in a position where, despite the pain of your work and the beauty of your play, a man may announce with superb casualness at any given moment that you have been counted out. ◆

IT TAKES A STADIUM

(APRIL 2004)

Matthew Stevenson

BY THE AGE of twenty-five, Jim Bouton, who had struggled to play even high school baseball, was an all-star, had won twenty games in one season for the New York Yankees, and had pitched in two different World Series, winning two games in 1964 against the St. Louis Cardinals. A teammate of Mickey Mantle, Whitey Ford, Yogi Berra, and Roger Maris, Bouton was a great Yankee hope to bridge the dynasties of Casey Stengel and Ralph Houk to others that would carry pennants to the Stadium in the middle and late 1960s. But both Bouton's and the Yankees' promise faded in 1965, and neither fared better in the years that followed. Bouton developed a sore arm and lost more games than he won, and in 1968 he was sold to a yet-to-play expansion team.

By good fortune, for both books and baseball, Bouton's new club became the Seattle Pilots, a team that lasted only one season, 1969. That year for the Pilots, and later for the Houston Astros, Bouton pitched with some distinction as a knuckleball reliever—the heat having left his fastball. But his real contribution was the locker-room diary he kept that was published in 1970 as *Ball Four,* which more recently the New York Public Library named one of its "Books of the Century." The initial press run was 5,000. But after the commissioner of baseball condemned the book, charging Bouton with the equivalent of blasphemy and baseball heresy, *Ball Four* sold 500,000 copies in hardback and another 5 million in paperback.

Bouton understands baseball's hierarchy, observing correctly that "if Mickey Mantle had written *Ball Four* he would have gotten away with it. A relief pitcher on the Seattle Pilots has no business being a deviant." Because he had tarnished the reputation of, among others, Mantle, he was cashiered from baseball. Among the blasphemies that Bouton committed was describing Mantle hitting home runs while hungover and leading ballplayers to hotel roofs to peep into windows—a recreation known to those in the trade as "beaver shooting." Writing of Joe Pepitone, he reveals that the first baseman "has two different hairpieces. He's got a massive piece, which he wears when he's going out, and a smaller one to wear under his baseball cap. He calls it his game piece."

To be sure, Bouton remembers Mantle pushing "little kids aside when they wanted his autograph, and the times when he was snotty to reporters." But Bouton, better than most of Mantle's biographers, also captures his warmth, boyishness, and sense of humor. "What we do know, though," Bouton writes, "is that the face he showed in the clubhouse, as opposed to the one he reserved for the outside world, was often one of great merriment." For a long time a rumor circulated that Mantle would not attend Old Timers' Day at Yankee Stadium if Bouton were there. But before Mantle died, he and Bouton had a warm reconciliation—further proof that although *Ball Four* broke literary form in 1970, by the mid-1990s it was as quaint as wool uniforms and the suicide squeeze.

Although celebrity Yankees, like Mantle, Maris, and Pepitone, make cameo appearances in *Ball Four,* the heart of the book describes the expansion Seattle Pilots, who have as many memorable crewmen as one of Herman Melville's whaling boats. The manager, Joe Schultz—"short, portly, bald, ruddy-faced, twinkly-eyed"—is a genial Ahab who weaves allusions to Budweiser into many of his sentences. The pitching coach is the former New York Giant Sal Maglie, a.k.a. Sal the Barber: "He still looks like he'd knock down his grandmother." When some of the Pilots are filling out a questionnaire from the team publicity department—"What's the most difficult thing about playing major-league baseball?"—first baseman Mike Hegan responds: "Explaining to your wife why *she* needs a penicillin shot for *your* kidney infection."

Despite the book's camp-bus humor, the baseball commissioner said Bouton had done the game a "grave disservice." Dick Young called him a "social leper." The literary criticism of Pete Rose was more direct. He stood on the steps of the dugout, the next time the Cincinnati Reds faced Bouton, yelling, "Fuck you, Shakespeare." (When they bumped into each other at a sports banquet two years ago, Rose admitted, "You know, I never even read your fucking book.") But the threat posed to baseball was not the revelation about Pepitone's game piece or that "Yastrzemski has a bit of dog in him." Instead, as Bouton writes in the afterword to the re-issued *Ball Four,* the book "revealed, in great detail, just how ballplayers' salaries were 'negotiated' . . . how owners abused and manipulated players by taking advantage of their one way contract"—the so-called reserve clause under which professional baseball, with antitrust exemption from Congress, operated like the Texas Railroad Commission. Although it was not Bouton's intention, *Ball Four* loaded the bases for the million-dollar runs that came with free agency.

Baseball may have wanted to be through with Jim Bouton in 1970, but he still had more innings left, both with his knuckleball and his pen. He retired from the Houston Astros after the 1970 season, then worked as a New York sports broadcaster, covering some of the same players who had panned his book. For love of the game, he continued to play independent and minor-league baseball in the summer, for such teams as the Teaneck Blues, the Portland Mavericks, and the Englewood Rangers. In 1978, at age thirty-nine, Bouton convinced Ted Turner to let him pitch in the Atlanta Braves farm system, getting called up to the big leagues in September, where he started several games and won one—his last victory in the majors. During this time he also appeared in a Robert Altman movie, invented Big League Chew (bubble gum that is shredded like tobacco), and traveled the country as a businessman, motivational speaker, writer, and inventor. Sometimes he would call on his old teammates, such as Steve Hovley, known as "Orbit" for his spacey qualities. Among other subjects, they touched on religion. Always insightful, Hovley remarked: "Religion is like baseball . . . great game, bad owners."

Remarried, children grown, Bouton moved to the Berkshires in the 1990s, his only connection to baseball being occasional starts for a team sponsored by Mama's Pizza and for the Saugerties Dutchmen. In the Berkshires organized baseball has been played since 1892 at Wahconah Park, located in Pittsfield, Massachusetts, a town that has had eight teams in the last thirty-five years. Both Casey Stengel and Lou Gehrig played at Wahconah. In one of his many comebacks, Bouton had a tryout there for the Texas Rangers. The roof and the toilets leak, and the seats are wooden benches. But, like Fenway Park and Wrigley Field, it is a connection to baseball before Astroturf, domed stadiums, steroids, corked bats, and the San Diego Chicken. And it is one of the oldest minor-league parks in America, which may explain why Pittsfield wanted to tear it down.

Before Bouton got involved, the local political establishment tried to spend $18.5 million that it didn't have to build a new stadium. By chance, the lot selected for the new ballpark was owned by the local newspaper, the *Berkshire Eagle*, which ran a series of editorials equating the proposed stadium with a new birth of freedom and the chance to revive the city's sagging economy. Not feeling a spare $18.5 million in their pockets, the voters of Pittsfield turned down the proposition, but that did not stop either the mayor, the newspaper, their benefactors at General Electric, or the Parks Commission from trying to revive the idea.

In his introduction to *Foul Ball,* bringing to local politics what *Ball Four* brought to baseball, Bouton writes: "A historic ballpark soon to be abandoned, a government that ignores its citizens, a newspaper at war with its readers, the curious involvement of General Electric. It was about this time that I began taking notes."

The result is the diary of the political campaign to save Wahconah from the wrecker's ball, and to bring to Pittsfield a locally owned team that could not be moved to another city when the owners found bigger subsidies in other pastures. "You are no doubt familiar," Bouton writes, "with America's most costly hostage crisis, perpetuated by the owners of professional sports teams: 'Build us a new stadium,' they warn, 'or you'll never see your team again.'" As an alternative, Bouton and his faithful offer "100% private funds to restore and improve a public ballpark to house a 100% locally owned professional baseball team." All this, says Bouton, "at no cost to the taxpayers. We'd even sell stock to local investors so no one could ever move the team out of town." At a public meeting on the subject, he implores: "Wahconah Park should be a working museum . . . the Museum of Minor League Memories."

Ignoring friendly advice that the political establishment "has been 'touched' on this new stadium issue," Bouton teams up with Chip Elitzer, an engaging local investment banker, and Eric Margenau, who owns several teams. Together, they draft plans to save Wahconah Park and to purchase a minor-league franchise. Bouton and Elitzer file petitions, write letters, appear on radio, and testify before the city council and the Parks Commission. But no one around city hall or among those pushing for a new stadium is listening to their requests. "It was like trying to have a conversation with animated robots at Disney World," Bouton reports. Among these is Pittsfield's mayor, Gerald S. Doyle Jr., who exhibits "a combination of regular-guy affability and unjustly accused fury, creating the overall impression of a pugnacious maitre d'."

One of the mayor's friends is the *Berkshire Eagle.* The paper is part of MediaNews Group of Denver, which has invested $250,000 in a promotion company, Berkshire Sports & Events, to convince local voters that it is in their interest to spend $18.5 million, mostly from the public trough, for a new minor-league park. When Bouton speaks to the *Eagle*'s publisher about saving Wahconah Park, he is told: "The guy you have to convince is my boss in Denver."

Why such fixation on a new stadium? One tantalizing possibility is that the location selected, that owned by the *Berkshire Eagle*, was part of an old junkyard where in the 1940s and '50s, General Electric and others may have dumped waste contaminants, including PCBs. Thus having a field of dreams instead of a waste site would save local interests millions in cleanup costs: build it and the Environmental Protection Agency will stay away.[*]

For the Bouton and Elitzer plan to work, they need to get a thirty-year lease for Wahconah from the city, with the condition that they will purchase a franchise from one of several minor-league teams playing in New England. They pledge to invest $250,000 in Wahconah upgrades prior to opening day 2002, and they unveil plans to maintain the stadium's turn-of-the-century charm with improvements such as a Taste of the Berkshires food court and what they call Not-So-Luxury Boxes. Omitted from the plans were some of the minor-league promotions that Bouton saw in his playing days, such as "Bladder Buster Night," when the beer is free until someone goes to the rest room, or "Diving for Dollars," when fans scramble for $1,000 in single bills scattered around the stadium.

Bouton, Elitzer, and their many supporters lobby to have an open forum to debate the merits of the proposals for Wahconah and, later, to have the question included on the November ballot. When Bouton asks a Parks official, "whatever happened to the public hearings you said they were going to have?" he is told: "I spoke to Cliff [Nilan, head of the Parks Commission], and he said, 'I don't want to have to talk to everybody and defend what we're doing. Everybody's just going to have to live with it.'"

The city council votes against putting the question of Wahconah's lease on the November ballot, a move that prompts one local politician to tell Bouton, "The council meeting last week was really about the abdication of democra-

---

[*] *During their campaign Bouton and Elitzer are told what everyone knows about Pittsfield: "This city is marinating in PCBs." In 1998 it reached a settlement with General Electric to clean up some of the sites. Critics of the settlement, which was negotiated by Mayor Doyle, among others, said that Pittsfield should have gotten double the amount to fund the cleanup.*

cy, not the ballpark." Bouton reflects: "This is democracy in action, advise and consent, Pittsfield style: The power structure *advises* the council what it wants to see happen, and asks them to play ball or else. Once the council *consents,* which can take all of fifteen minutes, the matter goes to the lower chamber—DelGallo's or The Brewery—for enactment by people like the mayor or the commissioners."

About the same time as the Parks Commission vote the *Berkshire Eagle* criticizes Bouton and Elitzer for their "continued divisive mentality," prompting one of Bouton's few piques of anger in a frustrating political battle:

> The mayor says "the fix is in." The City Council president says he's getting "an unbelievable amount of shit" from new-stadium councilors "and others." A mayoral candidate says state officials told him "the city was lying about not having to put up money." A state senator says he "knows" decisions are being made at a bar. And the Parks chairman is going around telling people we're "out" before the Commission has voted.
>
> And Chip and I are somehow responsible for "this continued divisive mentality"?
>
> Well, too bad. "Everybody's just going to have to live with it."

Instead of granting the Bouton group a thirty-year lease for independent, locally owned baseball in Wahconah, the mayor and his pals on the Parks Commission give the field to Jonathan Fleisig, then owner of the Massachusetts Mad Dogs, despite his lack of a comprehensive plan. Watching Fleisig's presentation to the Parks Commission, Bouton writes, is "hard to describe, although the word 'rambling' would be a good place to start." But Fleisig "is just a place holder." Two and a half years later, as I write this, he is moving his team, now called the Berkshire Black Bears, from Pittsfield to New Haven, not having found sufficient subsidies to keep baseball in Wahconah.

Whatever the outcome in Pittsfield in the years ahead, 109 minor-league baseball stadiums have been built since 1985 with taxpayer dollars. Bouton observes: "The amount of public money spent on sport stadiums over the past fifteen years is estimated to be in excess of $16 billion. And that's just what's visible." In most cases stadiums are built to attract a team from another city or to keep an existing franchise on location, but other threads link these projects, which all play the game of "hide the subsidy."

According to Bouton, those who favor new stadiums tend to be local oligarchs: the law firms, the banks, the politicians, the contractors. Invariably, if there is a door-to-door campaign, it is to oppose a new stadium, the proposals for which rarely make it onto any ballot. The consensus is that a public vote on the issue would go against new building. No matter what team owners say about putting up new stadium money, nearly all the finance for these ballparks comes from public sources, although the shell game of land swaps, zero-coupon bonds, state grants, match funding, and the like usually makes it difficult to trace the flow of funds.

In Bouton's view, local newspapers nearly always support new stadiums, because, like the *Berkshire Eagle*, they are part of vertically integrated "media" conglomerates that have side bets in real estate, cable television, radio, and sports. (For example, the *New York Times*, which publishes the *Boston Globe*, owns 15 percent of the Boston Red Sox, who were recently discussing a new Fenway Park.) In most cases neither the team owner nor the league puts up much new-stadium money. But Bouton believes the ultimate reason that so many stadiums get built with other people's money is because the opposition gets "worn down" while the sentimental support of a local team touches a cord of civic pride, under which the costs are buried. Only in San Francisco, thanks to a loyal opposition, were private funds raised for a new ballpark.

A great many of these conditions were present in New York when former mayor Rudolph Giuliani put forward plans to build new stadiums for both the Yankees and the Mets, at an estimated cost of $1.6 billion. At the time, post–September 11 New York had a budget deficit of $4 billion, and Giuliani had already given both Messrs. Steinbrenner and Wilpon, the respective owners of the Yankees and the Mets, the gifts of more than $100 million toward minor-league stadiums, one in Brooklyn and the other on Staten Island. When someone had the temerity to ask the mayor why a vote had not been held on the proposed major-league ballparks, Giuliani responded, "Because they would have voted it down."

Nor does Bouton believe that new-stadium economics trickles wealth into pockets other than team owners'. Once the construction is completed, those employed around baseball fields, other than the players, tend to earn minimum wage selling hot dogs and beer, cutting grass, and parking cars—not exactly the stuff on which economic revivals are made. "The only people, besides team owners, who want new stadiums are politicians, lawyers, and the media," Bouton concludes. "Politicos like to swagger around a palace—and stadiums are the modern palaces—the bigger the better, especially for mayors suffering from stadium envy. They like to watch games from the owner's box in full view of the TV cameras and hang out in the clubhouse with the players. This is in addition to the usual perks, graft, kickbacks, and patronage that accrue to politicians on big construction projects."

Seen through Bouton's eyes, baseball appears as a feudal guild, a restricted trade manipulated so that a few appointed nobles maintain their designated fiefs. Of the office of the commissioner, he writes: "Since he is hired and paid by the owners and not the players or the fans, he should more accurately be described as the Person in Charge of Protecting the Financial Interests of the Twenty-Six Business Groups Which Make Profits from Baseball."

The current commissioner, Bud Selig, was the owner of the Milwaukee Brewers, which he created after buying the franchise of the bankrupt Seattle Pilots. He maintains the ban on Pete Rose for financial indiscretions, but when Selig had to divest his ownership in the Brewers, he put them in a blind trust, albeit one overseen by his daughter. He also presided over the condemning of the Montreal Expos, who were purchased by the owners' guild at a distressed price and who are now entertaining offers to move to a new city, provided the package includes a new stadium. When Selig and the other owners turned down the possibility of the city of San Diego owning the Padres, they also made it clear they would not tolerate a community-owned team in the major leagues. Who do you blackmail if the fans own the team?

Although *Foul Ball* is mainly a book about minor-league politics, both in it and in the updated edition of *Ball Four* one can glimpse Bouton's attitude toward the modern game itself. He deplores the way baseball thrives on a series of ugly confrontations—between players and owners, between one team and another. "Baseball has become a cheaper game, designed for unknowing fans accustomed to gross action over subtle beauty." He remembers the respect once accorded players on visiting teams, not to mention modesty in achievement. At times he finds baseball "cartoonish." When he started playing, he writes, "A homer was just a homer—not a religious experience."

Nor are the minor leagues thriving, despite all the new ballparks. When Bouton signed with the Yankees in 1959, they had eleven minor-league teams, and he played in a system that moved him from Auburn, New York, to Amarillo, Texas. Now the Yankees have only six minor-league affiliates, since the major leagues rely more on college baseball to stock the professional pond. Modern players come to the game more prepared for the major leagues and have had the benefit of well-funded programs. But college baseball has made the game, in Bouton's view, "more corporate." As a game of rival corporations, baseball loses some of the character that it drew from sandlot America. Gone are the days when a scouting report consisted of the advice to "smoke 'em inside." Or the times when Bouton was told "the word on Tim McCarver of the Cards was that Sandy Koufax struck him out on letter-high fastballs." (As Bouton later reflected: "Which is great advice if you can throw letter-high fastballs like Koufax could.")

When *Ball Four* was published in 1970, I purchased the hardback edition for $6.95, a lot of money for a high school sophomore to spend on a book. That summer and throughout high school I read it endlessly, flipping back and forth across the diary entries. I wish I had spent as much time with Shakespeare or Henry James as I did with the Seattle Pilots. But *Ball Four* was the perfect coming-of-age account for anyone who grew up between the salad days of the Yankee dynasty and the fog of Vietnam and Watergate. In the same vein, *Foul Ball* reconciles baseball's constructed nostalgia—as expressed in Baltimore's Camden Yards or the stereopticon of Ken Burns—with what Howard Cosell called "the ugly business of carpet-bagging."

Another pleasure of *Foul Ball* and the updated *Ball Four* is to catch up with Jim Bouton after thirty years and not find him, as is the case with former Yankee Fritz Peterson, shuffling cards in a casino. At one point his wife complains he's spending too much time trying to save a run-down stadium. "It's such a long shot," she says. "My whole life is a long shot," he tells her. Now Bouton has moved from challenging hitters to busting one inside on a cozy political establishment. He does it with language that lays bare the extent to which town democracy is played on a field of schemes. But in using baseball to write an important book about local politics, Bouton does credit to the original editor of *Ball Four,* Leonard Shecter, who observed before he died that "a guy could make a living just telling the truth."   ◆

A Mickey Mantle Koan

(SEPTEMBER 1992)

David James Duncan

ON APRIL 6, 1965, my brother, Nicholas John Duncan, died of what his surgeons called "complications" after three unsuccessful open-heart operations. He was seventeen at the time—four years my elder to the very day. He'd been the fastest sprinter in his high school class until the valve in his heart began to close, but he was so bonkers about baseball that he'd preferred playing a mediocre JV shortstop to starring at varsity track. As a ballplayer he was a competent fielder, had a strong and fairly accurate arm, and stole bases with ease—when he could reach them. But no matter how much he practiced or what stances, grips, or self-hypnotic tricks he tried, he lacked the hand/eye magic that consistently lays bat-fat against ball, and remained one of the weakest hitters on his team.

John lived his entire life on the outskirts of Portland, Oregon—637 miles from the nearest major league team. In franchiseless cities in the Fifties and early Sixties there were two types of fans: those who thought the Yankees stood for everything right with America, and those who thought they stood for everything wrong with it. My brother was an extreme manifestation of the former type. He conducted a one-man campaign to notify the world that Roger Maris's sixty-one homers in '61 came in three fewer at bats than Babe Ruth's sixty in '27. He maintained—all statistical evidence to the contrary— that Clete Boyer was a better third baseman than his brother, Ken, simply because Clete was a Yankee. He may not have been the only kid on the block who considered Casey Stengel the greatest sage since Solomon, but I'm sure he was the only one who considered Yogi Berra the second greatest. And, of course, Mickey Mantle was his absolute hero, but his tragic hero. The Mick, my brother maintained, was the greatest raw talent of all time. He was one to whom great gifts were given, from whom great gifts had been ripped away; and the more scarred his knees became, the more frequently he fanned, the more flagrant his limp and apologetic his smile, the more John revered him. And toward this single Yankee I, too, was able to feel a touch of reverence, if only because on the subject of scars I considered my brother an unimpeachable authority: he'd worn one from the time he was eight, compliments of the Mayo Clinic, that wrapped clear around his chest in a wavy line, like stitching round a clean white baseball.

Yankees aside, John and I had more in common than a birthday. We bickered regularly with our middle brother and little sister, but almost never with each other. We were both bored, occasionally to insurrection, by schoolgoing, churchgoing, and any game or sport that didn't involve a ball. We both preferred, as a mere matter of style, Indians to cowboys, hoboes to businessmen, Buster Keaton to Charlie Chaplin, Gary Cooper to John Wayne, deadbeats to brownnosers, and even brownnosers to Elvis Presley. We shared a single cake on our joint birthday, invariably annihilating the candle flames with a tandem blowing effort, only to realize that we'd once again forgotten to make a wish. And when the parties were over or the house was stuffy, the parents cranky or the TV shows insufferably dumb, whenever we were restless, punchy, or just feeling as if there was nothing to do, catch—with a hard ball—is what John and I did.

We were not exclusive, at least not by intention: our father and middle brother and an occasional cousin or friend would join us now and then. But something in most everyone else's brain or bloodstream sent them bustling off to less contemplative endeavors before the real rhythm of the thing ever took hold. Genuine catch-playing occurs in a double limbo between busyness and idleness, and between what is imaginary and what is real. Also, as with any contemplative pursuit, it takes time, and the ability to forget time, to slip into this dual limbo and to discover (i.e., lose) oneself in the music of the game.

It helps to have a special place to play. Ours was a shaded, ninety-foot corridor between one neighbor's apple orchard and the other's stand of old-growth Douglas firs, on a stretch of lawn so lush and mossy it sucked the heat out of even the hottest grounders. I always stood in the north, John in the south. We might call balls and strikes for an imaginary inning or two, or maybe count the number of errorless catches and throws we could make (300s were common, and our record was high in the 800s). But the deep shade, the 200-foot firs, the mossy footing and fragrance of apples all made it a setting more conducive to mental vacationing than to any kind of disciplined effort. During spring-training months our catch occasionally started as a drill—a grounder, then a peg; another grounder, a peg. But as our movements became fluid and the throws brisk and accurate, the pretense of practice would inevitably fade, and we'd just aim for the chest and fire, *hissss pop! hissss pop!* until a meal, a duty, or total darkness forced us to recall that this was the real world in which even timeless pursuits come to an end.

Our talk must have seemed strange to eavesdroppers. We lived in our bodies during catch, and our minds and mouths, though still operative, were just along for the ride. Most of the noise I made was with the four or five pieces of Bazooka I was invariably working over, though when the gum turned bland, I'd sometimes narrate our efforts in a stream-of-doggerel play-by-play. My brother's speech was less voluminous and a bit more coherent, but of no greater didactic intent: he just poured out idle litanies of Yankee worship or even idler braggadocio à la Dizzy Dean, all of it artfully spiced with spat sunflower-seed husks.

But one day when we were sixteen and twelve, respectively, my big brother surprised me out there in our corridor. Snagging a low throw, he closed his mitt round the ball, stuck it under his arm, stared off into the trees, and got serious with me for a minute. All his life, he said, he'd struggled to be a shortstop and a hitter, but he was older now, and had a clearer notion of what he could and couldn't do. It was time to get practical, he said. Time to start developing obvious strengths and evading flagrant weaknesses. "So I've decided," he concluded, "to become a junk pitcher."

I didn't believe a word of it. My brother had been a "slugger worshiper" from birth. He went on embellishing his idea, though, and even made it sound rather poetic: to foil some muscle-bound fence-buster with an off-speed piece of crap that blupped off his bat like cow custard—this, he maintained, was the pluperfect pith of an attribute he called Solid Cool.

I didn't recognize until months later just how carefully considered this new junk-pitching jag had been. That John's throwing arm was better than his batting eye had always been obvious, and it made sense to exploit that. But there were other factors he didn't mention: like the sharp pains in his chest every time he took a full swing, or the new ache that half-blinded and sickened him whenever he ran full speed. Finding the high arts of slugging and base stealing physically impossible, he'd simply lowered his sights enough to keep his baseball dreams alive. No longer able to emulate his heroes, he set out to bamboozle those who thought they could. To that end he'd learned a feeble knuckler, a roundhouse curve, a submarine fastball formidable solely for its lack of accuracy, and was trashing his arm and my patience with his attempts at a screwball, when his doctors informed our family that a valve in his heart was rapidly closing. He might live as long as five years if we let it go, they said, but immediate surgery was best, since his recuperative powers were greatest now. John said nothing about any of this. He just waited until the day he was due at the hospital, snuck down to the stable where he kept his horse, saddled her up, and galloped away. He rode about twenty miles, to the farm of a friend, and stayed there in hiding for nearly two weeks. But when he snuck home one morning for clean clothes and money, my father and a neighbor caught him, and first tried to force him but finally convinced him to have the operation and be done with it.

Once in the hospital he was cooperative, cheerful, and unrelentingly courageous. He survived second, third, and fourth operations, several stoppings of the heart, and a nineteen-day coma. He recovered enough at one point, even after the coma, to come home for a week or so. But the overriding "complication" to which his principal surgeon kept making oblique references turned out to be a heart so ravaged by scalpel wounds that an artificial valve had nothing but shreds to be sutured to. Bleeding internally, pissing blood, John was moved into an oxygen tent in an isolated room, where he remained fully conscious, and fully determined to heal, for two months after his surgeons had abandoned him. And, against all odds, his condition stabilized, then began to improve. The doctors reappeared and began to discuss, with obvious despair, the feasibility of a fifth operation.

Then came the second "complication": staph. Overnight, we were reduced from genuine hope to awkward pleas for divine intervention. We invoked no miracles. Two weeks after contracting the infection, my brother died.

At his funeral, a preacher who didn't know John from Judge Kenesaw Mountain Landis eulogized him so lavishly and inaccurately that I was moved to a state of tearlessness that lasted for four years. It's an unenviable task to try to make public sense of a private catastrophe you know little about. But had I been in that preacher's shoes, I would have mentioned one or two of my brother's actual attributes, if only to reassure late-arriving mourners that they hadn't wandered into the wrong funeral. The person we were endeavoring to miss had, for instance, been a C student all his life, had smothered everything he ate with ketchup, had diligently avoided all forms of work that didn't involve horses, and had frequently gone so far as to wear sunglasses indoors in the relentless quest for Solid Cool. He'd had the disconcerting habit of sound-testing his pleasant baritone voice by bellowing "*Beeeeeee-Ooooooooooo!*" down any alley or hallway that looked like it might contain an echo. He'd had an interesting, slangy obliviousness to proportion: any altercation, from a fistfight to a world war, was "a rack"; any authority, from our mother to the head of the U.N., was "the Brass"; any pest, from the kid next door to Khrushchev, was "a buttwipe"; and any kind of ball, from a BB to the sun, was "the orb." He was brave: whenever anybody his age harassed me, John warned them once and beat them up the second time, or got beat up trying. He was also unabashedly, majestically vain. He referred to his person, with obvious pride, as "the Bod." He was an immaculate dresser. And he loved to stare at himself publicly or privately—in mirrors, windows, puddles, chrome car-fenders, upside-down in teaspoons—and to solemnly comb his long auburn hair over and over again, like his hero, Edd ("Kookie") Byrnes, on *77 Sunset Strip.*

His most astonishing attribute, to me at least, was his never-ending skein of girlfriends. He had a simple but apparently efficient rating system for all female acquaintances: he called it "percentage of Cool versus percentage of Crud." A steady girlfriend usually weighed in at around 95 percent Cool, 5 percent Crud, and if the Crud level reached 10 percent it was time to start quietly looking elsewhere. Only two girls ever made his "100 percent Cool List," and I was struck by the fact that neither was a girlfriend and one wasn't even pretty: whatever "100 percent Cool" was, it was not skin-deep. No girl ever came close to a "100 percent Crud" rating, by the way: my brother was chivalrous.

John was not religious. He believed in God, but passively, with nothing like the passion he had for the Yankees. He seemed a little more friendly with Jesus. "Christ is cool," he'd say, if forced to show his hand. But I don't recall him speaking of any sort of goings-on between them until he casually mentioned, a day or two before he died, a conversation they'd just had, there in the oxygen tent. And even then John was John: what impressed him even more than the fact of Christ's presence or the consoling words He spoke was the natty suit and tie He was wearing.

On the morning after his death, April 7, 1965, a small brown-paper package arrived at our house, special delivery from New York City, addressed to

John. I brought it to my mother and leaned over her shoulder as she sat down to study it. Catching a whiff of antiseptic, I thought at first that it came from her hair: she'd spent the last four months of her life in a straight-back chair by my brother's bed, and hospital odors had permeated her. But the smell grew stronger as she began to unwrap the brown paper, until I realized it came from the object inside.

It was a small, white, cylindrical, cardboard bandage box. "Johnson & Johnson," it said in red letters. "12 inches x 10 yards," it added in blue. Strange. Then I saw it had been split in half by a knife or a scalpel and bound back together with adhesive tape: so there was another layer, something hiding inside.

My mother smiled as she began to rip the tape away. At the same time, tears were landing in her lap. Then the tape was gone, the little cylinder fell away, and inside, nested in tissue, was a baseball. Immaculate white leather. Perfect red stitching. On one cheek, in faint green ink, the signature of American League president Joseph Cronin and the trademark REACH. THE SIGN OF QUALITY. And on the opposite cheek, with bright blue ballpoint ink, a tidy but flowing hand had written, To *John—My Best Wishes. Your Pal, Mickey Mantle. April 6, 1965.*

The ball dwelt upon our fireplace mantel—an unintentional pun on my mother's part. We used half the Johnson & Johnson box as a pedestal, and for years I saved the other half, figuring that the bandage it once contained had held Mantle's storied knee together for a game.

Even after my mother explained that the ball came not out of the blue but in response to a letter, I considered it a treasure. I told all my friends about it, and invited the closest to stop by and gawk. But gradually I began to see that the public reaction to the ball was disconcertingly predictable. The first response was usually, "Wow! Mickey Mantle!" But then they'd get the full story: "Mantle signed it the day he died? Your brother never even *saw* it?" And that made them uncomfortable. This was not at all the way an autographed baseball was supposed to behave. How could an immortal call himself your "Pal," how could you be the recipient of The Mick's "Best Wishes," and still just lie back and die?

I began to share the discomfort. Over the last three of my thirteen years I'd devoured scores of baseball books, all of which agreed that a bat, program, mitt, or ball signed by a big-league hero was a sacred relic, that we *should* expect such relics to have magical properties, and that they *would* prove pivotal in a young protagonist's life. Yet here I was, the young protagonist. Here was my relic. And all the damned thing did, before long, was depress and confuse me.

I stopped showing the ball to people, tried ignoring it, found that this was impossible, tried instead to pretend that the blue ink was an illegible scribble and that the ball was just a ball. But the ink *wasn't* illegible: it never stopped saying just what it said. So finally I picked the ball up and studied it, hoping to discover exactly why I found it so troublesome. Feigning the cool rationality I wished I'd felt, I told myself that a standard sports hero had received a letter from a standard distraught mother, had signed, packaged, and mailed off the standard ingratiatingly heroic response, had failed to think that the boy he inscribed the ball to might be dead when it arrived, and so had mailed his survivors a blackly comic non sequitur. I then told myself, "That's all there is to it"—which left me no option but to pretend that I hadn't expected or wanted any more from the ball than I got, that I'd harbored no desire for any sort of sign, any imprimatur, any flicker of recognition from an Above or a Beyond. I then began falling to pieces for lack of that sign.

Eventually, I got honest about Mantle's baseball: I picked the damned thing up, read it once more, peered as far as I could inside myself, and admitted for the first time that I was *pissed.* As is always the case with arriving baseballs, timing is the key—and this cheery little orb was inscribed on the day its recipient lay dying and arrived on the day he was being embalmed! This was *not* a harmless coincidence: it was the shabbiest, most embittering joke that Providence had ever played on me. My best friend and brother was dead, dead, dead, and Mantle's damned ball and best wishes made that loss even less tolerable, and *that,* I told myself, really was all there was to it.

I hardened my heart, quit the baseball team, went out for golf, practiced like a zealot, cheated like hell, kicked my innocuous, naive little opponents all over the course. I sold the beautiful outfielder's mitt that I'd inherited from my brother for a pittance.

But, as is usual in baseball stories, that wasn't all there was to it.

I'd never heard of Zen koans at the time, and Mickey Mantle is certainly no roshi. But baseball and Zen are two pastimes that Americans and Japanese have come to revere almost equally: roshis are men famous for hitting things hard with a big wooden stick; a koan is a perfectly nonsensical or nonsequacious statement given by an old pro (roshi) to a rookie (layman or monk); and the stress of living with and meditating upon a piece of mind-numbing non-sense is said to eventually prove illuminating. So I know of no better way to describe what the message on the ball became for me than to call it a koan.

In the first place, the damned thing's batteries just wouldn't run down. For weeks, months, *years*, every time I saw those nine blithely blue-inked words they knocked me off balance like a sudden shove from behind. They were an emblem of all the false assurances of surgeons, all the futile prayers of preachers, all the hollowness of Good-Guys-Can't-Lose baseball stories I'd ever heard or read. They were a throw I'd never catch. And yet ... REACH, the ball said. THE SIGN OF QUALITY.

So year after year I kept trying, kept hoping to somehow answer the koan.

I became an adolescent, enrolling my body in the obligatory school of pain-without-dignity called "puberty," nearly flunking, then graduating almost without noticing. I discovered in the process that some girls were nothing like 95 percent Crud. I also discovered that there was life after base-ball, that America was not the Good Guys, that God was not a Christian, that I preferred myth to theology, and that, when it came to heroes, the likes of Odysseus, Rama, and Finn MacCool meant incomparably more to me than the George Washingtons, Davy Crocketts, and Babe Ruths I'd been force-fed. I discovered (sometimes prematurely or overabundantly, but never to my regret) metaphysics, wilderness, Europe, black tea, high lakes, rock, Bach, tobacco, poetry, trout streams, the Orient, the novel, my life's work, and a hundred other grown-up tools and toys. But amid these maturations and transformations there was one unwanted constant: in the presence of that confounded ball, I remained thirteen years old. One peek at the "Your Pal" koan and whatever maturity or wisdom or equanimity I possessed was repossessed, leaving me as irked as any stumped monk or slumping slugger.

It took four years to solve the riddle on the ball. It was autumn when it happened—the same autumn during which I'd grown older than my brother would ever be. As often happens with koan solutions, I wasn't even thinking about the ball at the time. As is also the case with koans, I can't possibly describe in words the impact of the response, the instantaneous healing that took place, or the ensuing sense of lightness and release. But I'll say what I can.

The solution came during a fit of restlessness brought on by a warm Indian summer evening. I'd just finished watching the Miracle Mets blitz the

Orioles in the World Series, and was standing alone in the living room, just staring out at the yard and the fading sunlight, feeling a little stale and fidgety, when I realized that this was *just* the sort of fidgets I'd never had to suffer when John was alive—because we'd always work our way through them with a long game of catch. With that thought, and at that moment, I simply saw my brother catch, then throw a baseball. It occurred neither in an indoors nor an outdoors. It lasted a couple of seconds, no more. But I saw him so clearly, and he then vanished so completely, that my eyes blurred, my throat and chest ached, and I didn't need to see Mantle's baseball to realize exactly what I'd wanted from it all along:

From the moment I'd first laid eyes on it, all I'd wanted was to take that immaculate ball out to our corridor on an evening just like this one, to take my place near the apples in the north, and to find my brother waiting beneath the immense firs to the south. All I'd wanted was to pluck that too-perfect ball off its pedestal and proceed, without speaking, to play catch so long and hard that the grass stains and nicks and the sweat of our palms would finally obliterate every last trace of Mantle's blue ink, until all he would have given us was a grass-green, earth-brown, beat-up old baseball. Beat-up old balls were all we'd ever had anyhow. They were all we'd ever needed. The dirtier they were, and the more frayed the skin and stitching, the louder they'd hissed and the better they'd curved. And remembering this—recovering in an instant the knowledge of how little we'd needed in order to be happy—my grief for my brother became palpable, took on shape and weight, color and texture, even an odor. The measure of my loss was precisely the difference between one of the beat-up, earth-colored, grass-scented balls that had given us such happiness and this antiseptic-smelling, sad-making, icon-ball on its bandage-box pedestal. And as I felt this—as I stood there palpating my grief, shifting it around like a throwing stone in my hand—I fell through some kind of floor inside myself, landing in a deeper, brighter chamber just in time to feel something or someone tell me: *But who's to say we need even an old ball to be happy? Who's to say we couldn't do with less? Who's to say we couldn't still be happy—with no ball at all?*

And with that, the koan was solved.

I can't explain why this felt like such a complete solution. Reading the bare words, two decades later, they don't look like much of a solution. But a koan answer is not a verbal, or a literary, or even a personal experience: It's a spiritual experience. And a boy, a man, a "me," does not have spiritual experiences;

only the spirit has spiritual experiences. That's why churches so soon become bandage boxes propping up antiseptic icons that lose all value the instant they are removed from the greens and browns of grass and dirt and life. It's also why a good Zen monk always states a koan solution in the barest possible terms. "*No ball at all!*" is, perhaps, all I should have written—because then no one would have an inkling of what was meant and so could form no misconceptions, and the immediacy and integrity and authority of the experience would be safely locked away.

This is getting a bit iffy for a sports story. But jocks die, and then what? The brother I played a thousand games of catch with is dead, and so will I be, and unless you're one hell of an athlete so will you be. In the face of this fact, I find it more than a little consoling to recall how clearly and deeply it was brought home to me, that October day, that there is something in us which needs absolutely *nothing*—not even a dog-eared ball—in order to be happy. From that day forward the relic on the mantel lost its irksome overtones and became a mere autographed ball—nothing more, nothing less. It lives on my desk now, beside an old beater ball my brother and I wore out, and it gives me a satisfaction I can't explain to sit back, now and then, and compare the two—though I'd still gladly trash the white one for a good game of catch.

As for the ticklish timing of its arrival, I only recently learned a couple of facts that shed some light. First, I discovered—in a copy of the old letter my mother wrote to Mantle—that she'd made it quite clear that my brother was dying. So when The Mick wrote what he wrote, he knew perfectly well what the situation might be when the ball arrived. And second, I found out that my mother actually went ahead and showed the ball to my brother. True, what was left of him was embalmed. But what was embalmed wasn't all of him. And I've no reason to assume that the unembalmed part had changed much. It should be remembered, then, that while he lived my brother was more than a little vain, that he'd been compelled by his death to leave a handsome head of auburn hair behind, and that when my mother and the baseball arrived at the funeral parlor, that lovely hair was being prepared for an open-casket funeral by a couple of cadaverous-looking yahoos whose oily manners, hair, and clothes made it plain that they didn't know Kookie from Roger Maris or Solid Cool from Kool-Aid. What if this pair took it into their heads to spruce John up for the hereafter with a Bible camp cut? Worse yet, what if they tried to show what sensitive, accommodating artists they were and decked him out like a damned Elvis the Pelvis *greaser?* I'm not trying to be morbid here. I'm just trying to state the facts. "The Bod" my brother had very much enjoyed inhabiting was about to be seen for the last time by all his buddies, his family, and a girlfriend who was only 1.5 percent Crud, and the part of the whole ensemble he'd been most fastidious about—the coiffure— was completely out of his control! He *needed* best wishes. He needed a pal. Preferably one with a comb.

Enter my stalwart mother, who took one look at what the two rouge-and-casket wallahs were doing to the hair, said, "No, no, no!", produced a snapshot, told them, "He wants it *exactly* like this," sat down to critique their efforts, and kept on critiquing until in the end you'd have thought John had dropped in to groom himself.

Only then did she ask them to leave. Only then did she pull the autographed ball from her purse, share it with her son, read him the inscription.

As is always the case with arriving baseballs, timing is the key. Thanks to the timing that has made The Mick a legend, my brother, the last time we all saw him, looked completely himself.

I return those best wishes to my brother's pal. ✦

WINDING UP

(JUNE 1979)

Robert H. Zieger

I HAVE BECOME a pitcher, no longer merely a thrower. I have learned to hit the spots. To pace myself. To change speeds. I can no longer overpower, both because my fastball has lost velocity and because my opposition has become more confident, more aggressive, and more powerful. Had I not learned the location of the black part of the plate and the uses of the change-up, my career would have been over. As it is, I'm far from invincible, and I'm sure that one day—soon, no doubt—even my guile, cunning, and thirty-three years' baseball experience will not be enough to still my fourteen-year-old's slashing bat.

I began to notice the decline three years ago. Increasingly, he handled the fastballs I poured over the plate, driving them down the right-field line or into the alley in right center. Last summer he began to pull the high hard one, catapulting several whiffles over the stone grill that stands at the edge of our property. He hit the lilac bushes in center field twice. I could still get strikes with the hollow, latticed ball, but too often only two. Then he would shorten his swing, nudge fastballs foul, wait for the conceder, and hammer it. More and more, I relied on my still trusty glove to bail me out, snatching liners before they gained height to clear the wall, grabbing one-hoppers through atavistic reflexes.

But this year started off badly. After sending three fastballs into the high grass, he bade me stop lobbing them in. Strikeouts became rare and were usually achieved with my dipping slider or my nickel curve, after wasting fastballs up and in or down and away. After one particularly brutal assault, I resorted to old reliable: my Ewell Blackwell side-arm fastball, delivered from third base, sending the batter reeling off the plate, swinging feebly from the heels as he bailed out. He missed the first offering in surprise, drilled the second into the right-field corner, hitting the dog that had learned that that area was safe. One day the kid began batting *left-handed,* offering me the concession that *I* had for years so magnanimously granted.

Clearly, my Allie Reynolds days were over. Was there a future for me? Or would I become a pathetic hulk, pounding my glove, trying to find someone to indulge me in a game of whiffle, trying to recapture a dead past? Old Pete, sleeping in the bullpen. Winter's child in the summer game. Clearly, unless I was ready to face condescension and indulgence, I had to rethink my pitching habits.

It was then that I began for the first time to read attentively the interviews with the older pitchers in *The Sporting News.* The clichés took on meaning. One *did* have to learn to pitch, not just to throw. One did have to locate the ball, move it around. One did have to nibble at the corners, saving the hummer for when it would do the most good (or the least harm). I experimented with the Hoyt Wilhelm–Jim Bouton solution, but my knuckle ball did not knuckle; it just rotated slowly up to the plate, a ripe melon.

By midsummer last year, however, I was on my way back. I had begun the season with the old fastball, hoping that perhaps memories of last year's late-season debacles had become magnified and that perhaps the pounding I had taken in October had to do with arm fatigue. It took three innings to dispel these illusions. I got out of the first with two leaping catches. A soaring home run, one-hopping against the stone pillar, brought back a taste of the previous autumn in the second. The roof fell in in the third. Only a spate of left-handed hitters—who tend to hit low line drives rather than arching shots—slowed the rally and enabled me to retire the side. Damage? Seven runs on nine hits, including four home runs (one of them left-handed, a low shot that skimmed the top of the wall just above the relocated dog).

So in the fourth I became Stu Miller. I had thought about this approach, had rejected it as unmanly. Now it seemed inspired. I busted him with a fastball, up and in. Then I nibbled. Down and away. Down and away. An overhand change-up. A couple of sharp sliders, in on the fists. Since we have no walks or hit batters in our games, I was able to experiment—perhaps a little unfairly, because the batter, after three or four bad pitches, will swing at anything rather than face incessant retrieval of the four whiffles we normally play with. But it worked. A comebacker on a change-up. A pop foul off a slow curve in on the fists. A *strikeout* on a sweeping hook, coming off several set-up, lame fastballs too far inside to handle. Pitching could be fun. I celebrated by pounding out four hits. (Alas, just one run: of late, while my average kept reasonably high, my power quotient seemed to suffer. Was I becoming Pete Runnels as well as Eddie Lopat?)

During the last ten weeks of the summer we played a succession of tense, hard-fought games. For all his batting prowess, my son tended to tire on the mound in the late innings, unless he dispatched me quickly in the first three or four. At the plate, he showed cunning himself. He learned to adjust: to lay off the ephus ball—my Rip Sewell special—that I had learned to rely on for an easy first-pitch pop-up; to step into the outside pitch and go with it to right field; to fight off the high inside fastball and hit it to right center. He learned my pattern. If I got him on inside sliders one inning, he was ready the next. If I set him with curves down and away, all too often he was ready for the inside fastball that was supposed to be my out pitch. Still, the home runs diminished and the games that had been going 9–1 and 11–3 were now 7–5 and 4–3 affairs. A balance had been reached, especially when I adjusted to my new Billy Goodman style of hitting and found that sometimes four weak singles were more discouraging to the defense than one towering blast.

We had what I think was our final game of the season this week. In October, we tend to spend the glorious afternoons and the shortened evenings watching the other ballplayers on television. In our season's ender, he jumped on a couple of thoughtless fastballs early on and sent them into the leaf pile. An unusual lapse of fielding on my part, together with a Chinese home run, yielded two more in the fourth. But I kept tattooing away, a looping double and two sharp singles getting one back in the second, a nice line drive that hit the fence post that serves as the foul pole in left getting another back in the third. Five to two in the ninth.

I drilled a double off the wall in right center, jumping on one of his now-decelerating fastballs. He made a good play on a tricky hopper in the hole. But I rolled a single through his legs and followed it with another just past his glove. I jumped on a fat fastball and popped up (a major-league pop-up, the kind he used to get dizzy under and drop) for out No. 2. Two strikes, and then—could I believe it?—a belt-high conceder. I wrapped it around the broomstick foul pole in right for a three-run home run and a 6–5 lead.

He gave me a scare in the bottom of the ninth. Concentrating, bearing down, weighing every pitch, I got a third strike on a tantalizing curve ball, down and away. Hoping for a quick second out, my stamina spent, I grooved one and he hit me in the stomach with it. The ball spun out of my grasp for a base hit. He followed with a two-strike ground single, but I got the second out on a soft liner that I plucked out of the dusky air with ease.

It came down to this. Two wasted pitches, followed by a good low fastball that did not elicit a swing. Then a guilty offer at a wide curve (no called strikes, but the batter is more or less obligated to swing at the next pitch if he lets an obvious strike go by). Two inside sliders. Now down and away. He swung. The ball started out heading for the wall in right center. But it died, as some lucky wind current caught the louvers on the underside. I spun back to the wall, reached up, and pulled it in. He tossed the bat aside. "Get you tomorrow," he said, heading for the kitchen and a slug of cider. ✦

PART III: THE UPPER DECK

✦

No Joy in Sorrento

THE STORY OF THE DAVIS CUP

(SEPTEMBER 1938)

John R. Tunis

THIS IS THE story of the growth of a game. Because lawn tennis is an international sport played in almost every nation on earth the changes both in the game itself and in our attitude toward it are more dramatic than in some purely national pastime. But essentially what is true of this sport can be duplicated in all: the history of lawn tennis is the history of the Olympic Games, of rugby and cricket in England, of intercollegiate football in the United States. With the passing of time and the changes in our habits, with the spread of sport among the people and their consequent expanding interest in records, with the gradual growth of leisure time since 1900, the result was inevitable. Given the increasing importance of games, it was inevitable that first big business and then politics should fasten upon what was once merely an amusing interlude in our lives, and use it for their own ends. "Sport the bitch goddess," Mr. Lewis Mumford calls it today.

I THE AGE OF INNOCENCE

1903: the third year of the Davis Cup. The United States, holder, was playing the British Isles, challenger. From the picket fence which bordered the grounds of the Longwood Cricket Club my brother and I watched the matches of the opening afternoon. Occasionally the driver of a brewery wagon would rein in his horses, lean out, and yell "Forty Love" in a high falsetto voice.

On the second day we were cutting Mr. Harmon's lawn. For this we received a quarter apiece, enough to take us in on the final afternoon. (This 1903 match was apparently the first international tennis event at which admission was charged.) To save the Cup the United States must win both matches; but as patriotic youngsters we believed that Bill Larned and Bob Wrenn would each defeat the Dohertys.

Once inside the grounds we discovered that reserved seats were fifty cents extra. They might as well have been fifty dollars. Otherwise you took a chair and sat down opposite the low grandstand, your chin over the green baize fence and almost on the playing surface itself. But all the chairs were gone. Impossible for us to see over the heads in the front row, so we scouted back of the clubhouse—a small, one-storey wooden dressing room—and discovered a small box. This barely supported us if we stood with our arms round each other. From it we could see over the seated front row.

The Saturday crowd kept coming. Soon all grandstand seats were gone. A row of standees pushed in behind us. Boxes like ours were valuable as more persons lined up. Someone poked my brother in the ribs and offered us a dollar for our perch. One dollar! We gasped. Then we looked back to the street where we'd seen the matches of the first afternoon. The club had erected a high green curtain to shut off the view of the courts. We declined the offer.

Both matches began simultaneously. The calls of the umpire and the cheers of the spectators from one court interrupted a tense rally on the adjoining one. Precarious on our flimsy box, we overlooked a sideline of the Larned–Doherty match. There may have been greater players than Laurie Doherty but I was not to see one until the Tilden era. Larned, however, was a giant too. His virile American game, with more punch if less finesse than young Doherty's, kept him in the running until the middle of the fifth set.

The score was four games all, while six black balls were hung on the iron standard of the adjacent court; the two matches were exactly even and the Cup had to be won. On Doherty's service Larned reached gamepoint. The Englishman served and came to the net. Larned passed him and the score was 5–4 in his favor with his own service to follow.

Then Doherty questioned that service. Was it good? The umpire glanced at the linesman. His chair was vacant. The linesman had agreed to take the line until time for the last boat to Nantasket, when he was to be relieved. No one had observed his departure. Play stopped on both courts until Dr. Dwight, the referee, decided to call a let and replay the point. As Doherty served again we leaned forward. So did a dozen others. Crack! Down went the box and seven or eight men on top of us.

Did the commotion upset Larned, hardly five yards away? Or was he bothered by having to play the point again? At any rate he netted the service and the score was deuce. We picked ourselves up, rubbing bruised shins and elbows. We saw little of the rest of the match. Maybe this was just as well.

Doherty finally won the game and took the set, 7–5. For the first time England had captured the Davis Cup.

The four-mile walk home was long for a couple of battered twelve-year-old boys. We were battered in body and spirit. Our side had been robbed. That ball was good. Weren't we right on top of the line? Only seven feet from where the shot fell? Nearer even than the umpire. It was good. We knew it was good. A drizzle was falling as we stumbled up the front walk at home and there were tears in the eyes of two tired and disappointed youngsters.

II TENNIS COMES OF AGE

1914: the thirteenth year of the Davis Cup. In 1903 the matches had been a family affair between teams from the United States and the British Isles. By 1914 three continents were sending teams to fight for the famous salad bowl. That summer teams were competing from France, Belgium, and Germany on the Continent, the British Isles, from the United States (which after years of struggling had regained the Cup) and Canada in North America, and from Australasia representing Australia and New Zealand.

Lawn tennis had also grown. Instead of the sylvan setting of the Longwood Cricket Club under the Massachusetts elms, a larger arena had been provided. By this time the family-party atmosphere had vanished. No need to erect curtains to prevent twelve year-old boys from watching on the street. The vast stands at the West Side Tennis Club did that. They towered to the sky and offered space for eleven thousand spectators. (At two dollars a seat; the days of a quarter admittance were gone too.) Here the American talent for organization showed at its best. No hasty arrangements with linesmen leaving at their own sweet will, but three days of sport efficiently planned, advertised, and staged.

The Challenge Round that year was a fight between the Australasian veterans, Brookes and Wilding, and two youngsters, Maurice McLoughlin and R. Norris Williams (then a sophomore at Harvard). Twelve thousand fans jammed into the stands and sat on the porches of the clubhouse, the largest number ever to see a match of tennis anywhere in the world. That bleacher at Longwood could have been placed in one section of the wooden amphitheater.

The crowds had changed. So had the tennis. Instead of the fluent strokes of Larned and the Dohertys, instead of the long rallies, the fencing for position, the game was speeded up. It was faster and more vital. This was also due to the vivid personalities of the players and chiefly to McLoughlin. The first of the long line of Californian champions which has extended to the present day, he popularized lawn tennis in the United States. He was young. He was husky. When he served his adversaries stood watching the ball flash past them. No one was calling "Forty Love" in a high falsetto voice to McLoughlin.

In daring and brilliancy Williams was little behind. For the first few games of his match against Wilding he had the Australian gaping at the boldness of his shots. He could pilot the ball into the tiniest opening, and with a half-volley take it on the rise, opening up the angles of the forecourt, the area between the net and the service line that had never before been exploited. Then leading 4–1, he suddenly lost his precision. Those dazzling shots would be just out. The burly Anzac saw his chance and merely kept the ball in play. The American went to pieces. In less than an hour the first point was marked for the challenging team.

Then appeared the heroes of the day: the red-headed picturesque American boy who was selling tennis to the plain people, and the left-handed veteran Brookes, the cool, crafty, resourceful tactician. McLoughlin's flaming thatch contrasted with the golf cap Brookes pulled down over his eyes. There have been greater matches in Davis Cup history; none so grim or so spectacular. The speed of shot was tremendous. The rallies were few. It was a different game from the poised, polite garden-party tennis of the Dohertys. Tennis had changed as the world was changing.

The goal of both men was the net. Points were quickly won, usually by the volleyer. Service was important and games were even to 8–all. In the 18th game Brookes was 0–40 on the American's service. Three times the redhead served. At the first ace the crowd cheered. At the second they shouted. When he smacked over a third to tie the score, and finally won the game, ending with an untouchable delivery, they stood and yelled like madmen. A new era in sport had arrived.

There was no answer to such tennis. McLoughlin had weak ground shots but he had that service, a mighty weapon. Finally he won the set, 17–15, the longest singles set to be played in a completed match in Davis Cup history. In fact that struggle burned both men out; neither ever played top-class competitive tennis again.

Within the clubhouse afterward talk buzzed of the battle, but a few serious-faced men in one corner of the big room were grouped about a late edition telling of British troops landing at an unnamed port in France. Tony Wilding had been waiting for the end of the Challenge Round; he soon enlisted and a few months afterward was killed in the trenches in France. Meanwhile someone suggested that the war would be over by Christmas. Theodore Roosevelt grunted. "Which Christmas?" he said.

III DOLLAR DECADE

1927: twenty-second year. In 1903 two nations had battled for the Davis Cup; by 1914 there had been 6 challenging nations; in 1927 there were 25, the largest number so far. Tennis was now a universal game. Save Russia and Turkey, hardly a country was impervious to the prestige value of winning the Cup donated by Dwight F. Davis of St. Louis in 1900. In 1927 teams came from the north of Europe, Denmark, Poland, and Sweden. They came from the Antipodes, from below the Tropic of Capricorn in Africa, from India and Japan, from Italy and Greece, from Mexico and Cuba, and even from the Balkan nations.

First the British Isles (now England, because Ireland had become a separate nation) then the United States had dominated international play. Since 1920 when the two Bills, Tilden and Johnston, had won the Cup at Melbourne, they had defended it against all challengers. Against astute Japanese like Kumagae and Shimidzu, against fresh Australian reinforcements, Anderson, Patterson, Hawkes, and Wood. Now a new tennis-playing nation appeared on the sporting horizon. For the first time a Latin country was dangerous.

This was the dollar decade of American sport. The era of million-dollar prize-fight gates, the period when citizens would pay sixty dollars for a ringside seat a hundred yards from the fighters, or twenty dollars to sit behind the goalposts at an Army–Navy football game, the time when Jones and Sande and Ruth and Hagen among others were performing for the multitudes. Not to mention a Philadelphian named Tilden.

No wonder the stands at the Germantown Cricket Club were insufficient to hold the throng who clamored to pay three dollars on the last afternoon of the Challenge Round which brought the young French team against the United States. Twelve thousand were jammed into the seats but three or four thousand more paid to get in, sat Chinese-fashion on the turf near the court or hung to one end of the bleachers to watch Tilden and Lacoste in the opening match of the day.

There were new changes in the game. American organization had finally captured sport. The shelf of the umpire's chair now supported a pair of scissors, a can of talcum powder, a rule book, a penknife, a pair of pliers, a shoe horn, a couple of extra belts, some garters, a bottle of smelling salts, a steel pick for removing dirt from player's spikes, some powdered rosin in a large shaker, safety pins of all sizes, adhesive tape in several widths, aromatic spirits of ammonia, and a cloth for cleaning eyeglasses. Under the chair was a bucket of iced barley water and a box of sawdust, and had Bitsy Grant been playing, there would have been a couple of bottles of Coca-Cola.

By this time the linesmen were not, as in 1903, chosen just before the match from prominent spectators who happened to be sitting in the front row. A man would as soon dare to run for the Nantasket boat in the middle of a match and leave his line untenanted as throw a tear gas bomb on the court. Now a Challenge Round necessitated an umpire and thirteen assistants. These men all belonged to an association; they were carefully selected weeks ahead and drilled, trained, and regimented like Prussian guardsmen. One bad decision might possibly cost us the Davis Cup, and the Davis Cup was important. We had come a long way from that informal afternoon's entertainment under the Massachusetts elms in 1903.

The tennis was different also. From the all-court game of the Dohertys and Larned, we had passed to the crafty and penetrating game of Brookes and Wilding, the daring and spectacular strokes of McLoughlin and Williams; now we were watching the powerful games of Tilden and Johnston with no weaknesses, backed by every shot in tennis. We had made the turn of the wheel. Once more we seemed to be in the epoch of the Dohertys, for Tilden was a kind of super-Doherty. But he was past his prime.

The American had more power off the ground than either of the Dohertys. In addition he had an American cannon-ball service, a service perhaps as fast as McLoughlin's, better placed, and one over which he had better control. Moreover, where McLoughlin had a cannon-ball delivery, Tilden had that plus two or three other kinds. In all during that match he made twenty-one service aces. But Lacoste, the French crocodile, had the ability to parry these shots. He possessed one of the greatest tennis brains of all time. First he pulled Tilden far to one side with a spinning service, then made him grope for a low shot in the corner. Then he would yank him into the forecourt and send him chasing back after a perfect lob. The American was always reaching for the ball. He was giving away twelve years to Lacoste. Twelve years is lots in a young man's game.

Then Cochet and Johnston took the court. The crowd rose because Little

Bill, then losing his power, was the most popular athlete in the country. The crowd wanted him to win. They were frankly partisan. The Longwood crowd had come for the tennis, the game; they had applauded everyone's good shots. But this was a different crowd, a gallery eager for sensations. Mixed with the players and lovers of the sport were many who came for excitement. They were rooters, the sort of people who howled at the umpire in a World's Series, who yelled at fighters to "knock the big bum out."

The end came in a frenzy of vociferation. They cheered every point Johnston won; every error of Cochet's was greeted with applause. The little Frenchman tried merely to keep the ball in play. His defense was sagacious. Johnston finally beat himself, and Cochet on the final point tossed his bat high in the air. For the first time Latins had beaten Anglo Saxons in their own specialty, on the fields of sport. No more could the French be called a decadent race.

IV TENNIS ACROSS AN OCEAN

1932: the twenty-second year. There was a cordon of gendarmes thrown wide round the gates of the Stade Roland Garros on the last afternoon of the Challenge Round, and you had to show your tickets to get through that line. Once inside, I climbed to the top of the stadium with César Saerchinger, the European Director of Columbia Broadcasting System. Short-wave transmission had been perfected and for the first time an oral, play-by-play account was going across an ocean. Millions were following each move on that red court in Paris during the afternoon.

By this time France had gone tennis-mad. Every little café had its loudspeaker on the sidewalk and a knot of listeners standing about. "La Coupe" was a household word. Interest was intense, single tickets for the matches cost four hundred francs or sixteen dollars—if you could find a speculator who had one to sell. Dwight Davis, former cabinet minister and donor of the Cup, tried to enter the section of the stadium reserved for players and their friends but was refused admittance and returned to his hotel unnoticed. The Davis Cup had become an event of world-wide importance, but who was this Monsieur Davis?

We climbed the rickety ladder to the broadcasting perch eighty feet in the air behind the court. At Longwood the press had been represented by one man from the Boston *Transcript* and by Fred Mansfield, the umpire, who for the love of the game used to telephone an account of the matches to the

Herald. At Roland Garros a special section of the stands was devoted to the press, with reporters by the dozen from every capital of Europe, sob sisters, special writers, columnists, and sports authorities from half a dozen nations. There was even a man from Egypt. Meanwhile across the court, our platform—which ran the length of the stands but was only six feet wide without any railings—swayed under its burden of reporters in a new medium. A dozen camera men with their guns trained on the court and twice that number of radio commentators and mechanics filled our narrow perch. Beside me a French youth rippled phrases into his mike, on the other side a German gutturaled the story to Berlin, and farther down the line an Italian was talking. It was a lovely scene. Over the leafy chestnut trees surrounding the Stade, the Eiffel Tower cut the blue sky in the distance. Below, round the reddish court, in the packed stands sat the restless French gallery eager for a triumph in the Coupe. And the four streets bordering the stadium were solidly jammed with ticketless thousands who saw only one edge of the big electric scoreboard or simply stood listening to the cheers from within.

I had guessed three-thirty as the moment to take the air. We were in luck, for Borotra and Allison, a man from Bayonne and a boy from Austin, Texas, appeared just at that moment following the intermission after the third set. By this time the famous Four Musketeers who had won the Cup at Philadelphia were losing ground. Lacoste was through. Cochet was weakening and Borotra was a veteran too old to withstand the challenge of a generation of young Americans. He dropped the first two sets to the fine volleying of Wilmer Allison. But tennis matches of a Musketeer never went by default. In the third set he became suddenly the Borotra of his prime. In the fourth he went from strength to strength, drawing reserves of courage from his fanatical supporters in the stands. The crowd was almost beyond control as he began to stab his volleys past the tiring American.

"Un peu de silence s'il vous plait," pleaded the umpire vainly. From the swaying platform—so flimsy it might topple any moment—I tried to describe this amazing scene to dispassionate Americans three thousand miles away, to explain what it meant to the French to have their champion come from behind, to portray the emotional crowd in the stands waving the little red-white-and-blue paper parasols which colored the stadium as Borotra won game after game. So we came into the fifth set. Allison, volleying with a firm hand, at last reached matchpoint. Borotra exerted an extra bit of pressure and drew an error. Another matchpoint. Again the Basque saved himself and

France, this time with a netcord shot. You could hear his groan of relief from the platform. Now the gallery was beyond control.

"Borocco, Borocco, Borocco," they yelled, their nickname for their favorite. The umpire appealed for quiet but no one paid any attention and it took a gesture of agony from Borotra himself to still them. Then the third match-point came up.

Borotra served. A fault. The second service. Over the line. A doublefault and the match was won. Allison tossed his bat high in the air.

No . . . wait a minute. That ball was called good. I was speechless. I forgot I was broadcasting. That ball *good* . . . ? Pandemonium. For some minutes everybody was shouting. Finally order was restored and the match resumed. But the punch was gone from the American's game. Exhausted, he let Borotra storm through to victory. The *Coupe Davis* was saved for France. Ten thousand cushions rained upon the court as the Basque, still wet, came to the box below us, where he was embraced by the President of the Republic.

Our time on the air was up. In fact we had gone half an hour over, but so exciting was the struggle that New York had kept the wires open. Had I described the match correctly? Had I mentioned that decision? Yes, but it was not till six weeks later—when a friend who had listened with a portable set on a Jersey beach told me that he had heard my exclamation as a linesman saved the Cup for France—that I found out. I had described the first sporting event across an ocean and the last victory of France in the Davis Cup.

V LIFE AND DEATH

1937: the thirty-second year. Possibly the French had been the first to perceive the national prestige attaching to a victory in this world sport. They were by no means the last. By 1937 every nation in Europe laid plans during midwinter for the next summer's campaign. Likely candidates were excused for months on end from their military service. Governments stood ready to furnish unlimited sums for expenses. For by this time money was a necessity if you hoped to capture possession of the Davis Cup.

On what was money spent? First you must have a professional trainer, a Tilden, a Kozeluh, or a Nusslein. These men come high. Then you must find a captain, some older player willing to spend all his time developing champions, and a masseur to keep the team in shape. *En voyage* you must live well. The Dohertys in 1903 stayed at private houses; now Davis Cup stars stop only at Grand Palace Hotels—our team always puts up at Grosvenor House in London. Last year the Germans started their campaign early in May, playing in Milan, Prague, Brussels, and Paris before reaching Wimbledon early in July to take part in the Interzone Final against the United States. You must either transship your side across an ocean or send them jaunting around the capitals of Europe for three or four months. Sometimes gate receipts help out, sometimes not. What does it matter? The Davis Cup is important. Government chiefs realize this—none better than the dictators.

1937 was not a record year for entries because only 24 nations challenged to try to take the Cup from England, the holder; but it was significant as showing the strength of countries hitherto little known as sporting nations. France, holder of the Cup only a few years previously, was badly beaten by Czechoslovakia. The summer before they had lost in the first round to the Yugoslavs. Nor have we heard the last of that country in the matches for the Davis Cup.

In July, 1937, it was the Germans—conquerors of the Czechs—who stepped upon the Center Court at Wimbledon, headed by their blond champion, Gottfried von Cramm, to meet the Americans led by another redheaded Californian named Donald Budge. Three weeks earlier in the English championships Budge had beaten the German rather easily in three straight sets, and he seemed likely enough to repeat when, with the teams even at two matches apiece, the champions of Germany and the United States faced each other in the deciding contest.

By this time we were in an era of shorts, but they were not worn by either Budge or Cramm. Curiously enough, champions seem able to handicap themselves in this way and still conquer all comers in abbreviated garments. Notice also another change since the early days. Instead of the one extra racket which Larned and Doherty each carried on court, Budge and Cramm appeared with seven or eight bats in their arms. So great is the speed of the modern game, so tensely strung are the champions' bats, that three or four may snap a string in the course of a match. Observe that the balls are taken from a frigidaire back of the umpire's chair, where they have been kept at a fixed temperature all night. Originally they were just tennis balls, of any weight, size, bound, or temperature. Now all balls are standardized, conforming to mechanized tests which limit the bounce to 53 inches when dropped on concrete from a height of 100 inches, the weight to 2–2 $\frac{1}{16}$ ounces, and the compression to between .265 and .290 inches. This shows the point to which the American talent for systematization and organization has taken what was once a friendly match for a Challenge bowl.

The struggle began. Old-timers have said it was the greatest match ever played at Wimbledon. Great is a large word, but probably never had the standard of play on both sides of the net been so high. For points were not lost; they were won. There is a difference. Moreover, they were won several times in each rally. You were watching super-tennis by super-players. Tilden afterward declared it the finest match he had ever seen.

Cramm won the first set. Budge waited for the avalanche to pass. But the second set came and the avalanche persisted. Two sets up for Cramm. Not until the third did a reaction start in the German's game, and Budge working to the net managed to make some winning volleys. Slowly the tide turned. The American won the third set after a fight, and the fourth. Only a player armed at every point, with no physical or moral weakness, could have evened the score against a champion playing like Cramm.

It was seven o'clock when the fifth set began. The German showed he had a kick left by serving and driving faultlessly. He was soon 4–1. Then Budge became the grand champion. His service in pace and accuracy was hardly inferior to Tilden's at its best. Slowly he fought back and evened the score. In the fourteenth game he had five matchpoints before he finally won the set and the match. Both players were completely exhausted and so was every single spectator.

One must admit that Budge's tennis that afternoon was a step forward in the game. The technic of sport does not stand still. Nor yet does the power and influence of the Davis Cup. Looking back, some things about that magnificent struggle are clearer. Most champions play better for their country in team matches than in tournaments when they are on their own. But Cramm had never played like that before. Nor ever did again. How to explain this?

Possibly because the German was playing for his country and something more. It was common knowledge that Cramm had never been a member of the Nazi party. Despite his efforts in sport for the Fatherland, he had never been in Hitler's good graces. Those who are not for a dictator are against him. What a chance Cramm had at Wimbledon! Imagine his triumphal return to Berlin, that emblem of world supremacy in sport by his side. Germany on top. First the Olympic Games, then the Davis Cup. Would the Führer not forgive anything of the man who was the artisan of the first German victory in this international event?

But he failed. Cramm failed by a few inches which separated the ball from the baseline in several critical rallies in the critical games of the last set. By a shot or two in the alley, and not just inside the court, by a few inches on the wrong side, once when he was leading 4–2 and again at 4–3. By the merest fraction of a second in the timing of his racket.

Accordingly this summer he is in disgrace, a prisoner in his native land. Do you suppose that if those few balls had been inside the court in the last set, if Cramm had captured the Davis Cup, he would now be in a concentration camp? If so you misunderstand the mentality of dictators.

This is 1938. Tennis has changed and so has the world in which we live. Thanks to the press, to radio, to easy means of communication, and to widespread interest in athletics, the Davis Cup has been "sold" to the entire world. Today it is a matter of growing national importance. President Lebrun, Foreign Secretary Sir Samuel Hoare, and Secretary of State Cordell Hull have all presided in recent years at the drawings for the Davis Cup and set the governmental kiss of approval upon the contest. It has become a test of national superiority.

Longwood is no longer prominent in the sport. One hears little about it now; can that be because Longwood is still a club primarily for people who want to play and do not care overmuch for the prominence attaching to Davis Cup matches? And what will the Davis Cup be in 1960? Will there be a national holiday, will the President and his Cabinet attend the Challenge Round, will the Stock Exchange close as the matches between the United States and Japan are played and televised to hundreds of millions of fans in a waiting world? Will they be played in a double-decked Rose Bowl seating half a million spectators, and will the star of the Japanese team commit hara-kiri on the center court rather than return defeated to be killed in Japan by an angry populace?

Impossible? Absurd? Perhaps. But who in 1903 would have visualized the changes which the machine age has wrought in what was once a pastime and nothing more? Anyhow one thing is certain. In 1960 no small twelve-year-olders will watch the Challenge Round—except maybe the Sistie and Buzzie of that period. ✦

HOCKEY NIGHTS

(JANUARY 1998)

Guy Lawson

IN SEPTEMBER THE streets of Flin Flon, Manitoba, are deserted at twilight. The town has no bookshop, no record store, no movie theater, no pool hall. Main Street is a three-block strip of banks, video shops, and Bargain! outlets. The 825-foot smokestack of the Hudson Bay Mining and Smelting Company rises from one end of the street, and the Precambrian shield stretches out from the other. In the Royal Hotel, gamblers forlornly drop quarters into the video slot machines. Farther up the street at the Flin Flon Hotel, the front door has been broken in a fight, and inside strangers are met by suspicious glances from miners wearing baseball caps with slogans like YA WANNA GO? and T-shirts that read, with the letters increasingly blurry, DRINK, DRANK, DRUNK. Susie, who works behind the counter at the Donut King, says a major shipment of LSD has arrived in town and half the students at the local high school, Hapnot Collegiate, have been stoned out of their minds for weeks.

Described by *Canada: The Rough Guide* as an "ugly blotch on a barren rocky landscape," Flin Flon, population 7,500, straddles the border between Manitoba and Saskatchewan, 90 miles north of its nearest neighbor, The Pas, 500 miles up from Winnipeg, and a thirteen-hour drive due north of Minot, North Dakota. In this part of the world, Flin Flon is literally the end of the line: the two-lane highway that connects it to the rest of North America circles the perimeter of town and then, as if shocked to its senses, rejoins itself and hightails it back south.

But Flin Flon is also the heartland of Canada's national game. In a country where every settlement of consequence has a hockey arena and a representative team made up of players twenty years old and younger, the Saskatchewan Junior Hockey League is one of the grandest, oldest competitions. And Flin Flon is one of the grandest, oldest hockey towns. I had played hockey in towns like Flin Flon—in a league one level below the juniors—before I went to college. Many of my teammates had gone on to play junior hockey; some became professionals.

One hot day in August, seventeen years after I'd left western Canada, I flew north, arriving from Toronto in a twin-prop plane, to spend the first month of the new season with Flin Flon's junior hockey team. Hockey, as I remembered it from my own teams, was an untold story. It was also the path I had chosen not to take.

At the airport, I was greeted by the Flin Flon Junior Bombers' coach and general manager. Razor (like everyone else in hockey, he goes by a nickname) was in his early forties, solidly built, with a deep, raspy voice and the confident, slightly pigeon-toed stride of a former athlete. He had grown up in Flin Flon and had been a defenseman for the Bombers. He had gone on to play a long career in minor-league professional hockey as well as some games—"a cup of coffee here, a cup of coffee there"—with the Boston Bruins in the National Hockey League. As we drove into town, Razor told me that the previous year, his first full season as coach, the Bombers had finished with the second-worst record in the SJHL's northern division. This year, he said, was going to be different. He had big tough forwards, speed, and two of the best goalies in the league.

A blast of cold air hit me as I walked out of the 90-degree heat and into the Whitney Forum's simulated winter for the first time. Meeks, a veteran Bomber left-winger, was alone on the ice practicing his signature trick: tilt the puck on its side with the stick, sweep it up, then nonchalantly cradle it on the blade. Lean and large and slope-shouldered, he was one of the toughest players in the league. As he left the ice, I heard him say to Hildy, the team trainer, "Tell Razor I'm not fighting this year. This is my last year of hockey, and I'm not missing any games." He was twenty years old. He had sat out a third of last season because he had broken his hand twice in fights. His thumb was still out of place, the joint distended and gnarled.

In the Bombers' dressing room, Meeks's sticks were piled next to his locker stall, the shafts wrapped in white tape and covered with messages to himself written in black Magic Marker. One note read MEGHAN, the name of his girlfriend; another said HOCKEY GOD; and a third, WHAT TO DO? While he took off his shoulder pads and loosened his skates, other players, hometown kids like Meeks or early arrivals from out of town returning from last season's team, drifted in. Boys with peach fuzz and pimples—Rodge, Quinny, Woody,

Airsy, Skulls, Dodger—they seemed to transform into men as they pulled on their pads and laced up their skates. I went to the stands to watch them play.

The Forum is a squat, dark, tin-roofed building on the shores of what used to be Lake Flin Flon but is now a drained and arid wasteland of tailings from HBM&S's smelter. Dozens of tasseled maroon-and-white championship banners hang from the rafters. Photographs of nearly every Flin Flon Bomber team since the 1920s look down from the walls. And there is a pasty-faced portrait of Queen Elizabeth in her tiara at the rink's north end.

With no coaches and no fans, nobody but me around, the rink echoed with hoots and laughter. Scrub hockey, like schoolyard basketball, is a free-form improvisation on the structures and cadences of the real game. Passes were made between legs and behind backs. The puck dipsy-doodled and dangled, preternaturally joined to the stick, the hand, the arm, the whole body, as players deked left, then right, and buried a shot in the top corner of the net. In those moments, the Forum seemed an uncomplicated place where the game was played purely for its own sake: *Le hockey pour le hockey.*

The Bombers, like virtually every team in the SJHL, are owned by the community; the team's president and board of directors are elected officials, like the mayor and the town council; and the team is financed by bingo nights, raffles, and local business sponsorship. HBM&S once gave the Bombers jobs at the mine—with light duties, time off to practice, and full pay even when the team was on the road, an arrangement that was a powerful recruiting tool for prairie farm boys—but these days there are no jobs at HBM&S and there's little part-time work in town. Some of the players do odd jobs to earn spending money. Like junior-hockey players across Canada, most Bombers move away from home by the time they're sixteen. Long road trips, practices, and team meetings leave little time for anything but hockey. For decades, players were expected either to quit school or slack their way through it; now the Junior A leagues advertise hockey as the path to a college scholarship in the United States.

The Bombers' training camp began the morning after my arrival. Eighty-four teenagers turned up for tryouts at the Forum, most driven from prairie towns across western Canada by their fathers. Razor, dressed in a Bombers' track suit, maroon with slashes of white and black, positioned himself at center ice. His seventy-three-year-old father, Wild Bill, stood in the broadcast booth above, scouting the players. When Razor blew his whistle, the hopefuls skated at full speed; when Razor blew the whistle again, they slowed to a coast. At the scrimmages that weekend, Flin Flonners drinking coffee from Styrofoam cups wandered in and out of the arena, their ebb and flow marking the beginning and end of shifts at HBM&S. Like contestants in a beauty pageant, the players had only a fleeting chance to catch the eye of Razor and his coaching staff; unlike beauty contestants, these hopefuls were allowed full body contact and fights. Three, six, eleven—I lost count. The fights seemed to come out of nowhere, with nothing that could sanely be described as provocation but, for all that, with a certain unity of form: the stare-off, the twitching of a gloved hand, and the unmistakable message "Ya wanna go?" Then, striptease-like, the stick was dropped, gloves fell, elbow pads were thrown aside, helmets were taken off—a bravura gesture shunning any effete protection—and two players circled each other, fists cocked.

On Saturday morning, Sides arrived in Flin Flon from Moose Jaw. He was seventeen, skinny, shy; he wore a Christian Athlete Hockey Camps windbreaker. Razor and Wild Bill were excited that Sides, a late cut by the Warriors of the elite Western Hockey League, was in town. Rodge and Meeks, twenty-year-old veterans and leaders on the team, had heard about Sides, too, and decided to put the rookie arriviste to the test. Sides had played only a couple of shifts in an intrasquad match before Meeks was yammering at him, challenging him to a fight. Looking both terrified and afraid to look terrified, Sides skated away from Meeks. "Leave him alone," Razor called down from the press box. "Keep in touch with yourself."

"Meeks isn't the right guy. He's too good a fighter," Razor said to me. "We'll send someone else, and if the kid answers the bell and stands up for himself, he'll be accepted by the team. If he doesn't, we'll go from there." Sides scored three goals that session. The next afternoon he fought Ferlie, a man-child six inches shorter than Sides but an absurdly eager and able fighter. Skate-to-skate, lefts and rights were thrown in flurries. Sides's head bounced off the Plexiglas as he and Ferlie wrestled each other to the ice. The players on the benches stood and slapped their sticks against the boards in applause. Sides and Ferlie checked their lips for blood, shook hands, exchanged a grin.

Northern Exposure—An Exciting Kickoff Tournament of Junior A Hockey started the following Friday when the Bombers played the North Battleford North Stars. A few hundred miners stood along the guardrails, among them Meeks's father in a T-shirt that said TOUGH SIMBA and featured a lion cub chewing on a piece of steel. The Forum's southwest corner was dotted with students from Hapnot Collegiate, the boys near the top and the girls closer to the ice. Security guards in Dadson Funeral Home jackets circled the arena. The Bombers skated out to cheers; the crowd stood, baseball caps off; a taped version of "O Canada" played; then, with sudden ferocity, Flin Flon's preseason hockey began. Players swarmed off the bench, bodies slammed into boards, the puck flew from end to end. Less than two minutes into the game, the North Stars scored on Dodger, the Bombers' first-string goalie, in a scramble in front of the net. Thirty seconds later, Ferlie was sent off for roughing. Less than ten seconds after that, a teenage girl in the stands was hit in the face by an errant puck; she casually threw the puck back on the ice. Four minutes and ten seconds into the opening period, Dodger let in a second goal, a wrist shot from the top of the slot. During the playoffs the previous season, Dodger had made sixty-two saves in an overtime loss in Watrous, a feat his teammates spoke of with hushed awe, but today Dodger couldn't stop a thing. Two minutes and fifty-three seconds later Meeks got a penalty for slashing. Fourteen seconds later Rodge scored for Flin Flon. Air horns sounded and Bachman-Turner Overdrive's "Takin' Care of Business" blared over the speakers. And on it went: sticks whacked across legs, gloves rubbed into faces after the whistle, the game a relentless, Hobbesian cartoon of taliation and retaliation, misconduct, inciting misconduct, and gross misconduct. Rodge, the most gifted player on the Bombers, stopped on the way to the dressing room at the end of the first period to sign autographs for children calling out his name. "It's a *Gong Show* out there," he said to me. "It's always the same in exhibition season."

Between periods, I followed a crowd to the bar in the curling club next door to the arena. A dozen men were sitting at a table drinking rye whiskey. What did they think of their team this year? I asked. "Pussies," they said. What did they think of Razor? "Pussy." A former Bomber, slurring drunk, reminisced about his glory days—when Flin Flon, he boasted, was the toughest town anywhere. Picking up on the theme, a burly man who called himself Big Eyes and whose son had captained the Bombers a few years earlier, told a story about an all-you-can-eat-and-drink charity fund-raiser a few years back at which a brawl broke out. Big Eyes couldn't remember why or how the fight started; he did remember, he said with a glint in his eye, that the raffle tickets he was supposed to sell the next morning were covered in blood.

I stepped outside for a breath of fresh air. Aurora borealis was out in the northern sky. A few feet away a little boy pushed another little boy onto the gravel in the parking lot. "Faggot," he said. The other little boy got to his feet and shoved back: "Faggot."

In the gazebo in front of Razor's cottage near Amisk Lake a few miles out of Flin Flon, the swarming mosquitoes and no-see-ums kept out by the screen, a red cooler stocked with beer, steaks ready for the barbecue, Razor and Wild Bill and the assistant coaches held a long debate, complete with diagrams, about the dressing room: Who should sit where? Who had earned a prime spot? Who needed to be sent a message? There was also the matter of the tampering dispute with the Opaskwayak Cree Nation Blizzard of The Pas, who, Razor said, had had a Bomber player practice with their team. In compensation, Razor angrily had demanded $30,000 and the big defenseman or two he needed to round out his roster; the Blizzard were offering a forward they had imported from Sweden. The merits of a player from Thunder Bay on the verge of making the team were also discussed: he had the quickness to wrong-foot the defense, but he had a long mane of coiffed blond hair and wore an earring off the ice.

Razor wanted the Bombers to attack. On offense, in the grand banal tradition of Canadian hockey, the Bombers would "dump and chase": shoot the puck into the opposition's end, skate like hell after it, then crash bodies and hope to create a scoring chance. On defense they would "build a house": each player would be a pillar, spreading to the four corners of the defense zone, supporting one another, and moving the foundations of the house as one. Razor's team would forgo the flourishes of brilliance, the graceful swoop across the blue line, the geometrically improbable pass, the inspired end-to-end rush. They would play the man, not the puck. They would play what Razor called "ugly hockey." "You've got to play with balls, big balls," Razor had told the Bombers in the dressing room between periods in one of the Northern Exposure games. "Look at yourself in the mirror before you go back on the ice. Look in the mirror and ask yourself if you've got balls."

The Bomber players were very good, but two or three ingredients short of the strange brew that makes a professional athlete. Rodge lacked all-consuming desire. Woody was too thin, Quinny too plump, Reags too small. Meeks and Dodger were not dexterous enough in handling the puck. When I skated with them at morning practices, though, instead of seeing what they weren't, I saw what they were. They were fast and skilled and courageous: Rodge, with a low center of gravity, calm and anticipating the play; Woody grinning as he flew smoothly past a stumbling defenseman; Quinny letting go a slap shot and boom, a split second later, there's the satisfying report from the wooden boards; Dodger flicking a glove hand out to stop a wrist shot; Meeks trundling down the wing like a locomotive, upright, his legs spread wide, his face blank with pure joy.

Scrimmaging with the Bombers, the pace and sway of the game came back to me. Watching out for me—"Heads up, Scoop," "Man on, Scoop"—the Bombers hurled one another into the boards with abandon, the arena sounding with the explosive thud of compressed plastic colliding with compressed plastic. The speed of the game reduces the rink to the size of a basketball court. Things that are impossible to do on your feet—go twenty miles an hour, glide, turn on a dime—become possible. The body and mind are acutely aware of physical detail and, at the same time, are separated from the earth.

After *Northern Exposure*, Razor held the year's first team meeting in the Bombers' dressing room. Two dozen pairs of high-top sneakers were piled on the mats beside Beastie's Blades, the skate-sharpening concession next to the dressing room; Razor had recarpeted during the off-season, and no one except Hildy was allowed in without taking off his shoes. This season Razor had also put the team logo—the letter "B" exploding into fragments, a design donated by the company that had supplied HBM&S with its dynamite in the 1930s—on the floor under a two-foot-square piece of Plexiglas, as the Boston Bruins had done with their logo when Razor played for them. The dressing room was a dank cavern at the southeast corner of the arena, rich with the smells of decades of stale sweat. Its ceiling was marked with the autographs of Bombers of seasons past.

In front of their newly assigned stalls, Rodge rubbed Lester's ear with the blade of his stick and Reags rested his hand on Meeks's back. Dodger sat in a corner with his head in his hands. In their final game of the Northern Exposure tournament against the Dauphin Kings, with the Bombers trailing 4–1 in the first period, Ferlie had started a line brawl; in an orgiastic outbreak of violence, all the players on the ice had begun to fight at the same time. Now Razor addressed the topic of fighting. Because of the SJHL's penalty of compulsory ejection from the rest of the game for fighting, Razor said, other teams would send mediocre players out to try and goad Flin Flon's best players into scraps. "I know things are going to happen out on the ice. It's the nature of the game," Razor said as he paced the room. "But Rodge, Lester, Schultzie, the goal scorers, you can't fight unless you take an equally talented player with you. If we lose one of our best, we need them to lose one of their best."

"You told Ferlie to fight against Dauphin," Rodge said.

"No," Razor explained, "I didn't tell Ferlie to fight. We were getting beaten and I said, 'If you want to start something, now would be a good time.'"

The Bombers all laughed.

Razor turned to Meeks. "Meeks, I don't want you to fight. The other team plays two inches taller when they don't have to worry about you. We need the intimidation factor of you out there banging and crashing." Razor said he wanted to change Meeks's role. He wanted Meeks to be a grinder, not an enforcer. He wanted Meeks to skate up and down his wing, using his size to open up space on the ice.

At the barbecue in Razor's gazebo, Meeks had been a topic of concern. The coaches were worried that Meeks was under too much pressure at home. Meeks's father and brother wanted Meeks to ask for a trade; at practice one morning, Meeks's father had told me he didn't think the Bombers had a chance this season because they had too many rookies on the team. Maybe, one of the coaches had suggested, Meeks should move out of his family's house ten miles out of town and billet with another family in Flin Flon. "I want to give the kid the world," Razor said. "He deserves it. If I ask him to do anything, he'll do it. He's vulnerable, though."

The rhythms of the hockey season set in quickly: practice at eight in the morning so that the players still in high school could get to class on time, lunch at Subway, long empty afternoons, fund-raising appearances to sell Share of the Wealth and Pic-A-Pot cards to chain-smoking bingo players. Paul Royter, a hypnotist, came to town for a three-night stand at the R. H. Channing Auditorium, and half a dozen Bombers went up onstage to fall under Royter's spell, which, it turned out, meant lip-synching to Madonna and Garth Brooks. The legal drinking age in Manitoba is eighteen, and most of the players on the team were old enough to go to bars, but Razor had banned the Bombers from Flin Flon's beverage rooms, a rule he waived only once so that some of the boys could go to a matinee performance by Miss Nude Winnipeg. Nineteen of twenty-three Bombers were not from Flin Flon, and Razor told me that resentful locals would try to beat up the Bombers if they went into a bar.

On the second Saturday in September, Razor lifted the Bombers' eleven o'clock curfew to let the team watch the final game of the World Cup between Canada and the United States. Late that afternoon, carrying the twelve-pack of pilsner I had been advised to bring along, I went to Ev's place. Ev was one of the locals playing for Flin Flon, and his parents had taken in Bombers from out of town as billets for years. This season Rodge and Dodger were staying in Ev's parents' basement. With hockey posters and the autographs of the Bombers who had passed through their doors written on the basement walls, Ev's place was a fantasyland for a teenager living away from home: pool table, beer fridge, a couple of mattresses on the floor beside the furnace, a hot tub on the patio.

At twilight, Bornie, Reags, and I piled into a car and drove past houses, searching for the party. We found that Funk, who had played for Flin Flon a few years ago, was having a shake at his house. Rodge and Woody were sitting on the floor of the den playing a drinking game with Holly, Melanie, and Deanna, the girls who arrived fashionably late for the hockey games and sat slightly apart from the rest of the Hapnot section—the girls whom the players, and the town, called Pucks or Bikes.

"You want to play, Scoop?" Rodge asked me.

I looked down at a salad bowl filled with beer.

"No, no thanks," I said.

We got back into Bornie's car and went to Hildy's billet a few blocks away. More than half the Bombers were there, some sipping Coke, most with a twelve-pack of Molson Canadian or Labatt Blue between their legs. It had been front-page news that in the semifinal match between Russia and America, played in Ottawa, the Canadian crowd had cheered for the Russians and booed the Americans. Now Canada was playing the United States.

"All the guys who treat women with respect are here," Meeks said as the game started.

"Who's going to get on the phone and find the chicks?" Schultzie asked.

"Skulls knows where they are," Ev said.

"I do not," Skulls said.

"Don't hold out on us," Schultzie said.

"I don't know where they are," Skulls said. "I swear on hockey."

The game between Canada and America was played at an astonishing pace. Both teams were dumping and chasing, cycling the puck against the boards, relying as much on muscle and force as on skill. The majority of players in the NHL are Canadian, but because franchises in Quebec and

Winnipeg have relocated to major-market cities in the United States in recent years and because the economics of hockey are changing and growing vastly more expensive and lucrative, it is a common complaint that the game is being Americanized. Still, three of the players on the Canadian team had played in the Saskatchewan Junior Hockey League, and some of the Americans had played junior hockey in western Canada as their apprenticeship for the NHL. The SJHL influence on the style of play was obvious. This World Cup game was, in its way, ugly hockey.

"Gretzky sucks," Skulls said in the middle of the second period. "He's a pussy."

"You're full of shit," Quinny said. "He's the greatest player of all time."

"He's a floater," Skulls said. "He doesn't go into the corners. He's not a team player."

Lester turned to Dodger. "That Swede Razor might get from The Pas is gay, eh."

In the next second Canada scored to take a 2–1 lead. We leapt to our feet and let out a huge cheer. Chief, a big defenseman from Patuanak, a Native community in the far north of Saskatchewan, stayed sitting.

"I want the Americans to win," Chief said. "They're playing the same way as Canadians and they're playing better."

"Yankee lover," Bornie said.

In the third period the Americans scored to tie the game and then scored again to take the lead. Canada came back with increased desperation. The faces of the Team Canada players were drawn, anxious: Canada's destiny and national pride were at stake. But the Americans withstood the onslaught. In the dying seconds, a pass came to Wayne Gretzky in front of an open net. Gretzky, so many times the hero, missed the puck as it flitted off the ice and went over his stick. Canada had lost.

"I wouldn't mind losing to the Russians," Reags said on the ride back to my apartment. "But not the fucking Americans—always bragging all the time, so cocky. It's not fair. It's our game."

"Fishy fishy in the lake,
Come and bite my piece of bait. . . .
Fishy fishy in the brook,
Come and bite my juicy hook."

Meeks repeated his good-luck mantra as we trolled for pickerel on the southern shore of Amisk Lake. It was the morning after the Canada–U.S. game, and Razor had organized a team fishing trip. Meeks and I were in a small boat, the outboard motor chugging, a cool breeze creasing the black water. At a Bombers meeting a few days earlier, Razor had announced that Lester would be the captain; Rodge, Airsy, and Woody, the assistant captains. Meeks had hung his head in disappointment. Razor told me he didn't want to put too much strain on Meeks. "I'm still a leader on this team," Meeks said to me. During the exhibition season, he had often played doubled up in pain, his face contorted into a grimace. He had, he told me, ulcerative colitis, an extremely painful stomach disease brought on by stress, and he had forgotten to take his medication. He had moved out of his family's home and was living in town now with Reags's family.

I asked Meeks what it was like growing up in Flin Flon. "It was different," he said. "There were a lot of rock fights. Guys'd get hit in the head all the time. Once you got hit, everyone would come running and start apologizing. It was a good time."

When Meeks was thirteen, his father and brother had taught him how to fight in the garage after school. "I'd put the hockey helmet on, and they'd show me how to pull the jersey over a guy's head, to keep your head up, when to switch hands." Listening to Meeks, I couldn't help but remember when I was thirteen. My father had made it a rule that if I fought in a hockey game he would not allow me to keep playing. The first time he missed a game, I fought. After the game, the father of the player I fought tried to attack me. The fathers of my teammates had to escort me from the arena. It was terrifying.

A few of the Bombers had told me about the present that Meeks's older brother—a giant of a man and an ex-Bomber, with 30 points and 390 penalty minutes in one season—had given Meeks for his eighteenth birthday: a beating. "Yeah, he did, Scoop," Meeks said sheepishly. "My brother would say, 'I can't wait until you turn eighteen, because I'm going to lay a licking on you.' The day of my birthday he saw me and started coming after me. I grabbed a hockey stick and started swinging, nailing him in the back, just cracking him. It didn't even faze him. Next thing you know, my jersey's over my head and he's beating the crap out of me. My mom and one of my brother's friends hopped in and broke her up."

"Why did your brother do that?" I asked.

Meeks shrugged. "I turned eighteen."

He expertly teased his line. "I just want to turn into a professional fisherman," he said. "Stay out on the water and think about life."

Most days Dodger wandered the parking lots and streets of Flin Flon in search of empty pop cans, nonrefundable in Manitoba but worth a nickel across the border in Saskatchewan. Because his billet at Ev's place was at the other end of town, Dodger had taken to storing his jumbo plastic bags filled with crushed cans in the front yard of the apartment I had rented for the month. During training camp I had met Dodger's father, an anxious, eager-to-please man. "He's hard on himself," Dodger's father said of his son. "I tell him to relax, let life take its part."

Dodger, like many goalies, was probably the most skilled athlete on the team, agile and fast and alert. He was in his fourth season in the SJHL but had played poorly in the exhibition games and practices. He had let in soft goals and had even pulled himself from a game against the Nipawin Hawks after they had scored six times by the beginning of the second period. He had seemed to disappear into his equipment, his face hidden behind his mask, and the slow, ponderous way he had of moving off the ice had been replaced by nervous twitching. It is a hockey cliché that goalies, who stand alone in their net, are the game's eccentrics, and Dodger, who would sit quietly staring at the floor in team meetings and didn't much go for "the rah-rah and all that," was allowed that latitude. Still, Don, one of Razor's assistant coaches, was angry that Dodger wasn't taking the games seriously enough. "He's going around saying it's only exhibition season. I don't like that. That kid's got to be focused from day one."

But there was a reason for Dodger's lack of focus. "I've got a real story for you, Scoop," he said to me one morning after practice. "It's got nothing to do with hockey, though." Dodger's real story, the one that had been playing on his mind constantly, and which he told me in pieces over a few days when I passed the time helping him look for pop cans, began the Easter weekend of 1995, when Dodger was back home in Regina, Saskatchewan. He and Al, his best friend and an old hockey buddy, had been on a jag, hitting bars, going to parties, the same sort of things I did when I was around his age and living in the same city. On Sunday night, after drinking beer and Southern Comfort in the parking lot beside a hockey arena, Dodger was too ill to carry on. Al borrowed Dodger's fleece hockey jacket, took Dodger's bottle of Southern Comfort, and went downtown with another friend, Steve, to pick up a hooker. Unable to coax a prostitute into the car, Al hid in the trunk until they found a woman willing to get in with Steve. She was a Saulteau woman from the Sakinay Reserve named Pamela Jean George.

"I was watching the news the next night with another friend," Dodger said, "and a story came on about the murder of Pamela Jean George, and my friend said, 'Can you keep a secret?' I go, 'Sure.' He goes, 'They killed her.'" Al and Steve, white boys from the well-to-do south end of the city, both athletes, popular, good-looking, had, according to Dodger's friend, taken Pamela Jean George to the outskirts of town, where she had given them oral sex. Al and Steve then took her out of the car, brutally beat her, and left her for dead, facedown in a ditch. Al split for British Columbia the next day without saying good-bye to Dodger. Steve stuck around. One week passed. Another week. Dodger was constantly sick to his stomach. He thought it was only a matter of time before they would be caught. He didn't know about Betty Osborne, a Cree girl from The Pas, who was pulled off the street and killed by local white boys in 1971. In Betty Osborne's case, the open secret of who had done it was kept for nearly sixteen years until, at last, in 1987, three men were charged and one was convicted of second-degree murder.

Finally, with no news of the investigation and the growing prospect that Al and Steve would never be caught, Dodger felt that he was going to crack. At a friend's wedding reception, he told someone who he knew would tell the police. A couple of days later, while Dodger was watching an NHL playoff game, the police called him. "The cops wouldn't have had a fucking clue," Dodger said to me. "They were looking for pimps, prostitutes, lower-class people." Dodger was, he told me, scheduled to testify against Al and Steve in a few weeks, and he was finding it difficult to concentrate on hockey.

"I'll tell you what I'm really bitter about: people hinting that it's all my fault. The guy who told me about it in the first place came up to me at a party and said, 'I know this may sound harsh, but I'm going to have a tough time feeling sorry for you because I know it got out at the wedding reception.' And I was like, 'Who the fuck are you to talk to me? Show a little nuts.' This guy tries to play the role, like it's been really tough for him. I heard girls were calling him and saying, 'I feel so sorry for you, losing your friends. If you need someone to talk to I'm always here.' If girls called me I'd say, 'Fuck you. Don't feel sorry for me, feel sorry for Pamela Jean George.'"

Ever since I had arrived in Flin Flon and had heard about the Pucks and Bikes, I had wanted to meet them. Ev, one of the Bombers who was still going to Hapnot Collegiate, convinced the girls to meet and talk with me at twilight at the Donut King.

"I don't understand why anyone would write about Flin Flon," Susie said to me from behind the counter as I waited for the Pucks and Bikes. Because I had no telephone in my apartment, the Donut King had become a kind of makeshift office, and for weeks, with increasing bemusement, Susie had watched me shouting over the howling northern wind into the pay phone in the lobby. "There's nothing to write about," she said, smiling. I asked Susie if she ever went to Bombers' games. "I went this year to see if any of them were cute," she said. "They might look okay, but once you get up close they have zits or their teeth are crooked. I guess I went to see them lose, because they suck and I want to see them get killed."

"Would you date a Bomber?" I asked. "I'm not allowed to," she said. "My sister says, 'As if I'm going to let you walk around town and have people say, "There's your Bike sister."'"

Just then the Bikes pulled up in a blue Mustang and I took my leave of Susie. The car smelled of perfume and tobacco and chewing gum. We drove out to the town dump, where we sat and watched fifteen or so brown and black bears pick through the garbage and stare at the car's headlights. Holly, who had had a long plume of blonde hair when I had seen her at the Bombers' games and who now had a pixie haircut—the plume had been hair extensions, it turned out—was the femme fatale of Flin Flon: du Maurier cigarette, bare midriff. She told me that when she was dating Rodge last season her ex-boyfriend, a local she had dumped in favor of Rodge, had jumped up on the Plexiglas at the end of a game and screamed at Rodge, "I'm going to kill you!" This year, though, Holly said she wasn't interested in any of the players. "I don't have a crush. I wish I did. I'm guy crazy like hell, but I'm not even attracted to any of them."

Deanna, who was driving the car and had a pierced eyebrow, purple hair, and an inner-city hipster's Adidas sweat top on, allowed that she had a crush on one of the Bombers. Melanie, quiet in the back seat with cherry-colored lipstick and a sweater around her waist, told me she had one real crush and another crush she was faking so that an awkward, shy Bomber wouldn't feel left out.

"The players say we're Pucks," Holly said, "but they're the ones who phone us. We don't even give them the time of day and they're asking, 'What're you doing tonight? You want to come over?' Without us they wouldn't have any friends in Flin Flon."

The spectacle of the bears began to wear thin. The girls suggested we drive to the sandpit on the other side of what used to be Lake Flin Flon and watch the nightly pouring of the slag at the HBM&S smelter. The slag pouring was a disappointment: a thin line of lava red barely visible against pitch black, steam rising and joining the sulphur dioxide chugging out of the company smokestack. Afterward, over strawberry milkshakes at the A&W, the girls told me about teen culture in Flin Flon: cruising around looking for house parties, driving to hangouts in the forest outside town—the Hoop, the Curve, the Toss Off—lighting a fire and drinking beer until the police chased them. Deanna said, "Flin Flon was in *The Guinness Book of World Records* for the most beer bought per capita in a weekend, or something like that."

"I hate rye," Holly announced. "I get into fights when I drink rye." She told me about the Boxing Day social last year. "This girl pissed me off, so me and a friend tag-teamed her. My friend slapped her and I threw my drink on her and she started blabbing at me so I grabbed her and kicked her in the head and ripped all her hair out. She was bald when I was done." The girl had to go to the hospital to have her broken nose set, Holly said, now speaking in quiet tones because she had noticed the girl's aunt a few tables down from us. "And then she went to the cop shop and filed charges, even though she was four years older than me."

Melanie and Deanna exchanged a furtive glance. They had never been in a fight; Holly had never lost a fight.

Saturday night was hockey night in Flin Flon. Game-day notices in the store windows along Main Street advertised that evening's match against the Humboldt Broncos. The night before, in the opening game of the regular season, the Bombers had defeated Humboldt 2–1. Beastie, who drove the tractor that cleans the ice at the Forum, toked on an Old Port cigarillo. "Pretty tame last night," he said. On the ice, the Stittco Flames were practicing before the main event. A dozen girls, including Razor's eleven-year-old daughter, who had recently given herself the nickname Maloots, skated lengths of the ice and worked on passing and shooting the puck. At the end of the session one of the girls dropped her gloves as if she wanted to fight and then, in full hockey uniform, turned and did a graceful lutz.

It had been payday at the company the day before, and 700 fans, nearly a tenth of Flin Flon's population, came to watch the game. In the Bombers' dressing room, the players sat and listened to Razor, their foreheads beaded with sweat from the pre-game skate. The new jerseys had arrived, and the pants and gloves the Bombers had bought secondhand from the Peterborough Petes of the elite Ontario Hockey League, the only other team in Canada with maroon-and-white colors, had been passed out. Norm Johnston, the coach of the Broncos, had coached in Flin Flon in the early 1990s, and his teams had a reputation for fighting and intimidation. Razor, in his game attire of shirt and tie, black sports coat, and tan cowboy boots, paced the room and told the Bombers that Johnston would try to set the tone of play but that they should not allow themselves to be provoked. What *did* Razor want to see from his players? He wrote the homilies on his Coach's Mate as Bombers called them out rapid-fire:

HARD WORK
INTENSITY
INTELLIGENCE
UGLINESS

"How about the Whitney Forum?" Razor asked. The Bombers began to chatter: "C'mon boys!" "It's our barn!" "Fucking rights!"

"We're going to own the building," Razor said. "We're going to *rock* the Whitney fucking Forum! We're going to take the fucking roof off!"

Two and a half minutes into the first period Rodge and Schultzie had scored, and twice "Takin' Care of Business" had played on the loudspeakers. Razor's ugly hockey had the Broncos disoriented and backing off by half a step. I sat with Meghan and her friends in the Hapnot section as they tried, with little success, to start a wave. Meghan was a senior, a mousy blonde, petite and pretty in a woolly-sweater, Sandra Dee kind of way. She was the daughter of an HBM&S geologist; Meeks was the son of a union man. Most afternoons I would see Meghan and Meeks walking down Main Street holding hands. In the stands, she told me she had never seen Meeks fight. "I didn't come to the games last year, before we started dating. I tell him not to fight, because he's not like that. He's really gentle. He should write on his stick: LOVER NOT A FIGHTER."

By the second period, the Bombers were leading 4–1 and completely outplaying the Broncos, but the Flin Flon fans had turned on their own team. Johnston, as Razor had predicted, had seen to it that the Broncos were slashing and shoving and trying to pick fights. And the Bombers weren't fighting back. Humboldt would get penalties, Razor had told the Bombers, and Flin Flon could take advantage of power plays. "Homo!" Flin Flonners screamed at the Bombers. "Pussy!" Woody, the Bombers' best defenseman, fell to the ice and covered his head as a Humboldt player tried to pummel him. A minute later, Turkey, another Bomber defenseman, did the same thing, but the referee, who had lost control of the game by now, gave Turkey a penalty anyway. Ev was sticked in the stomach by a Bronco but didn't retaliate.

"You're a fucking woman!" Meeks's older brother shouted at Ev from the railing. In a scrum in front of the Bombers' net, Meeks was punched in the head, but he, too, followed Razor's instructions and didn't fight. It didn't matter, though: both Meeks and the Bronco got kicked out of the game. Meeks was jeered as he skated off.

A chubby twenty-one-year-old sitting near me, dressed in a leather jacket with the Canadian flag on the sleeve and unwilling to give his name in case the players read this article, explained why he was hurling abuse at Flin Flon: "It's embarrassing to the fans, to the team, the town. You look at all the banners hanging from the rafters, all the tough guys who have played here. The Bombers should have the balls to drop their gloves."

In the dressing room between the second and third periods, the faces of the Bombers' coaching staff were pale: Flin Flon was easily winning the game, but they were also, absurdly, losing. The Whitney Forum, territory, pride, tradition, manliness were being attacked. The game was, as Razor had told the Bombers repeatedly, war; it was, in the Clausewitzian sense, the continuation of hockey by other means.

At the start of the third period, after a quick shower, Meeks came and sat with Meghan and me. "I talked to my dad and my brother," he said. "My brother told me to fight. Fuck him." Meeks and Meghan held hands as we watched twenty minutes of mega-violence. When number twenty-two for the Broncos skated to center ice and dropped his gloves, challenging someone, anyone, to a fight, Bornie took him on. There was a loud cheer. Lester fought at the drop of the puck. Airsy beat up a Humboldt player and winked to the Hapnot section as he was led to the dressing room for the compulsory penalty. Schultzie ran his fingers through his peroxided hair before he swapped blows with a Bronco. "People are getting scared to play now," Meeks said. At the final siren, with both benches nearly empty because of all the players ejected from the game, a Bronco was still chasing Skulls around the ice.

The Bombers' dressing room was a riot of whoops and hollers. Flin Flon had won the game. Flin Flon had won the fights. "That's the way a weekend of hockey should be in Flin Flon!" Razor bellowed.

In the midst of the celebration the head of the local Royal Canadian Mounted Police knocked on the door and brought a little redheaded boy with a broken arm in to meet the Bombers. "All right guys, watch the swearing," Razor said. The tiny Flin Flonner went around and shook the players' hands.

Six days later, in the middle of a five-night, four-game road trip, the Bombers' bus barreled south through the narrow rutted back roads of Saskatchewan toward the prairie town of Weyburn. Razor and Wild Bill and Blackie, the radio announcer who broadcast the games back to Flin Flon, sat at the front of the bus, Razor thumbing through the copy of *Men Are From Mars, Women Are From Venus* that his wife had asked him to pick up while he was on the road. Behind them, the twenty-three Bombers were splayed in their seats. The dress code most of the boys follow for official team functions—shirt and tie, Bombers' jacket or suit jacket, baseball cap—eased as ties were loosened and gangly limbs stretched across the aisle. It was quiet on the bus; after losing to the Yorkton Terriers in the first game of the trip, Razor had told the team that he wanted them to visualize that night's upcoming game against the Red Wings. Razor had also told Dodger that he would be the starting goalie for the first time in the regular season. There had been a mistrial in Al and Steve's case, and Dodger's testimony had been postponed indefinitely; Razor hoped that, with the pressure off, Dodger would begin to play up to his abilities. A few rows behind Dodger, Meeks leaned his head against the window. He was growing his whiskers in a wild, slanted way, with seemingly random slashes of the razor running across his face. He had had a terrible dream the night before. He couldn't remember what it was, but it was terrible. And his medication wasn't working, so his stomach was giving him awful pain.

In the back row of the bus, where I had been assigned a seat, I sat with a few of the players and watched the harvest prairie roll by. "I think it's brutal if people say you can't play hockey and be a Christian," Bornie said to me. "I just watch my mouth, try not to swear, and do my job. If you have to fight, you fight."

"It's not up to Christians to judge others for swearing," said Schrades, the other Bomber goalie. "We don't judge them for *not* swearing."

"They can do whatever the fuck they want," Ev said.

"You'll go to hell," Sides said to Ev. "That's the truth."

"Judgment Day is so hypocritical," Ev said. "Christians are supposed to be forgiving, and then they say anyone who doesn't believe can't come into heaven even if they're a good person."

"It's hard not to sin out on the ice," Airsy said.

"I'll probably go to heaven," Shultzie said.

When we arrived in Weyburn and walked into the Colosseum I had a shock of recognition. The last time I had been in the Colosseum was in the late 1970s, just before I "got a letter" offering me a tryout with the Regina Silver Foxes, a now-defunct franchise in the Saskatchewan Junior Hockey League. Everything about the Colosseum had seemed huge then, the stands and ice surface and the red-and-white banners hanging from the rafters. I didn't want to take road trips and miss school, I had a bad knee, I wanted to drink beer and chase after girls. That's what I told my teammates, Boner and Dirt and Cement. I had lost touch with them long ago, but I knew they had all gone on to play professional hockey. The real reason I quit playing, though, what I didn't tell my friends, was that at the time, I had grown to hate hockey. It was in rinks like the Colosseum that I realized I had become, as they would say in Flin Flon, a pussy.

By game time, the Colosseum was nearly full. Many of the people in the stands were parents of Flin Flon players from farms and towns in southern Saskatchewan. Weyburn had won the league championship two of the last three years and had a team stacked with imports from Quebec and northern California and Latvia. When the Bombers skated out to a chorus of boos, Meeks, following his pre-game ritual, went straight to the bench and took off his helmet and gloves and lowered his head and prayed. In minutes the Red Wings were all over the Bombers. Dodger's play, unlike his nervous, uneven play in the exhibition season, was sensational—diving, sprawling, kicking shots away with his leg pads. On a clean breakaway for Weyburn, Dodger made an acrobatic save. A few seconds later he gloved a slap shot from the point. I stood and whooped. The Bombers began to come back, Rodge swooping past the Weyburn blue line with the puck and taking a wrist shot from ten feet out. Frustrated, the momentum now with Flin Flon, the Red Wings started to hack at the Bombers. With only seconds left in the first period, number seventeen for Weyburn hit Woody in the face with his stick.

In the second period, the score still 0–0, Seventeen skated past Sides and whipped his feet out from underneath him. Called for a penalty, Seventeen shot the puck at the linesman. It was, I thought, a familiar script: ripples become waves and rise rhythmically, climax-like, toward the fight. But then, suddenly and unpredictably, the Red Wings scored three quick goals on

Dodger. "Sieve! Sieve!" the crowd taunted Dodger. Meeks skated out to take a shift. The puck was dropped, and Skulls, who was playing center, went into the corner after it. Seventeen followed Skulls and slammed him into the boards. Skulls's helmet came off, and Seventeen, seemingly twice Skulls's size, kept shoving, ramming Skulls's face into the Plexiglas. Across the rink, Meeks had dropped his gloves. He skated toward Seventeen, throwing off his helmet and tossing his elbow pads aside.

Meeks had explained his fighting technique to me back in Flin Flon: "I can't punch the other guy first," he said. "That's why I've got a lot of stitches. The other guy always gets the first punch and then I get mad." Meeks took the first punch from Seventeen square in the jaw. Meeks's head jerked back. He grabbed Seventeen by the collar and threw a long, looping, overhand right. He pulled Seventeen's jersey over his head. Another shot, a right jab, an uppercut; switched hands, a combination of lefts. A strange sound came from the audience, a mounting, feverish cry: Seventeen was crumpling, arms flailing, as the linesmen stepped in and separated the two. Meeks waved to his teammates as he was led off the ice by the officials to the screams of the Weyburn fans. The Bombers scored four minutes later. Between periods in the dressing room Razor shook Meeks's hand. "Great job."

Two days later we crossed the border into the United States, heading for Minot, North Dakota, and an encounter with the Top Guns, the only American franchise in the Saskatchewan Junior Hockey League. The flat of the prairies became the dun-colored hills and valleys of the North Dakota Badlands, the face of each rise marked by massive stones arranged to spell "Class of 19—" for each year of the past five decades.

Ev, who had never been to the United States before, chanted every thirty seconds, "This is the furthest south I've ever been. This is the furthest south I've ever been."

"I don't like it here," Rodge said. "It's too far from home."

"People aren't as nice in the States," Bornie said.

"Look at that shitty little American town," Lester said as we drove through a roadside village. "It sucks cock compared to a little Canadian town." Lester and a couple of the Bombers began to hum the Guess Who song "American Woman."

When we arrived at the All Seasons Arena, Liberace's version of "Blue Tango" was echoing through the building as the Magic Blades, Minot's nationally ranked precision skating team, worked on their routine. The rink was in the middle of the fairground, a modern complex, new and brightly lit, with no banners hanging from the rafters and no memorabilia on display. Joey, a Minot player from southern Manitoba and a friend of Meeks and Woody and Ferlie, joked with the Bombers before the game. "They play the American anthem," Joey said, "and we have to stand there and listen, and we're, like, we couldn't give a shit."

For local high school hockey games, one of the Magic Blades told me, the place was packed with more than 3,000 fans, the crowd led by cheerleaders with pom-poms and fight songs, but only 452 turned up to watch the Bombers and the Top Guns.

"Let's get ready to rumble!" the announcer yelled over the loudspeaker as the Top Guns and Bombers skated out for the game.

In the stands, eating french fries covered in ketchup and vinegar, Meeks told me about the Weyburn game and his fight. He showed me his hands. The knuckles were badly swollen and cut. "Seventeen stuck Woody in the face in the first period," he said. "I wasn't on the ice then, but the whole game he was slashing and punching people, going after Sides and Skulls. Between periods, Razor came into the room and said to wait until the third period and someone's going to take care of Seventeen. He looked at me but he didn't say anything. I knew my role. I'd be the one taking care of it."

Meeks couldn't play and wasn't sure when he would be able to play again.

"I called Meghan and told her I broke my hand," he said. "She said, 'You did not.' I said I did, I had to fight. She said I shouldn't fight. She said that I always have a choice."

There was a long silence. On the first day of the road trip, less than an hour out of Flin Flon, Meeks had asked me how to write a love poem. Should it rhyme? he asked. What should a love poem say? For almost a week he had scribbled notes in the blue spiral notebook that he used to write to Meghan. For now, though, Meeks had given up on writing poetry; he could barely bend his fingers, and he thought his thumb was dislocated again.

After the game, driving through the fairground, it was quiet on the Bombers' bus. The Bombers had played four games on the road and had lost four very close games. Cokes and chocolate chip cookies Sides's mother had baked for the team were passed around. Ahead there was a thirteen-hour ride north through the ancient rock of the Precambrian shield, through swales of muskeg, endless stands of jack pine and spruce and trembling aspen, the bus swerving occasionally to miss caribou and wolves that had strayed onto the road.

The next day, before I left Flin Flon, I went to skate with the Bombers one last time. At the Forum, Beastie told me about Blackie's broadcast of Meeks's fight in Weyburn. "Blackie pretty near creamed his jeans," Beastie said. "He's describing the bout, all the shots Meeks is getting in, and he's yelling, 'There's a good old home-town Bomber beating!'"

In the dressing room, Reags came and sat beside me. He was upset that I was leaving with the Bombers on a losing skid. I should stay until Friday, he said, when they were sure to defeat the Melville Millionaires. I pulled on my jock pad, shin pads, shoulder pads, elbow pads, jersey; wrapped tape around pads, and fastened Velcro tags—a sequence I had repeated since I was scarcely old enough for kindergarten. I tightened the laces of my skates and stood and walked out of the Bombers' dressing room, past a sign with one of those sports clichés on it—IT'S MORE THAN A GAME—and glided onto a clean sheet of ice, the smack of pucks against the boards echoing around the empty stands.

After I left town, Flin Flon would suffer another losing streak, and, after a dispute with the team's board of directors over trading Schultzie for a defenseman, Razor would be fired. Dodger would testify against Al and Steve in the murder trial. The killers, relying for their defense on their intoxication and diminished responsibility, would be convicted of manslaughter and given sentences of six and a half years each, with parole possible in only three and a half years. Dodger would be traded to a team in another junior league. The Bombers' new coach would ask Meeks to fight all the time; Meeks would lose confidence and would have a screaming argument with the coach. Two games before the end of the season, he would get kicked off the team. He would not be allowed in the team photograph. The Bombers would finish last in their division.

On my last day in Flin Flon, after practice, Dodger stopped by my place to pick up the enormous plastic bags filled with crushed pop cans that he had collected in the past month. As he gathered his cans from the yard, Dodger showed me the letter he had drafted to send to Harvard, Brown, Cornell, and a bunch of other American schools, to inquire about playing for them next season. It was still September, but it had snowed in Flin Flon and the cold of the coming winter was in the air. Shifts were changing in the company, and Main Street was lined with pickup trucks. Dodger zipped up his fleece Bombers' jacket. Maybe he would try to play professionally in Europe, he said. He was in his final year of eligibility for junior hockey, but he wanted to keep playing. ◆

A Poisoned Russian King

(DECEMBER 1973)

Nicholas Bethell

On July 14, at the end of the European Championships in Bath, England, Boris Spassky came to dinner with me in London and afterward played chess against us. Of course it was quite ludicrous of us to take him on, like taking a swing at Muhammad Ali in a public bar. And to make our humiliation complete Spassky decided to lead with the chin. In one game he made a series of appalling moves, leaving his defenses wide open. We rushed into the attack only to be astoundingly checkmated with a short, sharp blow. Spassky then demonstrated how we *should* have played the situation, how with a little foresight we could easily have beaten him.

In another game he began by moving his king straight into the middle of the board, which is chess madness, and within a few moves we had chances to checkmate him. At first these were difficult problems, three- or four-move combinations, and every time we missed them Spassky moved a piece back and showed us what we should have done. He managed to make the task easier and easier until finally we got it and we had mated the ex-world champion. Everyone's eyes lit up, ours with a sort of perverse triumph, his with the simple pleasure of having made us happy.

It was a relaxed, self-confident Spassky, very different from the one I met in Reykjavik last year just after he had suffered one of the most publicized defeats in the history of sport. Then there was the same humor and modesty, the same gentlemanly, old-fashioned politeness, but there was also a frightening degree of stress and worry. His head was so full of the match that he kept losing his train of thought. For days after his final resignation on the morning of September 1 the match had dominated his thoughts and dreams. "Two of the mistakes I made were the sort which would not be made by a fifth-class player," he told me. "It's been like playing a movie through backward. Why did I play P-B3 in game fourteen? Why did I play Kt-Q2 in game eight?"

Most games involve speed, pain, and exertion, and are over in two hours, but chess is slow and the world championship lasted two *months*. There was nothing physical to divert or numb the players' worrying brains. In such a situation psychology becomes very important. Spassky told me, "In a match like this one, chess skill is probably less than half the battle. The main element is nervous energy." Anyone who has played chess seriously knows how the mind can be almost paralyzed by a strenuous five-hour session, but I had always imagined that in the end skill must triumph. Not always so, apparently. A blow to your opponent's ego, on or off the board, can be more valuable than a pawn.

At first it seemed that Fischer must lose this off-the-board battle. Surely his tantrums would affect his game. Spassky was already in Reykjavik, seemingly cool, keeping himself fit with afternoons of tennis. Hearing that Fischer had yet again missed a flight from New York, he said, "I think he is lying in his bath gazing at the ceiling and thinking of me here waiting for him." He did not realize that these displays, far from exhausting the American, were building him up toward a peak of creative sensitivity.

In the end it was Spassky's game that suffered. When Fischer failed to appear at the opening ceremony, Spassky was faced with a terrible decision: should he play the match at all? "I would have been fully within my rights to leave Iceland, and if I had done this all chess players would have understood me. I could have gone home and remained champion." The Soviet chess authorities with their decades of supremacy must have been tempted by the idea of retaining the title so easily, if only by a technicality. Spassky was aware of such feelings. They influenced and confused him.

So already Fischer had an advantage. Spassky could retain the title, but only by looking as if he were afraid to meet his challenger. Chess is usually a gentle game, but here was this wild American behaving so erratically and with such rudeness that the match was going to become a duel to the psychological death, a mental shoot-out. Whatever happened, one of the two was going to be broken.

Spassky was made to continue by other, equally exhausting, personal feelings: "I decided that my main job was to meet Fischer and play him, because the whole chess world wanted the match to take place. Also I had this idea—maybe it's a bit naïve and silly—but I thought that if this match collapses, when I come to the end of my life, when I know I'm going to die. I may think to myself, 'What a fool I was to refuse to play because of some quarrel over formalities, because I wanted to show that I was in the right.' It was going to be the most interesting match of my career, and it was this that made me decide to play, because if I'd gone home the match would be lost. Whether I was in the right or not, at the end of the day no one would be the winner."

It is here that Spassky feels he dissipated his nervous energy. For months he had been preparing for this moment with a program of strenuous exercise, physical as well as mental, and suddenly here was a problem which knocked him quite off balance. He feels this is one reason why he played so badly in the first ten games. He says that there were moments, usually after an hour of play, when he felt quite unable to concentrate. It never happened to him before and is still a mystery to him. Expert chess analysts have confirmed this, that in the middle of several games Spassky seemed to lose concentration. Either he made some terrible mistake and lost, or else he gave up a winning position and had to settle for a draw. It became so bad that some Soviet chess officials began to claim that Spassky was being drugged. He himself said that Fischer was "hypnotizing" him, though by this he meant nothing more than that Fischer had somehow disturbed him, and that this was affecting his play.

At this point Spassky conceived the idea that he was "a rabbit paralyzed by a snake"—an image he has referred to several times in the past year. And this is what the Fischer/Spassky duel is all about, who is the snake and who the rabbit. Until now there has been no doubt about the answer. As Spassky himself says, "In several games it got to the stage where Bobby was just sitting there, fooling around, scratching his face, making moves that were almost insulting, waiting for me to make a mistake. Then he really began to concentrate. He stopped playing around and became completely calm." The Russian player would feel the coils begin to tighten around him and would know that there was only one possible outcome: Fischer was going to eat him.

At the end of the match Spassky said: "I wish there was some machine that measured human stress. Then I could have taken regular readings and compared them with my results. As it was, I did what I could to keep a check. I took my pulse regularly, but it didn't vary, it was always around 68 or 70. They took my blood pressure. It was normal. I didn't feel the need to take any pills or medicines. As far as any doctor could tell I was fine." But he knew that he was not fine and was still looking for something to explain those "fifth-class" mistakes.

In those days which followed surrender there was no question of his being able to relax. Most of the nights he spent analyzing and worrying. The days were mercifully taken up with the ordinary problems of getting his wife, Larissa, and himself home to Moscow. And then there were the journalists. Somehow they had got the idea that he was frightened of returning to Russia and would be staying in the West. One or two of them actually asked him directly if this was true. It was totally false, but such rumors can cause Soviet citizens intense worry or even harm. Others built up exaggerated notions of the fate that awaited him. If he was not actually exiled to the frozen wastes of Siberia, it was suggested, he would certainly be punished severely for the "crime" of losing a title which the Soviet Union had come to accept as naturally hers.

Westerners saw him and his wife arrive at Moscow Airport. There were no officials to meet them and they drove away in a private car. The Soviet grandmaster Kotov wrote in the official newspaper *Pravda* that Spassky had played "passively and without sufficient accuracy." He was also criticized by the great player Botvinnik in the chess journal *Sixty-Four*. A few weeks later there were tournaments in San Antonio, Texas, and in Majorca, Spain. Spassky had told journalists that he would be playing in these, and when he did not appear they were ready to assume that he was in disgrace and would never play chess abroad again.

In fact Spassky's future depended on his potential for regaining the title, not on any futile need for official retribution. And this potential could not be evaluated until he had regained his mental balance. "Very soon now I'll begin to suffer from acute depression. It'll last about two or three months," he said to me, quite calmly, the evening before he left for home on September 10. I thought to myself that he had indeed plenty to be depressed about, but I was misunderstanding him. "It was the same three years ago, after the match against Petrosian." This was when he became world champion, the moment of his greatest triumph.

"The brain works itself up to a climax at the end of two months of solid chess. Then suddenly the match is over. The brain has nothing to do. It's more than the organism can stand. Something has to break," he went on. I realized that Fischer and Spassky were like two mothers who had just given birth. Fischer had won, Spassky had lost, but postnatal depression is normal whether the child is healthy or stillborn. Fischer too was going to have his problems. The two men were flying to opposite ends of the world, but into the same emptiness and loneliness for each other. For months they would miss each other and, in a sense, the mental battle would continue. The winner would be the one who came best out of the black mood.

At first the battle seemed over, the war at an end. At the concluding banquet, Fischer was presented with a laurel wreath, a gold medal, and a large check. Flushed with victory, he told Spassky he thought the twenty-four-game championship was too short, not a stern enough test of stamina. If he had his way, he said, there would be a forty-eight-game marathon spread over four months. The very thought was enough to make Spassky turn pale, for when he won in 1969 he announced that his main feeling on becoming world champion was one of tiredness and that "it is impossible to play in this exhausting system." Fischer's extraordinary suggestion may have been yet another off-the-board gambit. But it may have been genuine, because at the moment Fischer, a man of up and down moods, was on top of the world, so much so that he actually gave Spassky a present, a small camera. Spassky said, "It was kind of him, I thought of giving him a present back, but in the end I didn't. After all, I had already given him happiness."

So the sparring had begun, only two days after the last match was over. Spassky countered Fischer's insults and rudeness by announcing, to everyone's utter amazement, that he really *liked* Fischer: "He is a great man, a man of art, a worthy champion." He pointed out that even his appalling behavior had its positive side: "He wants to make chess as big a money-spinner as football or boxing. He is the chess player's most effective trade union boss. He has done more than anyone else to up our wages." Spassky actually feels close to Fischer as a friend: "It's not a pose. I really *do* like him. You see, I have to like him, otherwise I'd never get to know him. And if I don't know him, I won't beat him."

He has a large photograph of Fischer, he told me, which he has framed and hung in his flat in Vyesnina Street, Moscow. I reminded him of how General Montgomery hung a picture of Rommel in his headquarters in the North African desert. "Know thy enemy," I said. "Know thy brother," Spassky corrected me: "I want to make him my best friend, like Myshkin and Rogozhin." He was referring to two characters in *The Idiot* by Dostoevsky, his favorite author. In the book Myshkin makes it his business to make friends with Rogozhin, his rival. Only thus can he supplant him.

Spassky is therefore professionally pleased, though personally sad, to hear of Fischer's present torpor and inactivity. Last autumn he prophesied a bleak future for the new champion. He knew from his own experience that Fischer would be "a very poor man" for the next three years. Being champion had a bad effect on his own chess because it added more psychological burdens to those which a top-class player carries in any case. Every match he played was a "grand confrontation" with an opponent fighting tooth and nail, longing to beat the champion. He found it harder and harder to relax. The record shows that during 1970–71 his results deteriorated.

The world champion also has administrative work. He is an ex officio member of the World Chess Federation's "central committee." Spassky found this work boring and suspects that Fischer will find it intolerable. "I was tormented by all the duties and responsibilities. Now I can just play. That's another reason why I'm in a better position than Bobby. Being champion occupies part of your time and part of your mind. If we play again the position will be the reverse of 1972. He'll have had three years of troubles and I'll have had three years of chess."

There is also the unknown factor of Fischer's mental state. Unlike Spassky, Fischer has an obsession with chess which excludes most of the joys and good things of life. He had a consuming ambition to be world champion, and achieving it was bound to make him happy. But now that the speeches are over and the match has vanished from the newspapers, Fischer finds he has nothing more to achieve. Money-making, for instance, was something that seemed to interest him, and last autumn he may have thought that here was some new, exciting thing he could do well, some new way of winning. But he is not world champion of the money game and his efforts to make millions, successful at first, have ended badly.

He is not used to such failure and seems confused about how he should exploit his position. Spassky says, "I said this a long time ago, that Bobby was going to be a very unhappy man. He has terrible problems. He is afraid of people, he thinks they're trying to get at him. And he has this need to be admired and worshiped. All this, with the normal after-the-match depression and the problem of being champion, makes a strong cocktail. He is now *afraid* to play chess. He hasn't played seriously for a year and from what I hear it'll be some time before he's able to pull himself together. Meanwhile he's like a laid-up ship gathering barnacles."

Spassky himself has had a better year since he returned to a cool reception and an uncertain future. He has now analyzed the Reykjavik games in detail as well as the psychological situation, and is fairly confident he can beat Fischer if they play again. But he remembers ruefully that he was "100 percent sure" he would beat him in Iceland. One problem is the age difference between them. Ten years ago a player was reckoned to reach his peak about the age of forty-two. Since then the peak age has dropped steadily until, according to Spassky, it is about thirty-five or thirty-six. "That is a statistical fact," he says. The trouble is that he was thirty-six in January, while Fischer has seven more years before he begins to worry about decline. And however much he explains his defeat, the fact remains that some chess experts consider him quite simply the weaker player.

It was a depressing winter for Spassky. He was upset at not being able to play in San Antonio and Majorca. "They thought I was tired, that I might play badly. Maybe that's right, but I'm not afraid of playing badly. I was bound to after a match like that. I just wanted to keep playing. That's what a chess player has to do." He played at a tournament in Tallin, Estonia, and finished third. It was not very impressive. At last in June he was allowed to go abroad and play in Dortmund, West Germany. I saw him there and asked him about the chances of a quick return match with Fischer.

Now he excludes any chance of a replay before the next world championship at the end of 1975. He says, "Our chess authorities in Russia are against it. And they're right. In the first place to play Fischer I would have to be showing top results. But I'm not. I'm not at all happy with the quality of my game. I'll just have to play it out of my system. The other thing is that I know that my best chance of beating Fischer is by going through the qualifying rounds like the other challengers. There'll be eight of us, and of course I may not win, but if I do I'll have the right impetus and morale. To beat a world champion you have to be in the right spirit. You have to be sure inside yourself that you've beaten all the others and that now is the time to knock the eagle off his perch."

Spassky has several more tournaments before this struggle begins with the quarterfinals in January. In the late spring the four winners will have their semifinals, and in the fall there will be the final which will decide who has the right to play Fischer for the world title a year later. In July Spassky told me, "The Spassky shares are going up on the chess stock exchange. For the past few months I've been like a steam engine with a hole in the boiler. I've been making steam all right, but it's all been leaking out, it hasn't been getting me anywhere. Now I really think I'm on the mend. I have to be able to turn that steam into energy."

So, in spite of his exhaustion and disappointments, Spassky is again setting out on the killing championship track. If he does well it will mean two unimaginable years, one year of cutthroat games against the seven "eagles," who are mainly Russian, and another of preparation for the great revenge. Such a meeting could be the most exciting in chess history, though there are many "ifs" in the way of it, not the least being the problem of how to bring the champion up to scratch. Recently a figure of $1 million was mentioned to Fischer as the sort of sum that might be offered in 1975. "Why not $10 million?" was Fischer's only answer.

Meanwhile, says Spassky, "Bobby is like a snake which has swallowed a rabbit. He is lying on a warm stone having a long sleep." He says again, as an afterthought, "I am the rabbit." He calls Fischer "my dear cannibal," almost affectionately, as if he liked the thought of being swallowed by such a genius. What really cheers him, though, is the thought that maybe Fischer swallowed him only at the cost of poisoning himself. Every chess player knows the beauty of giving one's opponent a piece in order to obtain a checkmate a few moves later. He may hope that his defeat in Reykjavik will turn out to be the most imaginative sacrifice of his career, that he managed to turn himself into a "poisoned king," which Fischer took only at the cost of destroying his chances at the next meeting.

Spassky lost the Battle of Iceland, but the war continues, and the longer Fischer remains a recluse, the better chance Spassky has of beating him. The thought of 1975 brings Spassky to a mood of cool, ruthless contemplation. He said to me, "If we play, the result will depend on how we both feel when we sit down for the first game. I'll look across the board at him and then I'll *know*, before I move my first pawn." ✦

No Joy in Sorrento

(OCTOBER 2004)

Pat Jordan

THE MYTH IS: He walked out of a sugarcane field with a bat over his shoulder, an unknown, eighteen-year-old man-boy, 6'6", 240 pounds, with chiseled muscles and a talent as prodigious as Babe Ruth's.

He was born in the sugarcane fields of Sorrento in northwestern Louisiana. His feet were so big his aunt Nora nicknamed him "Toe," or maybe it was his grandmother. He learned to hit a baseball by swinging a broomstick handle at beer-bottle caps tossed to him by his father. When he was twelve a professional scout saw him strike out seventeen of twenty-one batters and hit two home runs, one left-handed, one right-handed, in a Little League game. He quit school at thirteen because it was "boring," and then disappeared. He lived in a trailer with "friends" and cut sugarcane for a living. By fourteen, he was playing in the semi-pro Sugar Cane League on hardscrabble fields littered with collard-green plants and oil drums. He played with much older men, migrant workers and washed-up ballplayers of distant repute, who called him "Hit Man." When he was eighteen, the scout who had seen him at twelve tracked him down and saw him hit two 400 foot home runs, one lefty, one righty, and throw 93-mph fastballs. The scout spirited him off to a Tampa Bay Devil Rays try-out where he hit ten home runs lefty and ten home runs righty. Tampa general manager Chuck LaMar told the media that "Toe" Nash had "Mark McGwire power and Doc Gooden arm." Tampa's scouting director at the time, Dan Jennings, said he was a "monster . . . like something out of the old Negro leagues. 'Toe' Nash is Babe Ruth." LaMar added, Nash's "life should be an inspiration to all young men." Then he signed Nash for a $30,000 bonus in September of 2000, and a few months later, in January 2001, "The Myth of Toe Nash" was born.

The Myth was started by Benny Latino, thirty-four, a part-time scout from Hammond, Louisiana, who said that discovering Toe was "the pinnacle of my short career." Then he introduced Toe to Larry Reynolds, a California sports agent, who came to represent Toe. Larry Reynolds told Toe he was living a fairy tale and then introduced him to his brother, Harold, a former major leaguer who is now an ESPN-TV commentator. Harold invited Toe to live with him in California, where he introduced him to famous big leaguers like Tony Gwynn, Eric Davis, and Shawn Green. Harold said he would help Nash get his GED because he was a "good kid. I'll be a father figure, a big brother, a friend, a place to live." Then he introduced Nash to Peter Gammons, an ESPN-TV commentator and writer, who wrote a story about Nash on the Internet on January 11, 2001, titled "Devil Rays Find The Natural in the Cane Fields." Gammons compared Nash to the mythical Roy Hobbs in Bernard Malamud's novel *The Natural*. His story had more than 3 million hits, and soon The Myth was picked up by newspapers throughout North America. Oprah Winfrey was interested in his story. Paramount, New Line Cinema, and Disney wanted to make a movie of his life. CBS-TV News profiled him. There was talk of $3 million. Gammons was approached to write a book about Nash. After playing in only fourteen games after Little League, and before he played his first professional game, Nash's baseball card was selling for $9.99; he once made $10,000 in two hours signing his cards.

Those stories posed more questions than they answered. His grandmother or his aunt? Why had ESPN got the location of Sorrento wrong? How could Nash strike out seventeen of twenty-one batters in a Little League game when Little League games were only six innings in duration? Why was he allowed to quit school at thirteen, and who were the "friends" he lived with? Many of the writers who wrote about The Myth of Toe Nash never actually went to Louisiana to report on it. They just took the word of people—scouts, agents, general managers—who had a vested interest in promoting The Myth. If Toe Nash really was living a fairy tale, and if his talent really was as prodigious as Babe Ruth's and Roy Hobbs's, I wanted to find out for myself. So over the next ten months I went to Louisiana twice and interviewed everyone involved in The Myth of Toe Nash.

I first flew to New Orleans in mid-February of 2002. I spent three days driving from one small southeastern Louisiana town to another (Hammond, Sorrento, Gonzales, Donaldsonville, Napoleonville, Thibodaux). I drove mostly on two-lane blacktops past rusted-out trailers and cars on cinder blocks, vast fields of sugarcane, swampy bayous, and an occasional plantation mansion set back off the road and shaded by the weepy moss of live oaks. I interviewed people in law offices, sheriff's departments, jails, restaurants, strip malls, trailer parks, gas stations, and in the bleachers of ballparks. Sometimes, driving from one interview to another, I talked to people in California and Florida via my cell phone. Here is what I learned.

Gregory "Toe" Nash was born around the sugarcane fields of Sorrento, population 1,300, a depressed little town of poor whites and poorer blacks living mostly in trailers in *southeastern* Louisiana. His mother was a drug addict who abandoned Nash and his little sister to his father, Charles Payton, when Nash was thirteen. Shortly afterward, Nash was expelled from two schools, one for fighting and the other for threatening a teacher with a knife. He was called "a delinquent" with "no ambition" and "a follower." At sixteen, he moved into a trailer, but with a forty-one-year-old white two-time divorcée and mother of numerous children, named Charlene, who had a few a.k.a.'s—Suttle, Potter— and so many bogus addresses that even the local D.A. didn't know where she really lived. (Last year she was a witness in a murder case.) By eighteen, Toe's body was less "chiseled" with muscle than marbled with baby fat. He never cut sugarcane, though he did mow his uncle's lawn a few times until he quit because his uncle was too strict with him. The baseball fields he played on were well manicured, and he wasn't unknown to professional baseball. The Pittsburgh Pirates scouted him but decided not to sign him when they discovered his long rap sheet at the Ascension Parish sheriff's office in Gonzales, Louisiana, where he was known as "a criminal, a bad citizen."

Chuck LaMar told me, "The scouting department was aware of *some* trouble but didn't know all the details. I didn't know about his probation." LaMar did admit, though, that Tampa Bay had agreed to monitor Nash's strict probation (no drugs, liquor, weapons, or criminal friends) if he agreed to be on his best behavior "and not embarrass the organization."

Once Nash's past surfaced in late January 2001, everyone who had a vested interest in The Myth rallied around him. His crimes were described as mere bumps in the road, minor offenses committed by a man-boy described as innocent, naive, trusting, a simple country boy who got lost in airports and was astonished to find out that he could order a pizza over the phone.

Harold Reynolds claimed Nash had "a great personality, fun to be around. He just got caught up with the wrong crowd. You're not dealing with a kid who's a gang member caught in drive-bys."

Jennings, now a vice president of player personnel with the Florida Marlins, said, "After the Gammons story it took on a life of its own. It was a feel-good story. He's a good kid who made some bad choices. Baseball will give him a second chance, because there are two sides to every story."

Toe Nash began his first pro season at Princeton, West Virginia, in the Class A Rookie Appalachian League, where "he was a model citizen," said Jennings. He arrived there already famous. People clamored for his autograph. They fed him dinner, braided his hair, drove him to the mall, loaned him money.

Roy and Ruby Beasley were his host family in Princeton. Ruby told me, "We took him out to eat, on a picnic, to the mall, to church. He was very quiet. Greg was a follower. He wasn't very mature. He was more like a child that depended on us. I told my husband that if he goes back to Louisiana he'll get into trouble again."

After Nash's first season, in which he batted a mediocre .240, with eight home runs and twenty-nine RBIs in forty-seven games, he returned to Sorrento, where on January 21, 2002, he was arrested for robbery and the forcible rape of a fifteen-year-old white girl.

"He's a street kid who had some potential and squandered it," said Tony Bacala, an Ascension Parish sheriff's deputy. "He surrendered his baseball career to crime." Bacala sat behind his desk leafing through Nash's arrest reports. "Somebody's got their hands full."

Nash was arrested for the first time on March 17, 2000, for driving without a license and possession of marijuana. He told the arresting officer he didn't know his address, Social Security number, or driver's license, and said, "I don't have nothing." In plain view was a bag of marijuana.

Thirteen days later, Nash and a friend, Dalacy Bureau, were arrested for beating up a youth named Chris Oncale and stealing $200 from him. Nash told the arresting officers, "We kicked his ass because he was talking shit." Dalacy Bureau took the $200 from Oncale and gave Nash twenty.

One day later, Nash was arrested for theft and simple battery and damage to property in a fight with Charlene in her trailer. When she asked him to leave her trailer, he punched her fifteen-year-old daughter, stole Charlene's purse, and broke two windows in her car.

Less than a month later, on April 19, 2000, Nash was driving with Charlene when they were stopped for a traffic violation. The officer found marijuana in one of Nash's socks and Valium in the other. He also discovered that there was an outstanding warrant on Nash for missing his court date in the Oncale beating. In November of the same year, Nash was arrested again on a marijuana charge.

On January 30, 2001, Nash was charged with simple battery when he and Charlene, who described their relationship as "loving," got into a fight. She threw a light bulb at him, and Nash banged her head against a wall. He claimed she came at him with a knife because she was angry he was leaving her to go off to play baseball, but there was no mention of a knife in the arrest report.

On February 18, 2001, Nash was arrested for a misdemeanor possession of alcohol by a minor, shortly before he was to go to spring training. The Ascension Parish D.A., Anthony Falterman, agreed to release Nash to Tampa Bay if Nash promised to leave the state, and Tampa agreed to supervise his probation, which the team did. Nash spent the following months until September in West Virginia. He then returned to Sorrento, where he was arrested for robbery and forcible rape on January 21, 2002, again shortly before he would go to spring training with Tampa Bay. There were questions about the fifteen-year-old girl's testimony (Nash admitted he had sex with her but claimed it was consensual and that "I didn't know how old she was"), so the assistant D.A., Robin O'Bannon, reduced the charges to carnal knowledge of a minor, and Nash pleaded guilty. He was sentenced to seventeen months in the Ascension Parish jail in Donaldsonville and served half that time, which covered the entire 2002 baseball season. When he was released from jail, Tampa Bay had cut him and he was signed by the Cincinnati Reds in the winter of 2002. One month later, on January 14, 2003, Nash was arrested for second-degree battery of his white friend James Eric Thomas, who, Nash claimed, had called him a "nigger." He was jailed again and denied bail when it was discovered he had "absconded from supervision" by failing to report to his parole officer. (Nash has spent two years in jail since he turned eighteen.) If he were found guilty of either charge he would be forced to serve ten years in jail for violating his carnal-knowledge parole. That hearing was scheduled for March 19, at which time Nash would learn whether he would spend his next years wearing an orange prison jumpsuit or a baseball uniform. Even before that hearing, the Reds had had enough of "Toe" Nash and released him in February, before he had ever played an inning for the organization.

Benny Latino lives in Hammond, northeast of Gonzales, where he runs a construction company that restores houses. I met him across the street from Southeastern Louisiana University at noon, and we went for lunch at a nearby restaurant. He's a good-looking man with a wispy, reddish goatee and sunglasses perched insouciantly on his forehead. After only a few minutes talking to Latino it became clear that he dreaded this interview. After he signed Nash, which "changed our lives," he was made a full-time scout. Then, after Nash's crimes were exposed, Tampa Bay made him the fall guy for failing to inform the team of Nash's past.

"I didn't know of any trouble he's got in," said Latino, as we ate our po'boy sandwiches. "I mean, it wasn't like I could go to his high school and check on him. Oh, I'd heard some things, but I was told it wasn't a big deal. When I was with the kid he seemed fine."

Latino described Nash as having "limited life experience. He had no problems in West Virginia, 'cause he's not smart enough to get in trouble on his own. If that girl flashed him her I.D., I don't think he could read it. I'm sure he didn't know statutory-rape laws. He's the kind of kid you've gotta pick him up and take him everywhere he's supposed to be."

Latino claimed that the Reynolds brothers "dropped the ball" with Nash every time they let him leave California to return to Sorrento. He pointed out that the rape occurred two days before Nash was scheduled to return to California, and this January's aggravated-battery charge came three days before he was supposed to return to California. The Reynolds brothers, he said, had high plans for Nash, but he was too much to baby-sit for all the time. Then, when they found out there was no movie deal after the rape charge, "they dropped him, because their big payday was gone. Everyone had their own motives with Toe. Even the D.A. [Anthony Falterman]. He's friends with Hot Rod [John "Hot Rod" Williams, a former NBA basketball player and Nash's uncle], and Hot Rod delivers the black vote. This is still Louisiana, you know."

Latino claimed that Williams convinced Falterman to release Nash on probation to Tampa Bay because of their friendship, and that it was Williams who discovered problems with the rape victim's testimony and cast a shadow over her claims.

"You gotta talk to Hot Rod," Latino said, picking up his cell phone. He got Hot Rod and told him I'd be driving down to Sorrento in an hour. Then he hung up. "Hot Rod's a good guy," he said. And then he told me that he thought many of Nash's problems stemmed from The Myth. He wished he'd never told Gammons about Toe Nash and the sugarcane fields. Latino looked pained. "The kid had so much raw ability. All he needed was 120 games a year for four years." Then he brightened. "I got this other kid now, the fastest kid in the Sugar Cane League. I met him in the parking lot one night after a game. His friends were betting whether he could jump over a car. I said, 'I'll take forty of that action.' And he did it. I signed him for $22,000, and he's in the Sally League now." He looked at me. "He's a helluva story."

Hot Rod Williams was waiting for me by the baseball stadium he built in Sorrento for his team, the Williams All Stars, which Nash played for in the Sugar Cane League. It's a beautiful field that reportedly cost Williams a million dollars. He's known for giving back to the community where he grew up. He had invested the money he made in the NBA in a construction company. While his men were repairing the road alongside the field, Williams and I sat in the stands behind home plate and talked. Williams is a handsome man, 6'11", with a beard, who resembles a black George Clooney. He talked exuberantly.

"Greg's a good kid, but easily led," he said. "He has a man's body, but he's a child inside. The friends he follows let him use their car so he'll be beholden to them. One of them's in jail with him for shooting a kid in the back with a shotgun, killing him." He shook his head. "I try to help the boy, get him outta jail, tell him he can do whatever he wants to do, but he just stopped. He lost his space, ya know? Gave up on life." When Nash was about to sign with Tampa, Williams offered him the services of his lawyer and his agent, "but the boy went behind my back and signed with Larry Reynolds. He's got power of attorney over Greg's money. Where'd it go? I'm the one bailed Greg outta jail. Larry sent a check, but it bounced. Him and Harold washed their hands of Greg. They don't even return my calls. Everyone wanted to jump on the bandwagon too fast—the book deal, the movie—and then after the rape charge they distanced themselves from him, and I'm still here."

Williams's account was not entirely accurate. It was Larry Reynolds who hired a high-priced, high-profile New Orleans defense attorney named Arthur Lemann III to fight Nash's rape charge. Williams said that was one of Nash's problems. He should have a local lawyer.

"Lemann didn't do nuthin'," Williams said. "*I* found out about the girl's past, that she said two other guys done the same thing to her, and *I* told Lemann."

When Williams finally caught a breath, I told him that I wanted to interview Nash in jail, but the warden wouldn't allow any media in the jail. Williams jumped up. "We'll see about that," he said. He went over to his crew and came back with a short, portly, sweet-looking black man who could pass for a beardless Santa Claus. "This here's his daddy, Charles," Williams said. Charles Payton smiled and turned his face away, a painfully shy man. He has worked for Williams for the last nineteen years. "His daddy will get you in the jail tomorrow," Williams said.

I asked Payton a few questions about his son. He gave me a sideways smile and mumbled, "I tried to talk to him. He say, 'Yes, Daddy,' and do what he want. I let him go his own way. I couldn't get him rid of his friends."

I asked Payton what happened to his son's $30,000. "I don't know. I ain't seen none of it."

Before I left, Williams introduced me to Cedric Robertson, twenty-three, a center fielder in the Tampa organization. We walked out to the tall tree behind the right-field fence. Robertson, a college graduate from Texas, said, "Tampa sent me to Hot Rod because he's the guy got Toe together. I'd heard about this legend, how he hits the ball 400 feet lefty or righty, and I wanted to compare myself to him. The first time I saw him he hit a ball over that tree. I found out the legend was true."

The next morning at ten, I went to the Lemann law offices in a restored old building on a cobblestone street in New Orleans. While I sat in the waiting room, the receptionist brought me a book written by Arthur Lemann III, titled *Hail to the Dragon Slayer*. In it Lemann recounts his privileged childhood on a sugarcane plantation in Donaldsonville, and then his most famous cases. He has defended more than a few Louisiana senators and governors, the Mafia don Carlos Marcello, and a priest accused of trafficking in child pornography. Lemann got the priest acquitted by recounting his own sexual exploits when he was thirteen to laughter in the courtroom. My cell phone rang. It was Larry Reynolds, who hadn't returned my calls in a week until he discovered that I was in Louisiana and that Nash was in jail again.

"That boy is trying everyone's patience," said Reynolds. "I don't know why I should even bother if the boy doesn't have a career." He asked me if the D.A. would let Nash loose to play baseball. I told him I didn't know. "Then I can't have any plans for the kid until I hear what the D.A. will do," he said. "I can't tell teams he'll stay outta trouble. I already got burned."

After Reynolds hung up, a boyish-looking man of thirty-four, slightly rumpled, without a jacket or tie, came into the room and introduced himself to me as Arthur Lemann, Nash's lawyer. Larry Reynolds may have thought he hired Lemann III, but it was Lemann's son, the IV, who handled Nash's case.

We went into the conference room and sat at a long table. The IV produced his files on the rape case, and said, "I first met Toe in jail. He didn't trust me. He's a chameleon. He can be quiet or menacing, a thug with his friends. He had a long rap sheet. His fee to retain us was $25,000. Most of his bonus went to us. But he didn't care. Money's not real to him. He's immature. He just doesn't care about right or wrong or think about consequences. I'm not even sure he wants to be a baseball player."

Then, without looking at his files, Lemann IV told me about the rape case. "She asked him to autograph her arm," Lemann IV said. She didn't accuse Nash of rape on her first visit to the police station. After she filed rape charges, "Hot Rod did what he could," said Lemann IV. "He told me the girl accused two other guys of rape too. Hot Rod's a political player, you know. He makes contributions. The charge was reduced to carnal knowledge, and he admitted he knew she wasn't of age."

Before I left, Lemann IV gave me copies of his rape-case files. I asked if he would represent Nash at his March 19 hearing.

"He's already used up his retainer," he said, "but I might do the revocations hearing." He smiled. "But I'll think twice about handling his next case."

I drove west out of New Orleans to Thibodaux, to talk to the man who would ultimately determine whether Nash ever played baseball again: his parole officer, Craig Berteau. His office was in a strip mall off St. Mary Street. The receptionist asked me if I was on parole with Officer Berteau. I said, "Not yet."

Berteau came into the lobby and led me down a hall to his tiny office. He sat behind his desk and I sat across from him. I told him what the receptionist had asked. He smiled, a slim, small man with the slicked-back hair and pencil-thin mustache of a riverboat gambler.

"My business cards are all over the parish," he said. "Nobody wants to admit they know me." I asked him about Nash's revocation hearing. He grimaced. "Aw, I can't talk about that. Let's just say he seemed mild-mannered and polite." That's how all the adults who come in contact with Nash describe him, even the officers who have arrested him. Berteau did agree to describe the hearing process, however. "The judge has the final say. I'll give him the facts. What I think. Sometimes the judge will ask for my recommendation, but he don't have to follow it." In Nash's case, Berteau's recommendation will take into account whether he will leave Sorrento, where he will reside, and with whom, and whether that person will supervise his probation. Berteau assumes that person will be one of the Reynolds brothers. If the Reynolds brothers don't present a detailed plan for supervision of Nash at the March 19 hearing, then it is a foregone conclusion Nash will spend the next ten years in jail.

I left Thibodaux at noon and drove north to Sorrento, where Charles Payton, dressed in his best jeans and a clean shirt, was waiting for me beside Williams's baseball stadium. We drove in silence to the Donaldsonville jail, a small, square, white brick building surrounded on all sides by a wire fence topped with razor wire.

Inside, Payton asked the officer behind a glass partition if he could talk to his son. A few minutes later, the warden, Bobby Webre, came out of a door. "I told you I can't allow no media to talk to him," he said. I pleaded my case. Webre looked at Payton. "Well, if it's awright with you, Mr. Payton?" Payton nodded.

We went into a narrow room with chairs and a telephone by each cubicle on either side of a glass partition. I saw the bottom half of an orange prison jumpsuit moving past the cubicles. Toe Nash sat down across from me. He was a huge, handsome kid with braided hair. We talked to each other through the telephone. I asked him first about his pro-baseball season.

"It was tougher than I thought," he said. "Rick Ankiel [the St. Louis Cardinals pitcher] struck me out three or four times." Then he said the toughest part of his season in West Virginia was living up to his myth. "I wish I coulda just played a few years like everyone else before that stuff."

Then Nash described life in jail. "We play basketball outside. Cards, dominoes. The loser got to do sit-ups. A good bit of my friends is here. The new guys ask me questions 'cause they read about me in the papers. But, shit, I wanna get out." He hung his head.

When I asked if his problems were caused by his friends, he showed a flash of anger. "It's not like anybody controls me. I can't blame no one else. I just wanna play ball so I can help my daddy and little sister. I ain't never had no money before." I glanced at his father, who'd told me he hadn't seen a penny of his son's $30,000.

"All my money's in a bank in L.A.," he said. "With Larry, whenever I need it."

Our time was almost up, so I let his father talk to him. Payton didn't say much to his son, just mumbled a few words, nodded, and we left.

On the morning of my third day I drove north to the D.A.'s office, in a Gonzales strip mall, to talk with Assistant D.A. Robin O'Bannon, who handled the rape case. Lemann IV had described her as "tough but fair."

O'Bannon is a vivacious blonde who had canceled our last meeting because she had to watch the last episode of *The Bachelorette*, which she described as "very funny." She sat behind a desk piled high with papers and said Nash was a "little hood who didn't appreciate the opportunity that was given him." She said he was lucky to get his rape charge reduced to carnal knowledge when the girl's credibility came into question. "I didn't believe we could prove a rape beyond reasonable doubt," she said. "But I do believe Nash raped her. Now the girl and her parents hate me."

I asked her if she believed Nash's problem was that he was afraid to leave Sorrento. She exclaimed, "Oh, puhleeze! He got in trouble because he's afraid to go away and play baseball for $30,000?"

Before I left Gonzales I stopped for gas. I remembered that someone familiar with the case had told me everyone dumped on the girl because she was poor white trash. I pulled out Lemann IV's files and began to read the arrest report:

At midnight of January 21, 2002, Nash, Bureau, and Thomas, known as "Money," went to the house of a seventeen-year-old girl in Donaldsonville. Bureau and Nash took turns having sex with the girl, and the other one carted off her father's safe, a Kentwood water jug filled with coins, and a CZ-Czechoslovakian semiautomatic pistol. At about 3:00 A.M., at a house in Gonzales, the alleged victim and two white male friends were drinking. One of the males called Toe for marijuana. When Nash, Bureau, and Thomas arrived they brought in the safe and the Kentwood jug. They told the girl they had pulled a "lick" in Donaldsonville. While the three were trying to crack the safe, the girl went into the bathroom. A few minutes later, she claimed, Nash and Bureau broke down the door and raped her. In her written statement to police, in a child's big, round, printed letters, she wrote,

> We were all chillin hanging around talking and stuff. . . . I sat my drink down to go to the restroom then I went back to the living room someone told me that delacy and toe put something in my drink I didn't believe them so I finished it off. 20 minutes later I went back to the bathroom. This time I heard a knock . . . and delacy he said Are we going to fxxx or not When I said No toe forced hiself on top of me. When he done . . . delacy got on and he did the samething. After that was over Toe put his you know what in my butt and he keep saying it feels good huh. I told them a bunch of times to stop but they did not. They just continue. After everything was over delacy, toe, and Eric left. That they were going to hurt me and family members if I was not quit. End

The problem with the rape victim's testimony was that she did not give it to deputies when she was first interviewed at the police station. The girl and her mother left, then returned a few minutes later, and then the girl told an officer she'd had sex with Nash and Bureau. When asked if she was forced, the girl said, "I can't remember."

On the page after the arrest report there was a petition from the court that claimed the rape victim, as a thirteen-year-old, had been an ungovernable child and a truant. In the middle of that petition was the girl's name, and her address in Gonzales. I called the operator and got the number. Her father answered. I told him who I was and what I was doing.

"A story on that fucking nigger," he said. Then he insisted I talk to his daughter, who was now sixteen and living with a boy. He gave me her number and I called her. She had the light voice of a child. "Yes, sir," she said, "my daddy told me to talk to you." She gave me directions to her trailer and I drove there. She lived at the end of a street lined with ramshackle trailers and rusted-out cars. There were four rusted-out "vehicles," as she called them, on her front lawn, and a number of mangy-looking pit bulls prowling around as well. The girl was sitting on the deck in front of the trailer, drinking a Pepsi. A boy, maybe eighteen, skinny, with a shaved head, was sprawled in a chair behind her. I climbed up onto the deck and introduced myself. I asked the boy who he was. He replied, sullenly, "I'm the one lives here."

I sat down across from the girl, who was pale and pretty and small, and asked her if she would mind recounting the night of the rape. She began to talk without emotion:

"I didn't know him before that night," she said. "Except as a known drug dealer. I thought he would just come to my house, we'd pay for the weed, and he'd leave. My older brother was passed out, and my younger brother was asleep. I had a glass of Bacardi and took two Valiums. After I done took them, Toe and Dalacy put something in my drink. I went to the bathroom to throw it up and they broke the door off the frame. Toe told me, 'This is the way a bitch is supposed to be treated,' all kinda stuff like that. Then they held me down with a hand over my mouth so I couldn't scream. First Dalacy did it, then Toe. I was bleeding real bad after it." When she was examined at a hospital the next day, doctors had discovered anal tears.

"Toe had a gun he said he got in Donaldsonville. I seen it. He threatened to kill my little brother if I told. The next day I didn't tell the police 'cause I was scared. My mother made me go back and tell 'em when I told her about the bleeding. But nobody believed me. Everybody said I was lyin', even my own defense attorney [Assistant D.A. O'Bannon], because Toe was a famous baseball star."

After she finished her story, I thanked her and went to my car. Just before I pulled out of the driveway she came over to my window. She asked me for proof that I was a reporter. I showed her a letter that satisfied her. Then I remembered something Lemann IV had told me.

I said, "If you didn't know Toe was a famous baseball player, then why did you ask him to autograph your arm?"

"I didn't," she said. "He autographed my butt after he, you know. He wrote on it, 'Toe Nash, Fuck Number 24.'"

It was already hot and sunny at 9:00 A.M. on March 19, outside the Ascension Parish Courthouse, a nineteenth-century red-brick building shaded by live oaks in the sleepy little town of Donaldsonville along the banks of the Mississippi River. Donaldsonville has a high, grassy levee to hold back the river, a small park with a gazebo, a number of partially restored antebellum Colonial and Victorian houses, and the Railroad Cafe, where black women wearing white aprons serve oyster po'boy sandwiches and sugary, homemade pralines.

The second-floor courtroom of Judge Alvin Turner Jr. was already packed to overflowing. Spectators sat on worn wooden benches and stood along the walls. Lawyers with wavy, silvery hair hustled back and forth with sheaves of paper. A number of beefy officers in blue stood guard over the twenty or so prisoners in orange jumpsuits who sat, handcuffed together, in two rows of long benches like church pews. Most of the prisoners waved and smiled at friends and family. They pantomimed instructions. Nash sat in the second row, his jaw in the palm of his hand as if he were bored, or sleepy, or maybe just anxious to get back to jail for lunch. When his case was called, he had to be told to stand up.

For the next thirty minutes O'Bannon and Berteau argued their case sotto voce to the judge, while Lemann IV stood between them looking bewildered. ("He had no clue what was going on," Berteau said later.) Nash stared at the floor, shifted his weight, then sat down. O'Bannon glared at him. "Please stand, Mr. Nash!" she said. He stood up again. He seemed unaware that a lot of people had an interest in his life, even if he didn't.

Judge Turner's decision was that Nash could be released *only* to Larry

Reynolds's supervision in California, or else Nash would have to remain in jail where, almost certainly, his carnal-knowledge probation would be revoked and he'd go to jail for ten years.

The next afternoon I called Larry Reynolds and asked what his plans for Nash were. "Well," he said, "we're in the process of making arrangements to get the situation handled." I told him the judge wouldn't let Nash out of jail unless Reynolds supervised his probation. Reynolds blurted out, "Hell, I'm not takin' responsibility for no parole."

In June of 2003, Toe Nash was released from jail. He boarded a flight for Ontario, California, where he was met by the twenty-six-year-old college student and mother of two small children with whom he would live. She was a close friend of Larry Reynolds, whom she referred to as "my uncle." For a number of reasons, she pleaded with me not to use her real name, so I will call her, simply, Mary.

Mary was majoring in early childhood studies at a community college and worked in the business office of her church. She lived in what she described as an "affluent condo in a drug- and crime-free zone that is right next to a golf course."

She had first met Nash during one of his stays with Larry Reynolds. She described him then as "a very sweet, sweet guy when he was around Larry. We became friends, then our relationship turned romantic." When Nash was arrested on his carnal-knowledge charge, Mary said, "He told me he loved me and that he was innocent."

While Nash was "incarcerated," said Mary, they communicated through letters, which still led her to believe "he was a nice guy." When she learned that Nash could be released from jail after a May hearing only if someone in California took him in and monitored his behavior, and that Larry Reynolds refused to be responsible for Nash, she called the judge and then wrote him a letter stating that Nash could live with her and that she would provide a stable environment. She assured the judge that "he would never hurt anyone again." Mary is an articulate woman, and the judge was so impressed with her letter that he released Nash to her care in June.

Shortly after Nash moved in with Mary, she realized he was "a totally different person than the one I'd met." Although she didn't know it at first, Nash began a sexual affair with Mary's twenty-six-year-old neighbor only days after he'd arrived. He started coming home late at night, and when Mary questioned him, "he would become violent and force himself on me." "When I went to work, he'd sit on my front porch drinking and smoking and talking on the phone all day to his friends in Louisiana. He ran up a $1,000 phone bill, and my phone was disconnected. I told him he'd promised to get a job and go to church with me, but he never did."

When Mary had minor surgery on her hand, the doctor gave her a prescription for Vicodin. Nash stole the pills and swallowed sixteen of them. When he started to come down from the effects he became violent and "threw" Mary around in front of her children. Then, about a month after Nash moved in with Mary, he came home at 1:00 A.M., after having had sex with her neighbor. When Mary confronted him about this and told him he wasn't adhering to his curfew, "he absolutely beat me up," she said. "He grabbed my hair and shoved my face into the ground. He ripped my small braids out of my head. I was crying when he lifted my denim skirt over my head and rammed his fingers inside me, both places. He was laughing, like it turned him on. 'This is what you want, bitch,' he said. That's when I called Jennifer and told her to come and pick him up."

Jennifer Marisnick is the director of marketing for Reynolds Sports Management. She is in her late thirties, married, with three sons. According to Mary, when Jennifer came to pick up Nash, and Mary told her what Nash had done to her, Jennifer warned Mary not to tell anyone. She told Mary no one would believe her, they'd just think Mary was jealous of Nash's relationship with Mary's neighbor, and that Mary had made up her accusations to get even. Besides, Jennifer told Mary, it would ruin her friendship with her "uncle," Larry Reynolds.

"To keep me quiet," Mary said, "Larry gave me $500. They said they'd pay my expenses, but they never did. They really used me."

Months passed, and Mary did nothing, while Nash lived in a trailer on Jennifer's property. "She told me Toe was a perfect angel," said Mary. "But he always is an 'angel' with adults." Mary said that Nash seduced adults with his soft-spoken deference, his humility, his ineffectualness, his ability to parrot back to adults what he knew they wanted to hear. But with his peers he was aggressive, violent, and sexually abusive.

When Mary began cleaning out her old phone numbers in October she came across mine. I had called her in late June to ask if Nash was living with her. She had just "kicked him out" but was too frightened to tell me this. Now she decided to call and tell me what had happened because "he's gonna hurt someone else if I don't," she said. "He turned out to be exactly what he was accused of. Exceptionally violent. He's got sexual hang-ups. It's pretty grotesque what he did to me. He should absolutely be in jail."

After speaking with Mary, I called Jennifer at Reynolds Sports Management. She told me Nash had gone directly from Louisiana in June to live with her. "He was fabulous," she said. "He went to school every day, worked out with the high school coaches. Of course, I had to take him to school, because he didn't know how to use the bus system." Jennifer insisted Nash had never lived with anyone but her and her family since he was released from jail in June and that "I was not aware he ever got in any trouble [out here]."

In late August, Nash told Jennifer he was "homesick" and uncomfortable living with her. "My husband and I ran a tight ship," she told me. "Very structured. He had to do chores. Toe began to cry. He said he just wanted to go home, and he didn't want to play baseball anymore. He was uncomfortable with the media attention. I was very disappointed, because at the time some major-league teams were interested in him. It's a sad story. He's a product of his environment, and he has no deep drive to change." Before she hung up, Jennifer beseeched me not to write anything negative about Toe Nash. She claimed he was just a good kid who had been misled by his peers.

On September 2, Jennifer called Berteau and told him Nash was returning to Sorrento because he was "homesick for his family." Nash arrived on September 4 and immediately went to the home of a friend Berteau described as "a hoodlum." Because Nash was still on probation for his carnal-knowledge conviction, he was required to report to Berteau the moment he set foot in Louisiana. When he didn't, Berteau had him picked up on September 5 and transported back to the Ascension Parish jail.

He remained in jail until his next hearing, on December 15, at which time the judge released him and reinstated his parole, which meant he had to report to Berteau. A few months ago I called Berteau and asked how Nash was doing; he told me that Nash was fulfilling the dictates of his probation. He was still in Ascension Parish, of course, but living with his father now and playing with the Hot Rod Williams All Stars in the Sugar Cane League. At twenty-two, he had more in common with his older, more world-weary teammates than with the eighteen-year-old phenom he used to be. He certainly was no longer a myth. ✦

226

The National Pastime

(May 1979)

Tom Wolfe

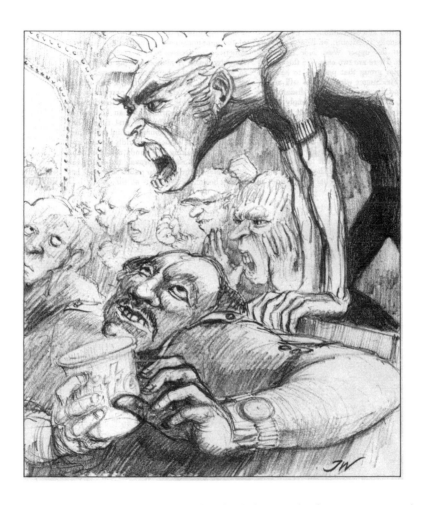

"Eight hundred thousand a year, a fast-food chain, a deodorant commercial, and a line of thermal underwear, and *you* throw to the wrong *base!*"   ✦

Time Loves a Haircut

(APRIL 1987)

Bill Cardoso

"ALL RIGHT, BUDDY, sit down and I'll see what I can do," said the old out-fielder, now thirty-nine and twenty pounds heavier at 201 than he was when he left the game in 1981, playing for Vera Cruz in the Mexican League.

Bernie Carbo, the Cincinnati Reds' No. 1 draft choice in 1965, chosen ahead of Johnny Bench. Bernie Carbo, clutch hitter, home run hitter. Bernie Carbo, who kept the many visages of Buddha in his locker. Bernie Carbo, who, it is said, never knew what day it was, let alone where he was.

Well, we're in Wyandotte, Michigan, downriver from Detroit. Bernie's neck of the woods these days. We are in a brown two-story building where Bernie Carbo's We Are Family Hair Stylists shares space with Nunzio's Construction Services Inc. The salon had been a real estate office until Bernie moved in with his clippers and his "family," Sonia and Dorothy, colleagues in the world of lock and tress.

"That tail, yeah," Bernie was saying of the single lock of hair starting to trail down the nape of my neck. "Extension, you call 'em? I like that. Ride 'em, cowboy. You see mine? I got a tail. I had mine new when I went to Saudi Arabia in, what? Three years ago. I went to Saudi Arabia to do a baseball clin-ic. I couldn't believe it. All these kids were running around, big gold necklaces and Mercedes-Benzes and everything like that. And they all had tails. Every one of them had a tail. And that's when I came back and said, those tails are pretty neat. And I started growing a tail.

"So, I've had it for a few years. And then I bleached it. Put some bleach in it. Back then I had my hair a little bit longer. Then I went shorter. I like it shorter, like yours. I'm gonna blow it a little bit." The blow-dryer purred.

"It looks all right. You're getting the works. I'm gonna give you what we used to call—remember the ducktail? The duck ass? Heh-heh. The DA? The *lively* DA! DA with a tail! The tail is really not off-center. But it's the way your hair grows. Oh, that tail looks good. You look like a movie star. Hah hah hah." Bernie was clipping away.

"Yeah, man, you know what? My first full year, in 1970. Sparky Anderson was my manager? I said, I'm going to get me a perm. I'll be the first white ballplayer to have an Afro. In 1970, in San Diego. Paid forty-five dollars. That was a lot of money then." Indeed.

"Went back to the ballpark. Sparky took one look at me and said, 'You ain't playing today. You ain't playing tomorrow. You ain't playing until you get that hair cut!'"

Now Sonia, who had been Bernie's instructor at Virginia Farrell's hair school before she joined the family, spoke. "Hey, look, Bernie, Bill ain't got no stockings on!"

I'm stuck in the Hamptons, Sonia. Socks ain't legal there.

"Hey, you know what?" said Bernie. "You laugh about the no stockings. Sonia laughs. Listen to this. When I was in St. Louis, this lawyer came in to read a letter from Mr. Busch. Mr. Busch was going to give us a pep talk: 'Hey, you guys, you gotta go out there and win. You know, you don't win a championship playing like this.' And the lawyer that was reading it didn't have any socks on. I walked up to him and said, 'Hey, you don't got any socks on. Do you mind if I read that letter?' He says, 'Yeah, you can read it.' And the next day I got released. I got released for asking him about his no socks."

My word! How's my extension?

"Good. Don't touch it! I'll tell you what, though. Your hair is not the easiest to cut. Swirls all over the place. It's cra-zy! Strong hair. Your hair sticks out on the sides there. The tail is—see how that is right now? That's in the middle of your hair. But watch how your hair grows. See? Look at that. That's something, isn't it? It grows right into a circle."

I'll have to *mousse* it?

"Not *mousse* it! I'll *grease* that son of a gun. We'll grease it. Get it all nice and greased. But look how nice the neck is. I'll comb it to grow toward the middle, into that DA. And worn a little close to the neck like this. And let that tail grow down like this. And when it gets long enough, we can braid it. Let that tail start growing out.

"See, mine's a little bit longer than that. Mine was long, but Sonia cut it. When yours gets a little bit longer, braid it. Do you trim your mustache? Do you like it off your lip?"

I like it bandito-style. Zapata.

"Oh, wild and crazy, eh?"

Yup.

"I'll just trim it a little bit here. Relax. Close your lips." Bernie snipped away. "Looking good! Yeah, when I went to that fantasy camp the Red Sox have in Winter Haven I took my clippers with me. It was the worst thing I did the whole damn week. I was giving the whole fantasy camp haircuts. Shaving their beards. Bill Lee had a beard. And his wife wanted me to shave it off. Bill's over in Rome now, doing a clinic. So, I shaved it off. The whole thing. Gave him a haircut."

Clip clip. "I thought the '75 Boston Red Sox was the best team I ever played on. That's including the Big Red Machine in '70. We played the World Series in '75 without Jimmy Rice. He had a broken wrist. Who's to say, if he played, I probably wouldn't have hit my two pinch-hit home runs. Do you want this above the ears, or do you like it on the ears?"

A little over the top of the ears.

"Just a little bit over the top? That's the style, to show your ears a little bit. You like it to cover the ears a little?"

No. The new style, Bernie. I want to be with it, now that I'm finally in the eighties.

"I tell you, Bill, the extension doesn't look that bad. Yeah, I did the Red Sox fantasy camp with Dom DiMaggio. I did the Cincinnati Reds, too. There ain't too many I can't do. I played on enough teams. I'll tell you that.

"The most fun team, though, was the Boston Red Sox. See, I don't actually say I was a Cincinnati Reds man. Although I'd like to see Rose and those guys win. But I'm a Boston Red Sock. The only reason was Mr. Yawkey. He's the one who made my day. He was in the clubhouse one day. I walked in and said, 'What'd we do? Hire another old man?' He had a pair of brown pants on. Old shoes. A work shirt. And he comes my way and says, 'Bernardo! How're you doing? I'm Mr. Yawkey.'

"And I went, 'Mr. Yawkey!' Wasn't he great? He really cared for his players, I'll tell you that. Too bad he had to go and pass away. Well, I'm almost done. You look like a movie star! All right now, I'll just clean you up a little bit. Well, what do you think? The tail's looking good! I wish it was longer. Then I could braid.

"Too bad the old man didn't live, eh? I'd probably still be playing for the Boston Red Sox if he was still living. You know what happened? In '75 I hit those two pinch-hit home runs. And that was the year my contract was up.

And I had to sign, right? So, I got a 20 percent cut in pay after that World Series. That damn Haywood Sullivan and Buddy LeRoux took over the club in '77, and they gave me a 20 percent cut. And then they traded me to Milwau—who'd they trade me to, Cleveland? They traded me to Cleveland, didn't they? No, that was in 1977. No, they traded me to Milwaukee. I went to Milwaukee. That's when my wife was nine months pregnant and stuff like that. Took a 20 percent cut in pay. Couldn't believe they treated me like that. Mr. Yawkey probably would've given me a nice contract. Just like he did prior to that.

"But I think your tail really turned out nice. I don't know if these tails are gonna be in style that long, or what. What do you think? Three years? Three years. You know who started the tail? The Japanese. The Japanese!

"Yeah. Bill, you need to let this grow just a little bit longer. There you go, looking like a movie star! I told my father I was gonna be a haircutter when I grew up, and he said, 'No you're not. You're gonna be a ballplayer.' See, one side of the family had too many boys and no girls, and the other side—my father's—was all girls. So, I'd get together with the girls and try to straighten my hair, or I'd do their hair."

And then one day, his career at an end, it all came true. Bernie was tending bar at the Bump Shop in Lincoln Park, in the downriver area of Detroit, when a customer, Allison McKay, talked him into going to hair school with her.

"You know, Bill, the most fun I used to have, even when I was having trouble playing ball and stuff, you know what I'd do? I'd stop at the side of a ballpark, where there were kids playing, you know, throwing the ball all over the field and everything. And I'd stop and watch them because of all the fun they were having, And I just tried to realize, hey, I had a lot of fun when I played when I was a kid, too. If I could just get that frame of mind. You know what I mean?"

Absolutely.

"But how do you like the haircut, Bill?"

Why, it's beautiful, Bernardo.   ✦

Brains, Baseball, and Branch Rickey

(April 1948)

John Chamberlain

By MIDSEASON OF last summer the Brooklyn Dodgers, a quiet, well-behaved lot of ball players who no longer swaggered under the name of the Beloved Bums, were clinging with tenacious claws to first place in the National League. Their hold on such an exalted spot was a tribute to the Brooklyn president, the portly, pious-talking, and shrewd Mr. Branch Rickey, who had figured in the spring that his team of youngsters ("Rickey's kindergarten") wouldn't really begin clicking until August 15.

Back in April the Dodgers were unsettled at first and third bases, their pitching staff was uncertain, and, worst of all, they had just been deprived of their aggressive manager, the loquacious Leo Durocher, who for no ascertainable reason had been banished from baseball for a year by ex-Senator Happy Chandler, the big leagues' High Commissioner and synthetic tough guy. Rickey had surmounted his managerial troubles by bringing the ancient and loyal Burt Shotton, a friend of four decades' standing, out of retirement to handle his athletes, and he had plugged the gaps in the infield with characteristic speed. But his pitchers kept going to pieces in the fifth inning, and in June his star outfielder, Pete Reiser, cracked his skull while pursuing and clutching a fly ball at the centerfield barrier at Ebbets Field in Brooklyn. It was all most disconcerting, yet the team continued to stay up there.

Rickey, who doesn't deal in legerdemain, sometimes wondered just how it was possible. For everywhere he looked from out beneath his shaggy eyebrows, which are strictly on the John L. Lewis order, he saw traps, snares, and elephant pits. Just how dangerous the footing was likely to become Rickey knew better than anyone else, for the traps and snares all bore one legend: "Constructed by Branch Rickey." Before hiring himself to the Dodgers in late 1942 Rickey had put in twenty-seven years of careful work on the St. Louis Cardinals—and here, in late July of 1947, the Cardinals were coming fast, moving up from last place to the first division with General Patton speed. It was no comfort for Rickey to realize that the entire Cardinal infield was a Rickey-recruited, Rickey-trained bunch of knock-you-down, run-you-over athletes, or that the Cardinal pitchers had been developed in a Rickey-devised minor league farm club system. Nor did it help Rickey to remember that Eddie Dyer, the Cardinals' manager who had won the pennant in 1946, had blurted out: "I owe it all to Rickey."

Rickey, who had originally put the Cardinals together, knew that the "old reliables" from St. Louis were the team to beat—and so it proved in September, when Brooklyn turned back the Cardinal threat. But as August approached there were other teams to beat, too. Curiously enough, they also were teams that owed their eminence to Branch Rickey.

First of all, there was a New York team powered by Walker Cooper and Johnny Mize, two ex-Cardinals from the old Rickey system who had collected fifty-three home runs between them by July 31. And up in Boston there were the Braves, managed by an ex-Rickey player and manager, Billy Southworth, who was getting a lot out of material that included the ex-Rickey outfielder Johnny Hopp. What Rickey had built threatened to tear Rickey down, and the man who is universally known in baseball as "The Brain" didn't relish the results of his own cerebration. In a fight calculated to prove which was the better man, Rickey or Rickey, Rickey could conceivably get the worst of it.

II

But if Rickey didn't have an opposition to spur him on, he would not feel at home, and the fact that he had invented the opposition himself merely saved him the trouble of doing it all over again. The president of the Dodgers, who is called The Mahatma when he isn't called The Brain, fears mediocrity as most men fear the plague, and he knows that lethargy steals upon a man when he lacks competition. An inveterate lighter and chewer of cigars, which he uses as adjuncts to conversation, Rickey has a habit of tossing lighted kitchen matches into his Montague Street office wastebasket, and his secretary, Jane Ann Jones, half suspects him of trying to kindle real fires under himself and the whole office staff. When doctors ask the sixty-six-year-old Rickey when he intends to slow down, he grins and says: "I certainly expect my funeral cortege to move at a dignified pace." Rickey's drive to isolate the secret of perpetual motion goes on in spite of an inner-ear complication that sometimes results in dizzy spells when he gets overtired. But when the dizziness has passed, he rises with a cry that his competitors are working nights—which means that if his office staff gets home to supper once a week a miracle has happened.

With his ball players, Rickey doesn't need kitchen matches to build fires under them. He does his best to keep them on low or medium salaries on a general level of sameness—and so makes them hungry for the extra cash which a World Series inevitably brings. When he has a veteran who seems to be fading, the old fellow is stirred to renewed life by peculiarly coincidental rumors of an impending trade. Rickey stocks his minor league farm clubs (and Brooklyn has twenty-five of these, ranging from Montreal to Ponca City, and from Abilene to Zanesville) with the best young talent that a superior scouting system can turn up, and the Brooklyn player who has a faltering spell knows that at least five and maybe twenty eager farm hands are ready to scrap and snarl for his place. When a star player is about to go over the peak, Rickey, who has a sixth sense about such things, sells or trades his contract without compunction or sentiment—although he will hire a good "organization type" man as a scout, a coach, or a front-office man if the fellow needs a job when his playing days are done. Rickey is a compassionate person when it doesn't interfere with his inexorable drive to his goal: the pennant. (Parenthetically, his piety—along with his feeling about his mother's wishes—keeps him from attending games on Sunday, although he has no objections to sharing the gate receipts derived from a Sunday doubleheader.)

The modern game of baseball, with its short right field fences, its hopped-up "rabbit" ball, and its concomitant home-run slugging, owes its character to Babe Ruth. Its integrity is undoubtedly due to the late Judge Landis, the High Commissioner who purged it of gambling influences after the scandalous behavior of the Chicago "Black Sox" of 1919 in throwing the World Series to the Cincinnati Reds. But the creativeness of modern baseball is almost entirely the product of Branch Rickey, who has been responsible for most of the innovations of the past four decades. When he was field manager of the St. Louis Browns and the St. Louis Cardinals, he used newfangled sliding pits in which to instruct his players in base running, and he tried to make baseball smartness plain via the institution of the blackboard talk. When a pitcher failed to come to rest on two feet after a pitch, Rickey would carefully explain that a man who was off balance couldn't very well leap for a high bounder or a line drive. The athletes were too dumb to master Rickey's complicated ideas about cut-off plays, or even to catch up with Rickey's common sense when it was presented in polysyllabic words, but when Rickey moved to the front office of the Cardinals back in 1925 he found plenty of scope for his ingenuity.

It was while he was still a field manager with the Cardinals that he devised the farm system, which enables a major league club to save money by developing its own players on minor league teams which it owns or controls. In its way, the farm idea was simple industrial "rationalization" applied to baseball: just as it made sense for Andrew Carnegie to own his own ore mines, his own ore boats, and his own coking coal supplies to support his steel mills, so did it make sense for the Rickey St. Louis Cardinals of 1920 to control their own supply of future stars. But if the idea was simple, it remains true that Rickey was the only man in baseball who had the wit to think of it. A dimly distant relative of the man who invented the gin rickey, he is still coming up with beautiful simplicities that are as obvious as a full moon once Rickey has made them obvious. Either Mr. Rickey is very smart, or the game which he adorns is as dumb as the late Ring Lardner thought it was.

Rickey didn't evolve the farm system idea out of any philosophical bias in favor of business rationalization. He did it because of a condition in St. Louis. The St. Louis National League club had no money back in 1919. When a Cardinal scout would put in a bid in Albuquerque for a potential Ty Cobb, the Albuquerque owner would call up the rich New York Giants or the flush Chicago Cubs and get a really good price for the rookie. This created a vicious circle in St. Louis: the rich Giants got better, but the poor Cardinals, unable to get and develop young stars with box office appeal, just couldn't earn any money at the gate to buy stars from anybody else.

Rickey tried various ways to counteract the Cardinals' poverty, even going so far as to borrow his wife's rugs for office use when he was trying to impress a visitor and put over a deal. Such makeshift shenanigans couldn't compensate for the absence of a good double-play combination, so Rickey, who had been a bright young school-teacher in Scioto County, Ohio, before going on to college at Ohio Wesleyan and to law school at the University of Michigan, bethought himself of a chain-store system of primary, secondary, and tertiary baseball schools. He talked over his proposition with Sam Breadon, a young automobile salesman whom he had persuaded to put $2,000 into the Cardinals, and together they pioneered the idea at Houston, Texas, and Fort

Smith, Arkansas. With Breadon's support and money, Rickey's Cardinals subsequently bought fifty per cent of the stock in the Syracuse club of the International League. First baseman Jim Bottomly alone was worth the purchase price. From here on the Cardinals branched out, buying into Sioux City and many smaller clubs. By 1928 the Cardinal investment in farm clubs amounted to $946,000. And likely looking youngsters were moving upward for nominal sums to the parent St. Louis team. Farmer Rickey's green fingers grew the sprouts that blossomed as Manager Gabby Street's pennant winners of 1930 and 1931 and Frankie Frisch's famous Gashouse Gang of 1934. St. Louis won six pennants and four World Series when Rickey was laboring under President Sam Breadon as the club's vice presidential general manager in charge of the farm system.

In twenty-seven years with the Cardinals Rickey made more than a million dollars in salary and commissions. But the St. Louis attendance could not equal the figures achieved in such metropolitan areas as Chicago and New York, so Rickey had to develop the selling of players into a fine art in order to create and justify his financial take. When Rickey was a big league catcher with the St. Louis Browns in 1906 and the New York Highlanders (ancestor of the modern Yankees) in 1907, he wasn't very good. (Indeed, thirteen Washington runners stole bases on his lame arm in a single game in 1907.) But he had an unmatched eye for a player's reflexes, which he further developed when he was coach of the University of Michigan ball team in 1910 and 1911—the team on which George Sisler, future major league .400 hitter, was both his special project and star. With his uncanny eye for the nature of reflex action, Rickey could tell just when the ripeness of a young star was about to become the rottenness of baseball middle age, which may even begin in a player's late twenties. In 1937 pitcher Dizzy Dean looked to Rickey to be through forever. Since he is constitutionally unable to tell a lie, Rickey announced to Phil Wrigley of the Cubs that Dean's arm was dead—but that he wouldn't take less than $185,000 for Dizzy's contract. Wrigley couldn't believe that Rickey would be holding out for $185,000 for a dead-armed pitcher, so he bought Dizzy anyway. But dead the arm was, and Rickey chuckled to himself as he pocketed his twenty per cent of the profits.

On the Dean sale and others like it (he marketed a slowing Ducky Wucky Medwick to the Dodgers for $125,000) Rickey built the Cardinals into the property which Sam Breadon recently sold to Bob Hannegan's syndicate for

$3,000,000. In Brooklyn, Rickey's reward is $50,000, plus bonuses based on attendance. And the canny player sales go on in Brooklyn, even though Ebbets Field can attract more spectators in the course of a year than St. Louis's Sportsman's Park ever succeeded in doing. Last year Rickey realized some $600,000 in cash for ball players' contracts sold to Pittsburgh, Boston, and Philadelphia—and the old Ebbets Field debt has been paid off with a rapidity that no longer pleases the Brooklyn Trust Company, which has had its profitable lien on the Dodgers ever since the estate of the late Charles Ebbets fell into disarray.

Rickey's pre-eminence as a baseball business man is based on the mastery of conceptual thinking that first produced the farm club idea. He has basic theories about everything, and he employs mathematical concepts in working them out. A mathematical theory of probability is at the back of his methods of creating and balancing a ball team. What Rickey aims at is a blend of speed, throwing arms, and power, with fast outfielders like Pete Reiser compensating for average-good pitchers, and with fast baserunners like Jackie Robinson stretching doubles into triples and potential infield outs into singles. In his salad days Rickey carried a little notebook filled with the names of promising sandlot, high school, and college ball players; now he has a card-index system covering the nation's schools and minor leagues. To move up in the Rickey chain gang, a young man must have at least two of the three qualifications of speed, throwing arm, and power; Rickey doesn't go for mere sluggers, or mere speed kings, or mere throwers.

When he was still with the Cardinals he sold Johnny Mize to the New York Giants because Johnny had little beyond slugging ability to recommend him—and also because St. Louis had two brilliant farm club first basemen, Ray Sanders and Johnny Hopp, ready to replace him. Always Rickey strives for the blend in a ball player, and a blend of blends in the team. He likes pitchers who can vary their pitching direction, first sweeping the ball in from halfway to third or first base, then zooming it down from extension-ladder height. And he keeps track of his blends and blend of blends with mathematical precision; he now has a statistician at work at $7,000 per annum traveling with the team and jotting down the nature of every pitch by a Brooklyn pitcher and every hit by a Brooklyn batter.

The theory of mathematical probability is reinforced by the keen Rickey eye, which takes in all details of physiology, anatomy, and psychology. It was

Rickey who made George Sisler over from a pitcher into the greatest first baseman of all eras. Once at a Cardinal training camp, Rickey heard the crack of a bat against horsehide, and looked up to see the ball hit the fence. "Judas Priest," he shouted, "who hit that ball?" "Hafey," came the reply. "He's a pitcher." "You mean he *was* a pitcher," said Rickey. "Tell him he's no longer one. He's an outfielder." The keenness of this instantaneous judgment was corroborated when Chick Hafey developed into one of the heaviest hitters in the National League.

Last spring Dixie Walker, popular Dodger right fielder, was hitting well above the .300 mark. But to Rickey, the reflexes of the thirty-six-year-old Dixie seemed to be slowing up. He started in with the inexorable mathematical analysis, and discovered that Dixie, a left-handed batter, was slicing a big percentage of his hits into left and left-center fields instead of "pulling" them straight and true into right field in the old Walker manner. The Rickey statistician reported a difference of 100 points in Dixie's effectiveness against right- and left-handed pitchers. This all meant that Dixie was tired or going over the peak. In June rumors hit the sports pages that Rickey was contemplating the idea of peddling Dixie to Pittsburgh. Whether this would be good business or not involved a mathematical conjecture; he might get a good price—in cash or ball players—for Dixie's big name, but on the other hand, Dixie's Brooklyn fans might stay away from the park in droves to protest the deal. (They might even hang Rickey in effigy in front of Brooklyn's Borough Hall.) The question was: would Dixie bring in more in a trade than he would bring in at the gate? In the end Rickey postponed the sale of Dixie to the winter months in which even Brooklyn fans grow relatively lethargic. But the first rumors of the trade were followed by a revival of Dixie Walker's old-time playing form; the burr that Rickey put under the veteran's tail evidently worked.

In the late winter, when Rickey is wrangling about contracts with his young men, he trots out the systematic thinking all over again. His theory that scantily paid ball players will fight doubly hard for World Series cash naturally doesn't go down with the athletes, but Rickey has a plausible line which he buttresses with actual statistics. An overpaid ball player, he argues, will become satiated with the game at a younger age than might otherwise be the case; therefore the owner who dishes out too much money too early is cutting years of top earning power off a man's playing life. Rickey can keep the ball of salary palaver spinning so merrily and in such a confusing way that players sometimes accede to his demands out of sheer intellectual exhaustion. Once a holdout ball player was urged to get together with Rickey and settle their salary differences. "Not me," he answered. "I ain't going to see Mr. Rickey. Five minutes with him and I'll sign anything he hands me and I won't be a hold-out any more."

Since coming to Brooklyn, Rickey has been a trifle more generous with veterans' salaries than in his old Cardinal days. But he bases the generosity that paid Dixie Walker $25,000 for 1947 on the fact that Brooklyn is a richer gold mine than St. Louis, not on any change in his basic philosophy. The proper salary for a ballplayer, says Rickey, must be based on (1) the club's ability to pay, (2) the player's ability to earn, and (3) the relationship of the player's income to that of others on the team. What Hank Greenberg may be getting in Pittsburgh or elsewhere for the home runs he hit three years ago in Detroit has nothing to do with the case.

But if Rickey sees no other way of binding a man's loyalty he will loosen up the purse strings. In 1933 the Cardinals, needing a shortstop, purchased Leo Durocher from Cincinnati. Leo stormed into Rickey's office and informed his new boss that he wasn't going to take any Sunday school lecturing from a pious old cheapskate. "Leo," said Rickey calmly, "we've bought your contract from Cincinnati. It isn't as much as I'd like to pay you, but I don't believe in tearing up contracts. So there's a thousand dollar bonus waiting for you at the treasurer's office."

Scarcely able to believe his ears, Leo gulped and became a Rickey man for life. When he was ousted last season as Brooklyn manager by High Commissioner Chandler, Leo prefaced his departure with an earnest tribute to Mr. Rickey, who had given his tacit promise to fight to bring the errant bad boy back to the Dodgers as field boss in 1948. Rickey takes pride in his ability to reform Durocher at periodic intervals; as he says, "evil is transient." In 1934 when the Cardinals were in the thick of a pennant fight, Rickey persuaded a business woman friend of his, the attractive Grace Dozier, to consummate a romance by marrying Leo a few days before the St. Louis–Detroit World Series "just to clear his mind." With his mind cleared, the benedict Durocher played a bangup game to defeat Detroit. Unfortunately the marriage is numbered among those which didn't last, but Mr. Rickey has high hopes that Leo's romance with the moving picture star Laraine Day will steady the boy permanently: Miss Day neither smokes, chews, drinks, gambles, nor swears. The main reason why Rickey brought Durocher back to manage the 1948 Dodgers is that Leo never rests on old laurels; each game is a career with Leo. Burt Shotton, on the other hand, might have grown conservative after his 1947 pennant.

Rickey is naturally high on "sincere" types like Lou Boudreau, the college-bred, family-man shortstop-manager of Cleveland. He quickly weeds out the gamblers, drinkers, and "roosters" on his teams if he can't reform them; in fact, his dislike of high-stake gambling explains the departure of certain supposedly key Dodgers after Rickey came to Brooklyn in late 1942. But for all his dislike of liquor and gambling Rickey has an inordinate affection for real screwballs. He would die of inanition if he didn't have a Dizzy Dean or a Pepper Martin in his past to spin yarns about (he tells a wonderful novell-length story of how Dizzy Dean permanently lost track of his father when a mile-long freight train came between the two cars which were carrying the Dean family over the face of Texas). Undoubtedly the value of screwballs at the box office adds to the affection Rickey feels for them, but he also responds to the challenge which a hell-raising ball player presents. He knows that if he can "reclaim" a wastrel or a drunkard, he will bind the fellow to him with hoops of steel—and maybe make a hundred thousand dollars out of him. It was a reformed and grateful Billy Southworth who won the pennant as manager of the Cardinals in 1942.

The mathematics of reform may be somewhat tenuous in Rickey's mind, but when it comes to the mathematics of a swap he has things figured out to the last decimal point. Before going in to a trading session he first puts a money price on all the players he hopes to swap and all the players he hopes possibly to get. Then he proceeds to translate the money prices into simple units for quick addition in his mind—say, Pitcher Kirby Higbe equals 10 units, Pitcher Hank Behrman equals 5, Infielder Gene Mauch equals 2, Outfielder Gionfriddo equals 4, and so on. When the sessions get a little wild or fogged with cigar smoke, with the opposition throwing in extra rookies and aged pitchers, Rickey is likely to come out of the deal with $150,000 in cash and ball players for the $130,000 worth of baseball ivory he has just given away. Naturally, any evaluation of a ball player who is being swapped for another ball player is subjective, at least to some extent, but Rickey takes a fiendish delight in seeing a confused opponent putting two separate money valuations on a man during the course of a session. Rickey's own unit system of valuation keeps this from happening to himself; he always makes sure his units balance when the columns are added. He isn't telling the identity of the victims of his unitary figuring, for he has to deal with the same club owners and managers year after year. Even so, anyone who has dealt with Rickey half suspects that he has been hornswoggled; the gag around the National League circuit is that Rickey would sell a player he didn't expect to see live through the summer. The fact that he can't lie about a player's condition doesn't hurt Rickey's chances in a trade, for he is such a master of longwinded double talk that he can spout forever without divulging a thing.

III

Rickey left the St. Louis Cardinals in late 1942 when the war destroyed the basis for his customary $80- or $90,000-a-year take. With the military draft scooping up the promising farm club kids, the St. Louis club decided that it must hang on to its veterans—and there was literally nobody for Rickey to peddle to the other clubs for fantastic sums and fantastic commissions. Since Mrs. Jane Moulton Rickey, an Ohio country store-keeper's daughter whom Rickey had married after first breaking her down with more than a hundred proposals, had her roots in St. Louis, where she had raised a son and five daughters, this matter of pulling up stakes was an unwelcome prospect to the whole Rickey tribe. Rickey could have taken a job with the St. Louis Browns of the American League and gone on living in his charming home at Country Life Acres, where the Rickey family had spent fabulously happy years listening to "pa's" stories about being cornered in a boat by an alligator and missing pheasants which "flew out the back way." But there were two other prospects that beckoned: first, the prospect of taking over the Philadelphia Phillies and lifting them out of their customary berth in the league cellar, and second, the tantalizing prospect of giving Brooklyn a baseball organization commensurate with the enthusiasm of the one really baseball-mad town in the United States.

The choice was put up to nineteen of "Rickey's boys"—key scouts and business managers in the Cardinal chain system who could be counted on to follow Rickey anywhere. After hours of deliberation the decision was unanimous: "Go to Brooklyn!" And so Rickey pulled up stakes at the age of sixty-one, sold his home, and entered previously hostile Flatbush as general manager. (Later he and his friends bought stock control of the club.) With Wid Mathews, one of the great judges of neophyte baseball talent, with brother Frank Rickey, and with George Sisler, who is as good a talent scout as he was once a first baseman, Rickey started to build up a Brooklyn farm system to surpass the one he and his men had created for St. Louis. Today the Brooklyn system, with its twenty-five minor league clubs, is a multi-million-dollar investment. The Montreal, St. Paul, and Fort Worth clubs are owned outright. And the fact that three-fourths of the farm teams finished in the first division in 1947 argues plenty of talent for future Dodger teams.

To keep in touch with the soil after coming to the Flatbush pavements, Rickey has bought himself a salt water farm at Chestertown, Maryland. He commutes to his rural hideout whenever possible, gets up at dawn to run the disk-harrow, and has even been known to shave in a taxicab crossing the Brooklyn Bridge in order to get in an extra hour's sleep in the country before returning to his Montague Street office. Chestertown, however, sees but little of him during the summer season. Although he is afraid of high places (he even pulls the shades in a hotel room to keep from looking too precipitately at the distant ground), Rickey spends the working baseball season hopping about the country in a private plane. En route between farm clubs and crucial series he and his wife and cronies play a wildly interminable game of Hearts. They seldom look out unless they are passing over Rickey's native county in Ohio, in which case the Rickey family gazes at the old home scene and says "moo-o-o." At table the Rickeys play a strange game: one of the Rickeys will suddenly put a finger to his or her nose, which is a signal for all to follow suit. The last person to touch the nose is banished to a place beneath the table, where he or she must eat in darkness and ignominy. Mrs. Rickey's mother, who is nearing a hundred, is usually exempted.

Before the advent of Rickey, Brooklyn baseball had been on a hit-or-miss basis. Once upon a time, when Charles Ebbets and Steve McKeever were alive, the team had made money. But with the death of Ebbets, the confusion among heirs, and easy credit at the bank, the club had fallen under the sway of the Brooklyn Trust Company, which had everything to recommend it except a knowledge of inside baseball. During the pre-Rickey days Brooklyn sometimes won a pennant or staggered home in second place with ancient castoffs who were prone to "September wilt," but there was no more system to this procedure than there was to Manager "Uncle" Wilbert Robinson's eccentric method of benching outfielders whose names he had forgotten how to spell correctly for the starting lineup slip. And the Brooklyn civic inferiority complex, which demands a perpetual winner, went pretty much unassuaged.

The first attempt at soothing Brooklyn's feelings was made in 1937, when the Dodger directors, acting on Rickey's advice, hired the flamboyant Rickey protégé, Larry MacPhail, to rebuild the club from scratch. MacPhail installed new lighting fixtures, painted the stands, and purchased a whole army of Big Name ball players, including some extra-special ivory from Rickey's barracks in St. Louis. With Durocher as his manager (bought, incidentally, from Rickey), MacPhail finally won a pennant in 1941. But the cost of getting championship athletes such as Medwick, Mickey Owen, and Durocher from Rickey was staggering, and the profit-starved Brooklyn directors evidently thought it cheaper in the long run to buy Rickey direct. Accordingly the bid went out in 1942 and Rickey accepted.

Rickey and the nineteen "Rickey boys" had correctly doped Brooklyn's characteristics. They had figured that Brooklyn was a country town which needed a shrewd country boy—*i.e.,* Branch Rickey, from the Duck Run country of southern Ohio—to help it along in its baseball fortunes. When he was a hungry farm kid in Duck Run, Rickey had developed an overmastering desire to outslick all city slickers, and the drive persists to this day. Rickey is a vague fellow who gets lost on subways and commuters' trains; he wears a suit or a hat until his wife takes it away from him; he is perennially short of pocket money; he forgets to eat his meals, and he has even been known to mop his brow with two black socks taken absently from his hip pocket in the middle of an important speech. But the vagueness merely means that Rickey has a genius's ability to concentrate with overwhelming intensity on the problem at hand. When he missed his commuter's stop in suburban Forest Hills, where he lived until recently, it merely indicated that he was about to pull off a deal that would mean all the difference between a winner or a loser.

IV

The Rickey need for compensation just matches Brooklyn's need for the same thing. Rickey has been compensating ever since he taught school in Duck Run, where it was a mark of pedagogical success to keep the hulking louts in the front row from soiling teacher's shoes with tobacco juice. By dint of brain-power Rickey mastered the louts. He learned Latin and Greek in his spare time in his strenuous efforts to prepare for Ohio Wesleyan, where he finally managed to catch up with the rest of his class in senior year. As a big league catcher Rickey failed to set the world on fire. He lost his first major league job with Cincinnati when Manager Joe Kelley, a tough, irreverent old

Baltimore Oriole, fired him because of his refusal to play Sunday ball. Later he failed to stick with the St. Louis Browns and the New York Highlanders. The reason for his failure became obvious in late 1907, when the doctors told him he had tuberculosis.

The t.b. setback merely whetted Rickey's appetite for success. After a winter at Saranac, Rickey went to the University of Michigan, where he crammed three years of law school work into two years in the intervals when he wasn't coaching the baseball team. He failed to make ends meet as a lawyer in Boise, Idaho, where he hung out his shingle in 1912. Colonel Bob Hedges of the St. Louis Browns rescued him from poverty by hiring him as his Pacific Coast scout in 1913. During his year as a scout Rickey sent three winning ballplayers to the Browns—an outfielder named Patterson, a pitcher named Leverenz, and a catcher named Agnew. Leverenz and Agnew were Brown standbys for years. And when Rickey moved east from the Pacific Coast to manage the Browns he signed his college protégé, George Sisler, who promptly began to knock down the American League fences.

At sixty-six the ability to appreciate young ballplayers is still Rickey's chief business asset. But he no longer relies on chance abetted by his own eyesight—or even on the farm club idea which he pioneered with the St. Louis Cardinals. Brooklyn's farm system is first-rate: for example, its Montreal club in the International League, managed by the shrewd Clay Hopper, usually contains enough talent on its payroll to send up replacements guaranteed to give Brooklyn a winner for some years to come. Brooklyn's twenty-eight full-time scouts, many of whom came east with Rickey from St. Louis, are as keen as any in the game. But where other major league clubs have their farm systems to compete with Brooklyn's, Rickey has gone them all one better. Each year, in Florida, he runs a baseball finishing school for his own crop of farm-club rookies. A year ago, in Pensacola, he and his scouts processed some six hundred young ballplayers, giving them forced-draft instruction in sliding, batting stance, pitching follow-through, and other polished baseball savvy that it takes an ordinary Giant or Brave rookie, for example, two or three years' experience to learn. With the finishing school added to the farm system, Rickey figures that he has a two- or three-year advantage over the rest of the field. By the time the New York Giants and the Cincinnati Reds and the rest of the National League clubs have built up their own finishing schools, Rickey will undoubtedly have another idea to keep him at the head of the procession. Even though his competitors are "working nights," Rickey counts on his own superior wit and cleverness to turn up better ideas than can be provided by anybody else in the game.

V

The best recent example of Rickey's wit and cleverness is the Jackie Robinson story. When the New York State Antidiscrimination Law was passed, the late Mayor La Guardia appointed a Committee for Unity with a subcommittee to consider the problem of the Negro in baseball. The subcommittee included Larry MacPhail of the Yankees, Bill Robinson, the Negro tap dancer, Judge Jeremiah Mahoney, Arthur Daley, sports columnist of the New York *Times,* and—Branch Rickey. The slow deliberations of the committee drove Rickey mad, and characteristically he decided to bypass the committee business by going out into the field and hiring a good Negro player to play for Brooklyn or one of the Brooklyn farm teams. While others were debating the Negro problem in doubletalk as a sociological issue, Rickey was spending $25,000 to search the continent.

Scouts finally reported that a certain Jack Roosevelt Robinson, shortstop for the Kansas City Monarchs, a crack Negro club, had major league potentialities. Rickey had him signed at once, and sent him to Montreal. As the Montreal second baseman, Robinson led the International League in batting with .349 and spark-plugged his team to the pennant. An ex-U.C.L.A. athlete whose speed had enabled him to star at football, baseball, basketball, tennis, and broadjumping, Robinson was a better answer to the "Negro problem" than anything that the La Guardia subcommittee could turn up.

Last year Rickey brought Robinson up to Brooklyn and had him installed as the club's first baseman. During the early weeks of the season Robinson labored under a strain. Some sixty per cent of the National League's ballplayers are from the Southern states, and Robinson was fearful of plunking the ball too hard into a Mississippian's ribs or of taking out a Georgia-bred shortstop with a rolling block calculated to break up a double play. But early in June Jackie's natural adventurousness cropped out; he scored all the way from first in Chicago on a sacrifice, and in Pittsburgh he stole home. By the end of July he was hitting .300 and leading the Dodger regulars in batting. He was also leading the league in stealing bases and in scoring runs. By September he was the Rookie of the Year.

Now that he has become an accepted institution, Robinson is ready to become one of the real stars of the National League. Other Negroes were quickly signed in the wake of Robinson's exploits—Doby by Cleveland, and Thompson and Brown by the St. Louis Browns. But Rickey, with his usual acumen, has already cornered the best talent in the Negro baseball world. Roy Campanella, the Montreal catcher, is a Negro—and Campanella played a game in 1947 that makes him a logical candidate for this year's Dodgers. And Rickey's Dan Bankhead, Negro pitcher, has the makings of a comer.

Rickey normally takes an hour to answer a simple question: his method of illustration is to develop a parable with the drawling, long-winded but quite telling art of that other Ohio story-teller, Sherwood Anderson. The round-aboutness of Rickey's conversational and literary habits makes it impossible to quote him extensively without bursting an article or a sports column at the seams. But in the case of Robinson, Rickey is succinct. Asked if he had brought Robinson up to "solve a sociological problem," Rickey said: "I brought him up for one reason: to win the pennant. I'd play an elephant with pink horns if he could win the pennant."

Such an answer puts the "Negro problem" in its right perspective. It also puts Rickey in his right perspective. In St. Louis they used to say that "turmoil follows Rickey around and perches on his shoulder." In Brooklyn they pronounce it toimurl, and it poiches on the shoulder. Keeping up with Rickey is a hectic procedure. But as long as the turmoil pays off with a first-place perch for the Dodgers, Brooklyn is going to be for the strenuous life as lived by Branch Rickey. Even if he plays a pink elephant in the outfield.   ✦

It's Only a Game

(MAY 1956)

Shirley Jackson

THE LITTLE LEAGUE is new in our town this year, which may be the reason my friend Dot and I were so ill-prepared on opening day. Dot had learned how to keep a box score, of course, and I had my movie camera, and I noticed that Marian—we are speaking to Marian again now, although she has not been quite so cordial since her son Artie's batting average went way down—had a pair of field glasses.

On the day of the first game Dot and I established ourselves on a car robe up on a little hill near the third-base line, and looked complacently down on the neat little field our husbands had helped build. Dot asked me if I remembered most of the rules of baseball and I said well, of course, I knew both our boys were on the team with dark blue hats named the Braves, and my son Laurie had been coaching me a little, and Dot said Billy had tried to explain a lot of it to her, too.

"It's so good for the boys to get in on something like this," I said.

"Learning sportsmanship and all," Dot said.

"I was telling Laurie last night," I said, "that the important thing is to work together as a team, not as individuals, and it doesn't matter *who* wins as long as the game is well played."

"It's *only* a game, after all," Dot said.

"That's what Laurie told me." I said. ("It's *only* a game, for heaven's sakes," he had said to me, "try to remember, for heaven's sakes, it's only a *game.*") "I just hope the boys aren't nervous," I said.

"I think maybe they might be, just a tiny bit," Dot said. "But after all, it's such a big day for them."

We settled ourselves comfortably. Dot got out her score card and pencil and I put a new magazine of film in my movie camera. We could see our husbands standing around in back of the Braves' dugout, along with the fathers of all the other Braves players. They were in a group, chatting with great humorous familiarity with the manager and the two coaches of the Braves. The fathers of the boys on the opposing team, the Giants, were down by the Giant dugout, talking to the manager and the coaches of the Giants.

Marian, a friend of Dot's and mine whose boy Art was first baseman for the Giants, came hurrying past looking for a seat and we offered her part of our car robe. She sat down, breathless, and said she had lost sight of her husband, so we showed her where her husband was down by the Giant dugout with the other fathers. Then, suddenly from far down the block, we heard the high-school band playing "The Stars and Stripes Forever" and coming closer. Everyone stood up to watch and then the band turned the corner and came through the archway with the official Little League insignia and up to the entrance of the field. All the ball players were marching behind the band, tall and proud. The band went out onto the field and the ball players ran behind, lining up along the base lines. The sky was blue and the sun was bright and the boys stood lined up in their bright new uniforms, holding their caps while the band played "The Star-Spangled Banner" and the flag was raised.

"If you cry I'll tell Laurie," Dot said to me out of the corner of her mouth.

"Same to you," I said, blinking.

It was announced over the public-address system that the Braves were the home team, and after a minute I was able to make out that Laurie was on second base. I told Marian that I was relieved that Laurie was not pitching, since he had been so nervous anyway that pitching would have been too harrowing an experience for him, and Marian said that Artie had been perfectly willing to sit out the game as a substitute, or a pinch runner, or something, but the manager insisted upon putting him at first base because he was dependable.

"You know," she added with a little laugh, "*I* don't know one position from another, but of course Artie has always been quite a baseball authority."

"I'm sure he'll do very nicely," I said, trying to put some enthusiasm into my voice.

It turned out that Billy was on first base for the Braves, and Marian leaned past me to tell Dot that first base was a *very* responsible position and required a large knowledge of baseball, but she was certain that Billy would play as well as he could. Then she smiled in what I thought was a nasty kind of way and said she hoped the best team would win. Dot and I both smiled back and said we hoped so, too.

When the umpire shouted, "Play Ball!" people all over the park began call-ing out to the players, and I raised my voice slightly and said, "Hurray for the Braves," and that encouraged Dot and *she* called out, "Hurray for the Braves," but Marian, of course, had to say, "Hurray for the Giants."

The first Giant batter hit a triple, although, as my husband explained later, it would actually have been an infield fly if the shortstop had been looking and if he had thrown it anywhere near Billy at first. By the time Billy got the ball back into the infield the batter—Jimmie Hill, who had once borrowed Laurie's bike and brought it back with a flat tire—was on third. I could see Laurie out on second base banging his hands together and he looked so pale I was worried. Marian leaned around me and said to Dot, "That was a nice try Billy made. I don't think even Artie could have caught that ball."

"He looks *furious*," Dot said to me. "He hates to do things wrong."

"They'll settle down as soon as they get playing," I assured her. I raised my voice a little. "Hurray for the Braves," I said.

The Giants made six runs in the first inning, and each time a run came in Marian looked sympathetic and told us that really, the boys were being quite good sports about it, weren't they? When Laurie bobbled an easy fly right at second and missed the out she said to me that Artie had told her that Laurie was really quite a good little ball player and I mustn't blame him for an occa-sional error.

By the time little Jerry Hart finally struck out to retire the Giants Dot and I were sitting listening with polite smiles. I had stopped saying, "Hurray for the Braves." Marian had told everyone sitting near us that it was her boy who had slid home for the sixth run, and she had explained with great kindness that Dot and I had sons on the other team, one of them the first baseman who missed that long throw and the other one the second baseman who dropped the fly ball. The Giants took the field and Marian pointed out Artie, standing on first base slapping his glove and showing off.

Then little Ernie Harrow, who was the Braves' right fielder and lunched frequently at our house, hit the first pitched ball for a fast grounder which went right through the legs of the Giant center fielder and when Ernie came dancing onto second Dot leaned around me to remark to Marian that if Artie had been playing closer to first the way Billy did he might have been ready for the throw if the Giant center fielder had managed to stop the ball. Billy came up and smashed a long fly over the left fielder's head and I put a hand on Marian's shoulder to hoist myself up and Dot and I stood there howling,

"Run run run," and Billy came home and two runs were in. Little Andy put a surprise bunt down the first base line and Artie never even saw it and I bent down to tell Marian that Artie's extensive knowledge of baseball had apparently never included the study of fielding bunts; Laurie got a nice hit and slid into second and the Giants took out their pitcher and put in Buddy Williams, whom Laurie once beat up on the way to school. The score was tied with two out and Dot and I were both yelling and then Ernie Harrow came up for the second time and hit a home run, right over the fence where they put the sign advertising Jim Morrow's sand and gravel. We were leading eight to six when the inning ended.

Little League games are six innings, so we had five more innings to go. Dot went down to the refreshment stand to get some hot dogs and soda; she offered very politely to bring something for Marian but Marian said thank you, no; she would get her own. The second inning tightened up considerably as the boys began to get over their stage fright and play baseball the way they did in the vacant lots. By the middle of the fifth inning the Braves were leading nine to eight, and then in the bottom of the fifth Artie missed a throw at first base and the Braves scored another run. Neither Dot nor I said a single word, but Marian got up in a disagreeable manner and excused herself and went to sit on the other side of the field.

"Marian looks very poorly these days," I remarked to Dot as we watched her go.

"She's at *least* five years older than I am," Dot said.

"More than that," I said. "She's gotten very touchy, don't you think?"

"Remember when Artie used to have temper tantrums in nursery school?" Dot said.

In the top of the sixth the Braves were winning ten to eight, but then George Harper, who had been pitching accurately and well, began to tire, and he walked the first two batters. The third boy hit a little fly which fell in short center field, and one run came in to make it ten to nine, and then Georgie, who was by now visibly rattled, walked the next batter and filled the bases.

"Oh, no," Dot said suddenly, "don't you dare, you can't *do* it." I stood up and began to wail, "No, no, no." The manager was gesturing at Laurie and Billy. "No, no," I said to Dot, and Dot said, "He *can't* do it, don't let him. That's my little boy," she explained to a man sitting on the other side of her.

"It's too much to ask of the children," I said.

"It's her little boy, too," Dot said.

The man on Dot's other side leaned forward to speak to me. "Your boy a pretty good pitcher?" he asked.

"I'm sure he ought to be home in bed," I said. "He looks pale and from here even, I can see that he has a fever."

"Billy had a fever this morning," Dot said. "And he hurt his foot the other day."

While Laurie was warming up and Billy was getting into his catcher's equipment I suddenly heard my husband's voice for the first time. My husband has been a fan of the Brooklyn Dodgers all his life, and this was the first baseball game he had ever attended outside of Ebbets Field. "Put it in his ear, Laurie," my husband was yelling, "put it in his ear."

Laurie was chewing gum and throwing slowly and carefully, with a pitching windup he could only have learned from television. I stood feeling my shoulder shaking against Dot's, and I tried to get my camera open to check the film magazine but my fingers kept slipping and jumping against the little knob and I said to Dot that I guessed I would just watch the game for a while and not take pictures and she said earnestly that it was much better for Billy's precarious state of health to be in the shade around first base instead of the hot sun behind home plate and couldn't the manager see a simple little thing like that?

I said to Dot, "Laurie doesn't look very nervous," but then my voice failed, and I finished, "does he?" in a sort of gasp.

The batter was Jimmie Hill, who had already had three hits that afternoon. Laurie's first pitch hit the dust at Billy's feet and Billy sprawled full length to stop it and the crowd laughed and I said to Dot that I thought I would be getting on home. Laurie's second pitch sent Billy rolling again and a man in the crowd behind us giggled foolishly and said maybe the kids thought they were playing football or something, and Dot turned around and said in a voice like a knife edge, "Sir, that catcher is my son."

"I beg your pardon, ma'am, I'm sure," the man said.

The umpire called Laurie's next pitch ball three, although it was clearly a strike, and I was yelling, "You're blind, you're blind," and I could hear my husband shouting to throw the bum out. The same man behind us—I could tell by the silly giggle—said that *this* pitcher wasn't going to last very long and I clenched my fist and turned around and said in a voice that made Dot's sound cordial,

"Sir, that pitcher is *my* son. If there are any more personal remarks you care to make about any member of my family—"

"Or my family," Dot said, "we will call Mr. Tillotson, our village constable, and have you ejected from this ball park. Picking on little boys! Really!"

"Because it so happens," I said, "that my son—"

"Strike," the umpire said.

I shook my fist once more at the man with the silly giggle and he announced quietly and with some humility that he hoped both teams would win, and he subsided into absolute silence.

Laurie then pitched two more strikes, his nice fast ball. It was at about this point that Dot and I abandoned our spot up on the hill and got down against the fence with our faces pressed against the wire. "Come on, Billy boy," Dot was saying over and over, "come on, Billy boy," and I found that I was telling Laurie, "Only two more outs to go and we win, only two more outs to go and we win, only two more outs . . ." I could see my husband now but there was too much noise to hear him; he was pounding his hands against the fence. Dot's husband had *his* hands over his face and his back turned to the ball field.

"He can't hit it, Laurie," Dot yelled, "this guy can't hit," which of course was not true; the batter was Bob Weaver and he was standing there swinging his bat and sneering.

"Strike," the umpire said, and I leaned my forehead against the cool wire and said in a voice that had no power at all, "Just two more strikes, just get two more strikes."

Laurie looked at Billy, shook his head, and looked again. He grinned and when I glanced down at Billy I could see that behind the mask he was grinning too. I thought of how hours ago they had been playing catch with hamburger rolls and Dot and I made them stop. Laurie pitched, and Bob Weaver swung wildly. "Strike two," the umpire said. Dot and I held hands, and Laurie threw the fast ball for strike three.

One out to go, and Laurie and Billy and the shortstop stood together on the mound for a minute. They talked very soberly, but Billy was grinning again as he came back to the plate. Since I was incapable of making any sound I hung on to the wire and promised myself that if Laurie struck out this last batter I would never never say another word to him about the mess in his room, I would not make him paint the lawn chairs, I would not ever mention clipping the hedge.

"Ball one," the umpire said, and I found that I had my voice back. "Crook," I yelled, "blind crook."

Laurie pitched, the batter swung, and connected in a high foul ball back of the plate; Billy threw off his mask and tottered, staring up. The batter, the boys on the field, the umpire, waited, and Dot spoke into the silence.

"William," she said, *"you catch that ball."*

Then everyone was shouting wildly; I looked at Dot and said, "Golly." Laurie and Billy were slapping and hugging each other, and then the rest of the team came around them and the manager was there and I distinctly saw my husband, who is not a lively man, vault the fence to run into the wild group and slap Laurie with one hand and Billy with the other. The Giants gathered around their manager and gave a cheer for the Braves, and the Braves gathered around *their* manager and gave a cheer for the Giants, and Laurie and Billy came pacing together toward the dugout, past Dot and me.

I said, "Laurie?" and Dot said, "Billy?" and they stared at us, without recognition for a minute, both of them lost in another world, and then they smiled and Billy said, "Hi, ma," and Laurie said, "You see the game?"

I realized that my hair was over my eyes and I had broken two fingernails. Dot had a smudge on her nose and had torn a button off her sweater. We helped each other up the hill again and gathered up the car robe and the camera and the box score which Dot had not kept past the first Giant run. On our way to the car we passed Artie in his green Giant cap and we said it had been a fine game, he had played well, and he laughed and said tolerantly, "Can't win 'em all, you know."

Back at our house Dot and I washed our faces and took off our shoes and put the kettle on for a nice cup of tea. After a while Dot said that she certainly hoped Marian was not really offended at us.

"Yeah," I said. "Why don't we plan a victory party for the Braves at the end of the season?"

"Listen," Dot said, "I heard the boys talking one day. They were going to take some time this summer and clear out your barn and set up a record-player in there and put in a stock of records and have some dances."

"You mean . . . " I faltered. "With *girls?*"

Dot nodded. "Oh," I said.

When our husbands came home some time later we were talking about old high-school dances and the time we went out with those boys from

Princeton. After a while Laurie and Billy stopped in, briefly, to change their clothes and pick up some cookies. There was a pickup game down in Murphy's lot, they explained, and they were going to play some baseball.   ✦

IV: STANDING-ROOM ONLY

✦

HUNTING THE DECEITFUL TURKEY

Hunting the Deceitful Turkey

(DECEMBER 1906)

Mark Twain

WHEN I WAS a boy my uncle and his big boys hunted with the rifle, the youngest boy Fred and I with a shotgun—a small single-barrelled shotgun which was properly suited to our size and strength; it was not much heavier than a broom. We carried it turn about, half an hour at a time. I was not able to hit anything with it, but I liked to try. Fred and I hunted feathered small game, the others hunted deer, squirrels, wild turkeys, and such things. My uncle and the big boys were good shots. They killed hawks and wild geese and such like on the wing; and they didn't wound or kill squirrels, they *stunned* them. When the dogs treed a squirrel, the squirrel would scamper aloft and run out on a limb and flatten himself along it, hoping to make himself invisible in that way—and not quite succeeding. You could see his wee little ears sticking up. You couldn't see his nose, but you knew where it was. Then the hunter, despising a "rest" for his rifle, stood up and took offhand aim at the limb and sent a bullet into it immediately under the squirrel's nose, and down tumbled the animal, unwounded but unconscious; the dogs gave him a shake and he was dead. Sometimes when the distance was great and the wind not accurately allowed for, the bullet would hit the squirrel's head; the dogs could do as they pleased with that one—the hunter's pride was hurt, and he wouldn't allow it to go into the game-bag.

In the first faint gray of the dawn the stately wild turkeys would be stalking around in great flocks, and ready to be sociable and answer invitations to come and converse with other excursionists of their kind. The hunter concealed himself and imitated the turkey-call by sucking the air through the leg-bone of a turkey which had previously answered a call like that and lived only just long enough to regret it. There is nothing that furnishes a perfect turkey call except that bone. Another of Nature's treacheries, you see. She is full of them; half the time she doesn't know which she likes best—to betray her child or protect it. In the case of the turkey she is badly mixed: she gives it a bone to be used in getting it into trouble, and she also furnishes it with a trick for getting itself out of the trouble again. When a mamma-turkey answers an invitation and finds she has made a mistake in accepting it, she does as the mamma-partridge does—remembers a previous engagement and goes limping and scrambling away, pretending to be very lame; and at the same time she is saying to her not-visible children, "Lie low, keep still, don't expose yourselves; I shall be back as soon as I have beguiled this shabby swindler out of the country."

When a person is ignorant and confiding, this immoral device can have tiresome results. I followed an ostensibly lame turkey over a considerable part of the United States one morning, because I believed in her and could not think she would deceive a mere boy, and one who was trusting her and considering her honest. I had the single-barrelled shotgun, but my idea was to catch her alive. I often got within rushing distance of her, and then made my rush; but always, just as I made my final plunge and put my hand down where her back had been, it wasn't there; it was only two or three inches from there and I brushed the tail-feathers as I landed on my stomach—a very close call, but still not quite close enough; that is, not close enough for success, but just close enough to convince me that I could do it next time. She always waited for me, a little piece away, and let on to be resting and greatly fatigued; which was a lie, but I believed it, for I still thought her honest long after I ought to have begun to doubt her, suspecting that this was no way for a high-minded bird to be acting. I followed, and followed, and followed, making my periodical rushes, and getting up and brushing the dust off, and resuming the voyage with patient confidence; indeed, with a confidence which grew, for I could see by the change of climate and vegetation that we were getting up into the high latitudes, and as she always looked a little tireder and a little more discouraged after each rush, I judged that I was safe to win, in the end, the competition being purely a matter of staying power and the advantage lying with me from the start because she was lame.

Along in the afternoon I began to feel fatigued myself. Neither of us had had any rest since we first started on the excursion, which was upwards of ten hours before, though latterly we had paused awhile after rushes, I letting on to be thinking about something else; but neither of us sincere, and both of us waiting for the other to call game but in no real hurry about it, for indeed those little evanescent snatches of rest were very grateful to the feelings of us both; it would naturally be so, skirmishing along like that ever since dawn and not a bite in the mean time; at least for me, though sometimes as she lay on her side fanning herself with a wing and praying for strength to get out of this difficulty a grasshopper happened along whose time had come, and that was well for her, and fortunate, but I had nothing—nothing the whole day.

More than once, after I was very tired, I gave up taking her alive, and was going to shoot her, but I never did it, although it was my right, for I did not believe I could hit her; and besides, she always stopped and posed, when I raised the gun, and this made me suspicious that she knew about me and my marksmanship, and so I did not care to expose myself to remarks.

I did not get her, at all. When she got tired of the game at last, she rose from almost under my hand and flew aloft with the rush and whir of a shell and lit on the highest limb of a great tree and sat down and crossed her legs and smiled down at me, and seemed gratified to see me so astonished.

I was ashamed, and also lost; and it was while wandering the woods hunting for myself that I found a deserted log cabin and had one of the best meals there that in my life-days I have eaten. The weed-grown garden was full of ripe tomatoes, and I ate them ravenously, though I had never liked them before. Not more than two or three times since have I tasted anything that was so delicious as those tomatoes. I surfeited myself with them, and did not taste another one until I was in middle life. I can eat them now, but I do not like the look of them. I suppose we have all experienced a surfeit at one time or another. Once, in stress of circumstances, I ate part of a barrel of sardines, there being nothing else at hand, but since then I have always been able to get along without sardines. ✦

THE BIGGEST
RACE TRACK KILLING EVER MADE

(JANUARY 1959)

Leo Katcher

When he was shot down in the Park Central Hotel in New York on November 4, 1928, Arnold Rothstein had long been the organizer and overseer of big-time crime in the United States. His activities had included bootlegging, labor racketeering, stock-swindling, and political fixing, but to the public he was known, beyond all else, as a gambler. (His death stemmed from a poker game in which he lost $322,000, a debt on which he welched.)

In 1921 he made what was probably the biggest winning of all time on a horse race—and he did it without doping a horse, bribing a jockey, or doing anything else illegal. How he brought off this coup—with only six seconds to spare—is told in the following excerpt from a biography of Rothstein, The Big Bankroll.

IN THE PERIOD when Arnold Rothstein operated on the race track, purses were small and expenses high. There were no $100,000 and $200,000 races. And there was also relatively little policing of the tracks. No saliva tests were given, no scientific examinations made of the sputum and urine of winning horses. Jockeys, trainers, and some owners used their horses on the track purely as gambling instruments.

And yet it was not by doctoring horses but by outsmarting the other gamblers that Rothstein made his biggest killings.

Competitors were alert to every move Rothstein made. They tried to bribe his stable help and people who worked in his offices—and sometimes succeeded. The Jockey Club long sought some means of barring Rothstein from the turf. When it was known that Rothstein was betting a horse the odds were shaved. Often the horses were wiped off the slates. And yet Rothstein could not be stopped.

His first coup, which took place at Aqueduct, was unplanned. It resulted from a hunch Rothstein played, plus an assessment of all the factors involved. It was a lightning decision, reached in a matter of minutes. It succeeded by the margin of six ticks of a watch.

The date was July 4, 1921. This was the second big day of the racing season. The first was Memorial Day and the third was Labor Day. On only those three days of the racing season were the tracks thronged. On only those days were the crowds so large that they filled the clubhouse and overflowed the big betting shed in the grandstand. The crowd played an important part in helping Rothstein.

The horse by means of which Rothstein won $850,000 was named Sidereal, by Star Shoot out of Milky Way. Herbert Bayard Swope had picked the fortuitous and fitting name for the colt. Though it was owned by Rothstein, it was registered in the name of Max Hirsch, now an elder statesman of the turf but then Rothstein's trainer.

The Rothsteins arrived at the track shortly after noon and went to the table that Rothstein always had reserved in the clubhouse restaurant. While his wife Carolyn ate, Rothstein attended to business.

The table resembled an anthill, with a continual parade of people moving to and from it. These were a motley group. Clockers and trainers. Men who were settling the losses of yesterday or collecting their winnings. Stage stars and producers. Big-time politicians. Betting commissioners. Touts and would-be borrowers.

THE OUTSIDER

After a time Rothstein left the table and went toward the stable area with Hirsch. They had to muscle their way through the crowds. The clubhouse bookmaking section was a solid mass of people, all trying to get down their bets. Under the grandstand thousands were surrounding the bookmakers who had their stands there. Rothstein said, "They're so busy, they don't have a chance to think. This would be a day to put a horse over. By the time they got wise they'd be paying off."

He did not like the idea of losing so rare an opportunity. He was not certain that another would arise soon. Hopefully he asked Hirsch, "Do you know anything?"

Hirsch shook his head. "Nothing. The only horse we were going to run today was Sidereal. I'm going to scratch him for a race on Friday."

Rothstein's head jerked up. "What shape is he in?"

"He's sharp." Hirsch looked at his program. "I think he could beat these other horses."

"Then run him." Rothstein was eager, scenting the chance of cashing in.

"I didn't van him in. He's in the stable at Belmont." That was three miles away. Hirsch looked at his watch. "I can get him here in time, though, if you want to run him." Getting the horse there "in time" meant twenty minutes before the horses went to the post.

"We'll never get another chance like this," Rothstein said. "Get the horse here." He walked away from Hirsch.

Now Rothstein had to make his plans. His own employees and betting commissioners were known to every bookmaker. If any of these started making bets of any size, the bookmakers would immediately scent trouble. Not even the size of the crowd would prevent that.

Rothstein's first step, therefore, was to ask a number of people if they would mind his using their commissioners during the day. He made the request casually. "I don't figure on betting today, but I may change my mind. I gave Nat [Evans] and the boys a day off."

Those whom he asked had no choice but to grant permission. You didn't refuse Arnold Rothstein a slight favor; you never knew when you might need a large one.

Rothstein immediately hunted up the various commissioners. He told all of them he might be using them during the afternoon. He added, "If I do use you, don't tell anyone for whom you're betting; bookmakers know I'm playing a horse, they'll shave the odds on a five-dollar bet." The commissioners knew that this was true. And, like their principals, they were only too eager to do a favor for Rothstein.

There were two races to be run before that in which Sidereal was entered. At the track, betting was primarily from race to race. It would be some time before the prices went up on Sidereal's race. However, the "overnight" line had Sidereal at prices ranging from 25 to 1 to 40 to 1. He was the outsider, his form unknown, in the figures.

Rothstein now went looking for Hirsch to see how arrangements were going. He located him at a telephone, sweat running down his face. The trainer had been unable to get anyone at Belmont to answer the phone. It was a holiday and no one was in the track office.

He told this to Rothstein quickly.

Rothstein's lips thinned. He wasn't going to have his plans upset. "Come with me," he said, and hurried back to where Carolyn was sitting.

Of course, if the horse couldn't be vanned to Aqueduct in time, Rothstein would lose nothing. But he was already counting his potential winnings and these had attained a reality to him. In addition, there was his ego to satisfy. He had to make chumps of the bookmakers.

Carolyn caught his signal, rose from the table, and joined Rothstein and Hirsch.

"Tell her what she has to do," Rothstein said. "Tom Farley's out in the car and he can run her over."

Hirsch grasped at this. He lived close to Belmont and his wife was at home. "Pick her up," he said, "and go to the stables with her. Tell her to have the horse's plates changed and then put him into a van and get him over here. Tell her and the foreman we don't have any time to waste."

This was literally true. One race had been run. The horses were being saddled for the next. And Sidereal was entered in the race after that. Hirsch, not having scratched the horse, was responsible for its being in the stable area in time to run. If the horse was not there, Hirsch could be fined and suspended.

Carolyn rushed from the track. Farley drove her to the Hirsch home, where Mrs. Hirsch was picked up. On the way to Belmont, Carolyn explained what was to be done. She knew something big was happening and was caught up in the excitement of it. This was one of the few times when she shared anything with Rothstein. She didn't want to fail him.

The car pulled up in front of the stable where Rothstein's horses were quartered. A stableboy was sent to find the foreman. When he appeared, Mrs. Hirsch told him what had to be done. He said, "You'll never make it."

"We have to," Carolyn said.

The foreman shrugged. "I'll see what I can do." He sent the stableboy to find a van and driver. No blacksmith being available, he changed the shoes on the horse himself. As he worked, the stableboy returned. He had found a driver. The van would be on its way soon.

Carolyn looked at her watch. Time was going fast.

The Battle of the Odds

Time was also going fast at the track. Rothstein had begun his betting campaign. He had given cash to some of the commissioners, told others to bet in the names of their regular employers. His orders were simple. "Get as much as you can down, but make all your bets small. Use anyone you need to help you."

The opening price on Sidereal was 30 to 1. At this price, a bookmaker might take a $100 bet in the clubhouse, a $50 bet in the grandstand. However, after taking the bet, the bookmakers would probably cut the price. It was up to the agents, and their agents, to protect the price as long as possible.

Normally, if one bookmaker cut a price, others received a report quickly and, even though not carrying any bets, they would cut their price too. This day, however, most bookmakers were so busy they could hardly keep track of their own books, let alone keep watch on the competition. This was what Rothstein was banking on.

He had forty men placing bets for him, placing bets at the same time. The bets were relatively small, but they started adding up. The odds dropped from 30 to 25, and then to 20.

Now some bookmakers began to wonder what was going on. They dispatched men to seek Rothstein out and observe what he was doing. These spies returned to say Rothstein was sitting in a box with friends and apparently totally unconcerned with the wagering.

Since none of the bets had been placed by men who worked for Rothstein, it was plausible that he had nothing to do with the wagering. The race track was filled with many amateur gamblers on this holiday and most of these were long-shot players. That was why holidays were red-letter days to bookmakers. These were the days when they got the sucker play.

Nonetheless, the price on Sidereal dropped steadily as the bookmakers sought to keep their ledgers in balance.

Meanwhile, Hirsch was waiting at the gate. He had virtually no leeway left. It was five minutes to saddling time, five minutes until the horse had to be in the saddling area or Sidereal would automatically be scratched.

Jimmy McLaughlin, the paddock judge, began to verify the presence of the horses. He saw Sidereal's stall was empty. Hunting for Hirsch, he found him at the gate.

"Where's your horse, Max?"

"On the way" was all Hirsch could say. He was staring down the dirt road. He wondered if that was a dust cloud he saw.

McLaughlin looked at his watch. "Two minutes, Max."

"I know." Hirsch kept peering and was sure that it was a dust cloud.

Then it was one minute. McLaughlin said, "I'll have to notify the stewards, Max. Sorry." He started to turn.

As he did so the dust cloud lifted. A van was rolling up to the gate. It came to a stop. It wasn't enough that the horse was on the track; it had to be in the paddock.

Hirsch ran and opened the tail gate. The ramp went up. Hirsch jumped into the van, led the horse down, brought him into the paddock.

McLaughlin looked at his watch. "You sure drew it fine, Max. You beat the gun by six seconds."

Hirsch had no time for McLaughlin. He was rubbing the horse down, quieting him. Grooms and stableboys went to work on Sidereal. The jockey, who had been standing about, joined them.

Carolyn Rothstein drove up while this was going on. She got out of the car. "Were we in time?"

"Yes," Hirsch said.

Carolyn went back to the clubhouse. Walking through it, she saw Rothstein. Casually, she stepped into the box; Rothstein gave her a quick look. Her nod was almost imperceptible. So was Rothstein's smile.

The saddling bell sounded. Then the bugle for the parade to the post. The horses came out slowly, led by the outrider.

Rothstein got word to the commissioners. "Take any price."

Now the money was poured in. The price kept dropping and dropping. To 15 to 1, to 12, to 10, to 8, to 5, to 4.

There is a contagion, a hysteria, at a race track. Word spreads without a word being spoken. Five people, fifty, five hundred—five thousand—suddenly become aware of the same thing at the same moment. That happened at Aqueduct. It seemed as though everyone at the track simultaneously decided to bet on Sidereal.

Professional bettors, casual visitors, and touts. The innocents and the smart money. All of them wanted to get in on this. It was the same at every book, clubhouse, or grandstand. Price meant nothing.

The books did the only thing they could. They marked "OUT" opposite the name of Sidereal, boosted the odds on every other horse in the race, hoping, somehow, to balance their sheets.

The horses were nearing the post. Marshall Cassidy, the starter, and his assistants were at the barrier. And still Rothstein sat in the clubhouse box, chatting and smiling.

But the bookmakers were no longer fooled. They knew that they had been hoodwinked, outsmarted. And there wasn't anything they could do about it. There was no place—no one—to which they could turn and try to lay off the bets they had taken. The man who had made those bets was the only place open for laying them off.

Some did try, however. And, surprisingly, Rothstein was willing to take back some of the bets. But at "closing" odds. That meant the last price that had been posted against Sidereal, 8 to 5. He accepted bets amounting to $125,000 at those odds.

Why? Because it meant that, no matter what happened in the race, he had to be a winner. He was playing with the bookmakers' money. If Sidereal won, even after paying out $200,000, he would still be $850,000 ahead. If Sidereal lost, he would be about $40,000 winner. Not bad for an afternoon.

Of all the gamblers at the track he was the only one who could relax and watch the race. He had taken advantage of every bit of percentage. The odds were working for him. This was the gambler's dream, the sure thing. That is, if the gambler was Arnold Rothstein.

THE STRETCH

Sidereal was a golden chestnut with a glistening coat. He was a handsome horse, thick in the withers. There was a full field in the race—thirteen horses—but the crowd as interested in only one, Sidereal.

Cassidy and his assistants lined up the horses. This was before the starting gate was in use, and the horses ranged behind a barrier. It took time to steady the horses, to have them get over their nervousness. But Sidereal appeared without nerves. The horse stood ready, poised to break when the barrier went up. Its jockey, Billy Kelsay, was crouched low.

The chart on the race reports: "Start good." The horses broke almost in a straight line. Kelsay broke Sidereal fast so as to avoid trouble at the first turn. Sidereal was fourth as the horses went around the bend. Ultimo, owned by Charles Stoneham, was in the lead, with Northcliffe, owned by Thomas Fortune Ryan, the traction magnate, second, and Harry Payne Whitney's Brainstorm running third.

The horses ran in that position up the backstretch, made the turn, and then came around again into the stretch, with a quarter mile to go. Here Kelsay made his move. He loosed his grip on the reins, slapped the horse.

Sidereal passed Brainstorm and ranged up alongside Northcliffe. A half-dozen strides and Sidereal was second, a length behind Ultimo.

The boy on Ultimo started using his whip. The roar that was thundering out of the stands told him something was moving up behind him. Ultimo gave his best, but it was not enough. He was a tired horse and a hundred yards from the finish he began to bear out slightly. Kelsay had racing room, went inside Ultimo. Sidereal was a neck in front, a half length, and then a full length.

The chart reported: "Won driving. Place same." The margin of Sidereal's victory was a length and a half.

The time for the race was 1:11 2/5. Good time, but not sensational. But in that short time Arnold Rothstein had won more money than most people earned in all their lives.

He appeared to give no sign of strain, of pleasure. But Carolyn Rothstein knew how much emotion he felt because, when he spoke to her, there was a quiver in his voice. It was the only time she ever heard the quiver when he was a winner. All the other times it was present he was a loser.

With the end of the race won by Sidereal came the birth of a new race. The bookmakers, many of them knowing they were in debt to—and some beyond—the limit of their resources, had their slates up again. The bettors began to place fresh wagers.

Rothstein had made a killing, but done nothing dishonest. Sidereal was a two-year-old maiden, a non-winner in the three races in which he had started. Two-year-olds were permitted, by racing custom and racing law, to "qualify" in their first few races. That meant that owners and trainers did not run them to win, but to "educate" them.

In this manner a horse's true form and ability were concealed by its owner. This was part of the game. The one rule of the betting ring was "Caveant omnes." Let everyone beware.

The "qualifying" rule still holds. However, the pari-mutuel machines prevent any such killing as Rothstein made. A horse can open at 100 to 1 but the final price on the board determines the pay-off. And the more money bet on a horse in a race, the smaller the pay-off.

Rothstein sat through two more races and then he and Carolyn were driven back to New York. He did not tell her the amount of his winnings, saying only, "I won a big piece. A very big piece."

After a time he said, "This is my lucky day. I feel it in my bones. I think I'll find a game tonight. Do you mind if I don't take you to dinner?"

For the first time in their marriage, Carolyn lost her temper. "Damned right, I do," she said. "We're eating together tonight."

Taken aback, Rothstein said, "All right. All right." He tried to appease her in the one way he knew. He took out his bankroll, peeled off a number of bills. "Buy yourself something with this. You earned it." It was $5,000.

They had dinner at Delmonico's. All evening men came to their table. Some came to congratulate Rothstein on his killing; the word had spread very quickly. Others were bookmakers, come to negotiate a settlement with Rothstein, trying to arrange some means of having him carry their debt to him. He acceded to some of the requests. At six per cent.

It was almost eleven o'clock when Rothstein brought Carolyn home. He went inside with her, checked his telephone messages, and then went out. Still looking for a game.

She went upstairs, read a while, and then went to bed. ✦

Yachting at Kiel

(AUGUST 1903)

James B. Connolly

KIEL,—TUCKED AWAY in the southwest corner of the Baltic Sea,—a sort of mediæval town and modern port in Germany, lies seventy miles from Hamburg, and on the road to Copenhagen. Centuries ago the old women of Kiel sold gooseberries in the Stadthuse square. On the tablets tacked up here and there to attest the antiquity of things there is no mention of that, but you know it; for in the queer shoes and the dress of long ago, with smiles and sweet old-fashioned words, they are selling them yet.

Like many another good old German town was Kiel, soaked in the traditions of the Middle Ages and trying quietly to sleep it off, when along came a lot of busy people with their disturbing notions of modern progress and shook it into painful wakefulness. A navy-yard was established, the Baltic fleet began to rendezvous there, and the social atmosphere took on new and braver tints; the Krupps installed an immense plant, and industrial activity set in; a canal was cut through to the German Ocean, and commerce picked up; and beside the old Kiel a new Kiel grew.

Old Kiel is still there—old Kiel with its winding streets and curious houses—streets of no greater width than a man could leap with a twenty-foot run—if he could get the run,—and houses that give out whiffs of those good old Hanseatic days when pirates hovered in the offing, and no respectable burgher thought of storing himself away for the night until he had seen the town put under lock and key,—old Kiel is yet there, but it is the two together, old Kiel of the Hanseatic architecture and new Kiel of the trolley-cars, that go to make up what appealed to the present Emperor as an ideal setting for "Kieler Woche,"—that midsummer's dream for which gather the yachting-men of a dozen nations, with their most pretentious steam- and their most ambitious sail-craft, to compete for expensive trophies, and to enjoy, under favor of the Emperor, a purple social time. Cowes, Newport, Copenhagen, Stockholm,

Cannes,—any marine place at any time,—they are supposed to cast but little shadows beside the glory that is Kiel's during this first gorgeous week in July.

The first thought of the man who drops in there when the affair is well under way is that some sort of military celebration is in progress. The streets are lit up with uniforms, officers and men both togged out in their parade clothes, with the one forever returning the salutes that the others are forever rendering. Sentry-boxes are all over the place, and the winding streets wiggle with marching columns which are doing escort duty, and in command of men who very well pose for photographs of the Emperor ahorseback; and preceding them are those crashing military bands—battle-axes and wash-boilers they suggest—great things to break a way through crowded thoroughfares. The striped sentry-boxes are in pairs about the town, and others are being hustled along on what in America would be called push-carts, each in charge of a corporal of the guard, and a squad of able warriors in white trousers, blue tunics, and a gay pompon above. Coming to the door or gate of the clubhouse, hotel, castle, or whatever sort of building it is at which the last-arrived Herr Commissioner or other highly titled dignitary has taken up his quarters, the corporal in charge wheels up the push-cart, they are stood on end—in their stripes they seem like portable barber-shops then,—two men are set up beside them, and thereafter the great man cannot come or go without freezing those sentries stiff.

All this is but a little shore background and incidental to the composition. Down in the harbor is another part of the picture. The ships of the German navy catch the eye first. Twenty-odd men-of-war are there—battle-ships, cruisers, gunboats, training-ships, and what not. There are magnificent steam-yachts—the black *Corsair* of Morgan inshore, the white *Nahma* of Goelet farther out, and scores of others that are famous enough, some of them, in their own home ports, but here going for only one in the count. The *Hohenzollern* of the Emperor is there of course, a yacht to write poetry about, if only she had ever done something.

For the sailing-craft there are hundreds or so of chipper little knockabouts tied up in rows between the piers, and out in the more open water the larger vessels—big sloops, able cutters, handsome yawls, and shapely schooners. The best of a dozen European nations and a few from our own country are there. Flying from every man-of-war is the impressive battle-flag of Germany, and from the trucks of the *Hohenzollern* the imperial standard that only she may fly—black and gold, black eagle and confident "God with us" flaming out. And strung from stem to truck and from truck to peak of the yachts, sail and steam, are all the signal-flags in the ship. It is five hundred screw and sail lying to moorings in the harbor, and decorated as they are for this festival, they make a brave show.

Lending movement to all this scheme—to the paints and enamels of many colors, to the gold stripes, polished brass, oiled decks, varnished spars, and sails of snow,—are little steam-launches beyond counting. Every steam-yacht and war-vessel of any size has one, the battle-ships have two or more each, and royalty a half-dozen or more for its exclusive use, and there are the dozens in public commission. And all are tooting excitedly and steaming desperately, with churning wakes and streamers trailing out behind. Fifty or sixty entries for a day's racing is an ordinary list. As for the story of the racing—it is pretty much the same as at any less-renowned gathering, pleasant for the most part, and now and then exciting—that is, so far as the actual business of racing goes, for yacht-racing is pretty much the same all the world over. A number of men, some smart seamen and some who pass for such, get out in low-railed vessels with large sails and light spars and go over buoyed courses. If it comes to blow heavy, and they do not care to go over the course, or if they mismanage, nothing happens generally—no vessel goes down, no men are lost. There is always a safe harbor handy. Those that get around and come in, one, two, three, are presented with trophies. Sometimes a more than local interest draws the attention of the world. In this racing at Kiel there was that larger interest. Ten or eleven nations had entries in the various events, and yet what was really interesting to the public at Kiel was the ceremony attending it. There was, among others, that race to Travemünde, in which the *Meteor* sailed, the schooner-yacht built in America for the Emperor William. Before then the *Meteor* had been outsailed by several of the larger schooners, a catastrophe which had been only partly explained away by the "She needs very much wind, does the Emperor's yacht," of the German boatmen. There was a race in which there must have been some wind, with the English *Cicely* logging a new record—seventy miles in five hours,—but that doesn't matter. The Emperor William himself was to be aboard her this day, "and to sail her himself," according to the portly shore mariners, who misspent the middle of these beautiful days playing scat up in the coffee-houses.

It happened to be the Fourth of July, and the Americans who were hurrying down that morning to see the start for Travemünde were surprised and edified when they heard the big guns boom out from one of the great battle-ships. Twenty-one they counted, and took note of the great cheering that fol-lowed. Getting nearer the water-front, they could see crew after crew crowd-ing aloft and cheering in turn. There were present Americans who felt like cheering themselves—Hurrah!—and did. "Four thousand miles away from home and twenty-one guns on the morning of the Fourth of July!" said some-body, and all hands cheered—Hooray! It was a fine bit of international cour-tesy—yes. A group of American girls on the seawall, pretty of course, stopped wigwagging iridescent parasols to a yacht out in the harbor long enough to remark that it was real nice of the Germans. It seemed a pity to learn a few moments later that the Fourth of July had nothing to do with it. It was the Emperor leaving the *Hohenzollern* to go aboard the *Meteor* for the race! Pondering over that, we began to understand more clearly that when the Emperor sets out to do anything, the nation, or at least that part of it on the official pay-roll, must stand by and hold its breath, except, of course, those who are cheering or manning the yards.

The *Meteor* crossed the line, with the Emperor on her quarter, and then followed her escort: first, the *Hohenzollern,* in all her cream-and-gold magnif-icence, and long as some ocean liners; secondly, the cruiser *Nymphe,* three hundred and fifty feet long, twenty-one knots, four hundred men, guard to the *Hohenzollern;* after her, the *Sleipner,* tender, or errand-boy, two hundred feet long, and twenty-five knots; and beside her the *Alice Roosevelt,* messen-ger, or despatch-boat, twenty-five knots or so; and to tail out the procession, four long, low, black torpedo-boats, known by letters and numbers— *S 8, S 75, S 79, S 80,*—with a speed of from twenty-eight to thirty knots—these eight as escort to the schooner-yacht *Meteor* while she should be sailing a race from Kiel to Travemünde on a placid July day. It was a man on the observation-steamer, to leeward, who gave it out, after a good deal of what appeared to be careful thought, that it was his opinion that even if the *Meteor* did carry away her spinnaker-boom or incur some equally grave peril—even if she did, the Emperor had still a chance to escape with his life.

Tacked on to the wake of the Emperor's escort was a fleet of steam-yachts, of large size mostly, and of expensive decorations, nearly all. The people aboard of them did not seem to be too deeply concerned with the more tech-nical manœuvres of the racing-craft, but they were enjoying their racing, nev-ertheless. In creased white ducks, buttoned blue coats, and yachting-caps of the correct model, and with the proper club button on front, they lounged under the awnings on upper decks and watched the *Meteor*. There were craft there that were doing queer things with the *Meteor*; but the Emperor was on the *Meteor*, and on him the glasses were levelled. Probably a better-equipped fleet of steam-yachts, in the line of varnish, brass, upholstery, and good things in the locker, never left port. The owners of some of them had boats entered in the smaller classes—they knew their entries by the numbers on their sails, if they could but distinguish the numbers. However, it was glorious sport. They sipped cool drinks and had luncheon on the bridge; kept the steward busy, and watched the *Meteor*.

Throughout all of that day the breeze stayed light. Four, five, and six knots an hour was as good as they could do, with the small boats getting along about as well as the big ones. The squadron of national ships-of-escort to the Emperor were hanging on respectfully in the rear, and there, with one other, torpedo-boat *S 37* in attendance on the Empress's yacht, the *Iduna*, they remained until along in the middle of the afternoon, when the *Hohenzollern* and the *Nymphe*, being signalled to prepare things ahead, steamed on to Travemünde, where by and by they were joined by the *Sleipner* and the *Alice Roosevelt*, whereat all cast anchor near the judges' boats, to be ready to receive the *Meteor* when she should arrive.

It was slow waiting in Travemünde. The long-enduring twilight of a summer's day at fifty-four north began to settle down. It had been a sort of holiday in Travemünde, with visitors and residents gazing out from the benches or parading the long sea-wall in anticipation of the coming of the fleet. Flags were flying from the balconies of the cottages, the restaurants were doing a great business, and every fisherman's boat in the place was sailing about the harbor, all chartered by parties who wished to be close by when the *Meteor* should cross the line. After a long time there was seen to the north long trails of smoke. All hands are stretching their necks. The trails of smoke came nearer. There were three of them, and they were seen to be issuing from three torpedo-boats that were coming on like black comets. It was not in the official book of Kiel Week, but these were having the only race of the day. At twenty-six or twenty-eight knots an hour they came on, each with a quarter-wave higher than her hull. They ripped up the harbor, and went tearing on by for the inner harbor, leaving three long trails of smoke hanging low, and all the little fishing-craft dancing in the swell of the quarter-waves they left behind.

The dusk comes on, and on the ships of war they seem to be getting nervous. From the deck of the *Nymphe* is heard a piping to quarters, with the hurrying of feet on deck. Then follows the lowering of the flag, with one swelling bar of the national hymn, and after that up goes the night light. On the *Hohenzollern* there seemed to be a similar ceremony, with frequent looks out to sea. One member keeps a long telescope pointed over the rail, and another patrols the little balcony astern. It is a great day when the Emperor races.

The dusk deepens. The people ashore are still promenading the long walk, but colored lanterns have replaced the flags on the balconies. The bunting of the restaurants has also given place to evening decorations. The judges' boats flash search-lights seaward, but there is nothing to see. A passenger-steamer coming in hails to say that she left a bunch of yachts an hour's run astern, which means that it will be two hours or more before they arrive.

It is getting chilly in the night air, with the rations running low, and the charterers of some of the fishing-boats decide to go home. Never before had such ceremony been made ready for the finish of the race, and now in the dark no more than a dozen people would be by to see it—half of them on the judges' boats, and the other half in the little fishing-boats. It is eleven o'clock—dark night—and the breeze is freshening, when the first of the fleet heaves in sight. It is a big knockabout that has probably gone the inside, or shorter, course. She is felt and heard long before she is seen. Whoever has been there will know— the swish of the sharp stern through the placid sea; the long low hull coming toward one in the dark. Her great sail flashes up all at once—unnaturally white under the search-lights. They pinch her up, and then, finding themselves across, swing her off and let her run. One waiting spectator looks up her number, and finding her to be from Stockholm, gives her a cheer in Swedish.

"We are first?" they hail in reply.

"Yes."

"Good," and they go on up the harbor. The *Nymphe* and the *Hohenzollern* bring search-lights to bear on her as she goes bowling by, but she is not the *Meteor*, and there is no explosion. She goes on toward the lights of the inner harbor, where it is long odds they will soon tie up, make snug, go ashore, have a good supper for themselves, and be in fine condition to tell the next crew in how it was they did it.

After that they arrive rapidly. A half-dozen of the smaller craft come before there is any word of the schooner class. At length one of them works across the line of light and past that again into the darkness. Even in the gloom of a dark night she bears the impress of speed. Her hull is invisible except for the shine of the paint above the phosphorescence. "The *Cicely*," says somebody;

"The *Clara*," says another; but the night breeze having its swing, her port side-light rushes by—a red point in the blackness.

At midnight there is still no *Meteor*. The only intelligible report of her, and that in a strange language, comes from the deck of a big sloop. "Oh, somewhere behind," is their hail. The last two of the little fishing-boats, tacking back and forth, and, tired of dodging each other in the gloom, decide to leave for home, and they do. Five minutes later the *Meteor* comes. The search-lights pick her up, her number is taken, and she passes on to her berth in the inner harbor up between the jetties—and that is all there is to it. In the morning, at Kiel, the whole navy standing by, guns booming, ensigns dipping, thousands cheering, tens of thousands looking on, and ships of the navy to see that nothing happened to her; at night, at Travemünde, no guns, no cheering, no flags, and in her rear only the wake of an outclassed vessel as she goes on by in the gloom; and for an audience,—half a dozen on the judges' boats—and they of course wouldn't dare to leave.

Through the entire night they keep coming, with the search-lights picking them up one after the other as they cross the line. Next morning, when the people awake, they find sixty-odd of them tied up to the jetty—three, four, and five tiers the entire length of it, and a celebration under way. The real yachtsmen are busy enough, overhauling gear in preparation for what may come next, but the holiday lads are up on the promenade escorting the ladies and recounting to them the excitement of racing—that is, those who are not taking late breakfast or still in bed.

There is a great deal of entertaining, with not a little manœuvring to secure the Emperor as guest. Even to get him to put his foot on the companionway will be something for the owner of a steam-yacht to talk about. But he is not easily caught. He stands aft on the *Meteor* with the usual allowance of clear water about her, and the people ashore look through their glasses and marvel. The old boatmen, when they arrive abreast of the *Meteor*, in with oars, and catching the royal eye, salaam to the thwarts, and row on in flustered silence when he lifts his cap slightly in return. The Emperor's party go ashore for a stroll in the meadow on the farther side of the harbor, and the children cheer them sweetly.

It is that sort of day in Travemünde—a holiday in a German seaport, with the Emperor in the glow-spot of it all,—and then back to Kiel, where the thing is wound up with felicitous speeches, presentation of prizes, and a great consumption of wine and beer.

It is at night that congratulations are being handed around, and night in Kiel is a story of its own. The military is still there—you cannot stay up late enough at night nor get up early enough in the morning to catch the military out of action,—but much of it is gone. The sentries are not so large on the landscape, and the marching columns are out of action altogether. To replace them the jackies are ashore, whole crews together seemingly. In the resorts that are hid away in the back streets leading from the water-front they congregate thickly.

Up where the electric lights are thicker, people who have more money to spend and more time in which to spend it throng the restaurants and the coffee-rooms of the hotels, or sit out under the trees and smoke and chat or sip and eat, and listen to the music; or maybe they will be sitting in the balconies of the handsome residences along the bluff, or lounging on the verandas of the big hotels, or idling on the benches of the marine park, or along the promenade seawall, and from there taking in the night life of the harbor.

They are jumbled together now, with the ensigns and signal-flags replaced by Japanese lanterns and signal-lights. The battle-ship of the Admiral may be picked out, because she carries aloft the single truck-light which none but he may show, and because also she is illuminated in honor of the Emperor by a row of electric lights marking her water-line all the way around, and again encircling her belt of armor, and higher up her turrets and fighting-tops, and showing in addition to all that a dazzling crown of immense size surmounting a great letter W, suspended between the masts—a flashing thing of purple-white, and all for His Majesty. The *Hohenzollern* also may be discovered, lit from stem to stern and carrying lights to every truck—her royal prerogative,—and all about her the lesser craft illuminated also, with lanterns fore and aft and below and aloft.

To sit somewhere along the waterfront, in some quiet restaurant ashore, yourself at a little table under the trees, taking your dinner leisurely, with clustering lights above and about, and a tuneful orchestra not far away; to take it all in—the lights from the heights above, the tinkle of life in streets just far enough removed to suggest without disturbing, the lanterns in the rigging and their reflections in the dark water, the hail of boatmen, the melody of a song, the faint echo of a cheer, the cadence of soft music from cushioned cabins; the whole thing, lights, music, trees, and echoing voices, the whisper of the night breeze and the play of rippling waters,—all that—the mystery of five hundred screw and sail, and of darkness, and of light flashing out of darkness,—it is enchanting, and you hate to leave it. And yet that is the time to leave it.　✦

MOSCOW GAMES

(OCTOBER 1980)

George Plimpton

> *"Tip-toe incognito," whispered Mister Bumpus.*
> *—The Travels of Dr. Doolittle*

THOSE WHO HAVE been here before are surprised at the emptiness, really an eerie one, of the city. Some are reminded of Paris during the August *fermature annuelle,* and indeed for the four summer months there is an annual exodus from Moscow of a large percentage of the population . . . to dachas, to the resorts along the Black Sea, and the youngsters (their absence is the most noticeable) to the Pioneer camps. But this year more people are gone. To make room for the visitors to the Olympic Games and to keep the best face on the city many people have been asked not to come into Moscow at this time unless they have official business, and some, such as alcoholics and various undesirables, have simply been removed—swept not just under the carpet, but into dustbins, carried out and deposited elsewhere. On the bus today, a group of Californians were wondering how this deportation process might be carried out in Los Angeles in 1984, when the Olympic Games are scheduled to be held there. The junkies, it was suggested, should be relegated to Needles, California, the alcoholics to tent cities in the Napa Valley, the drifters to Palmdale, and the elderly ladies in tennis shoes to Tijuana.

"In each case," a Californian pointed out, "Los Angeles would benefit from their absence, and where they went would benefit from their presence."

Giving a city a face-lift is called "Potemkin-izing," after Prince Grigori Potemkin, Catherine the Great's shrewd adviser, not to mention her lover and, after he had fallen out of her amorous favor, the custodian of her male harem. To impress the empress on a trip through the newly conquered Crimea, Potemkin constructed a fake portable village, complete with a population of healthy-looking shepherds and shepherdesses, which he would set up along her travel route, and when she was resting for the night, he would pack up the village and hurry it along past her to be set up anew where she would pass it the next day—trusting, I suppose, that she would fail to notice that the shepherds and shepherdesses looked startlingly like the ones she had seen the day before.

Potemkin-izing is not specifically a Russian trait: one thinks of the false fronts along the streets of the western cowpoke towns built to make the buildings look as if they had two or three stories. Christo, the Bulgarian-born artist who wraps buildings in canvas, once told me that his first job in his native country was to help with the painting of vast backdrops of fake vistas along the rail lines—a task that doubtless inspired some of the scenic fiddling of his later massive projects in the West, such as wrapping part of the coast of Australia.

As this is my first visit to Moscow, I find it difficult to gauge how much Potemkin-izing has gone on. It would be safe to say, in any case, that those who are critical of the society would consider the cleaning-up process to be Potemkin-izing; others, more tolerant, might say, "Well, the old girl"—referring to Moscow—"certainly got herself a splendid facelift last month."

I had been told by people before leaving for Moscow to watch myself—that because I had written in opposition to the U.S. boycott of the Olympic Games in a national magazine the Russian press would be around to see me, television cameras and all, and that whatever I said would be twisted to their purposes. Furthermore, because I have supported Amnesty International and have close friends who work actively for it, I would surely be followed, my luggage searched, and my hotel room bugged. This last, I was told by insiders, would be something of an advantage in that if I wanted my laundry back I should face all four walls of my room and to each in turn shout my discontent and "No starch, please." The best way to nudge the laundry room is to get the KGB involved.

A sense of this affects everyone who comes to the Soviet Union—a pervading feeling that one is playing a real-life role in a spy drama. So paranoid does the average tourist become, and so substantial is the American ego, that it comes not only as a surprise, but something of a disappointment, when nothing happens. One of my friends with the track-and-field group, with which I am traveling, told me that he felt a tap on the shoulder yesterday getting off a bus. He turned to see a policeman and his heart sank abruptly into his shoes. "This is it," he thought. The policeman bowed slightly and hand-ed my friend a piece of paper that had dropped from his pocket. My friend was enormously relieved, of course, but afterward he told me there had been just the slightest twinge of disappointment that the official had not said, in excellent English, "Mr. Lane, will you come with us, please."

It was in reaction to being ignored by the Soviet authorities that many sto-ries, most of them second, even thirdhand, circulated in the hotel lobbies and at mealtimes, apparently to salve the feeling, *What is wrong with me? Why hasn't there been a sharp knock on the door at midnight?*

The most common of these stories was that so-and-so had surprised a KGB agent in his or her hotel room rummaging through the luggage. Whistles of alarm from those listening, and nods of I told you so. But that was always as far as the story went—we never found out what happened then. What did the Soviet agent do? Did he leap for the window? It must have been awfully embarrassing for him. Why hadn't he jumped for the armoire when he heard the key in the door? Or pretended to be repairing the rug? But no, the descrip-tion was always of him with his hands in the suitcase, startled, looking up like a raccoon caught in the car light's beam amid the overturned garbage cans.

Paranoia even crept into the performance of my official function in Moscow, which was to cover the games for *Time* magazine in the guise of a tourist. I was told to stay away from the Time-Life offices. "There's a KGB man in the courtyard," I was told over the phone. "Your cover may be blown if you turn up here. So you're to meet your contact, a girl named B. J. Phillips, in Pushkin Park and pass your copy to her."

"How do I recognize B. J. Phillips?" I asked. I felt like putting a handker-chief over the mouthpiece of the phone.

"It won't be difficult," I was told. "She's got a broken leg. She'll be wear-ing a cast and supporting herself on two canes—one steel, one wood. She wears big aviator glasses."

"Oh," I said.

A while later, I called up to say that I wasn't sure anyone could read my handwriting (I had been advised to leave my portable typewriter at home) and perhaps it would be best if I came in to the office to type up my copy before going out to Pushkin Park. I didn't say this directly. I used a few hasti-ly made-up code words to confuse anyone who happened to be listening in. Rather than *copy* I used the word *poppy.* "After it's cultivated," I whispered, "I'll bring the poppy to Eugene Origin's garden."

"What the hell are you talking about?"

The editor finally gave up the subterfuge and let me come in to type. It turned out that B. J. Phillips was in the next office, her leg propped up on a chair, working on her stories. I asked if it was all right to come around the corner and give her my copy rather than going out to Pushkin Park. The editor said it was fine with him as long as we turned out the lights so no one could see us through the window.

Sometimes, with the U.S. team not there, it was difficult to know for whom to root at the games. One tended to support those from the Western countries when they competed—Allan Wells, Daley Thompson, Sebastian Coe, and Steve Ovett of England (it was especially difficult when, in the case of the last two, both were in the same race), Peitro Mennea, the Italian sprinter, José Marajo of France, any Finn (they were the merriest people around town), and, from the socialist bloc, the Polish polevaulter, Wladyslaw Kozakiewicz, if for no other reason than it was seemly if a Pole won the pole vault. He did, too, hoisting himself up just a half-inch under nineteen feet for a world record.

I kept a small list of people at the other end of the competitive scale—those who seemed almost sublime in their ineptitudes. Byong Uk Il, for example, a Korean boxer, who got so frustrated with himself that he began kicking at his opponent. Or the two fighters, Ismael Moustalov and Ahmed Siad, from Bulgaria and Algeria respectively, who fought such a dull fight that a friend of mine turned to his companion to say, "You can go to sleep watching this," and discovered that he *was*.

In the women's gymnastics, both the entire Mongolian and North Korean teams made my list. The measure of their ability was somehow symbolized by the musical accompaniment to their floor exercises. Everyone else had picked large orchestral pieces, the flow of a hundred violins or the disco beat seeming to pick up the gymnast and whirl her across the vast expanse of matting. But when the Mongolian girl, dressed in robin's egg blue, stood poised for her first cartwheeling run, we heard first the loud amplified *click* of a tape recorder being turned on, and then what sounded like perhaps a pair of ancient player pianos being played at the same time, but with different tunes, so that a cascade of arpeggios roared down in a confused jumble through which the gymnast hopped and cartwheeled and was tumbled over as if in a great draft of wind. Kang Myong Duk was my favorite. On the beam she moved from one end to the other like a boy crossing a log over a swift-moving trout stream. Susan Cheesebourough of England was another favorite. Orange suited, she began to fall off the beam during her routine, but, almost regaining her balance, she poised, one leg flung out grotesquely, for a long, appalling instant, long enough for someone to call out, "Hang on, old girl!" before she finally slipped off.

At track and field, heading my losers' list was a contestant in the twenty kilometer walk—a gentleman from Laos with certainly the loveliest name of the 1980 Olympics, Thipsamy Chantaphone. The race had long been thought to be over. Suddenly, an hour and a half behind the twenty-fourth walker, who was assumed to have brought up the rear, Mr. Chantaphone appeared—whisking through the great doors at the east end of Lenin Stadium onto the track for his last lap. When the huge crowd realized that the man hurrying along in that crazy strut of the distance walker was a contestant in a race long thought to be finished, they rose to their feet and began cheering Mr. Chantaphone. Pandemonium! Mr. Chantaphone was not in the least abashed. He began waving his arms; an enormous smile ignited his features. He stopped and bowed—thus increasing his time to an even more horrendous total. One had the sense of his carrying an imaginary sign above his head: I am Thipsamy Chantaphone, Walker of Walkers.

It was interesting how some of the poorer athletes measured up to the stress of the Olympics. Some gave up from the start. In the third heat of the 1500 meters, a Vietnamese named Quang Khai Le started out last, stayed comfortably there, and finished last by twenty-six seconds. On the other hand, Marzoug Mabruk, a Liberian, burst out to lead the pack in his heat, turning it on absolutely full blast for two and one-fourth laps, and then, of course, ran out of steam and was passed by everybody. But at least he had the satisfaction of telling the folks back in Monrovia that he had "set the pace" and shown his heels to the rest of them for a while. Maybe he would go so far as to say his coach had run him at the wrong distance.

Pizzazz, that was the thing! A fighter named Wamba from a West African country came rushing out yesterday at the five-second warning bell and began fighting, so stirring up his opponent that he got himself knocked out almost immediately. He made my list . . . right up there with Thipsamy Chantaphone.

But my two favorite losers remain those English yachtsmen at the Montreal games who were so disgusted at the turtlelike qualities of their Tempest-class yacht *Gift 'Orse* that they set fire to her and watched from a dinghy until she eventually sank. Of the two men, the crew member, merrily tanked up on booze, was especially critical, not only of the *Gift 'Orse* but also of his skipper; he accused him of lacking in style. "I told him his place as captain was with the ship but he refused to go down with her."

A lot of stories about fires drifted around the hotel lobbies today. A man wearing a straw hat was reported to have self-immolated this morning in Red Square. It was such a fragmentary story that it would doubtless have been discounted if it had not been for that detail about the straw hat. A boater? Rather a jaunty one?

We also heard that in the spirit of the boycott the British had burned all their allotted tickets to the games. The boycott was actually thought up by the British—at least they were the ones who proposed the idea at a hastily convened meeting in Moscow at the news that the Russian troops had crossed the border into Afghanistan. I was surprised to hear at the American embassy that the purpose of the boycott had little to do with informing the Russian populace about the Afghanistan situation. The Russians are amply supplied with news from the West, if they wish to be, through the BBC and the Voice of America broadcasts, which have not been jammed since 1973, and of course word of mouth spreads very quickly news that might not appear in *Pravda*. Rather, the intent of the boycott was to indicate to Brezhnev and Co. how seriously the Western powers took the Soviet encroachment . . . a gesture to the top brass. This news increased my skepticism about the value of the boycott. Surely a high official would be more upset by the moves in diplomatic and trade channels—such as the defection of the Romanians and North Koreans in the General Assembly voting over the Afghan issue, and the obvious disgust of the Third World at the Russian incursion. Besides, did leaders such as Brezhnev wring their hands over such steps as an athletic boycott? He is in the Crimea somewhere. He's apparently a great soccer fan, but he has not been on hand for the games, save for the opening ceremonies where he stood and applauded at moments that pleased him, clapping his hands together slowly, as if his internal machinery had run down.

In fact, the whole Soviet political presence seems absent from the games. In a city awash with flags, the only Soviet banners I have seen fly from atop the Great Kremlin Palace and off the sterns of the *vaporetti* that ply the Moscow River.

The official box at Lenin Stadium, roofed, and with a long row of red-covered seats, has been empty since the opening ceremonies. That's one thing the Soviet hierarchy does not do—give its tickets away to secretaries and friends.

In the Hotel Ukraine, where I am staying, there has been a lot of lobby talk among the track-and-field people about cheating out at the games— Soviet judges giving their countrymen the edge even in such events that require measurements, such as the hammer, the shot put, and the discus. I would think it highly improbable, even lunatic, for a troika of judges and assistants (three of these officials converge where the thrown object first dents the grass, scampering to the spot like boys rushing for a tossed coin) to jockey the measuring sticks around, especially under the gaze of 103,000 spectators, many of whom are equipped with high-powered binoculars. But the rumors persist. The most curious is that the great runway doors at the west end of the stadium have been swung open to allow the wind funneling through to aid the javelin tosses of the Russians, and that when a Pole or an East German steps up for his toss, the tall, hangarlike portals are swung shut to cut the windstream off. Nonsense, of course, unless the wind were literally roaring through, blowing the hair straight forward off the brows of the javelin throwers looking downfield. *That* sort of a wind might carry a javelin with it, but we haven't had anything like that at all: the high clouds hang almost motionless in the pink evening sky. Besides, javelin throwers are unnerved by a following wind, which tends to shove the tail of the javelin down so that it hits the ground first, thus disqualifying the toss.

Flimflamming has also been reported in the triple-jump (once called less decorously, if more accurately, "the hop-skip-and-jump"). Here, an Australian named Ian Campbell and a Brazilian named Joao de Oliveira were called for fouls on nine of their twelve jumps, which made it easier for the Russians to place first and second.

I had particularly noticed the Brazilian, Oliveira. After his last try, in what seemed to me a most sportsmanlike gesture, he leapt out of the landing pit and began shaking hands with everyone in sight—the pit sweepers, the man who sits in a small chair and leans forward to prepare the takeoff board after the previous jumper had marked it, the judges up the line—and from the stands the applause began to flow down in appreciation. The man next to me said, "Well, so much for how much these folk know about track. Don't they realize the Brazilian is being *ironic?* He's knocking them. He's showing everyone how awful he thinks the judging has been."

I had been applauding along with everyone else. I stopped.

"How do you know?" I asked. "I mean, why doesn't he punch them in the snoot if he feels that way about it?"

"Oh no," the man replied. "It's all a question of symbolic gesture. You've got to know how to read these things."

Don Rollen, the ubiquitous fan who wears a vertically-striped painted beehive hairdo and invariably sits in the stands where the TV cameras can pick him out—"Rock 'n' Rollin" he calls himself—was picked up next to the press center by the Soviet police for "looking odd" (as an official at the American embassy described the incident to me) and then released. "He *does* look odd," someone said to me, hearing the news. "With that hairdo of his he looks like St. Basil's Cathedral on the move."

The Hotel Ukraine is one of the seven skyscrapers built around Moscow in the 1950s. The style is Russian art deco, not unlike—unless my memory flags—the compromise architectural monstrosity that gets blown up in the climactic finale of Ayn Rand's *The Fountainhead*. The place is, nonetheless, an oasis to our group—a home base to which everyone repairs after the games for meals, however unpalatable the latter turn out to be. One of my table-mates, looking down at a small section of fish waiting for him on his plate, and debating whether to tuck his napkin under his chin before knuckling down to it, remarked on what a shame it was that the French had only spent three months in Moscow in 1812. "A few months more, and a bit of the French cuisine might have rubbed off," he said mournfully.

One of the more novel aspects of dining at the Ukraine was that the majordomo of the dining room, a stout figure in a light grey suit, felt it was uncompanionable (and possibly a bad, bourgeois habit) to wish to eat by one-self. If I came into the dining room alone, he would imperiously motion me to an empty seat at a table already occupied—very much as if he were a social director on a cruise ship trying to get his single passengers to mix. But it was difficult if my tablemates turned out to come from Nepal with no common language to share. One lunch he sat me next to a poultry farmer from east Texas who over coffee told me that in his business chicks are pumped up to the size of broilers in only six weeks. "We don't let them chicks sleep," he told me. "We jes' keep the lights on and let 'em *eat.*" The thought of those gorg-ing birds stayed with me, disturbingly, through an afternoon of watching weight lifting, when the entrance of every weight lifter through the small stage door off to one side of the stage was accompanied by a mental image of a vast, slow-stepping, big-thighed emu.

Hailing a taxi, the usual procedure if it stops and you're alone is to get in and ride, not in the back seat, but up front with the driver—a pleasant enough practice that evokes the egalitarian spirit. The trouble is that such proximity suggests one should strike up a conversation with the driver. It's rude—or at least it feels rude—to sit next to someone and stare stolidly out the window. It's like hunching up a chair to a restaurant table where someone is seated alone and then not saying anything. So I try. It has struck me that I know many more Russian proper names than I do words, and how difficult and limiting it is to carry on a dialogue by mentioning in turn Tolstoi, Chekov, Tchaikovsky, Maiokovski, Pushkin ("Ah, Pushkin!"), Beria (thrust of the thumb down), Khrushchev (sideways motion of the hand to denote ambivalence), Stalin (thumbs down), Olga Korbut (thumbs up), and so forth. It's exhausting, and I only did it once; after that, I sat in the back. The driver did not seem to mind. At least I could detect no sign of hurt feelings.

Nadia Comaneci is a woman now—long, ropy legs like a racehorse's, a bosom!—and she towers over the strange, Munchkinlike gamines who dominate that peculiar sport like a light standard. In the troughlike walkways around the performing areas, the tiny gymnasts keep loose with slow, lovely cartwheels (they are upside down much of the time) and with a myriad of relaxing exercises, one of which is a trembling of the leg muscles as if trying to shake a bug off a toe. Nadia stands apart. She seems like a teenager at a lower-school recess. She doesn't submit herself as much to the exercises; with her, the preparation seems more mental. What could be running through her mind? Her primary rival (who eventually dethroned her as overall champion) is Yelena Davidova, a Russian, who is exactly Nadia's age (eighteen), but who by some genetic chance has not been assaulted by womanhood: she is still as flat-chested as a boy; the sheen on her legs is smooth; she is elfin—seventy-five pounds. Her floor routine is sexy, with little, exquisite bottom-shake movements that a purist friend of mine haughtily referred to as "kiddieporn." True, if Nadia tried such things, it would seem undignified. But I found Davidova's routine whimsical and charming. "Oh Christ," a purist friend said in disgust.

In Gorky Park I stopped at a bowling alley housed in a barrage-balloonlike bubble at the edge of the wide river balustrade. The place, without air conditioning, was an inferno of heat. A dozen pinball machines along the wall were in operation. I doubt the Russians make such things, but at least they have adapted foreign models for home-country use, to judge from the flashing Cyrillic lettering. Some penny-arcade war machines were also busy—the familiar American sound of the thump and whine of miniature electronic holocausts. I looked over the shoulder of a player and saw a torpedo wake heading for a red tramp steamer ploughing along doughtily against a painted horizon.

Russian bowling, though, has a peculiarly unique style. Apparently the bowler pays by the hour rather than by the number of games bowled, so that the criterion of performance rests on the number of throws rather than any emphasis on scoring. Bowling balls were got rid of down the dilapidated, pocked alleys as if they were fused in some way, and about to go off; they were flung with abandon, often into the gutter, and on occasion they smacked into the guardrail of the Brunswick pin-setting apparatus while the tenpins were still being settled into place—the shattering crash of such impacts rising above the general din: the guardrail would lift as if in alarmed haste above the pins, which would teeter there for just an instant before a bowling ball, often with another immediately on its tail, would smack into them. I only saw one scorecard being kept along the row of alleys—a man scribbling full-bent to keep up with the frantic activities of the players in front of him.

Speed was also a requirement of the ball's delivery. I have never seen bowling balls *hurled* . . . like cannonballs they bounced a third of the way up the alley. The preferred method of throwing them was with a two-fingered grip, as if either someone had figured out that the care required to insert the third finger was too time-consuming, or perhaps that the three-fingered grip was too dangerous: one might not be able to extricate one's hand at the end of the follow-through and thus be carried along up the alley behind the ball like a human streamer.

I left the alley after fifteen minutes or so. Outside, even with the weekend crowds thick and festive, and the calliope sounds from the merry-go-rounds and ferris wheels, and the calls of the children from the boat ponds, my ears were soothed by the comparative quiet.

T-shirts everywhere—international slogans, ad copy, funnies, poems, epithets, epigrams, pronouncements, assertions, admissions, paintings—carried around on tens of thousands of walking billboards. A lot of Mickey Mouse sweat shirts. The most arresting message I saw was an American T-shirt on the back of a pleasant-enough looking chap—I wondered vaguely if he could speak English and knew that what he was brandishing read as follows:

JOIN THE ARMY
TRAVEL TO EXOTIC LANDS
MEET UNUSUAL PEOPLE
AND KILL THEM

The blue jean is the truly coveted item from the Western world. But the Russian youth are very particular about their blue jeans. They turn up their noses at the Hong Kong-made models, which are the fancy brands preferred in the United States—the Calvin Klein, Gloria Vanderbilt, Sassoon brand names with the tight behinds and the stitched back pockets—and instead the Russian teenagers opt for American-made Levis, Texas Wranglers, and Sharpshooter models. The jeans are worn beltless; they don't even rip off the size identification labels. There is a brisk black market in blue jeans. In our group are three young brothers from Michigan who were approached just off Red Square by their Russian counterparts, young men who were interested in buying the trio's blue jeans right off their bodies. Only one of the Americans was wearing underwear, apparently, so he went around a corner and, divesting himself of his blue jeans, got back to the hotel wearing a pair of blue boxer shorts, eighty rubles (over a hundred dollars) richer. He had taken a brave enough entrepreneurial risk, though not as brave as his brothers' would have been had they given up their jeans.

The light switches in my hotel room, and in every room I have been in so far in Moscow, are placed six feet up on the wall. How do small children, much less midgets and gnomelike men, turn on the lights in the evening? Do they wrestle chairs around and stand on them? Paintings are invariably hung up near the ceiling. Such interiors, it occurred to me, are very suitable for Peter the Great, who was almost seven feet tall; when he strode around St. Petersburg his courtiers had to run alongside full tilt to hear what he had to say to them. Yesterday I saw an odd wooden statue of Peter in Leningrad's Hermitage that was fashioned just after his death and is supposedly an exact replica—a *body* mask rather than one of the face. He is seated in a chair wearing blue-gray court clothes, the tunic very dusty; it looks as if, were it smacked smartly, dust would emerge in a large cloud. His hands and feet are tiny, absurdly out of proportion to the body. His head is as round as a soccer ball, with a small black moustache tacked on at a curious angle. His hair, which is coal black, is reported to be his own. The countenance is quite foolish. The replica works; that is to say it can be pushed around like a wooden artist's model in a figure-drawing class. I wish the curators of the Hermitage had him standing upright rather than slouched in a chair looking like a man who feels he is on the verge of suffering a severe gas pain. It would be interesting to have a correspondence with the authorities in the museum on this matter: "Dear Sirs. . . . " The fact is I wish I had not seen him at all. Once, his enormous empty boots were on display at an exhibition I saw in New York's Metropolitan Museum, and the imaginary portrait generated in my mind from seeing them is certainly one I prefer to what I saw in the Hermitage.

The Moscow subway, as everyone knows, is the eighth wonder of the world. However much one has heard about the opulence of the stations with their marble, their statuary, and their chandeliers, and the speed and cleanliness of the trains, one is unprepared. I am especially impressed with the escalators, which with alarming speed seem to disappear at a sharp decline down to the point of infinity—such a long and deep descent that at lunch today a professor from Chicago pointed out that only an aetheist culture could venture so close to the infernal regions.

I went to see Lenin in his mausoleum this morning—"his Nibs" as our contingent refers to him. Foreigners are able to get to the head of the long line and with special guides sweep in without delay, but I thought it would be more interesting to go to the end of the line, which, when I joined it, stretched down Red Square and around a corner into a leafy park under the western wall of the Kremlin. We shuffled slowly by the great terrace that contains the flame of the Unknown Soldier. Fresh flowers lie on the stone. We watched a raven move with big hops among the flowers and then shy away abruptly from the heat of the flame. What is it that attracts the raven to national monuments, especially those with murky pasts, such as the Tower of London and the Kremlin? Behind me in the line were two boxers from Nigeria. I fell back and got into conversation with them. Their boxing coach four years ago had been Archie Moore, the former light-heavyweight champion of the world and an old friend. We reminisced about him as we moved through the park. Moore's team had never gone to the Olympics in Montreal. Most of the Third World countries boycotted the 1976 games because of their collective annoyance with New Zealand for having hosted a rugby team from South Africa—a sensitivity that certainly showed the degree of their feeling about isolating the latter country, but also seemed a somewhat farfetched and arbitrary reaction. The Nigerians volunteered as much. When I asked their opinion of the 1976 boycott, one of them threw his hands apart in a gesture of futility. "Poof!" he said. He made much the same kind of sound when I asked him about the U.S. boycott. "Too bad. Too bad," his friend said.

We moved out of the shadows of the park and up into the sunlight and vastness of Red Square. Conversations in the column began to die away. We were directed into double lines—security men, some in plainclothes, every dozen paces or so, peered closely at us. A small, untidy man in front of me had a bulge in his coat pocket, which turned out to be a piece of dried fish wrapped carefully in an old newspaper. His lunch. He unwrapped it three times for the security people as we moved along. Now there was no sound but the shuffling of feet; one was subdued as much by the ministrations of the security people as by the grim facade of the tomb with its absurdly small door, room for two of us at a time to enter.

Once inside, the chill of the mausoleum increased markedly as our column turned sharply to the left and filed down a marble stairway—it was almost palpable, like stepping into a pool of deep shadow. Two turns to the right, and ahead I saw an odd white object that I suddenly realized was Lenin's right ear, shining, remarkably delineated compared to most ears, I remember thinking fleetingly as we turned into the catafalque, and I saw the high forehead, the pale face, the faint reddish beard, the hands luminous above the black of either a coverlet or a black suit . . . the chiaroscuro effect of the lighting and the dispatch with which we were being hastened around the foot of the glass-enclosed bier made it difficult to tell. I had no sense of his feet sticking up at the foot of the bier—protuberances that always add a small touch of absurdity to the mien of a human lying on his back.

Then in front of me, just as we made the turn to pass down the left side of the catafalque, a man suddenly started sobbing. Almost instantaneously, a soldier moved out of the shadows. He leaned forward, within inches of the man's face, and with a finger to his lips he hissed, "Sssh!" . . . explosively loud in that enclosed gloom—the sharp sound of a nanny admonishing a child— and the man's sob stopped in mid-flight, like a hiccup.

The sunlight was refreshing once we got outside. Our trip in the mausoleum had lasted less than a minute. The Nigerians and I walked slowly along the foot of the Kremlin wall looking at the names of those interred there. We passed a bust of Stalin. We were still subdued. We kept thinking of what we had seen in the mausoleum. One of the Nigerians asked me if Lenin had had any children. I said that he had been married but—as I remembered it—he felt that his child was the Revolution. Anything else would have been a distraction.

"That's too bad," the Nigerian boxer said. "His great-grandchildren could drop in back there and see just how he looked."

One of our tourist group was a stage-lighting technician from Minnesota. He told me he was curious to see how his fellow artists had (as he put it) "lit Lenin," and he went to Red Square specifically to check up on them. He also had tickets to the Bolshoi Theater; he had hoped to get backstage to look at the lighting panels and the rest of the equipment but he had not been able to manage it.

"Well, how did you think they lit Lenin?" I asked when I saw him.

He said he was much more impressed with the lighting in the mausoleum than what he had seen at the Bolshoi. "It's a hard theater, that place, because you can't do your lighting from the front. So they use follow-spots; the actors and dancers move around in pools of light. Some people like that, but I don't: it's too artificial. I was surprised how little subtlety there was—just blue, white, red, and bright yellow. Too much white, I thought, but then who am I to criticize? It's the Bolshoi."

"What about Lenin?"

"Oh, that's just great, how they lit him. Really great," he said. "A spot on his face, and one for each hand . . . against the black background . . . a little rose gel used, I'd guess . . . a smokey pink to give the effect of life . . . oh *very* well done. I wanted to crouch down and look up to see the spots and how they'd done it, but it's not the sort of place you can stop to do that sort of thing, is it?"

"No, sir," I said.

B. J. Phillips told me today that a Russian friend of hers had reported that the stones or markers over the bodies of Russian soldiers killed in Afghanistan bear the inscription "Died on International Duty" followed by the dates. The Russian was contemptuous of the phrase. He said, "For those who died in the

Great Patriotic War the inscription was always 'For the Motherland.' That meant something. But this new inscription—it is meaningless. Two of my friends from school are buried under it." He had spat furiously at the grass.

In a Marxist society a considerable onus is put on being a servant or a waiter or anyone in a servile position. In Russia everyone wants to be an engineer. It takes forever to eat in a Moscow restaurant because whoever is supposed to appear at the table is back there in the kitchen pouting and banging the pots around, wondering what went wrong. That is why one can wait for an hour in a restaurant, often falling asleep (the best position, I am told, is with the head on the table edge rather than lolling back in the chair, which is not as steady, and can result in toppling off with a crash) waiting for the aggrieved waiter to show up with a temper just barely under control. It does not help matters that no one can be fired.

These thoughts crossed my mind as I sat in the stands of Lenin Stadium watching the games, because obviously in athletic events there are many serviles—people who have to sweep the broad-jump pit, mop up the sweat if a basketball player tumbles to the court, carry out the weights for the weight lifters to heft, tote back the shot put for the shot-putters to put, and so forth.

I watched carefully, and noticed that the Soviet authorities have done their imaginative best to keep the serviles happy by making their work as mechanically oriented as possible. For example, when the javelins, discuses, and hammers land out at the far end of the pie-shaped target area, they are picked up by the serviles and carried off just a short distance to the side where the objects are attached with clips to a motorized cable contraption, which transports them back to the throwing area where another servile unhooks them and puts them in the proper racks. No one is embarrassed by having to walk a long distance carrying a ball with a chain on it. As for the shot, which doesn't go as far as the other missiles, it is picked up and carried a few yards by the servile and settled into a long inclined trough, down which it rolls like a mammoth pinball, not propelled hard enough, returning back down the starting trough to the plunger.

I went to the weight-lifting events wondering if the great barbells were somehow going to be manipulated and shifted about by forklift trucks operated by men with engineering degrees. But no. To my surprise, the hefting is still done manually—by men wearing smart jumpsuits with a green arrow motif down the sleeves, often three of them at a time straining at the great weights. "Hernias," we thought might be a good name for these specialists.

One wonders, in fact, if the Russians have not found exalted descriptives for those who perform menial tasks to take the sting out of what they do. For example, might not those who labor at the jumping pits in track and field, sweeping them smooth after a broadjumper has landed, be referred to as "earth restabilizers," or perhaps "sand agronomists"?

Yesterday evening I saw a man jump higher over a bar than anyone in history—seven feet, eight and three-quarters inches, an almost obscene height (I can just barely reach up that high). The man was an East German, Gerd Wessig, and when he had done it, he lay on his back on the blue, square mattress, itself about four feet thick so that jumpers don't damage themselves on the way down from that prodigious height, and with his arms and legs akimbo, just as he had landed, he lay looking up into the pale evening sky for almost a minute, exulting, and letting the roar from the crowd wash over him. What a remarkable moment for him—to have done a simple act better than anyone else in the world! Above him, the bar, which had not even trembled as he had gone over it, must have seemed as solidly fixed as a tree branch.

We hear from travelers and tourists coming in from the West that in the press little play is being given to the games and such feats as Wessig's. There is much more coverage about the squabbling over the officiating, the alleged cheating, the food-throwing episodes in the Olympic Village disco, the lack of top-flight (i.e. U.S.) competition . . . almost as if the free-world press felt obliged to downgrade the Moscow show as much as possible. Only three minutes of the games are available daily to the networks in the States. Some newspaper publishers are refusing to publish any accounts of the Olympics, making the games a nonevent and its participants nonpeople in the best tradition (if they thought about it) of the Soviet practice of manipulating history.

Very discouraging, this, and it made me remember Ralph Ellison inveighing against the side effects of the boycott in the civil rights struggle in the 1960s. When it was suggested that industrial companies with discriminatory practices should be publicly listed and their products boycotted in protest, Ellison argued persuasively that too many people who were not responsible would be affected and caused anguish and hardship.

Certainly one thing to be said about the boycott was that it made everyone feel punk and frustrated. It hadn't changed anything. It demeaned without effect. It didn't make anyone feel righteous or smug, unless they were prigs and had forgotten about Vietnam. It created division and confusion. This morning I had breakfast with a girl who was worried about what people would say back in the United States because she had come to Moscow to see the games. "Do you think they'll say I'm a traitor?" she asked.

I watched her remove the top of her egg. "It's going to be all right this morning," she said. "Yesterday, it was a one-minute egg."

"Is that what they're saying?" I asked.

"What?"

"That you're going to be called a traitor."

"Everybody in our tourist group is talking about it. The Russian salesgirls in the Gum department store said to Pat—you know Pat—how sorry they were that President Carter wasn't going to let the tourists who came to the Olympics back into the United States. Where was she going to go, they wondered."

"We can all go and live in Tashkent," I said.

"Gorky's more likely," the girl said. "The Forbidden City—that's what the Intourist guide calls the place. I'm depressed. If it weren't for how nicely they've done the egg this morning, I'd cry." ✦

THE CESTUS OF HYGEIA

(JULY 1937)

Bernard DeVoto

THERE ARE SO many explanations of the great increase in popularity of games, sports, and athletics, and so many theories about what it is doing to the national life, that no one has bothered to determine whether in fact there has been any increase. Yet, knowing no more about finance than any expert in the weekly press, the Easy Chair ventures to assert that, next to starting a religion, the surest way to make money in America has always been to manufacture sporting goods. The nation has always been devoted to every kind of muscular proficiency and diversion, though the interpreters of our culture, being themselves a sedentary class, have only recently learned of that devotion. As usual, they got wind of domestic affairs by way of foreign events. Fifteen years ago they were convinced that the Americans did not play games but hired people to play them while they watched. When the European dictators began to nationalize sport, however, it became possible to forecast the eventual triumph of fascism in this country from the number of passengers on ski trains. Clearly the regimentation implied by a hillside covered with people all doing slaloms together meant that we should be a set-up for the next Huey Long, and the mass hysteria associated with nature-walks and golf tournaments meant that we had changed overnight from a slothful to an athletic people— and must lead straight to war.

Granted that a lot of people play games nowadays, neither the national tastes nor the national habits have changed, but only the kind of games played and the conditions under which they can be played. Such changes have nothing to do with fascism or regimentation but proceed, most of them, from a familiar abstraction, the urbanization of American life. A family whose home is one-eighth of a floor in a ten-storey apartment house just off the business district can neither amuse itself nor exercise its muscles as it could have done a mile out of the village in grandfather's time. Junior cannot go coasting in

299

the west forty, Sister cannot have a swing in the back yard, and their father cannot drive his horseshoe pegs just beyond the side porch; neither west forty, back yard, nor side porch any longer exists. Our fathers could usually shoot ducks without having to go farther than the next marsh, and our grandfathers could hunt deer or even bear in the next township; we ourselves, as boys, could play baseball on the vacant lot at the corner. Now the bears are in game preserves, the ducks are three States away, and the big leagues have had to organize schools of instruction to develop not only first-basemen but even bleacherites.

If the facilities for sport are less common, so are the opportunities. Village life permitted the bookkeeper to knock up a few flies with the boys at noon or at odd moments during business hours; the hour or more a day that the subway now consumes could once be spent in extemporized sports in your own neighborhood. Again, innumerable sports that once flourished because they had a faint survival-value have withered away in an urban culture. The innumerable shooting matches that entertained our ancestors disappeared not only for want of room but also because marksmanship ceased to be a craft; axemanship has gone the same way, and with it a good many other sports associated with the handicrafts. Farm and village life call for the natural development of muscular and motor skills that have to be cultivated artificially in the city. The man who masters a jackknife dive is only doing under glass what his grandfather did in plain air when he felled a tree or built a stack that would turn the weather.

All this has necessitated an intricate organization of sport—and that is what creates the appearance of fundamental change. The city dweller has only a limited time to spend on sport: he cannot possibly extemporize it. There must be allotment and preparation; the facilities must be ready for him; the means of getting to them must be assured. Hence the gymnasium instead of the corner lot, the swimming pool instead of the creek, the toboggan instead of Nob Hill; hence the ski train, the bridle path, the tout-encas surface, the routed bird walk, the surveyed and charted mountain trail. Hence also another development, instruction in sports and games. With his leisure time rigorously limited, an adult does not care to waste it developing skill by trial and error; he tries to cut short his novitiate by getting guidance by experts. And children have to be taught, because in the city they have no way of picking up skills for themselves. Thirty years ago the grade schools did not even have coaches for team athletics, still less instructors in dancing, swimming, mumblepeg, wrestling, and hopscotch; children learned such things from one another, more or less well depending on their doggedness and their natural abilities. Nowadays both the schools and the playgrounds provide such instruction as a matter of course. The educators, inevitably, have grafted hope of saving society on the apparently simple matter of teaching children to play ball: group effort is to swing America from private ownership and the profit system into a socialized economy. That seems a heavy burden to hang from a volley-ball net, and will probably get no farther than the cognate effort to remold society by teaching basket-weaving to the children of the machine age—but we may trust the children to get a lot of fun out of it and, what is the main thing, they are learning skills.

It is no longer undignified for a graybeard to play tennis or run a mile in a sweat shirt, and that probably indicates that men now continue vigorous exercise to a later age than they used to, but it is unlikely that more of them take exercise. Women, however, are much more athletic than they were even a generation ago; more of them engage in sports and they are more adept than they ever have been before. In our own time we have seen an amusing cycle. Fifteen years ago the sex put away its corsets in order to be athletic; now it has had to put them on again in order to smooth out the muscles produced by athletics. (Some day a student is going to have an amusing time writing the history of the corset in America. It has been discarded on every possible ground since Dio Lewis's time: as a symbol of woman's subjection, as a menace to the unborn children of democracy, as an agency of the economic exploitation of women, as a luxury incompatible with either health or purity, as an impediment to the aspiring spirit, as a sex-gaud unworthy of free and enlightened American womanhood. And it always comes back; the corset is one of the most stable and constant elements in our civilization. To-day freedom and constraint have been beautifully compromised: it isn't a corset if it isn't called one.) The mothers of this year's debutantes seldom competed with men in athletics; but the debutantes play golf and tennis just about as well as their beaux, swim quite as well, and worry just as much about athletic condition, a phrase unfamiliar to their mothers and unknown to their mothers' older sisters. They sail, ski, pole vault, put the shot, shoot clay pigeons, and, if the picture press can be trusted, even wrestle. A girls' camp has to have as much apparatus as a boys' camp and has to offer as many forms of muscle strain. The one undeniable achievement of the feminist movement has been the enfranchisement of the female charley horse.

Melancholy prophecies about athletics for women based on various moral, physiological, and obstetrical grounds have been vitiated. Some thinkers expected women to be brutalized or at the very least to lose their chastity wholesale; others expected the birth rate to fall off because exercise would impair femininity. Neither expectation has been fulfilled, nor have the pains and difficulties of childbirth increased, as other prophets foretold. Perhaps a slight æsthetic realism has been forced on the male; for until natural selection attaches the female leg to its torso at a different angle a woman in rapid motion will never be beautiful. On the other hand, enthusiastic predictions based on orthodox feminism have also failed: American womanhood has not remade politics or reformed society since it learned the Australian crawl. Probably the one permanent change is the one that can be observed in shoe stores. Fashion having gone round the circle, the girls again have petticoats under which their feet may steal in and out, but they no longer have little feet. The first two sizes of adult shoes for women are practically obsolete. ... There is no evidence that the pores of the nose are larger, but there has been a heavy increase in the sale of bath salts.

The social changes produced by the organization of sport are of that kind: adaptations rather than shifts of direction. It is impossible to determine what effect the institutionalization of exercise has had on the national health. It has demonstrably improved and the expectation of life increased; so has the average height, and other indexes show the same trend. But every demonstrable fact of this sort may be accounted for by such things as improved pediatrics, better dietary habits, public sanitation, the advance of medicine and therapy, more widespread knowledge of hygiene, and many indirect forces. It is a curious fact that, despite the organization of athletics, the diseases supposed to be associated with the non-athletic life are certainly on the increase. Dysgenic forces are also at work. A blameless effort to keep the waistline down may put an impossible burden on the heart, and the lengthening of a man's athletic life may react by killing him early, so that the golf course has become a harder problem for insurance actuaries than floods or the Dust Bowl.

It seems likely that the physiological forces soon reach an equilibrium and that the more effective ones must be sought in psychology. One has to stand off only a little way to see these as a form of social adaptation. The decreasing opportunities in modern life to experience the primitive account for much of the popularity of camping, canoeing, hunting, and the like. More firearms are sold and more powder exploded than ever before in our history—

why, unless a deep need is thus satisfied artificially that was once satisfied in the natural routine of a man's life? The man who goes on a camping trip reverts to a simpler psychological level merely by cooking his food over a fire, sleeping on the ground, and letting his beard grow. The need for such a reversion is profound, and it is probably present also in the more generalized urge that takes the city-dweller out into the country to walk, to climb mountains, or just to drive on dirt roads. Add to this the need to develop and practice skills, which urban life does not satisfy, and you have accounted for a good part of the function of sport. Tinkering with the radio or adjusting the carburetor substitutes for the routine carpentry, taxidermy, cooperage, harness-making, veterinarianism, cabinet-making, blacksmithing, and general dexterity that our forefathers were forced to practice by the circumstances of their daily life. Skiing, swimming, roller-skating, shuffleboard, surf-boating, and the myriad other kinds of skills exercised in modern sport minister to precisely the same need.

Or, more simply, the function of sports, games, and athletics is that of release from the complexities of modern life. In Freud's famous phrase, modern man is forced to live psychologically beyond his means, and sport is a kind of retrenchment in an effort to balance the budget. The demands made on consciousness by mere existence in the world to-day are so great that there must be constantly available ways of lowering consciousness and escaping to simpler levels, to muscular and instinctive levels where the exigent demand for thinking is not felt.

It has been amusing to see sport, which William James preached as one of the moral equivalents of war, interpreted as an ominous sign of approaching war. Because Hitler has undertaken to fit the non-athletic German people for war by making athletes of them, our cerebralists have explained the traditional American enthusiasm for sports as proof that we are ripe for Fascism. True, the nonathletic Russians have also been forced into a similar wholesale training, but the Russians are merely trying to achieve the good life and to improve the modern mind by supplying it with a disciplined body. (Or, if you prefer, the Russians find that they like athletics, whereas the Germans are commanded to like them.) As a matter of fact, neither militarism nor foreign influence nor yet any leaning toward Fascism is discernible. The Europeanization of American sport has stopped short with the importation of a couple of words from the Scandinavian and the establishment of some shacks for hikers which, in melancholy imitation of the *Wandervögel,* are called hostels. It is like that other menace, our magnificently uniformed fraternal orders. Fascism has hard going where the lowest rank is lieutenant-general with four stars and the adjective Mystic, and you will not regiment youth by means of athletics in any country where the home-town fans lay for the invading hockey club with bricks.

It isn't Fascism, and it isn't even the paganism which part of the thoughtful press insists on considering it. You will travel a long way before you find anyone who goes in for skiing or bicycling because he believes in what is called the cult of the body, and when you find your first one he is likely to be a hypochondriac. He will be worrying about his weight or his blood pressure, not trying to be a faun. There is, in fact, no cult of the body, outside of literary essays. In the hostels, the bathhouses, and the locker rooms you will hear much talk about styles, conditioning, contests, and liniments, but you will hear no one talking like Petronius. The American pagan is just someone who is trying to crack par, someone who breeds gamecocks, or someone who thinks he can make Loon Lake with only three carries. We are breeding up no race of narcissists and exhibitionists; we are only having a good time.

The principal social moral to be drawn is that that is probably a good thing. It always has been and it always will be. There will be no falling off of the national intelligence through the fogginess produced by fatigue and sprained tendons: the most intellectual classes are by definition not fond of games, and the merely intelligent can probably think better after the oxygenation produced by exercise. For the rest, probably more of our people will be expert at games than ever have been before. If they are, they will be a little more graceful, a little more pleasing to the eye, a little more even-tempered. The rest is only an immemorial love of gadgets and the undying hope of serving four aces straight in tournament play. Better look elsewhere for omens. ✦

THE JOGGER'S PRAYER

(DECEMBER 1978)

Tom Wolfe

Almighty God, as we sail with pure aerobic
grace and striped orthotic feet past the blind
portals of our fellow citizens, past their chuck-
roast lives and their necrotic cardiovascular systems
and rusting hips and slipped discs and desiccated lungs,
past their implacable inertia and inability to persevere and
rise above the fully pensioned world they live in and to push
themselves to the limits of their capacity and achieve the
White Moment of slipping through The Wall, borne aloft on one's
Third Wind, past their Cruisomatic cars and upholstered lawn
mowers and their gummy-sweet children already at work like
little fat factories producing arterial plaque, the more quickly
to join their parents in their joyless bucket-seat landau ride toward
the grave—help us, dear Lord, we beseech Thee, as we sail past
this cold-lard desolation, to be big about it.   ✦

MUDVILLE

(MARCH 2008)

Lewis H. Lapham

> *Oh, somewhere in this favored land the*
> *sun is shining bright;*
> *The band is playing somewhere, and*
> *somewhere hearts are light,*
> *And somewhere men are laughing, and*
> *somewhere children shout;*
> *But there is no joy in Mudville—mighty*
> *Casey has struck out.*
>
> —Ernest Lawrence Thayer

IT'S BEEN THREE months since former Senator George Mitchell published his 409-page report confirming the use of illegal drugs by many if not most of the players in Major League Baseball, and we've yet to come to the end of being told sad stories of the death of kings. Somewhere the bands are playing for the season's presidential candidates, and in Florida the sun presumably is shining bright, but in the stadium press boxes the hearts are heavy and no birds sing. The makers of tabloid romance paste asterisks into the record books, rule the noble Clemens and the mighty Bonds ineligible for the Baseball Hall of Fame, declare the national pastime corrupted, the hallowed ground despoiled. Meanwhile, on Capitol Hill, the elected keepers of America's moral accounts entertain the prospect of stricter laws and harsher punishment, baseball players to be put on the endangered-species list, subjected to more rigorous inspections of their blood, their urine, and their souls.

The judgments are un-American and behind the times, the anguish unwarranted and overwrought. What else is the American dream if not the theory and practice of self-invention? How otherwise define the American way of life if not as a ceaseless effort to boost performance, hype the message, enhance the product? Deny an aging outfielder the right to inject himself with human-growth hormone, and what does one say to the elderly philanthropist who steps out of an evening with a penile implant and a flower in his lapel? To the lady in distress shopping around for a nose like the one she saw advertised in a painting by Botticelli? To the distracted child restored to his study of the multiplication tables with a therapeutic jolt of Ritalin? To the stationary herds of industrial-strength cows so heavily doped with bovine-growth hormone that they require massive infusions of antibiotic to survive the otherwise lethal atmospheres of their breeding pens?

In one of the New York newspapers toward the end of December, I came across a letter to the editor from a reader henceforth unwilling to let his young sons participate in competitive sports for fear of exposing them to an environment polluted with unnatural additives. I admired the parent's resolve but wondered where in the society he could find it safe to take the kids. Not to a nearby hospital, or to a local supermarket stocked with chemically preserved applesauce and genetically modified chicken potpie; not to the neighborhood Cineplex presenting computer animations programmed to act like movie stars and movie stars made up to look like robots; not into an Internet chat room frequented by jaded algorithms and naked avatars.

The voices of Christian conscience in our midst still like to draw a medieval distinction between what is "natural" (the good, the true, and the beautiful) and what is "artificial" (wicked, man-made, false). The distinction no longer exists. For better or worse, in one way or another, and to a greater or lesser extent, the whole of our environment—skyscrapers, highways, emotions, orchards, oil wells, terrorists, icebergs, tomatoes organic and inorganic, aquatic plants and Jason Bourne, pigeons, dogs, the smog in Brentwood, and the mountain dew in Colorado—is a virtual reality, fabricated by the hand and mind of man. We shape our tools, and our tools shape us. It's a fair and free exchange, our technology a process of evolution by accelerated means, machines reconfiguring their capacities and states of consciousness in ways comparable to those by which dinosaurs become birds and apes change into Mormon choirs. Vice President Dick Cheney's electronic heartbeat is born in Mudville together with YouTube, the Golden Gate Bridge, and Richard Wagner's *Parsifal*. The road forward to a better tomorrow is no farther away than the next generation of microchips or the nearest all-night pharmacy.

I don't mean to take anything away from the consolations of philosophy or the joys of motherhood, but how else is Heaven made if not with artificial sweeteners—with the elixir of Cialis and the embalming fluids of celebrity? Given the society's order of merit and measure of value, the hope of salvation is a transformed self somehow worth its weight in gold. Consider the revelation in the desert vouchsafed to the minor-league third baseman, age twenty-two, traveling on a monthly pittance to Texas or Alabama towns so poor or so closely monitored by Jesus that the motels don't sell hard liquor or provide the courtesy of an adult film channel. The young man knows that if in this or next year's season he can hit another fifteen or twenty home runs, lift his batting average by thirty or forty percentage points, his pay maybe will rise to $1 million a year, his travel upgraded to first-class accommodation at an altitude of 30,000 feet, his name and shoe size the stuff of legend among the girls at Scores. A variant promise of redemption appears as if in a burning bush to a thirty-four-year-old relief pitcher who knows that if he can keep his curve ball breaking across the corners of the plate, he stays for another two or three seasons in the big money, long enough to make good his mortgages on the property in Puerto Rico and maybe find himself transported into a broadcasting booth at NBC or ESPN.

Where is the dilemma? How not choose the sportsman's path to glory? The Mitchell report framed the questions on a losing premise—"The players who follow the law and the rules are faced with the painful choice of either being placed at a competitive disadvantage or becoming illegal users themselves. No one should have to make that choice." Why not? Was not that the choice stoutly made by the builders of America's railroads, by the Minutemen at Concord and General William T. Sherman marching from Atlanta to the sea? Our television commercials speak of little else except the gaining of a competitive advantage—cell phones equipped with applications as omnipotent as were those available to Zeus on Mount Olympus, headphones piping Mozart symphonies into the ears of six-month-old infants already enrolled on the waiting list for Harvard.

That steroids bring with them an element of risk is a fact that must be faced. What true American would want it any other way? Too easily we forget Marine Corps Sergeant Dan Daly at the Battle of Belleau Wood, leading his men into a storm of German machine-gun bullets with the heroic cry, "Come on, you sons of bitches—do you want to live forever?" How often do we hear the phrase "visionary risk-taking" in the speeches of our A-list business leaders (to explain, among other things, the brief but brilliant blowing of the subprime-mortgage bubble), read the message emblazoned on the pages of *The Wall Street Journal*, see it shining in the moonlight over Las Vegas?

The bull market for prescription drugs amounts to the sum of $249.3 billion a year; add to it the money spent on illegal drugs (at least another $63 billion), as well as the capital lost on state lotteries and legal gambling ($85 billion), and we find a strong majority of our fellow citizens bent on the quest for immortality. Visionary risk-takers one and all, willing to take their chances with a surgeon's knife, to buy a mansion in Arizona with non-existent credit, bet the marriage on the jack of diamonds, dance to the music of Ecstasy. How does one say to such people that the game isn't worth the candle, or that the candle can't be burned at both ends?

As with most other questions of interest to the society, the answers follow the money, and when carried with the bats and balls into the locker rooms of Major League Baseball, they move up in grade from the temporal to the spiritual. The product is entertainment, but the brand is the democratic ideal made flesh, Adam at play in the fields of the Lord before partaking of the contract with Steinbrenner, the belief that America in 2008 is somehow just the way it was in Chicago in 1907, when the Cubs were tossing the baseball around the diamond from Tinkers to Evers to Chance. The performance-enhanced memory sells tickets and souvenirs; as with most other forms of modern poetry, it needs a little help from its friends. Exceptional talent is as rare among ballplayers as it is among bond traders and politicians, and if the sandlots don't grow Rousseau's noble savages in an abundance sufficient to seed and staff the myth of America's idyllic boyhood, what happens to the gate receipts?

The chance of rain in the forecast threatened to delay or call the game during the early 1990s, when Major League Baseball was extending its franchise to twenty-eight teams eager to build luxury skyboxes overlooking the fields of dreams. To cover the spread between the expectations of the newly enfranchised fans and the shortage of number 2, 3, 4, and 5 hitters up to the standard of the immortal Babe Ruth, the owners narrowed the strike zones, shortened the distance to the outfield fences, sent scouts to tap the gene pools in South Korea and Japan. The players made chemical adjustments.

The Mitchell report notes the exemplary degree of cooperation between management and labor ("Everyone involved in baseball over the past two decades . . . shares to some extent in the responsibility for the steroids era . . . "), but instead of giving credit where credit is due, the former senator from Maine downgrades the sure-footed teamwork into "a collective failure," observes that the commissioners, the club officials, and the Players Association somehow failed "to recognize the problem as it emerged and to deal with it early on." The suggestion is insulting. Nobody was quicker to recognize the problem than the owners in need of crowd-pleasing spectacle to sell at increasingly spectacular prices; nor were the players slow to grasp the fact that a ninety-five-mile-an-hour fastball, no matter what its immigrant status, is always a well-paid wonder to behold. Together they brought joy to Mudville, and with it the sound of music and the sale of caps. Together they kept pace with the broad technological advance occurring elsewhere in the society—with the computer-generated trades breeding money in the credit markets, with the miracles of modern medicine being implanted in the bodies of widows and orphans as well as in the throats of New York real estate tycoons and the hearts of Arab oil sheikhs. That Major League Baseball continued to score game-winning profits despite the fears and suspicions noted in the margins of the official program (more players seen to resemble inflatable beach toys, mandatory and more frequent searches of antisocial urinary tracts, more pain-killing balms and ointments added to the roster of illegal contraband) testifies, as did Karl Rove's marketing of President George W. Bush, to the patriotism of the nation's sportswriters and the resilience of the American spirit.

The new season's presidential candidates speak of breaking old barriers and crossing new frontiers, of riding boldly into the future on the eagle wings of change. Let the proprietors of Major League Baseball do likewise. They say they wish to "level the playing field," to bring to a close a "troubling chapter" in the history of the game, above all else to "move on." The fulfillment of their desire lies as close to hand as a note from the friendly team physician. Supply the locker rooms, free of charge and in every color of the rainbow, with the best and brightest that the pharmaceutical industry has on offer, with or without prescription, performance-enhancing, and recreational. The competitive disadvantage disappears, the level playing field regains its egalitarian state of grace. Spread the good news to the paid attendance—Lucy in the sky with diamonds sold with the beer and hot dogs at prices referred to Medicaid—and great would be the joy in Mudville.

To mighty Casey at the plate the ball looks as big as a grapefruit; infielders rigged with silicon circuits in their heads turn double plays at broadband speed; the game might last for three days, running up bonus points for extra innings and providing its fans with the benefits of an extended stay in paradise.

All present in the stadium come fortified with self-improvements both chemical and surgical, fit for service aboard the *Starship Enterprise*. To the children suffering attention deficit disorder in the distant bleachers, the foul lines become as plainly visible as the replays on the JumboTron; the senior statesmen in the stands, growing hair as strong as Donald Trump's, unafraid of heart failure and immune to the risk of erectile dysfunction, bask content-edly in the glow of usherettes copied from designs in *Playboy*. Rich in equal opportunity and re-engineered with biofuels, the national pastime recovers its footing as America's foremost source of independent energy and strength, once again embodies, in reconstructed bone and re-integrated marrow, the ever-evolving truth of America's immortal dream. ✦

The Boys of Winter

(JUNE 2002)

Rich Cohen

I USED TO dread the day when I would be older than the oldest athlete in the pros. This occasion, I was certain, would mark a sad, desperate show-stopping diminishment of my possibilities. No longer would I play catch, or shoot around, or skate on the frozen park with the secret hope of being spotted by a wayward scout, of being recruited, fitted for a uniform, allowed to choose a number, of appearing on the ice in midseason, the long prophesied hope from the East, or the Midwest, or wherever. For this reason, I always kept a watch on the old guys, who seemed to mark the very edge of known existence. There was Phil Niekro, the knuckleballer, who pitched for the Atlanta Braves and the New York Yankees into his late forties! There was Gordie Howe, the power forward from long ago, big in a way you don't see anymore, who came into the National Hockey League in 1946, when there were just six teams, and was still playing in 1980. On the Houston Aeros of the World Hockey Association, Gordie centered a line with his sons on either wing. Son Marty called him "Gordie" on the ice; son Mark called him "Dad." There was Nolan Ryan, the power pitcher, who threw a no-hitter at forty-four. In what he had said would be his final season, Ryan got into a scrap with Robin Ventura, a big kid who charged the mound. As Ventura reached Ryan, you could see him suddenly pull up, as if waking from a dream, as if realizing what a bad idea it was to beat up on an old hero in public. Ryan, taking advantage, quickly got Ventura in a headlock and whaled on him. Ryan's career ended just shy of his planned retirement. A power pitch, one too many, and the big ligament in his throwing arm popped like a string—a fitting end for a man who made his living on the mound.

There was Bill Buckner, a first baseman who played primarily for the Los Angeles Dodgers, the Chicago Cubs, and the Boston Red Sox, in whose beginning, as the poet once said, was his end. In 1970, his second season in the major leagues, Buckner played in just twenty-eight games and hit for a .191 batting average. In 1990, his last season, he played in just twenty-two games and hit .186. In the summers between, he collected close to 3,000 hits, won a batting title, and played on an All-Star team. His final years read like a mad dash from the inevitable, or a search for redemption—perhaps from his fielding error in the 1986 World Series[1] that cost Boston its first championship in more than sixty years. Buckner played in Anaheim and then in Kansas City before returning to Boston to retire. He hit a single home run that last season. As a physical act, this would not have been very different from his first home-run hit nineteen years before, yet in our imagination it stands on the other side of a lifetime of hard work. And so it is epic, the last blow of an old man.

There was Gary Matthews, a paunchy outfielder who, in 1972, his rookie season, played alongside Willie Mays—who himself had played in the time of Ted Williams and Joe DiMaggio—and who, in 1987, his final season, played with Greg Maddux, still among the most dominant pitchers in baseball. In other words, the old player allows you, with just a pencil mark or two, to draw a direct line from the present clear back to the era of DiMaggio, and from there back to Gehrig and Ruth.

There was Grover Cleveland Alexander, a pitcher who, at forty, looking like a mean old country dentist, won twenty-one games for the St. Louis Cardinals. At the end of his career, he became the hero of the 1926 World Series, pitching his team to victory in Game 6 and then making a spot appearance in Game 7, where, although badly hungover, he struck out Tony Lazzeri of the New York Yankees with three pitches. Alexander was remembered by fans of that era less for his youthful dominance than for that long October walk in from the bull pen. Unlike modern stars, who carefully orchestrate their retirement, Alexander vowed to play until stopped, and not for some romantic love of the game but because he knew that life outside the game would be hard. Released by the Phillies in 1930, he went back to semi-pro ball, playing in the Texas League and then for the House of David, an independent club that featured players in long holy-man beards. Eventually, he turned up as an attraction in a Times Square sideshow.

These are athletes who reached the end of their ability but lived and played on—because they wanted to compete, because they did not want to

---

[1] *A sharply hit ball skipped through Buckner's legs. In the coming years, the ball itself became famous. A symbol of futility, it was passed from hand to hand until finally auctioned off to the actor Charlie Sheen for $93,500. For a time, Buckner tried to deny that it was the same ball.*

work in a factory, because, in the end, there is only the game. A television camera will sometimes catch such a star at the end of the bench—maybe Mark Messier, the forty-one-year-old captain of the New York Rangers—looking old yet reassuring in the way that a grandfather clock is old yet reassuring; and what is the body but a more elaborate kind of clock? Such athletes serve a function at least as important as does the kid with blazing speed. In showing that they can still find a role, that, even on the wane, they are determined to contribute, they prove that the end is no less real than the beginning. In my opinion, a superstar has an obligation to play until he can play no more, until the tank runs dry and the wheels burn.

In the present age, with the hegemony of youth culture, with, for example, F.D.A. approval, for cosmetic use, of Botox, which combats wrinkles by freezing the muscles of the face into an expressionless mask, it is increasingly difficult for a superstar to play out the string. Writers and fans simply will not stand for it. No one wants to see his hero, the idealized image of himself, become tired and old. With the first hint of decline, the first sad steps down the mountain, the superstar is urged to "Go out on top," a useless phrase that only diminishes the connection between sports and life; in life, no one goes out on top. It is a sentiment that reflects the neurosis of our society: the fear of age, the disregard of history. So we drive our veterans off to the golf courses and the television studios, and thereby cheat ourselves of the finest moments in sports—Ted Williams batting .388 at thirty-nine; Michael Jordan, having lost his spring, inventing a new style based less on body than on mind. Only the old player can re-enact that great American myth: the aging gunslinger strapping on his pistols for a last trip to town. I remember seeing one Sunday, in a game that had little meaning, Billy Kilmer, by then just an echo of an earlier era, replace an ailing Joe Theismann, the starting quarterback of the Washington Redskins. On the sidelines, Kilmer wore a maroon ski cap and popped a mouthful of gum. He already had a lifetime behind him—seasons with teams all over the league but also a near-fatal car wreck that almost lost him a leg. Jogging to the huddle, Kilmer, smiling and slapping backs, took control with a few brisk words. His passes were short and wobbly, he was impossibly slow, and yet he kept finding his target. No big flourish, just a man ending his career with a few more snaps. "He's fat," said my father. "And he can't run anymore, but he knows the game. He's like a brain out there on the field."

Increasingly, we call on great athletes to frame their final moments in the manner of Michael Jordan hitting his last jump shot, or John Elway finally winning that Super Bowl for the Broncos. But when Jordan quit, for the second time, in 1999, he still had much to contribute, which is one of the reasons he came back last year—for Michael, and for his fans, there had been no proper conclusion, no third act, no decline. And yet he was urged to retire. As was Joe Montana, as was Cal Ripken. In 1999, when Wayne Gretzky, the greatest player in the history of the NHL, took his final face-off, he was still among the elite scorers in the game. But at thirty-eight, he simply could not match his own earlier efforts and so had to leave. A farewell ceremony, a free car driven out to center ice, tears and more tears, and we no longer had to think of Gretzky. It was like watching a man prepare his own coffin. Michael Jordan called Gretzky and sang the glories of retirement; Jordan himself came back just two and a half years later.[2] An hour after the final horn of his final game, Gretzky gave a press conference at which, reporters noticed, he was still wearing his equipment: his skates, his jersey, his cup. Here was a man clearly not ready to exit. Later he said it was not the games he would miss so much as just sitting around with the other players, playing cards in hotel lobbies, doing nothing at all. Buses and airports, dank locker rooms: that is life for the athlete.

Because I need to believe that there is still something to look forward to; because I know that I am going to die; because my favorite athletes are going to retire; because I feel diminished by the death, actual or professional, of my heroes; because, as things are said to get better, as people get healthier and faster, they actually get worse; because Britney Spears is our biggest pop star and her catchiest hit is a Pepsi commercial—for these reasons, and others, I am a fan of the long career. I want the Austro-Hungarian Empire to last a few years more, I want Gordie Howe to take one more shift. And yet even I must admit that a great player now and then stays too long. There was Ryne Sandberg, for example, the second baseman of the Chicago Cubs, who, as his skills diminished, retired and then came back only to retire again—a twitchiness that called into question his legendary cool. This retirement and re-retirement may, for the time being, have even taken Ryne out of the running

[2] *A few highlights have already made Jordan's comeback worthwhile. In a game against Chicago, Jordan blocked Ron Mercer's breakaway lay-up in a two-handed catch, somehow freezing the ball against the backboard and, for a moment, freezing the very game itself. It was as if someone had pressed pause on a video machine.*

for the Hall of Fame. Of course, the most obvious example of retirement and re-retirement is Muhammad Ali, though boxing is another story: sticking around too long generally means brain damage.

But I am sympathetic even to those who stay far too long. For what is this refusal to retire but a determination to keep on living? The annals are filled with those who burned up on re-entry. Thirteen years after he retired, Jimmie Foxx, who led the Philadelphia Athletics to three straight World Series, couldn't pay his rent. Honus Wagner, a charter member of the Hall of Fame, for a while went to work in a sporting-goods store. Bleakest of all was Joe Louis, who lost all his money, who became broken in body and mind. Louis's son said of him, "I couldn't help thinking of Arthur Miller's *Death of a Salesman*. In the play, the man's name was Willy Loman, wasn't it? . . . Wasn't Willy a grand guy, just like my father, and then he started growing old and losing his customers? He was never really aware that he had lost his territory. That's the tragedy of it, just like my father's."

In sports, where every player is in a state of flux, always rising or falling, great athletes are haunted by portents. Each hitting streak implies its own end, and the end of the hitting streak implies the end of the career. The happiest athletes tend to live like the happiest people—in a state of ignorance, with little realization of the lurking dangers. But the superstar is of a different nature—he is jumpy and uptight, a temperature taker, a fretter. He knows that his skill, which seemingly came from nowhere, can just as easily return to that place. For him, all the conditioning is no more than a hedge against the inevitable. Now and then, you will see this twitchiness at a press conference, or in a cascade of broken bats, but for the most part it remains hidden beneath a facade of effortless joy. The great player must suffer through his wane with a kind of grace, for only in the end can you see his true character.

Most final moments in sports are manufactured where much of our history is manufactured: in the newsrooms. For a sports reporter, as for other reporters, being the first on a story can make a career; for years afterward colleagues will say, "He was the one to call for Gretzky to retire." Reporters tend to jump at the first signs of decay—the first four-strike-out game, the first big collision—as if to say, "No, no, we can't bear to look at it." Such a call, though it may begin as a voice in the wilderness, soon elicits calls from other reporters not wanting to miss a big story, and that lone voice soon swells into a chorus, from which emerges a question the athlete must respond to: "Will you go, or won't you?"

In other words, the reporter has created the moment he or she at first meant to predict. Now the athlete must decide: "Do I follow the logic of the moment, or do I follow my own?" Stubborn players like Messier, who in essence say, "I will play until they pull the skates off my feet," are then portrayed as selfish men who refuse to follow logic. A *New York Times* article, illustrated with a shot of a glowering Messier—he has a dark, handsome, granite face—recently ran under the headline: "Some Stars Don't Know How to Quit." An online article, written in classic tough-love style, sounds the typical tone:

> Messier has become a sad shadow of himself. A liability. It is time somebody told the emperor that he's standing there buck naked. . . . There are very few players I have enjoyed more in 40 years as a fan. But it is over. It is time to exit with some dignity. Time to put number 11 up in the rafters. . . . Time for Mark Messier to show that he still puts the team first. Time for him to hang up the skates. It's time.

In arguing for the end, sportswriters often invoke Willie Mays, the superstar who, we are told, hung around too long and so diminished his historic value. "There's a fine line great players walk," Larry Wigge writes in *The Sporting News*. "Jordan left when he still could have led the NBA in scoring and highlight moves. Willie Mays hung around too long. Gretzky is somewhere in between." Yes, in the 1973 World Series, playing for the Mets, Mays made the sort of error he never would have made as a young man. Less mentioned is the fact that, later that same day, outmatched physically but not mentally, Mays worked relief pitcher Rollie Fingers for a bouncer up the middle to win the game.[3] For me, this Mays, the late Mays, the slender-hipped boy hero gone soft in the middle, stands as one of the great icons of sports—the man determined to extract one more season from fate. This is not to say that late-inning success alone proves my point: one of the great photos in sports shows Y. A. Tittle, the thirty-eight-year-old quarterback of the New York Giants, on the grass after being leveled, blood trickling down his forehead, face so tired and desperate it strikes even the casual observer as Roman. A long career, like a long life, begins and ends in senility.

[3] From Mays's autobiography, *Say Hey*: "As I stepped into the batter's box I called time. I said to the catcher, Ray Fosse, 'Gee, you know, Ray, it's tough to see the ball with that background. I hope he doesn't throw me any fastballs. I don't want to get hurt.' Then I waited for Fingers's fastball. It came, and I nailed it."

No one much cares how the end comes to the mediocre or the merely good. Such athletes are allowed to wander away when no one is watching, to elicit, at most, a paragraph in the local paper. They are a friend of a friend leaving the party: you look up and he is gone and you cannot remember whether he has been gone for an hour or five minutes. Bob Dernier, Reggie Theus, Jeff Bukeboom: who remembers their last game? Their last hit? The memory of such departures, like the memory of physical pain, burns off, leaving behind only scattered moments: a diving catch, a mid-ice collision. But a superstar sucks the energy out after him, and so he is denied the easy getaway. The best are given appreciation days, parades, keys to the city. Or the living obituary, the newspaper farewell, which itself has become a set piece no less regulated by time than the sonnet or the beer commercial. Whereas the beer commercial will contain hot chicks, sober-looking professionals, and allusions to sex ("Head for the mountains, the mountains of Busch"), the living obituary will contain a final press conference—as bittersweet and redemptive as the Last Supper—a final ovation, and many melancholy phrases such as "hanging up the skates" or "putting down the glove." There is about such stories the suggestion of mythology, magic swords and aging kings, which reminds us that the best sports writing is an outgrowth of the literature of boyhood.

Here is Peter Gammons, writing in the *Boston Globe* in October 1983 about the retirement of Carl Yastrzemski, who played in Boston for twenty seasons:

> There were hundreds, maybe thousands still out on Yawkey Way when Yaz came out of his final press conference in the dining room atop Fenway Park. He was signing autographs for some security guards and ballpark workers who were waiting for him on the roof when he heard the "We Want Yaz" roar from the street and looked down.
>
> He stepped to the edge of the roof and waved out to them with another Papal gesture in his uniform pants, team undershirt and shower clogs, then turned to Red Sox public relations director George Sullivan and suggested that he'd like to go down into the street, and 10 minutes later, there were women and children and red-eyed truck drivers in a line that stretched down around the corner of Van Ness Street.

This brings up a question that has puzzled me since I watched the retirement of Jose Cardenal, a superb outfielder with a tremendous Afro, generate no more ceremony than the departure of an elevator: What sets one athlete above the others? What makes an athlete a star? What makes Yastrzemski into Yaz? Or a wave into a "Papal gesture"? And why were those truck drivers crying? Career totals, championships, the black-and-white of the record book—those are the easy answers. Sport is, after all, the kingdom of statistics, and, for the most part, the holders of the records were the stars of their day. In hockey, almost every scoring record was shattered by Gretzky, who, on first sight, many veterans thought too small and too slow to play professionally. The miracle of Gretzky's records is familiar to fans: 2,857 points, 10 scoring titles, 4 Stanley cups, 9 M.V.P.s. In a league where scoring forty goals puts you in the All-Star game, Gretzky, in the 1981–82 season, scored ninety-two goals—the equivalent of hitting ninety home runs in baseball. Other great players have set other great records: 755 home runs hit by Hank Aaron, Cal Ripken's streak of 2,632 consecutive games, Rickey Henderson's 1,395 (and counting) stolen bases. Yet the numbers don't really tell the story; they may even obscure a truth that was plain to fans at the time. As the other poet said, poetry is what is lost in translation.

What about Babe Herman? On paper, that lesser Babe, who played for the Brooklyn Dodgers in the twenties and early thirties, reads like a titan. Between 1928 and 1932, he batted, in succession, .340, .381, .393, .313, and .326, truly one of the all-time great runs. Yet if Babe Herman is remembered at all it is by very old Dodger fans who mutter or sadly shake their heads. What we miss is the clown essence of Babe, the light he gave off. John Lardner published a story about the Babe in *Sport* in 1952, before the man had dimmed into statistics.

> Floyd Caves Herman, known as Babe, did not always catch fly balls on the top of his head, but he could do it in a pinch. He never tripled into a triple play but he once doubled into a double play, which is the next best thing. For seven long years, from 1926 through 1932, he was the spirit of Brooklyn baseball. He spent the best part of his life upholding the mighty tradition that anything can happen at Ebbets Field, the mother temple of daffiness in the national game.

In other words, the Babe is what is lost in translation.

The record book exaggerates; it also diminishes. Jackie Robinson played just ten years in the majors, batted in the low .300s, and hit only 137 home runs. He looks good in the record books, yes, but certainly not as good as dozens of other players, and certainly he is not in the league of Babe Ruth, or even Babe Herman. But those who actually saw Jackie Robinson play consider him one of the greatest in history, an idea informed but not explained by the fact that he was the first African American in the majors.[4] It was his mystique, his style. He had a scrappy, pigeon-toed run and a risky streak that could electrify a stadium. He set the game to his own tempo, his own heartbeat, scraping and clawing his way to first base and agitating when he got there, taking giant leads, crouching, trailing his fingers in the dirt, and bang! He was gone! On occasion, he would bunt his way to first base, then steal second and third, making something from nothing. Amazingly, he stole home plate nineteen times, a particularly hard task since home plate, unlike the others, is under permanent guard. Robinson even stole home in the 1955 World Series, from Yogi Berra.

Gretzky's statistics, amazing as they are, freeze to the page a talent that was defined by movement. Gretzky is a lot like Bob Dylan: small and sinewy, he worked by misdirection and towered above the other stars of his era, in the process reinventing his game, or maybe inventing a new game that is now being played under the old name. Even in photographs, these two men, Dylan and Gretzky, who, of course, look nothing alike, look a lot alike: both seem to be laughing at a joke only they can hear, and both seem nonchalant and set apart in the way of all visionaries.

It is style that makes the difference. Joe Namath, Bobby Orr, Joe DiMaggio—it was not their numbers, or their championships; it was their way of walking, of running, of skating, of doing nothing at all. A great player without style, no matter how great, will fade, as Patrick Ewing now fades. A great player with style becomes a superstar. Such players come into the league in the manner of the revolutionary. They change not merely how the game is played but how it looks. As a rookie, Gretzky wore a big jersey that he tucked in on one side in the back; the other side was left to flag. To this day, his look, a sort of studied casualness, can be seen on suburban rinks all across North America. Before Gretzky, the best players wore single-digit numbers, usually in emulation of Gordie Howe, who wore number 9, or Bobby Orr, who wore number 4. Gretzky, perhaps in a sly reference to Howe, who had been his own boyhood hero, simply doubled the equation, as in, "Wayne will be twice the player

[4] *That is, the modern majors. The first black in major-league baseball was actually Moses "Fleet" Walker, who in 1884 played for Toledo in the American Association. A bare-handed catcher, he was popular with fans, less so with his teammates.*

Gordie was": he took number 99. Ambitious players have worn high numbers ever since. Mario Lemieux flipped Gretzky on his head, wearing 66. Jaromir Jagr two-upped Lemieux, taking 68.[5] Eric Lindros, steering a characteristic middle course, wears 88.

Michael Jordan is probably the best example of the triumph of style. What people remember of his great games is less the score than the lope of his run, or his slow backpedal after hitting a jump shot, how he turned up his palms as if to say, "Who knew?" Or the way, as he bent to catch his breath, he pinched the fabric of his long shorts. Before him, it was all short shorts in the league, a look that now, when I see an old game on ESPN Classic, strikes me as embarrassing. What JFK did to the fedora, Jordan did to short shorts. When he first wore baggies in the NBA—I think it was during his third season—he was mocked, then emulated. That has always been the life of the trailblazer: mocked, then emulated. Now all the players in the NBA wear long shorts, and so do all the kids on the playground, and all the parents on vacation. These days, when Jordan picks his way through a defense, he is moving through a world that he himself created. Style without talent is affectation; style with talent is revolution.

The record books are filled with the names of athletes whose careers describe the gentle arc that has always given sports its most intense pathos—not the action of a game or a season but the drawn-out play of a career, from first fumbling through prime to decline. It is a movement that, like certain pieces of music, simulates the lifespan, the growth and death, of the individual, and as such it is beautiful.

Sport is not something you can get beyond or on the wrong side of; it dramatizes every season of a person's life. For this reason, a forty-one-year-old like Mark Messier, though still a young man in street clothes, is, on the ice, a stand-in for old men everywhere. By struggling to stay in the game, he plays out the universal end. A fan with any sense of his own weakness will therefore feel a special attachment to the veteran, a fear to see him fail but also a knowledge that he must be allowed to play long enough to fail, that in failure is the drama of the shifting skies. The loss of speed and skill, the running into barriers—that is where the athlete comes closest to his fans. It is what A. J. Liebling, the great poet of boxing, was getting at when he followed the

[5] *Jagr, who is from Czechoslovakia, later said that he chose this number to commemorate the Prague Spring of 1968.*

last years of Joe Louis: "When Louis knocked Savold out, I came away singularly revived—as if I, rather than Louis, had demonstrated resistance to the erosion of time." Writing of Louis's match with Rocky Marciano, that big, cruel bruiser from up north—and isn't that how the future must always appear to the aging champion?—Liebling caught that terrible moment when the air hissed from the tires: "I think that punch was the one that made Joe feel old. Between the rounds, I could see Seamon pressing an ice bag against the back of Louis's neck, and when I turned my binoculars on [Marciano's trainer] Charlie Goldman's face, he was grinning."[6]

It is no surprise that when writers and filmmakers turn to sports they almost always focus on the old-timer, the geriatric on the verge of overstaying his welcome. Such stories tend to follow the same basic plot: the fading star, the youth-hungry front office, the blue-collar fans who make up the true backbone of the republic—as much a myth now as the cheap seats they are said to inhabit. In the end, the superstar breaks one more play, or makes a last catch in the rain, or sends a ball deep into the night—an act itself seen as a powerful rebuke to fate. Even before you hear the names of such films, you can picture the movie posters: the banged-up old veteran, the girl who has stood by him, the mean coach with the humorless little mouth, the front-office drone with his flip charts. *Bang the Drum Slowly, Bull Durham, For Love of the Game.* In *North Dallas Forty,* Nick Nolte, the aging, dope-smoking, floppy-haired receiver, tells the prudish young player, "You last long enough, you'll realize the only way to survive is the pills and the shots." *The Natural,* with Robert Redford, is probably the most ambitious of these films, a dream in cheesecloth with sexy magical realism leading to a happy ending of cornfields and new beginnings; but the novel, written by Bernard Malamud, is full of sin and might-have-beens. A man turns up from points unknown, somewhere out west, a sunny echo of the great big country, miles of empty road and telephone lines. This is the saddest of all types—the man who has squandered his youth. His appearance signifies a last chance: for the player but also for the city, for all those fallen Clevelands and Chicagos that, closing fast on middle age, crave rebirth. The athlete offers redemption, but a redemption so sappy it makes the sophisticates cringe. In the end, because it is Malamud, this redemption fails, and the last sentence of the novel reads like a kicker from the old book: "When Roy looked into the boy's eyes, he wanted to say

[6] *This is one of the few times in the story that Liebling calls Louis by his first name. Liebling was also named Joe. In defeat, the spectator and the fan have become one.*

it wasn't but couldn't and he lifted his hands to his face and wept many bitter tears."

In the Metropolitan Museum of Art in Manhattan, where the American Wing meets the Egyptian Wing, there is a display of trading cards, the only art form created by sports and still the best at telling its story. The earliest cards, printed in the 1800s, depict baseball players who came and went long ago, leaving no more trace than those other men who rode the trains and filled the offices. Now and then a name rings a tiny bell—Tris Speaker, George Sisler, Walter Johnson—each in his heavy sweater and beanie of a cap, looking embarrassed to be wearing such clothes so far on in life.[7] The collection tells the familiar story of America but in a different key: the coming of the photograph, of color, of stretch pants, of a greater slice of humanity—first the infusion from the Negro leagues, then from scrub leagues all over South and Central America. And something else, too, a change not of race but of character: a new look, a new easiness, a new shagginess, the fade of old coal-mine America. The cards from the mid-1970s show players with bushy sideburns and huge Afros, in rainbow-colored uniforms and handlebar mustaches. In my childhood, everyone knew that Dock Ellis had pitched a no-hitter on acid.

Through it all, the cards have remained the same; they are still the most compact and suggestive way of recording a career. For the young player, the card will have only a few lines, the empty space filled by hobbies, or by boyhood feats. For the veteran, the card will be so crammed with statistics that the numbers themselves become almost unreadable. In the end, the authority of the veteran derives from all those tiny numbers, from the many times that he has tried and failed and from the few times that he has tried and succeeded. With each at bat, fewer at bats remain, an equation that lends an urgency to the old-timer's appearance, the built-in tension of watching time run out. What might otherwise read like a meaningless stat on the back of a baseball card will therefore strike a true fan as poetry. Those two bases stolen by Davey Lopes in 1987, when he was forty-two years old, conjure the image of a broken-down old ballplayer, once among the best in the game, struggling merely to find a role. In that one small stat is all the sadness and all the courage of the aging player: he studies the pitcher, reads the signal, breaks for

[7] *In this era, Philadelphia manager Connie Mack wore a suit and tie in the dugout.*

second, and finally, his mind and body occupied, perhaps for the last time, by the need to make it safely to second, he is beyond the concerns of age and time; he is simply an athlete.

Late last year, I went to see the New York Rangers play the Buffalo Sabres. It was a pointless game between mediocre teams, but really I had gone to see Mark Messier, who had been in and out of the Rangers lineup with injuries. Messier is nowhere near as dominant as he once was, but his presence still has a way of transforming a bland game into history. In a sense, any game in which Messier plays becomes historic, because Messier embodies so much of the game. Even those who call for his retirement must realize that when he goes something important will be gone forever, as each retirement in some way diminishes the game. There were only a few thousand fans at Madison Square Garden, and it seemed as if most of them had come to heckle. Unlike crowds at basketball or baseball games, hockey fans haven't changed much over the years. You will still see much drunkenness, mullets, and the blood lust of children. Between periods, there is often an on-ice contest, with fans trying to shoot a puck from the red line, through an obstacle, and into a goal, thus winning a prize—a prize that, compared with the cash prizes given away at NBA games, seems shockingly modest: an Amtrak ticket to Philly or Wilmington, the opportunity to compete in yet another such contest. The contestants usually can be broken into three categories, which, in the manner of the Pass, Punt, and Kick Competition, gives the outing its informal name: a Bimbo, a Kid, and a Drunk Guy. A sad milieu in which to play out one's final days.

Messier no longer plays on the top line, so he usually makes his first appearance while you are looking elsewhere. Suddenly there he is, cutting in front of the net, his chin leading him into and out of confrontations. When he first came into the league, Messier was the biggest center in the game, the prototype of a new kind of forward. He has since been surpassed, overwhelmed by the tide of bigness he once portended. Eric Lindros, Bobby Holik, and Keith Primeau all dwarf Messier. Even on his more effective shifts, he therefore stands as a kind of relic, a reminder of an older standard. Like the Chrysler Building or the Brooklyn Bridge, he is a monument to a future that came and went, a cutting edge that passed into antiquity.

As the game slogged on, things got rough and then chippy, with sticks and pucks drawing blood up and down the boards. At one point, a young player took a run at Messier. Whenever a young player goes at an old star, there is the stink of regicide. For a moment, the Garden got quiet, the kind of quiet only a crowd can make. Messier turned slowly, his face set in that familiar hard and icy stare. It was the kind of stare it takes an entire career to perfect. The fact that it was mostly bluff made it only more courageous. That stare, that intensity, that stubbornness—it is all that remains of Messier's old game. On most nights it is enough.   ◆

About the Editors

Matthew Stevenson is a contributing editor of *Harper's Magazine.* He is the author of *Letters of Transit, An April Across America*, and *Remembering the Twentieth Century Limited*, which are available at the *Harper's* online store. He lives outside Geneva, Switzerland.

Michael Martin is a freelance writer and editor living in the Netherlands. His fiction and poetry have appeared in a variety of literary journals; he was cofounding editor of the literary magazine, *Hogtown Creek Review.* A contributing editor to *Amsterdam Weekly*, he is currently writing his first book.

Dedications

Matthew Stevenson: For the contributions that so many writers, editors, staff and board members have made to *Harper's Magazine* and its illustrious readers.

Michael Martin: For Rex Martin, my father.

Special thanks to: Lynn Carlson, Eve Brant, Ellen Rosenbush, and Kathy Park Price.

About the Authors

Pete Axthelm was a writer and columnist for *Sports Illustrated*, the *New York Herald Tribune*, and *Newsweek*, and the author of *The City Game* (1970). He also worked as a sports commentator for NBC and ESPN. He died in 1991 at the age of forty-seven.

Nicholas Bethell (1938–2007) was a journalist, author, historian, and a member of Britain's House of Lords from 1967 to 1999. He was fluent in Polish and Russian, and translated into English the works of Aleksandr Solzhenitsyn, among others. Bethell's own books, such as *The Last Secret* and *Betrayed*, explored Cold War history and politics.

Roy Blount Jr. has written more than twenty books—most recently, *Alphabet Juice*—on a wide range of subjects. *The New Yorker* recently cited his first book, *About Three Bricks Shy . . . And the Load Filled Up*, as "the best of all books about pro football." A former staff writer for *Sports Illustrated*, he is a panelist on NPR's *Wait, Wait . . . Don't Tell Me*, a member of the Fellowship of Southern Writers, and president of the Authors Guild. Raised in Georgia, he now lives in western Massachusetts.

Bill Cardoso worked as a magazine writer and editor at the *Boston Globe* and is the author of *The Maltese Sangweech and Other Heroes*. He was close to Hunter Thompson and coined the word "gonzo" to describe his friend's journalistic style. Cardoso died in California in 2006.

Gary Cartwright grew up in Texas and for many years wrote a sports column for newspapers in Fort Worth and Dallas. He has been a senior editor at *Texas Monthly* since 1982. Several of his books, including *Blood Will Tell*, have been made into movies.

John Chamberlain (1903–1995) had a long career in American magazines. In the 1930s he was on the staff of *Scribner's* and *Harper's Magazine*, and later worked at Time-Life publications, *National Review*, the *Wall Street Journal*, and King Features.

Rich Cohen's work has appeared in *The New Yorker* and *Harper's Magazine*, among other publications, and he is a contributing editor to *Vanity Fair* and *Rolling Stone*. His books include *Israel Is Real: An Obsessive Quest to*

Understand the Jewish Nation and Its History, Tough Jews, and the memoir *Lake Effect.*

James B. Connolly (1868–1957) worked his way through Harvard (where he studied classics) and then withdrew to compete in the first modern Olympic games, in Athens in 1896, where he won the first medal awarded. He was a veteran of the Spanish-American War, ran twice for Congress, and wrote extensively on maritime subjects.

Bernard DeVoto (1897–1955) was born in Utah, taught English at Northwestern University, and wrote a number of celebrated books (*The Year of Decision: 1846, The Course of Empire*) about the settlement of the American West. He was an authority on the life of Mark Twain and edited many of his papers. From 1935 to 1955, he wrote the Editor's Easy Chair column for *Harper's Magazine.*

David James Duncan has published short stories, essays, a memoir, and the best-selling novels *The Brothers K* and *The River Why.* He lives on a trout stream in the shadow of Montana's Bitterroot Mountains.

Joseph Epstein was for many years the editor of *American Scholar,* and has written for numerous magazines. Many of his books, such as *Snobbery* and *Friendship,* have been bestsellers. In 2005, he was awarded the Presidential Medal of Freedom for his contributions to American letters.

A. Bartlett Giamatti (1938–1989) was President of Yale University from 1978 to 1986. In 1986, he became president of baseball's National League, and eventually was appointed Commissioner of Major League Baseball. His academic love was Renaissance literature, but his passion was baseball and the Boston Red Sox. Among his many published books are *Take Time for Paradise, A Free and Ordered Space: The Real World of the University,* and *Exile and Change in Renaissance Literature.*

Shirley Jackson (1916–1965) was a prolific short-story writer whose work appeared in *The New Yorker, Mademoiselle, The New Republic,* and other magazines. Her most famous story, "The Lottery," was first published in 1948 in *The New Yorker.* Among her novels are *The Haunting of Hill House* (made into a movie in 1999), *The Road Through the Wall,* and the recently reissued *We Have Always Lived in the Castle.*

Pat Jordan was paid $50,000 in the late 1950s as what was called a "bonus baby" to pitch in the minor-league system of the Milwaukee Braves. He never made the big leagues, a story told in his classic memoir, *A False Spring*, but he stayed close to baseball and other sports. His journalism has appeared in *Sports Illustrated*, *The Atlantic Monthly*, *The New Yorker*, *Playboy*, and *The New York Times Magazine*.

Leo Katcher (1911–1991) was a reporter, screenwriter, novelist, and biographer who achieved acclaim with his book *The Big Bankroll: The Life and Times of Arnold Rothstein*, which was made into a movie, *King of the Roaring Twenties*. In the 1930s he was city editor of the *New York Post*.

Lewis H. Lapham is the editor of *Lapham's Quarterly*. He was editor of *Harper's Magazine* from 1976 to 1981, and again from 1983 to 2006. During that time he wrote the monthly Notebook column. He has published more than a dozen books, among them *Gag Rule*, *Theatre of War*, and *The Wish for Kings*; produced a movie, *The American Ruling Class*; and been the host of popular television and radio programs.

Guy Lawson is an award-winning investigative journalist whose articles on war, crime, culture, and sports have appeared in *The New York Times Magazine*, *GQ*, *Rolling Stone*, and many other publications. He is the author of *The Brotherhoods: The True Story of Two Cops Who Murdered for the Mafia*.

George Plimpton (1927–2003) was a founding editor of *The Paris Review* and the author of numerous best-selling books, such as *Paper Lion* and *Out of My League*, that recount his life and amusing times trying to play a professional sport. He contributed to *Harper's Magazine* for more than thirty years, often writing about sports.

Peter Schrag was for many years the editorial-page editor and a columnist for the *Sacramento Bee*. He is the author, most recently, of *California: America's High Stakes Experiment* and *Not Fit for Our Society: Nativism, Eugenics and Immigration*.

Wilfrid Sheed, essayist and author, has written short stories, novels, and memoirs, including one about his life at Oxford, *A Middle Class Education;* a biography of his parents, *Frank and Maisie;* and a book on music, *The House That George Built with a little help from Irving, Cole and a Crew of About Fifty*.

Matthew Stevenson's association with *Harper's Magazine* began in 1978, when he joined the magazine as an assistant editor. His books include *Letters of Transit* and *An April Across America*.

John R. Tunis (1889–1975) is the author of numerous works of juvenile sports fiction. With such characters as "Fat Stuff" Foster and "Razzle" Nugent, he inspired a generation of future sports reporters. He graduated from Harvard, fought in World War I, and was the first person to broadcast Wimbledon to an American radio audience.

Mark Twain (1835–1910) was the pen name of Samuel Clemens. He grew up, as he often recalled in his writing, on the Mississippi River and later worked as a newspaper reporter. He was the author of such American classics as *The Adventures of Tom Sawyer, Adventures of Huckleberry Finn, The Prince and the Pauper,* and *A Connecticut Yankee in King Arthur's Court.* He had a long association with *Harper's Magazine.*

Tom Wolfe is considered the inspiration for what is often called New Journalism, a style that he developed at the *New York Herald Tribune, Esquire, Harper's Magazine,* and many other publications. He minted the phrases "Me Decade" and "radical chic," and many of his books, such as *The Electric Kool-Aid Acid Test, The Right Stuff,* and *The Bonfire of the Vanities,* have sold millions of copies. *In Our Time* is a collection of his drawings from *Harper's.*

Robert H. Zieger is Distinguished Professor of History Emeritus, University of Florida. He also taught at universities in Wisconsin, Kansas, and Michigan. His books include *American Workers, American Unions*; a history of the CIO; and a biography of John L. Lewis.

ACKNOWLEDGMENTS

"Confessions of a Washed-Up Sportswriter," by Gary Cartwright. Copyright © 1968 by Gary Cartwright. Reprinted by permission of the author.

"The Final Season," by George Plimpton. Copyright © 1977 by George Plimpton. Reprinted by permission of Sarah Plimpton.

"Down and Out at Wrigley Field," by Rich Cohen. Copyright © 2001 by Rich Cohen. Reprinted by permission of the author.

"Obsessed with Sport," by Joseph Epstein. Copyright © 1976 by Joseph Epstein. Reprinted by permission of Georges Borchardt, Inc., on behalf of the author.

"The City Game," by Pete Axthelm. Reprinted by permission of SLL/Sterling Lord Literistic, Inc. Copyright by Brown Megan Axthelm.

"Mens Sana in Corpore Sano" and "The Jogger's Prayer" from *In Our Time* by Tom Wolfe. Text and illustration © 1980 by Tom Wolfe. Reprinted by permission of Farrar, Straus and Giroux, LLC.

"Tennessee Lonesome End," by Peter Schrag. Copyright © 1970 by Peter Schrag. Reprinted by permission of the author.

"Find Me a Writer," by Wilfrid Sheed. Copyright © 1984 by Wilfrid Sheed.

"Pilgrim's Progress," by Lewis H. Lapham. Copyright © 2003 by Lewis H. Lapham. Reprinted by permission of the author.

"These Sporting Poets," by George Plimpton. Copyright © 1977 by George Plimpton. Reprinted by permission of Sarah Plimpton.

"Hyperbole's Child," by A. Bartlett Giamatti. Copyright © 1977 by A. Bartlett Giamatti. Reprinted by permission of Marcus Giamatti.

"It Takes a Stadium," by Matthew Stevenson. Copyright © 2004 by Matthew Stevenson. Reprinted by permission of the author.

"A Mickey Mantle Koan," by David James Duncan. Copyright © 1992 by David James Duncan. Reprinted by permission of the author.

"Winding Up," by Robert H. Zieger. Copyright © 1979 by Robert H. Zieger. Reprinted by permission of the author.

"The Story of the Davis Cup," by John R. Tunis. Reprinted by permission of SLL/Sterling Lord Literistic, Inc. Copyright by John R. Tunis.

"Hockey Nights," by Guy Lawson. Copyright © 1998 by Guy Lawson. Reprinted by permission of the author.

"A Poisoned Russian King," by Nicholas Bethell. Copyright © 1973 by Nicholas Bethell. Reprinted by permission of James Bethell.

"No Joy in Sorrento," by Pat Jordan. Copyright © 2004 by Pat Jordan. Reprinted by permission of the author.

THE AMERICAN RETROSPECTIVE SERIES

VOICES IN BLACK & WHITE:
Writings on Race in America from *Harper's Magazine*

TURNING TOWARD HOME:
Reflections on the Family from *Harper's Magazine*

THE WORLD WAR TWO ERA:
Perspectives on All Fronts from *Harper's Magazine*

THE SIXTIES:
Recollections of the Decade from *Harper's Magazine*